Why Learn C

Paul J. Lucas

Why Learn C

Go Behind the Curtain of Modern Systems with C23

Apress®

Paul J. Lucas
Oakland, CA, USA

ISBN-13 (pbk): 979-8-8688-1596-6   ISBN-13 (electronic): 979-8-8688-1597-3
https://doi.org/10.1007/979-8-8688-1597-3

Copyright © 2025 by Paul J. Lucas

This work is subject to copyright. All rights are reserved by the Publisher, whether the whole or part of the material is concerned, specifically the rights of translation, reprinting, reuse of illustrations, recitation, broadcasting, reproduction on microfilms or in any other physical way, and transmission or information storage and retrieval, electronic adaptation, computer software, or by similar or dissimilar methodology now known or hereafter developed.

Trademarked names, logos, and images may appear in this book. Rather than use a trademark symbol with every occurrence of a trademarked name, logo, or image, we use the names, logos, and images only in an editorial fashion and to the benefit of the trademark owner, with no intention of infringement of the trademark.

The use in this publication of trade names, trademarks, service marks, and similar terms, even if they are not identified as such, is not to be taken as an expression of opinion as to whether or not they are subject to proprietary rights.

While the advice and information in this book are believed to be true and accurate at the date of publication, neither the authors nor the editors nor the publisher can accept any legal responsibility for any errors or omissions that may be made. The publisher makes no warranty, express or implied, with respect to the material contained herein.

Managing Director, Apress Media LLC: Welmoed Spahr
Acquisitions Editor: Melissa Duffy
Coordinating Editor: Gryffin Winkler

Cover Photo by Pawel Czerwinski on Unsplash (unsplash.com)

Distributed to the book trade worldwide by Springer Science+Business Media New York, 1 New York Plaza, Suite 4600, New York, NY 10004-1562, USA. Phone 1-800-SPRINGER, fax (201) 348-4505, e-mail orders-ny@springer-sbm.com, or visit www.springeronline.com. Apress Media, LLC is a California LLC and the sole member (owner) is Springer Science + Business Media Finance Inc (SSBM Finance Inc). SSBM Finance Inc is a **Delaware** corporation.

For information on translations, please e-mail booktranslations@springernature.com; for reprint, paperback, or audio rights, please e-mail bookpermissions@springernature.com.

Apress titles may be purchased in bulk for academic, corporate, or promotional use. eBook versions and licenses are also available for most titles. For more information, reference our Print and eBook Bulk Sales web page at http://www.apress.com/bulk-sales.

Any source code or other supplementary material referenced by the author in this book is available to readers on GitHub. For more detailed information, please visit https://www.apress.com/gp/services/source-code.

If disposing of this product, please recycle the paper

To my mentors and colleagues throughout my career who taught me much and made the journey more fun:

Richard Acevedo, Tameem Anwar, Mitch Blank, Andrew Brown, Mike Carey, Iuri Chaer, Thomas Chimento, James Coplien, Henry Corin, Kevin Densmore, Jon Detert, Jack Dixon, Steve Eick, Brad Euhus, Dana Florescu, Rich Gaushell, Bob Graham, Tom Green, Jon Handler, Chris Hillery, Joseph Huckaby, Jeff Isenberg, Ivan Jager, Gordon Kotik, Andrew Lippai, Nicky Masjedizadeh, Richard McKeethen, Abhinav Nekkanti, Mike Nelson, Tommy Nguyen, Fredrik Nygaard, John Oyston, Randy Paquette, Vishal Patel, Linda Pinck, Nathan Pope, Chris Pride, Fabio Riccardi, Sai Sajja, Jeff Schmidt, Pratiksha Shah, Logan Shaw, Helen Stewart, Igor Stojanovski, and Sundar Vasan.

Contents

Part I Learning C   1

1 A Tour of C   3
    1.1   A First Program   3
    1.2   Copying Input to Output   5
    1.3   Strings   9
    1.4   Functions 12
    1.5   Memory 14
    1.6   Pointers 15
    1.7   `const` 17
    1.8   Dynamic Memory 20
    1.9   Structures 23
    1.10   Epilogue 25

2 Comments, Names, and Types   27
    2.1   Comments 27
    2.2   Names 29
    2.3   Namespaces 30
    2.4   Scope 30
    2.5   Built-In Types 31
          2.5.1   Modifiers 31
          2.5.2   `bool` 32
          2.5.3   `char` 33
          2.5.4   `int` 34
          2.5.5   `_BitInt` 34
          2.5.6   `float`, `double`, and `long double` 35
          2.5.7   `_Decimal32`, `_Decimal64`, and `_Decimal128` 36
          2.5.8   Complex Numbers 36
          2.5.9   Imaginary Numbers 37
    2.6   `typedef` 37
    2.7   Fixed-Width Integer Types 38
    2.8   Unicode Character Types 38
    2.9   Other Standard Types 39
    2.10   Numeric Limits 39
    2.11   Signed Integer Overflow 40

	2.12	Choosing an Appropriate Integer Type	41
	2.13	Type Conversions	42
	2.14	Epilogue	43

3 Operators   45
3.1 Associativity vs. Evaluation Order   45
3.2 Arithmetic Operators   46
3.3 Unary Plus and Minus Operators   47
3.4 Increment and Decrement Operators   47
3.5 Relational Operators   48
3.6 Logical Operators   48
3.7 Conditional Operator   48
3.8 Bitwise Operators   49
3.9 Assignment Operators   52
3.10 Function Call Operator   52
3.11 Array Indexing Operator   52
3.12 Address-of and Dereference Operators   53
3.13 Member Access Operators   53
3.14 Casting Operator   54
3.14.1 Casting to `void`   55
3.14.2 Casting Away `const`   55
3.14.3 Casting Pointers   56
3.15 Comma Operator   56
3.16 `sizeof` Operator   57
3.17 `alignof` Operator   58
3.18 Epilogue   58

4 Declarations   61
4.1 Multiple Declarations   62
4.2 `auto`   62
4.3 Storage Classes   63
4.3.1 `auto`   64
4.3.2 `extern`   65
4.3.3 `static`   65
4.3.4 `register`   66
4.4 `constexpr`   67
4.5 `const`   67
4.6 `typeof`   67
4.6.1 Declarations without Initializers   68
4.6.2 Clarifying Complicated Declarations   68
4.7 `typeof_unqual`   69
4.8 `alignas`   69
4.9 Attributes   70
4.9.1 `deprecated`   70
4.9.2 `fallthrough`   70

		4.9.3	`maybe_unused`	71
		4.9.4	`nodiscard`	71
		4.9.5	`noreturn`	72
	4.10	Epilogue		72

5 Statements 73
	5.1	Expression Statement	73
	5.2	Compound Statement	73
	5.3	`if-else`	74
	5.4	`while`	75
	5.5	`do-while`	75
	5.6	`for`	76
	5.7	`break` and `continue`	76
	5.8	`switch`	77
	5.9	`return`	79
	5.10	`goto`	79
	5.11	Empty Statement (`;`)	80
	5.12	Epilogue	80

6 Arrays and Pointers 83
	6.1	Array Declaration		83
	6.2	Array Initialization		83
	6.3	Array Indexing		84
	6.4	Multidimensional Arrays		84
	6.5	`void` Pointers		86
	6.6	Pointers to Pointers		87
	6.7	Arrays and Pointers		88
	6.8	Arrays vs. Pointers		89
	6.9	Arrays of Pointers		89
	6.10	Pointers to Function		90
	6.11	Array Compound Literals		92
		6.11.1	Compound Literal Lifetime and Storage Class	93
	6.12	Multidimensional Arrays vs. Pointers		93
	6.13	Dynamically Allocating 2D Arrays		94
	6.14	Variable Length Arrays		96
	6.15	Epilogue		97

7 Enumerations 101
	7.1	Declarations		102
	7.2	Name Collisions		102
	7.3	Underlying Type		103
	7.4	Implicit Conversion		103
	7.5	Enumeration Constant Values		104
		7.5.1	Externally Imposed Values	104
		7.5.2	Serializing Values	105

	7.5.3	Duplicate Values 105
	7.5.4	"None" Values 106
	7.5.5	Checking Values 106
	7.5.6	"Count" Values 107
	7.5.7	Bit Flag Values 108
7.6	Epilogue 109

8 Preprocessor 111
- 8.1 Compilation Phases 111
- 8.2 Language 112
- 8.3 Object-Like Macros 112
- 8.4 Predefined Macros 113
- 8.5 Conditional Compilation 113
  - 8.5.1 `defined` 115
  - 8.5.2 `__has_c_attribute` 116
  - 8.5.3 `__has_include` 116
- 8.6 File Inclusion 116
- 8.7 Function-Like Macros 117
  - 8.7.1 Parameters 117
  - 8.7.2 Arguments 117
  - 8.7.3 Variable Numbers of Arguments 118
  - 8.7.4 Stringification 119
  - 8.7.5 Concatenation 120
  - 8.7.6 # and ## Pitfalls 120
- 8.8 Multiple Statements 122
- 8.9 X Macros 122
  - 8.9.1 Serializing Enumeration Values 123
  - 8.9.2 Counting Enumeration Values 124
- 8.10 Filename and Line Information 124
- 8.11 Errors and Warnings 124
- 8.12 Not Expanding a Macro 125
- 8.13 Paste Avoidance 125
- 8.14 Undefining a Macro 126
- 8.15 Embedding 126
- 8.16 Pragmas 127
- 8.17 Useful Macros 128
- 8.18 Epilogue 132

9 Functions 135
- 9.1 Declarations vs. Definitions 135
- 9.2 Parameters 135
- 9.3 No Overloading 136
- 9.4 "Array" Parameters 136
  - 9.4.1 Non-Null Array Syntax for Parameters 138
  - 9.4.2 Qualified Array Syntax for Parameters 138

		9.4.3	Variable Length Array Syntax for Parameters	139

         9.4.3   Variable Length Array Syntax for Parameters 139
         9.4.4   Multidimensional Array Syntax for Parameters 139
         9.4.5   Multidimensional VLA Parameters 140
         9.4.6   Array Syntax for Parameters Pitfalls 141
  9.5   Return Values 141
  9.6   Error Handling 142
  9.7   main 143
         9.7.1   Declaration and Parameters 143
         9.7.2   Return Value and Exit Status 144
  9.8   Static Functions 144
  9.9   Static Local Variables 145
         9.9.1   __func__ 145
  9.10 Inline Functions 146
         9.10.1 Differences from Macros 146
         9.10.2 Only a Hint 147
         9.10.3 When (and When Not) to Inline 147
         9.10.4 Inline Definition 148
  9.11 Variadic Functions 149
         9.11.1 Variadic Pitfalls 150
         9.11.2 Calling Other Variadic Functions 152
  9.12 Epilogue 153

10 Structures   157
  10.1 Definition 157
  10.2 No Nesting 158
  10.3 Initialization 159
  10.4 Structure Compound Literals 160
  10.5 Padding 162
  10.6 Flexible Array Members 162
  10.7 Bit-Fields 165
  10.8 Epilogue 167

11 Unions   169
  11.1 Definition 169
  11.2 Initialization 170
  11.3 Union Compound Literals 170
  11.4 Which Member? 171
  11.5 Type Punning 171
  11.6 Restricted Class Hierarchies 172
         11.6.1 Safeguards 175
  11.7 Epilogue 176

12 Input, Output, and Files   179
  12.1 Output 179
         12.1.1 Formatted Printing 181

12.2	Files		183
	12.2.1	Open Modes	186
	12.2.2	File Information	186
	12.2.3	File State	187
	12.2.4	File Position	188
	12.2.5	Low-Level File I/O	189
	12.2.6	Memory as a File	190
	12.2.7	A File as Memory	191
	12.2.8	Deletion	191
	12.2.9	Temporary Files	192
12.3	Directories		192
12.4	Input		194
	12.4.1	Formatted Reading	194
	12.4.2	String-to-Number Conversion	197
	12.4.3	Line Reading	198
	12.4.4	Environment Variables	200
12.5	Epilogue		201

13 Program Organization — 203

13.1	Include Guards	203
13.2	Opaque Types	205
13.3	Self Sufficient Headers	206
	13.3.1 Including Headers in a Header	206
	13.3.2 Include Everything Necessary	207
	13.3.3 Interdependencies	207
13.4	Cooperating with C++	208
13.5	Including Headers in a .c File	209
13.6	Initialization and Clean-Up	210
13.7	Header Example	211
13.8	File Organization	212
13.9	Build Tools	213
13.10	Epilogue	214

14 Multithreading — 215

14.1	Creating and Joining Threads	217
14.2	Detaching Threads	218
14.3	"Atomic"	219
	14.3.1 A Bad Example	219
14.4	Mutexes	221
	14.4.1 Timed Mutexes	224
	14.4.2 Deadlocks	224
	14.4.3 Recursive Mutexes	226
14.5	Condition Variables	226
	14.5.1 Timed Condition Variables	229
14.6	Doing Something Once	229

14.7	`thread_local`	230
14.8	Thread-Specific Storage	231
14.9	Epilogue	232

Part II Selected Topics   233

15 Undefined Behavior   235
15.1	Implications and Example	236
15.2	Two Parts to Undefined Behavior	237
15.3	Optimization Can Make Things Worse	238
15.4	Undefined Behavior in Other Languages	239
15.5	Epilogue	240

16 Assertions   241
16.1	Sample Implementation	241
16.2	Assertions vs. Errors and Exceptions	242
16.3	Disabling Assertions in Production Code	243
16.4	Adding a Message	244
16.5	Static Assertions	244
16.6	Epilogue	245

17 `_Atomic`   247
17.1	Alternative to a Mutex	248
17.2	Atomic Functions	248
17.3	Memory Barriers	250
	17.3.1 `memory_order_seq_cst`	250
	17.3.2 `memory_order_relaxed`	251
	17.3.3 `memory_order_acquire` and `memory_order_release` .	253
	17.3.4 `memory_order_consume`	254
	17.3.5 `memory_order_acq_rel`	255
17.4	Compare and Swap	255
17.5	Lock-Free Operations	258
17.6	The "ABA Problem"	259
17.7	Versioned Pointers	261
17.8	False Sharing	262
17.9	Epilogue	263

18 Debugging   265
18.1	Printing Values	265
18.2	Debug Information	266
18.3	Optimization	266
18.4	Core Dumps	266
18.5	Signals	267
18.6	Common Bugs	268
	18.6.1 Array Bounds	268

CONTENTS

- 18.6.2 Buffer Overflow ... 268
- 18.6.3 Double Free ... 269
- 18.6.4 Null Pointer Dereference ... 269
- 18.6.5 Off-by-One ... 269
- 18.6.6 Use After Free ... 269
- 18.6.7 Memory Leak ... 270
- 18.6.8 Uninitialized Variable ... 271
- 18.7 Warnings ... 272
  - 18.7.1 Recommended Warnings ... 272
  - 18.7.2 Disabling Warnings ... 276
- 18.8 The Curious Case of the Disappearing `if` ... 276
- 18.9 Profiling ... 281
- 18.10 Epilogue ... 281

19 `_Generic` — 283
- 19.1 Motivating Example ... 283
- 19.2 A `printf` Example ... 284
- 19.3 `const` Overloading ... 286
- 19.4 Static `if` ... 287
- 19.5 No SFINAE (Substitution Failure is not an Error) ... 288
- 19.6 Type Traits ... 289
- 19.7 Epilogue ... 297

20 `setjmp` and `longjmp` — 299
- 20.1 Basics ... 299
- 20.2 `setjmp` Restrictions ... 300
- 20.3 `volatile` Variables ... 301
- 20.4 `longjmp` Details ... 301
- 20.5 Exceptions in C? ... 302
- 20.6 Epilogue ... 302

21 `restrict` — 305
- 21.1 The Problem ... 305
- 21.2 The Solution ... 306
- 21.3 Pitfalls ... 306
- 21.4 When (and When Not) to Use `restrict` ... 307
- 21.5 Miscellaneous ... 308
- 21.6 Epilogue ... 308

22 `volatile` — 309
- 22.1 Optimization Suppression ... 309
- 22.2 Signal Handling ... 310
- 22.3 `setjmp` ... 311
- 22.4 `volatile` in Other Languages ... 311
- 22.5 Wrong Uses ... 312
- 22.6 Epilogue ... 312

Part III Extended Examples — **313**

23 Strings — **315**
- 23.1 `string` 2.0 315
  - 23.1.1 More `put` Variants 315
  - 23.1.2 Formatted Printing 316
  - 23.1.3 Taking Ownership 317
- 23.2 `strbuf`: A String Buffer Type 318
  - 23.2.1 Reserving Space 319
  - 23.2.2 Putting 319
  - 23.2.3 Formatted Printing 320
  - 23.2.4 Taking Ownership 321
  - 23.2.5 Resetting 321
- 23.3 Epilogue 323

24 Lists — **325**
- 24.1 Initialization and Clean-Up 326
- 24.2 Pushing 326
- 24.3 Front, Back, and Empty 328
- 24.4 Popping 328
- 24.5 Removing from the Middle 329
- 24.6 Iterating 331
- 24.7 Epilogue 332

25 Maps — **333**
- 25.1 Hash Tables 334
- 25.2 Hash Table Types 336
- 25.3 Initialization and Clean-Up 338
- 25.4 Insert 339
- 25.5 Growing 340
- 25.6 Finding 341
- 25.7 Deleting 342
- 25.8 Iteration 342
- 25.9 Epilogue 343

26 Dynamic Dispatch — **345**
- 26.1 Pointers to Function 346
- 26.2 Function Tables 347
- 26.3 Fat Pointers 348
- 26.4 Epilogue 350

27 Exceptions in C — **351**
- 27.1 Requirements 351
- 27.2 `try` 352
- 27.3 `throw` 353
- 27.4 `catch` 356

27.5	`finally`	357
27.6	Restrictions	358
27.7	Epilogue	359

A Standard Headers — 361

B Standard Functions — 363
- B.1 `ctype.h` . . . 363
- B.2 `string.h` . . . 364
- B.3 `time.h` . . . 366

C C23 Differences — 371
- C.1 Aggregate Initialization . . . 371
- C.2 `alignas` and `alignof` . . . 371
- C.3 Attributes . . . 372
- C.4 `auto` . . . 372
- C.5 Binary Literals . . . 372
- C.6 `bool` . . . 372
- C.7 `constexpr` . . . 373
- C.8 Declarations After Labels . . . 373
- C.9 Digit Separators . . . 374
- C.10 `#embed` . . . 374
- C.11 Fixed-Type Enumerations . . . 374
- C.12 Function Definition Unnamed Parameters . . . 374
- C.13 K&R-Style Function Declarations and Definitions . . . 374
- C.14 `noreturn` . . . 376
- C.15 `nullptr` . . . 376
- C.16 `static_assert` . . . 377
- C.17 Storage Classes for Compound Literals . . . 377
- C.18 `thread_local` . . . 377
- C.19 `typeof` and `typeof_unqual` . . . 378
- C.20 `__VA_OPT__` . . . 378
- C.21 Variadic Functions . . . 378
- C.22 `#warning` . . . 379

Index — 381

Preface

"Should I still learn C?"

That's a question I see asked by many beginning (and some intermediate) programmers. Since you're reading this preface, perhaps you have the same question. Considering that C was created in 1972 and that many more modern languages have been created since, it's a fair question.

Somewhat obviously (since this book exists), I believe the answer is "Yes." Why? A few reasons:

1. Modern languages have many features for things like data structures (e.g., dynamic arrays, lists, maps), flow control (dynamic dispatch, exceptions), and algorithms (e.g., counting, iteration, searching, selection, sorting) as part of the language (either directly built-in or readily available via their standard libraries). While convenient, the way in which those features are implemented "behind the curtain" has to be done in a general way to be applicable to a wide variety of programs. Most of the time, they work just fine. However, occasionally, they don't.

    C is a fairly minimal language and has almost none of those things. If you want any of them, you're likely going to have to implement them yourself. While onerous, you'll be able to tailor your implementations to your circumstances. Knowledge of how to implement such features from scratch and understanding the trade-offs will serve you well even when programming in other languages because you'll have insight as to how their features are implemented.

2. Many systems and some scripting languages (e.g., Python) provide C APIs for implementing extensions. If you ever want to write your own, you'll need to know C.

3. Many open-source software packages upon which modern computers and the Internet still depend are written in C including Apache, cURL, Exim, Git, the GNU compiler collection, Linux, OpenSSL, Postfix, PostgreSQL, Python, Sendmail, Wireshark, Zlib, and many others. If you ever want either to understand how those work or contribute to them, you'll need to know C.

4. Embedded systems are largely developed in C (or C++, but with restrictions). If you ever want to work on embedded systems, you'll likely need to know C.
5. C has influenced more languages than any other (except ALGOL). If, in addition to programming, you also have an interest in programming languages in general or from a historical perspective, you should know C.

I'm *not* suggesting that you should learn C intending to switch to it as your primary programming language nor that you should implement your next big project in C. Programming languages are tools and the best tool should always be used for a given job. If you need to do any of the things listed in reasons 2–4 above, C will likely be the best tool for the job.

"Wouldn't learning C++ be good enough?"
"I already know C++. Isn't that good enough?"

Since C++ has supplanted C in many cases, both of those are fair questions. The answer to both is "No." Why? A couple of reasons:

1. Even though C++ is based on C, their similarities are superficial. Aside from sharing some keywords, basic syntax, and toolchain, they are very different languages. The ways in which you get things done in C is necessarily different from C++ due to C's minimal features.
2. From the perspective of learning how features are implemented behind the curtain, C++ is already too high-level since the language has modern features and its standard library contains several data structures and many algorithms.

"Why *this* book?"

If all that has convinced you that C is still worth learning, the last question is "Why *this* book?" Considering that *The C Programming Language*[†] (by Brian Kernighan and Dennis Ritchie, C's creator, known as "K&R") is *the* classic book for learning C, that too is a fair question.

The second (and last) edition of K&R was published in 1988 based on the then draft of the first ANSI standard of C (C89). C has evolved (slowly) since with the C95, C99, C11, C17, and C23 standards. This book covers them all.

This book is split into three parts:

[†]*The C Programming Language*, Brian W. Kernighan and Dennis M. Ritchie, AT&T Bell Laboratories, Prentice-Hall, Englewood Cliffs, New Jersey, 1978 (1st ed.), 1988 (2nd ed.).

Preface   xix

1. **Learning C**: teaches the C23 standard of C, includes many additional notes on C's history and philosophy, and also includes best-practices I've learned over my thirty-five year career.
2. **Selected Topics**: explains several additional advanced or obscure parts of C that I've found not to be explained well elsewhere, if at all.
3. **Extended Examples**: gives detailed examples with full source code of how features in other languages might be implemented including discussion of the tradeoffs involved so you can understand what's really going on behind the curtain in whatever language you program in.

Additionally, there's an appendix that lists differences between C23 and C17, the previous version of C.

Notes to the Reader

This book is intended for professional programmers, computer science students, or serious computer hobbyists who either want to learn C or get up-to-date on C23.

Consequently, this book assumes familiarity with programming language concepts such as variables, statements, loops, functions, arrays, classes, objects, etc. Though no knowledge of any particular programming language is assumed, a few concepts from C++ are alluded to (not surprisingly).

This book also assumes familiarity with algorithm characterization given in "big O" notation in terms of n, the size of the input, the most common of which are:

$O(1)$ **Constant time**: same amount of time regardless of n.
$O(\lg n)$ **Logarithmic time**: base-2 logarithm ($\lg n$) time, e.g., $\lg 10000 \approx 13$.
$O(n)$ **Linear time**: time proportional to n.

This book's content is presented as follows:

- Concepts that are essential for learning C are presented normally like this.
- Commentary, explanations for why something is the way it is, historical context, and personal opinion, i.e., things not essential for learning C, but nonetheless interesting (hopefully), are presented as inline notes that are indented and bracketed by little squares.

    ■ Like this. ☐

- Unless otherwise noted, cross references like §*X*, §*X.Y*, or §*X.Y.Z*, refer to chapter or appendix *X*, section *X.Y*, or subsection *X.Y.Z*, respectively, of this book.
- Footnotes[†] are used for references to other sources.

[†]Like this.

- Italics are used for one of emphasis (e.g., "... is *not* the same ..."), for the first occurrences of important concepts (e.g., *pointer*), an excerpt from or the title of another work (e.g., *The C Programming Language*), or for Unix manual pages when followed by a digit in parentheses that specifies its section (e.g., *grep*(1)).
- Anything followed by a superscripted asterisk like this* means zero or more of the preceding item; anything followed by a superscripted plus like this$^+$ means one or more.
- C constructs are often presented like this:

    for (*init-expr*$_{opt}$; *cond-expr*$_{opt}$; *next-expr*$_{opt}$)
        statement

    Within such a presentation:

    - The Courier typeface like `this` is used for literal text that's part of a C program. Courier Bold like **`this`** is used for C keywords.
    - Italics like *this* are also used as placeholders (formally, "non-terminals") for concepts that are to be replaced by more literal text.
    - Anything followed by a subscripted *opt* means it's optional.

- Occasionally, brackets [like this] are used instead of a subscripted *opt* to enclose something optional.

The source code for many of the examples in this book is freely available online at `https://github.com/Apress/Why-Learn-C`.

Some Preliminary Notes on C

The standard for C23 is ISO/IEC 9899:2024[†] that describes both the C23 programming language and its standard library. There's also the related standard of IEEE Std 1003.1-2024, aka, POSIX.1-2024[‡] (portable operating system interface), henceforth POSIX ("pahz-icks"), that describes a Unix-like operating system, command-line interpreter (aka, "shell"), and common utility programs.

POSIX extends the C standard library with both additional functions and additional semantics for existing functions. Various operating systems are POSIX-certified or at least "mostly" POSIX-compliant. While this book primarily teaches standard C, it would be a disservice to ignore POSIX due to its significance. The few places in this book that are POSIX-specific are tagged with "[POSIX]."

[†] *Information technology — Programming languages — C*, International Organization for Standardization (ISO), *ISO/IEC 9899:2024*, 2024, `https://www.iso.org/standard/82075.html`

[‡] *POSIX.1-2024*, aka, *IEEE Std 1003.1-2024*, IEEE and The Open Group, 2001-2024, `https://pubs.opengroup.org/onlinepubs/9799919799/`

As described in K&R, C is a general-purpose programming language with a simple syntax. Part of C's philosophy† includes things like:

- **"Trust the programmer."**
  That means the compiler assumes you know what you're doing (even when you don't). Sometimes, this leads to a *core dump*. (If you don't know what that is, you will.)
- **"Make it fast, even if it's not guaranteed to be portable."**
  C prioritizes generating efficient code. By many benchmarks, a program written in C runs faster than equivalent programs written in other languages. One of the ways C achieves speed is by leaving many facets of the language *implementation defined* meaning that each C compiler generates code for what works best (is fastest) for a particular CPU. Examples include the number of bits comprising an integer and whether characters are signed or unsigned. Consequently, it can be too easy to write non-portable code. That is, it may work perfectly on your machine, but if compiled and run on another machine, it may fail in surprising ways.

Despite these things, there are best practices for avoiding bugs and writing portable C code.

"C is quirky, flawed, and an enormous success."
— Dennis M. Ritchie

Indeed, despite its quirks and flaws, the fact that you're considering learning C over half a century after its creation should demonstrate its success.

Acknowledgments

I would like to thank Andrew Brown, Dana Florescu, Mark Musante, Vishal Patel, and especially Simon Tatham for their thoughtful comments, gentle criticisms, and helpful suggestions on drafts of this book.

Now, let's begin.

April 2025   *Paul J. Lucas*

---

†*Rationale for International Standard—Programming Languages—C*, Revision 5.10, April, 2003, `https://www.open-std.org/jtc1/sc22/wg14/www/C99RationaleV5.10.pdf`

About the Author

Paul J. Lucas started programming on Commodore PETs at his high school. Courtesy of his parents, the first computer he owned was an Apple][*plus* that he programmed in BASIC, Pascal, Fortran, and 6502 Assembly language. At some point, he upgraded to a Macintosh. During his undergraduate studies, he taught himself C. He's been programming in C (on and off) ever since. He's also programmed in Bash, Go, Java, Perl, and Python. Of all those, C and C++ are still his favorites.

He started his career at AT&T Bell Labs in telephony, log file visualization, testing *cfront* (the original C++ compiler), and wrote the *The C++ Programmer's Handbook*.[†] He's also worked at NASA Ames Research Center, various start-ups, and lastly at Splunk. He holds patents on data visualization class libraries, visual log file analysis, programming language type systems, skewing of scheduled search queries, and cache-aware searching.

He developed open-source projects including *CHSM*, a finite state automata compiler and run-time system, used by both telecommunications companies and CERN for managing complex reactive systems; and maintains `cdecl` ("see-deh-kull"), the C and C++ gibberish-to-English translator.[‡]

[†] *The C++ Programmer's Handbook*, Paul J. Lucas, AT&T Bell Laboratories, Prentice-Hall, Englewood Cliffs, New Jersey, 1992.
[‡] `cdecl`: *Composing and deciphering C (or C++) declarations or casts, aka "gibberish,"* Paul J. Lucas, `https://github.com/paul-j-lucas/cdecl`

About the Technical Reviewers

Simon Tatham is the author of multiple free-software projects in C, most notably PuTTY. He also maintains the *Simon Tatham's Portable Puzzle Collection* series of games, and was the original author of NASM. He has published articles on creative uses of the C preprocessor. In his day job, he develops C compilers and C libraries.

German Gonzalez-Morris is a polyglot software architect/engineer with 20+ years in the field, with knowledge in Java, Spring-Boot, C/C++, Julia, Python, Haskell, and Javascript, among others. He works with cloud (architecture) web-distributed applications and micro-services. German loves math puzzles (including reading Knuth, and is proud of solving some of Don's puzzles), swimming, and table tennis. Also, he has reviewed several books, including books on application containers (WebLogic) and languages (C, Java, Spring, Python, Haskell, Typescript, WebAssembly, Math for coders, regexp, Julia, data structures and algorithms, Kafka).

Part I
Learning C

Part I covers the core of the C23 standard of C:

1. **A Tour of C**: Gives a "tour" of C's major features to give you a feel for the language including `main`, I/O, arrays, strings, functions, memory organization, pointers, `const`, dynamic memory management, and structures.
2. **Comments, Names, and Types**: Covers comments, names, scope, built-in types, `typedef`, standard library types, signed integer overflow, choosing an appropriate integer type, and type conversions.
3. **Operators**: Covers C's arithmetic, unary plus and minus, increment, decrement, relational, logical, conditional, bitwise, assignment, function call, array indexing, address, dereference, member access, casting, comma, `sizeof`, and `alignof` operators.
4. **Declarations**: Covers the C declaration syntax, multiple declarations, `auto`, storage classes, `constexpr`, `const`, `typeof`, `alignas`, and attributes.
5. **Statements**: Covers C's statements of expression, compound, `if-else`, `while`, `do-while`, `for`, `break`, `continue`, `switch`, `return`, `goto`, and empty.
6. **Arrays and Pointers**: Covers array declaration, initialization, indexing, multidimensional arrays, `void` pointers, pointers to pointers, arrays and pointers, arrays vs. pointers, pointers to function, multidimensional arrays vs. pointers, compound literals, and variable length arrays.
7. **Enumerations**: Covers enumerations, declaration, name collisions, their underlying type, implicit conversion, and values.
8. **Preprocessor**: Covers the C preprocessor, its language, compilation phases, object-like macros, predefined macros, conditional compilation, file inclusion, function-like macros, X macros, and gives some useful macros.
9. **Functions**: Covers function declarations, definitions, parameters, array parameters, return values, error handling, `main`, static functions, static local variables, and `inline` and variadic functions.
10. **Structures**: Covers structure definitions, initialization, compound literals, padding, flexible array members, and bit fields.
11. **Unions**: Covers union definitions, initialization, compound literals, type punning, and restricted class hierarchies.
12. **Input, Output, and Files**: Covers output, `printf`, files, directories, input, `scanf`, environment variables, and other related functions.
13. **Program Organization**: Covers include guards, opaque types, self sufficient headers, cooperating with C++, program initialization and clean-up, how to organize program source files, and build tools.
14. **Multithreading**: Covers creating, joining, and detaching threads, "atomic," mutexes, condition variables, `thread_local`, and thread-specific storage.

Chapter 1
A Tour of C

To begin, the first chapter gives you a "tour" of C's major features to give you a feel for the language including the `main` function, I/O, arrays, strings, functions, memory organization, pointers, `const`, dynamic memory management, and structures.

1.1 A First Program

The canonical first program shown in any programming language is "hello, world," a simple program that prints that phrase. In C, it's:

```
#include <stdio.h>

int main() {
  printf( "hello, world\n" );
}
```

■ The first "hello, world" program was written by Kernighan as part of his *A Tutorial Introduction to the Language B*.[†] (As you might guess, B is a precursor to C. B never gained widespread use.) When K&R was written, "hello, world" was the first C program shown. It's since become the canonical first program shown for any programming language. □

C program source files conventionally end with a ".c" extension, so, assuming this program is in a file `hello.c`, it must be *compiled* (converted from source code into an executable) with a *C compiler*. On most Unix systems, the C compiler is named "`cc`" (short for "C compiler"). To compile a program, at a shell prompt ($), type `cc` followed by the name of the source file to compile:

[†]*A Tutorial Introduction to the Language B*, Brian W. Kernighan, *Bell Laboratories Computing Science Technical Report*, #8, Murray Hill, New Jersey, Jan. 1973.

```
$ cc hello.c
```

■ If `cc` is not on your system, popular alternatives are "`gcc`" and "`clang`." To compile all of the examples in this book, you may need to specify a `-std=c23` or a `-std=c2x` option since, as of this writing, C23 is not yet the default C language version for some compilers. ☐

If there are no errors, nothing will be printed (no news is good news), but an executable file named "`a.out`" will have been created in the same directory.

■ Originally, C compilers produced assembly language source code for the CPU of the computers they were being run on. The assembly source was then fed into an *assembler* that *assembled* (converted from assembly source into machine code) producing the file `a.out` (by default) for "assembler output." Many modern C compilers generate machine code directly yet still produce executables named `a.out` for continuity. ☐

To run the executable, simply type its name (following `./` since it's in the current directory):

```
$ ./a.out
```

at which point it will print:

```
hello, world
```

In C, a program begins execution in a function named "`main`" (§9.7). All function declarations:

1. Begin with the type of the value returned — its *return type*. By definition, `main` *must* return `int` (a signed integer type, §2.5.4) whose value indicates the *status*, either the success or failure, of the program. By convention, zero means "success" and any non-zero value means "failure" where the value is a code for the type of failure.

   ■ Why not zero for failure? Because there is only one way to succeed by having zero failures, but there are many ways to fail and many non-zero integers. ☐

2. Followed by the name of the function (here, `main`).
3. Followed by a list of zero or more *parameters* (§9.2) between `()`.
4. Followed by a sequence of zero or more *statements* (§5) between `{}` comprising the function's *body*.

C is liberal when it comes to formatting and whitespace is largely insignificant.

■ In particular, C doesn't care if you use either spaces or tabs to indent, nor by how much, nor if the `{` of a function is on the same line as its name or the next line so that it lines up vertically with its corresponding `}`.

1.2 Copying Input to Output

On the one hand, not having to memorize and obey a rigid set of formatting rules is nice; on the other hand, insufferable debates have raged for decades about which is the "one true style." This book uses *my* style. □

C has no built-in input/output (I/O) facilities (§12). Instead, they're provided by C's standard library. The statement:

```
printf( "hello, world\n" );
```

calls a function named `printf` (for "print formatted," §12.1.1) from the standard library passing `"hello, world\n"` as an *argument*.

A sequence of characters between double quotes is known as one of *character string*, *string literal*, or simply *string*. The sequence \n is C's notation for representing the *newline character* that, when printed, prints subsequent output on the left edge of the next line.

The:

```
#include <stdio.h>
```

says to include the text (§8.6) of the file `stdio.h` (part of the C standard library) that declares functions for performing I/O such as `printf`.

There are actually two types of C program source files:

1. `.c` files contain *definitions* of functions (and other things).
2. `.h` files (known as *header files* or simply *headers*) contain *declarations* of functions (and other things) providing the API for the corresponding `.c` file. The C standard library has a few dozen headers (§A), but you can also create your own.

You might be wondering:

If main returns an int, where is it?

Normally, every function declared as returning `int` (or any type) *must* return a value. But `main` is special (§9.7.2) in that if no return value is given, it's equivalent to returning zero (success).

1.2 Copying Input to Output

The next program in listing 1.1 will simply copy its input to its output verbatim by reading, then writing, one character at a time. This program shows a number of new things about C:

- Comments (§2.1) can be specified either between `/*` and `*/` that may span multiple lines or after `//` that spans until the end of the line.
- Line 7 defines a *local variable* `c` to hold the value of the character read to be of type `int`. In C, variables must be declared prior to their first use.

```
1   #include <stdio.h>
2
3   /*
4      Copy input to output, v1.
5   */
6   int main() {
7     int c;                    // declare variable 'c' as int
8     c = getchar();            // get char. from "standard input"
9     while ( c != EOF ) {      // while it's not end-of-file ...
10       putchar( c );          //    print it to "standard output"
11       c = getchar();         //    read the next character
12     }                        //    and repeat
13  }
```

Listing 1.1: Copy input, version 1

- Line 8 calls the standard I/O library function `getchar` that reads a single character from *standard input* and *assigns* the character to `c`.

  ■ By default, standard input comes from your keyboard, but can alternatively come from a file or even from another program.
  In a Unix shell, you can redirect standard input and output for a command from files using < and >, respectively:

  $ *command* < input.txt > output.txt

  In an *IDE* (*integrated development environment*, §13.9), there's typically a configuration setting for standard input and output. □

  In addition to returning characters, `getchar` also returns a special "EOF" value to indicate that the "end of file" has been reached. Necessarily, EOF must be distinct from any actual character, so its type is int, not char; hence, c is declared int to match.
- Line 9 makes use of a `while` loop (§5.4). It evaluates the expression between ( ) and, as long as it remains true, the *loop body* (the statements enclosed by { }) is executed repeatedly. In C, `!=` is the *not-equal-to* operator (§3.5).
- Line 10 calls `putchar` that prints the character to *standard output* (by default, the terminal).
- Line 11 gets the *next* character from standard input, if any, or EOF.
- After the last statement in the loop body has been executed, the program "loops" back to the `while` and the expression is re-evaluated.

Let's tweak the main part of the program to be as shown in listing 1.2. This version is equivalent to the first, but it shows more idiomatic C:

- The first change is that the assignment and comparison to EOF have been combined into a single expression. In C, an assignment is itself an expression. The extra ( ) are needed since `!=` has a higher *precedence* (§3) than =. Without them,

1.2 Copying Input to Output

```
int main() {
  int c;
  while ( (c = getchar()) != EOF )
    putchar( c );
}
```

Listing 1.2: Copy input, version 2, using idiomatic C

c would be assigned the "truth" value of whether the result of `getchar` is not equal to `EOF`.

- The second change is that the `{}` have been elided from the `while` loop. This can be done whenever there is only a single statement. Of course, you can keep the `{}` if you want.

While the first two versions of the program are fine for illustrative purposes, they're not production-quality because copying input a character at a time is inefficient. While calling the functions `getchar` and `putchar` is fast, it's not zero-cost. Better would be to read and write "chunks" of characters as shown in listing 1.3.

```
1  #include <stdio.h>
2  #include <stdlib.h>
3
4  constexpr size_t BUF_SIZE = 4096;
5
6  int main() {
7    char     buf[ BUF_SIZE ];
8    size_t   bytes;
9
10   do {
11     bytes = fread( buf, 1, BUF_SIZE, stdin );
12     if ( ferror( stdin ) )
13       goto error;
14     if ( fwrite( buf, 1, bytes, stdout ) < bytes )
15       goto error;
16   } while ( bytes == BUF_SIZE );
17   return EXIT_SUCCESS;
18
19 error:
20   perror( "copy" );
21   return EXIT_FAILURE;
22 }
```

Listing 1.3: Copy input, version 3: production-quality

This version also illustrates more things about C:

- Line 4 defines a *constant* for the size of a buffer into which we'll read a chunk of characters. Using constants rather than "magic values" is a good practice. In C, it's conventional to name constants in all capital letters.

  The type of `size_t` (§2.9) is a standard library unsigned type used when dealing with numbers of bytes.

> ■ Any name that ends with `_t` is a standard library type. You should avoid naming anything of your own with that suffix. □

> ■ The ideal buffer size would match your system's *memory page size*. It's always a power of two and likely either 4096 or 8192. While there is a way to obtain the actual value at run-time, we'll just use 4096 to keep the example simpler. □

- Line 7 declares an *array* (§6.1) of `BUF_SIZE` char, that is a contiguous set of characters. In C, `[ ]` denotes an array.
- Line 8 declares a variable to hold the number of bytes read.
- Lines 10 and 16 introduce an alternate `do-while` loop (§5.5). Unlike `while` that evaluates its condition at the start of the loop (and therefore may not execute its body at all), a `do-while` loop evaluates its condition at the end of the loop (and therefore always executes its body at least once). It's useful here because we don't know whether to loop until *after* we've attempted to read some bytes.
- Line 11 calls the standard function `fread` (§12.4) that reads bytes into `buf` of 1 chunk of size `BUF_SIZE` from `stdin` (a global variable that refers to standard input) and returns the number of bytes read and assigns it to `bytes`.
- Since `fread` returns the number of bytes read, it can't also return whether an error occurred. Hence, line 12 calls the standard function `ferror` to check whether there was an error while reading: if so, it uses `goto` (§5.10) to go to the statement *labeled* `error` on line 19.
- Line 14 calls the standard function `fwrite` (§12.1) to write the bytes from `buf` for 1 chunk of size `bytes` to `stdout` (a global variable that refers to standard output) and returns the number of bytes written. Unlike `fread`, if its return value is less than the number of bytes requested to be written, it means there was an error, so it also uses `goto` to go to the statement labeled `error` on line 19.
- Line 16 checks if `bytes` equals `BUF_SIZE`: if so, it loops back to the `do`; if not, the loop will exit. (The only times `bytes` will not be equal to `BUF_SIZE` is when the last chunk of the input has been read and written or when there was an error.)
  In C, `==` is the *equal-to* operator (§3.5) — not to be confused with `=` that's the *assignment* operator (§3.9).
- Unlike previous examples, line 17 explicitly returns a "success" value from `main` because we don't want the code to "fall through" into the `error` code below.
- Line 19 is the label for the target of both `goto` statements. While overuse of `goto` is a bad practice in that it can lead to "spaghetti code," having shared error-handling code is better than duplicating it, and is a common practice in C.
- Line 20 calls the standard function `perror` that prints the text of the most recent error. The argument will be printed before the error message to identify the program that printed the message.
- Line 21 returns `EXIT_FAILURE` that's a standard error value. Both it along with `EXIT_SUCCESS` are defined in the `stdlib.h` standard header.

1.3 Strings

Before the next example, we need to digress on strings in C. In listing 1.3, there is:

```
char buf[ BUF_SIZE ];
```

that declares `buf` to be an array of `BUF_SIZE` `char`. There, it's only being used as a buffer for the raw bytes read and written. It's not a "string." In C, strings also use arrays of `char` with the convention that the last character *must* be a *null character* (having the value zero). The following string declarations are equivalent:

```
char msg1[6] = "hello";
char msg2[]  = "hello";
char msg3[]  = { 'h', 'e', 'l', 'l', 'o', '\0' };
```

The declaration for `msg1` explicitly specifies the size of the array and initializes it with `"hello"`. Even though "hello" has 5 characters, a string literal like `"hello"` implicitly has a null character appended by the compiler, hence 6 in total.

Having to count the number of characters and remember to add one for the null character is both tedious and error-prone. As shown in the declaration for `msg2`, you can omit the explicit size in which case the compiler will count the number of characters in the string literal for you, add 1 for the null character automatically, and make *that* the size of the array.

Finally, the declaration for `msg2` is simply "syntactic sugar"[†] for the declaration for `msg3` where the individual characters (between single quotes) are explicitly given between `{}`. When being explicit, the compiler does *not* append a null character — you have to do it yourself. The sequence `\0` (zero) is C's notation for representing the null character similar to `\n` for the newline character.

The next program in listing 1.4 is a special-case of copying in that it only copies sequences of four or more consecutive printing ASCII characters similar to the Unix *strings*(1) command. It does this by saving characters into a buffer until at least four have been encountered.

- Line 7, as in previous examples, defines a variable `c` to hold the value of the character read.

  Not mentioned previously, however, is that, by default, local variables are *not* initialized. That means their value is *indeterminate*. Attempting to read an uninitialized variable results in *undefined behavior* (§15). However, if you ensure that an uninitialized variable is written to before it's read (as all the examples have done), then everything is fine.

  ■ Leaving a local variable uninitialized is an instance of the compiler assuming you know what you're doing. Uninitialized variables can be

---

[†]*The mechanical evaluation of expressions*, P. J. Landlin, *The Computer Journal*, 6(4), Jan. 1964, pp. 308–320.

```
 1  #include <ctype.h>
 2  #include <stdio.h>
 3
 4  constexpr size_t STRING_MIN = 4;
 5
 6  int main() {
 7    int    c;
 8    char   str_buf[ STRING_MIN ] = { };
 9    size_t str_len = 0;
10
11    while ( (c = getchar()) != EOF ) {
12      if ( isprint( c ) ) {
13        if ( str_len < STRING_MIN - 1 ) {
14          str_buf[ str_len++ ] = (char)c;
15          continue;
16        }
17        if ( str_len == STRING_MIN - 1 ) {
18          str_buf[ str_len++ ] = '\0';
19          fputs( str_buf, stdout );
20        }
21        putchar( c );
22      }
23      else {
24        if ( str_len == STRING_MIN )
25          putchar( '\n' );
26        str_len = 0;
27      }
28    } // while
29  }
```

Listing 1.4: Print only strings of 4 or more characters

---

a source of bugs (§18.6.8). Some compilers in some cases may be able to warn you when you attempt to read an uninitialized variable, but you can't rely on the compiler doing so.

Why not automatically initialize local variables? It takes time. Not initializing them is another way C achieves its speed. If you're going to write to the variables before reading them anyway, why bother? □

- Line 8 declares str_buf as an array of STRING_MIN char and initializes each to the null character via the = { } syntax (§6.2). When the braces are empty, it means initialize the entire array to zero or equivalent.
- Line 9 defines str_len and initializes it to zero.

  To emphasize what was written earlier, in C, strings are *only* arrays of char ending with a null character. Arrays don't "know" how big they are, so neither do strings — you have to keep track separately, hence str_len.

- Line 12 calls the standard library function isprint declared in the ctype.h standard header (§B.1), hence the #include on line 1. It returns true only if a character is "printable," that is one of a space, a punctuation symbol, a letter, or a digit.

1.3 Strings

- If c is a printable character, then line 13 checks whether we've encountered fewer than 3 printable characters. If so:

    1. Line 14 appends c to str_buf by storing it at position str_len. In C, all arrays start at an index of zero, hence the valid indices for str_buf are 0–3.

       The ++ is the *post-increment* operator (§3.4) that increments a variable by one *after* returning its *old* value. There's also a *pre-increment* operator version that also increments a variable by one, but *before* returning its *new* value. For example:

       ```
       int x = 0;
       int y = x++;   // post-increment: y = 0, x = 1
       int z = ++y;   // pre-increment : z = 1, y = 1
       ```

       is equivalent to:

       ```
       int x = 0;
       int y = x;
       x = x + 1;
       y = y + 1;
       int z = y;
       ```

       but more concise. There's also -- that is both a *pre-* and *post-decrement* operator that decrements by one. Idiomatic C invariably uses ++ and --.

       ■ This is the origin of C++'s name. It's kind-of tongue-in-cheek implying that C++ is an incremental improvement upon C. □

       The (char) before the c is a *type cast* or simply *cast* (§3.14), that is the name of a type enclosed by ( ). It converts ("casts") an expression to the given type. In this case, since c is not EOF, it must be an ordinary character. However, in order to store it into str_buf, it should be cast from an int to a char.

       ■ You can actually omit the cast and the character will be stored just the same, but the compiler will likely warn you that you are storing the value of a larger type int into a smaller type char and may lose information. With the cast, you're telling the compiler that you're aware of the possible loss of information and it's intentional, i.e., you know what you're doing, so it won't warn you. □

    2. After appending c, line 15 performs a continue statement (§5.7) that jumps back to the start of the loop.

- Line 17 checks whether we've encountered exactly 3 printable characters. If so:

    1. Line 18 both null-terminates the string (as all strings must be) and increments str_len so it will now be 4 (important for line 24).

2. Line 19 prints str_buf by calling the standard function fputs (for "file put string," §12.1).

- Line 21 unconditionally prints c since we've encountered at least 3 printable characters previously.
- Line 23 shows that an if statement may have an optional else statement that is executed only if the condition for the if is false.
- If c is not a printable character, then line 24 checks whether we've reached the minimum of 4 printable characters and have been printing them. If so, we must now print a newline (line 25).
- Additionally, we also reset str_len to zero (line 26).

1.4 Functions

Except for the most trivial, programs in C are composed of multiple functions that allow a large, complicated program effectively to be broken down into smaller, simpler mini-programs.

Consider the function putubin in listing 1.5 that prints an unsigned integer in binary and returns the number of characters printed.

```
 1  #include <stdio.h>
 2
 3  unsigned putubin( unsigned n ) {
 4    if ( n == 0 ) {
 5      putchar( '0' );
 6      return 1;
 7    }
 8    unsigned digits = 0;
 9    for ( unsigned bit = ~(~0u >> 1); bit != 0; bit >>= 1 ) {
10      bool const is_1 = (n & bit) != 0;
11      if ( is_1 || digits > 0 ) {
12        putchar( '0' + is_1 );
13        ++digits;
14      }
15    }
16    return digits;
17  }
```

Listing 1.5: Function to print an integer in binary

It does this by starting out with bit equal to the integer where only the left-most bit is 1, print the corresponding bit in n, then for the next iteration, "shift" it to the right by 1, and repeat for however many bits comprise n.

- Line 3 declares the function to take and return unsigned, a non-negative version of int.

  In C, unsigned is a *modifier* (§2.5) that makes a declaration of an integer type be unsigned, for example:

1.4 Functions

```
unsigned char uc;
unsigned int  ui;    // same as: unsigned ui;
```

When the type is `int`, it can be omitted and usually is.

- Line 4 checks for the degenerate case of `n` being zero: if it is, simply print `0` and return `1`.

  ∎ In general, it's a good practice to handle easy, degenerate, or special cases first and return early. This allows the rest of the code not to be concerned with such cases thus making it simpler. □

- Line 8 declares `digits` that will count the number of digits printed.
- Line 9 introduces yet another loop statement: `for` (§5.6). It's a generalization of a `while` loop:

  for (*init-expr$_{opt}$*; *cond-expr$_{opt}$*; *next-expr$_{opt}$*)
      statement

where:

1. The *init-expr* performs any initialization once before the loop. Optionally, it can also declare the variables it's initializing. The scope (§2.4) of such variables is limited to the loop's body.
2. The *cond-expr* is the same as in the `while` loop.
3. The *next-expr* performs any steps necessary to go to the next iteration of the loop. It is performed after the last statement in the loop body or a `continue` statement (§5.7).

A `for` loop is roughly equivalent to:

init-expr;
while (*cond-expr*) {
  body
  next-expr;
}

but more concise. All expressions are optional, but the `;`s must remain. If *cond-expr* is omitted, it's equivalent to `true`.

For this `for` loop:

– The *init-expr* expression starts with `~0u >> 1` that uses the *bitwise-not*, aka, *one's-complement* operator (§3.8) on 0 to yield all 1s to which the *right-shift* operator shifts right by 1 bit to yield an integer with the left-most bit of 0 and the rest all 1s. Finally, `~` is used again to yield the desired integer where only the left-most bit is 1.

   By default, integer literals are of type `int`, i.e., signed. The `u` suffix makes it an unsigned literal.

– The *cond-expr* simply checks that `bit` is not 0.

- The *next-expr* of bit >>= 1 uses the *right-shift-assign* operator (§3.9) to right-shift bit by 1. In C, any assignment with an expression using any operator *op* of the form:

    x = x *op expr*;

  can be rewritten using the assignment version of the same operator like:

    x *op*= *expr*;

  hence bit >>= 1 is equivalent to bit = bit >> 1 but more concise.

- Line 10 introduces the bool type (short for Boolean, §2.5.2) for storing either of the "truth" values true or false. In this case, is_1 is assigned whether n & bit, the *bit-wise and* of n and bit, is not zero, i.e., a 1 — that is whether the bit'th bit of n is a 1.
- On line 11, the || (*logical-or*, §3.6) and > (*greater-than*, §3.5) operators are used to check whether either is_1 is true or digits > 0 so that we print a 0 only if we've previously printed a 1 so as not to print leading zeros. If true:

  1. Line 12 prints a '0', or a '1' if is_1 is true. In C, you can perform arithmetic on characters the same as on integers. (They *are* tiny integers behind the curtain.) Since the ASCII code for '1' is one greater than that of '0', this works.
  2. Line 13 increments digits.

- Line 16 returns digits.

As this function demonstrates, C is particularly good at working with individual bits comprising integers.

1.5 Memory

Before continuing the tour, we need to digress on computer memory. It's basically a (very long) sequence of *bytes*, each having a unique integer address. In C, a byte maps to the char type.

■ This is an oversimplification due to both register and cache memory, but those can be safely ignored for now. □

An analogy is a set of post office boxes, e.g., P.O. Box 1000, as shown in figure 1.1.

Assuming 8 bits, a byte is large enough to store any ASCII character, any signed integer –127 to 128, or any unsigned integer 0 to 255. To store larger values, multiple consecutive bytes are used. The number of bytes used is an object's *size*.

With the exception of char whose size is 1 by definition, C does not mandate specific sizes for any other type, only *minimum* sizes. On modern 64-bit computers,

1.6 Pointers

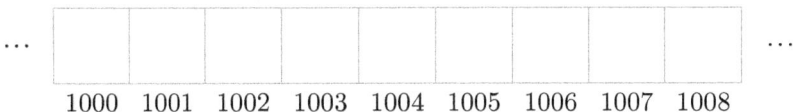

Fig. 1.1: Memory as a sequence of bytes

`int` is typically 32 bits and therefore has a size of 4 bytes. In the post office box analogy, you would need to rent a larger box to store an `int`. For example, storing the integer value 1941 would be done as shown in figure 1.2 where its address is the number of its first box, here 1000.

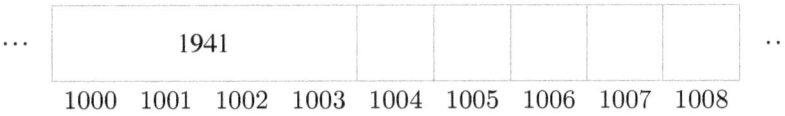

Fig. 1.2: Storing a 4-byte `int`

Once an object has been created at an address, it *stays* at that address forever unless explicitly moved. Moving it to some other address requires that the bytes comprising it be read from its current addresses and written to its new addresses. It's best to avoid moving larger objects (size $\geq$ 16 bytes) whenever possible. Rather than moving objects around, you can simply pass their addresses around instead.

1.6 Pointers

In C, a *pointer* is a variable that contains the address of some other object — it points to where in memory the object is. In the post office box analogy, a pointer would have its own box like any other variable, but inside the box would be a slip of paper with the address of the object to which it points written on it.

Like the types of variables we've already seen, such as `int` and `char`, pointers have types corresponding to the type of the objects to which they're pointing, e.g., *pointer to* `int` and *pointer to* `char`.

To declare a pointer, put the type to which it will point and a `*` before the name:

```
int *p;        // pointer to int
```

To initialize a pointer to point at no `int` in particular, use the special `nullptr` literal:

```
p = nullptr;   // p points to no int
```

One way to make a pointer point at something is by using the `&` (*address-of*) operator (§3.12):

```
int i = 1941;
p = &i;          // p points to i
```

The expression &i gets the memory address of i that = then assigns to p as shown in figure 1.3.

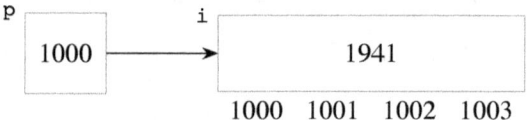

Fig. 1.3: Pointer to int

To get the value of the int to which p points, use the * (*dereference*) operator (§3.12):

```
int j = *p;      // j = 1941
```

■ Note that C "overloads" some operators. In listing 1.5 (p.12), & was the bitwise-and operator, but here it's the address-of operator. Similarly, the * is the multiplication operator, but here it's the dereference operator. The compiler knows which ones you mean based on context. □

In the post office box analogy, to *dereference* p would be to go to p's box, open it, take out the slip of paper having the int's address on it, read it (here, 1000), go to the box having *that* address, and finally read the int's value (here, 1941).

For a use for pointers, consider the program in listing 1.6 that intends to swap the values of two integers.

```
1   #include <stdio.h>
2
3   void swapi( int a, int b ) {         // v1 -- WRONG
4       int temp = a;
5       a = b;
6       b = temp;
7   }
8
9   int main() {
10      int x = 1, y = 2;
11      swapi( x, y );
12      printf( "x=%d, y=%d\n", x, y ); // prints: x=1, y=2
13  }
```

Listing 1.6: Swapping integers, version 1 (the wrong way)

- Line 3 declares a function swapi:
  - The use of void instead of a return type means this function returns nothing.
  - The function has two parameters, the values to swap.

- Line 10 shows multiple variables can be declared in the same declaration separated by commas.

- Line 11 calls swapi passing x and y.
- Line 12 prints the values.

This example also shows how printf can be used to print things other than string literals. When printf prints, it scans its first argument (the *format string*) looking for % characters. When one is encountered, it looks at the characters that follow that specify what is to be printed and how. Every % in the format argument *must* correspond to a subsequent argument (except when followed by another % that means to print a % literally).

In this example, each % is followed by d that means its corresponding argument is an int and to print it in decimal.

If you were to compile and run this program, it would print x and y with their original values — not swapped. Why not? Because C functions pass arguments *by value* that means the value of an argument is copied into the local parameter (variable) of a function. When main calls swapi, the value of x is copied into a and the value of y is copied into b. The function will then swap a and b (the copies), not x and y (the originals). The correct way to write swapi is shown in listing 1.7.

```
 3  void swapi( int *pa, int *pb ) {    // v2 -- correct
 4      int temp = *pa;
 5      *pa = *pb;
 6      *pb = temp;
 7  }
 8
 9  int main() {
10      int x = 1, y = 2;
11      swapi( &x, &y );                      // note '&'
12      printf( "x=%d, y=%d\n", x, y ); // prints: x=2, y=1
13  }
```

Listing 1.7: Swapping integers, version 2 (the right way)

- Line 3 now declares the two parameters as pointers to int.
- Lines 4–6 now swap the values of the integers to which the pointers point.
- Line 11 passes the addresses of x and y instead.

1.7 const

In addition to constexpr first shown in §1.2, C also has const. Before continuing the tour, we need to digress on their differences.

- As shown previously, the purpose of constexpr is to give names to constant values rather than using magic values directly.
- The purpose of const is to mark an object *immutable* after it's been initialized, not constant, hence it's a misnomer.

The details of each would be too much of a digression, so they will be deferred until §4.4 and §4.5. For now, the rules for when to use constexpr vs. const can be summarized as:

- Use constexpr to give names to things that otherwise would be magic values:

  ```
  constexpr size_t BUF_SIZE    = 4096;
  constexpr char   GREETING[] = "hello, world";
  ```

- Use const to mark an object immutable after initialization. For example, we can revise listing 1.7 to use const as shown in listing 1.8.

  ```
  void swapi( int *pa, int *pb ) {   // v3 -- with const
    const int temp = *pa;            // temp won't change
    *pa = *pb;
    *pb = temp;
  }
  ```

  Listing 1.8: Swapping integers, version 3, with const

Using const in such a small function doesn't really matter; but in larger functions, an object marked const:

1. Prevents accidentally changing its value. (If you try, the compiler will warn you.)
2. Documents to programmers that an object will not change rather than having to scrutinize the code to see if the value is ever changed.

It's a good practice to make objects const whenever possible. This is known as *const correctness*. Subsequent examples will all be const correct.

> ■ Admittedly, having to sprinkle const all over your programs is both tedious and verbose. Ideally, const would be the default and you'd have to specifically declare an object as, say, mutable to modify it. Unfortunately, C didn't originally have const so you can't simply add a mutable keyword and retroactively make all other declarations immutable by default without breaking every C program in existence. Hence, adding const to C was much less disruptive and better than not adding it. □

When it comes to pointers, there are two things that can be const: the object pointed to and the pointer itself. Listing 1.9 summarizes const pointer declarations. A few declarations need further explanation:

- On line 5, even though pcc is a pointer to const char, it can point at a non-const char. This means you can't modify the char via *that* pointer. Whether the char is actually const is irrelevant. The same is true for cpc1 on line 11.
- On lines 8, 9, 11, and 12, the pointers are const as indicated by a const to the right of the *. Since they're const, they must be initialized in their declarations. For such declarations, reading them right-to-left helps, for example cpc1 is a "constant pointer to a char that is constant."

1.7 const

```
1   char nc = 'x';                  // non-const
2   const char c = nc;              // const
3
4   const char *ncpc;               // non-const to const
5   ncpc = &nc;                     // ... OK
6   ncpc = &c;                      // ... OK
7
8   char *const cpnc1 = &nc;        // const to non-const: OK
9   char *const cpnc2 = &c;         // ... error
10
11  const char *const cpc1 = &nc;   // const to const: OK
12  const char *const cpc2 = &c;    // ... OK
```

Listing 1.9: Pointer declarations with const

- On line 9, the declaration is illegal because a pointer to non-const may not point to a const.

One final stylistic thing about const is that C doesn't care where you put it within a declaration. For example, the following declarations are equivalent:

```
const char x = 'a';     // "west" const
char const y = 'b';     // "east" const
```

The latter is known as "east const" because the const is to the right or "east" of the type it's making const. For declarations that don't involve pointers, there's no benefit; but for pointer declarations, the benefit is that const is always east of what it's making const. For example, in:

```
char const *const cpcc = &x;    // const is always "east"
```

the first const makes the char to its left const; the second const makes the * to its left const. Hence, it's consistent. Again, reading right-to-left helps: cpcc is a "constant pointer to a constant char." Subsequent examples will all use the east const style.

An example that illustrates many of the things presented so far is an implementation of the strcpy standard function (§B.2) that copies a string from src to dst and returns dst is shown in listing 1.10.

```
char* strcpy( char *dst, char const *src ) {
    char *const dst_orig = dst;
    while ( true ) {
        *dst = *src;
        if ( *dst == '\0' )
            return dst_orig;
        ++dst;
        ++src;
    }
}
```

Listing 1.10: strcpy implementation, version 1

By now, the code should be fairly straightforward. It copies a string a character at a time. If the last character copied was the null character, the function returns. Otherwise, it increments both dst and src and continues.

While this function works efficiently, a much more idiomatic version is shown in listing 1.11.

```
char* strcpy( char *dst, char const *src ) {
  char *const dst_orig = dst;
  while ( (*dst++ = *src++) )
    ;
  return dst_orig;
}
```

Listing 1.11: strcpy implementation, version 2, using idiomatic C

All the work of assigning *src to *dst, checking that result for zero (in this case, the null character), and incrementing both dst and src, is done within the while expression, so nothing is needed for the body, hence an empty statement (§5.11) of just ;. The extra () are used to suppress a warning about using = when you might have meant ==. It's necessary to use the post version of ++ here since we need to copy the first character before incrementing the pointers.

Such conciseness is a hallmark of C. While it may seem like gibberish now, it will eventually become second nature.

1.8 Dynamic Memory

Compared to modern languages, strings in C are primitive. As mentioned in §1.3, strings are only arrays of char. When you declare an array, you must specify a size.

Suppose you have a string, but want to append another to it as in listing 1.12.

```
1  #include <stdio.h>
2  #include <string.h>
3
4  int main() {
5    char greeting[13] = "hello";   // 5 + 7 + 1 = 13
6    strcat( greeting, ", world" );
7    puts( greeting );
8  }
```

Listing 1.12: String concatenation (the hard way)

- Line 2 includes the string.h standard header (§B.2) that declares several string functions including strcat used on line 6.
- Line 5 declares greeting so it's big enough to hold its initial contents "hello" (5), plus the string to be appended ", world" (7), and the null character (1).
- Line 6 concatenates the second string onto the end of the first. The array for the first *must* be big enough to hold their combined lengths. If not, it would result

1.8 Dynamic Memory

in a *buffer overflow* that is a source of many bugs (§18.6.2). The C compiler will not warn you when the program is compiled nor will the C runtime alert you when a buffer overflow occurs except perhaps via a core dump (§18.4) — if you're lucky.

- Line 7 calls the standard function `puts` that prints the string and a newline.

Fortunately, there is a better way. But first, a digression on memory kinds.

In any running program (written in any language), there are three broad kinds of memory:

1. **Global, aka, static memory**: holds all of a program's global variables. Its size is determined by the compiler and is fixed.
2. **Stack memory**: holds all of a function's local variables on a "stack" while that function is executing. Its size is determined by the compiler based on the number of local variables, but the size of the stack grows as functions are called and shrinks as they return.
3. **Heap, aka, dynamic memory**: holds anything you want for as long as you want on a "heap" independent of functions. Its size is determined by you. However, in addition to you allocating such memory, in C, *you* must free it explicitly.

Rather than guess how big to make an array, you can *dynamically allocate* exactly how much you need and make a pointer point to it. This can be done to concatenate strings with no chance of a buffer overflow. In listing 1.13, we define a function `mstrcat` (a dynamic memory version of `strcat`) to do exactly that.

```c
#include <stdio.h>
#include <stdlib.h>            // for malloc & free
#include <string.h>

char* mstrcat( char const *s1, char const *s2 ) {
  size_t const s1_len = strlen( s1 );
  char *const s12 = malloc( s1_len + strlen( s2 ) + 1 );
  strcpy( s12, s1 );
  strcpy( s12 + s1_len, s2 );
  return s12;
}

int main() {
  char *const msg = mstrcat( "hello", ", world" );
  puts( msg );
  free( msg );
}
```

Listing 1.13: String concatenation (the better way)

- Line 5 declares that `mstrcat` takes two constant strings (pointers to constant arrays of `char`) and returns a new concatenated string.
- Line 6 calls the standard function `strlen` (§B.2) that gets the length of `s1` and assigns it to `s1_len` since we'll need it twice.

- Line 7 calls the standard function `malloc` that dynamically allocates the given number of bytes (in this case, `s1_len`, plus the length of `s2`, plus 1 for the null character) and returns a pointer to the first byte.
- Line 8 calls the standard function `strcpy` (§B.2) to copy the characters comprising `s1` (including its terminating null character) to the start of `s12`.
- Line 9 calls `strcpy` again to copy the characters comprising `s2` to the start of `s12` *plus* `s1_len` that's at the end of the string as shown in figure 1.4. C allows arithmetic on pointers (§6.7). The null character is overwritten with the first character of `s2` followed by the rest of its characters and a new null character.

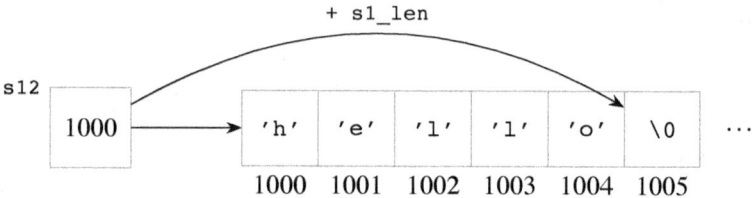

Fig. 1.4: `mstrcat`: copy `s2` to `s12 + s1_len`

- Line 10 returns a pointer to the new, concatenated string.
- Line 15 calls the standard function `puts` that prints the string and a newline.
- Line 16 calls the standard function `free` that frees the memory.

C doesn't have *garbage collection*, hence every call to `malloc` should be balanced by a call to `free` eventually, but generally as soon as the memory is no longer needed. A *memory leak* (§18.6.7) occurs when the value of a pointer to allocated memory is somehow lost thus making it impossible to pass to `free`. Repeated leaks will eventually exhaust memory. For listing 1.13, if `mstrcat` were called from within a loop and the concatenated strings returned by it were not freed, then each iteration would leak more memory.

As an exception, if some memory is allocated *once*, it's actually OK not to free it. When any program terminates, all memory used by it is reclaimed by the operating system.

If at this point you're thinking that's a lot of work just to concatenate two strings together, you're right. However, modern languages that have proper strings that can be concatenated easily are doing the same work behind the curtain to give the illusion that strings "just work." There are several ways to implement proper strings, each with their own storage and performance trade-offs. In a language with proper strings, you're generally stuck with whatever trade-offs the language implementers made. In C, you get to decide for yourself (§23).

1.9 Structures

Whereas an array is many objects of one type, a *structure* (§10) is one object of (potentially) many types. Suppose you want to create a proper string object that can grow automatically. You can declare a structure using `struct` followed by its name:

```
struct string {
    char    *contents;   // pointer to actual contents
    size_t  len;         // length (not including null at end)
};
```

This structure has two *members*: the first for a pointer to the actual characters comprising the contents of the string and the second for its length.

You can declare a variable of a structure type and optionally initialize it using {} where the order of the values corresponds to the order that the members were declared (§10.3):

```
struct string str = { "hello", 5 };
```

Alternatively, you can use *designated initializers* (§10.3), that is use the member names preceded by . (dot) and followed by =:

```
struct string str = { .contents = "hello", .len = 5 };
```

Designated initializers can be given in any order. To access a member, use a . (*member-access* operator, §3.13) followed by the name of the member:

```
puts( str.contents );
```

To access a member via pointer:

```
struct string *pstr = &str;
puts( (*pstr).contents );
```

You need the ( ) since . has a higher precedence (§3) than *. Fortunately, C provides a -> (*pointer-member-access* aka, "arrow") operator variant of the dereference operator that's a shorthand:

```
puts( pstr->contents );  // same as: (*pstr).contents
```

However, we don't want to manipulate the members manually; we want to write functions that manipulate the members on our behalf. One such function is to put (append) a string as shown in listing 1.14.

- Line 3 uses the standard function `realloc` that's similar to but unlike `malloc` in that `realloc` takes an existing pointer and *reallocates* the pointed-to memory to make it have the new length and returns a new pointer. (If the original pointer is null, then `realloc` allocates fresh memory.)

```
1  void string_puts( struct string *str, char const *s ) {
2    size_t const new_len = str->len + strlen( s );
3    str->contents = realloc( str->contents, new_len + 1 );
4    strcpy( str->contents + str->len, s );
5    str->len = new_len;
6  }
```

Listing 1.14: `string_puts` function

- Line 4 uses `strcpy` to copy `s` to the memory address `str + str->len` similarly to listing 1.13 (p.21), line 9.

We also need a function to clean up a `string` by freeing its contents as shown in listing 1.15.

```
1  void string_cleanup( struct string *str ) {
2    free( str->contents );
3    *str = (struct string){ };
4  }
```

Listing 1.15: `string_cleanup` function

- Line 2 calls `free` to free the memory used by the string's contents.
- Line 3 uses a *compound literal* (§10.4) that's used to create a literal for a `struct` by putting the name of a `struct` between `()` (similar to a cast) followed by the values between `{}`. As with initializing arrays, if the `{}` are empty, it means initialize every member to zero or equivalent. Initializing the `struct` to zero isn't strictly necessary here, but it's a good practice.

■ This function isn't named `string_free` because my personal style is to name a function with a `_cleanup` suffix if it cleans-up an object's resources but does *not* free the object itself and with a `_free` suffix only if it *also* frees the object. □

Given those two functions, we can now write code as shown in listing 1.16.

```
int main() {
  struct string str = { };
  string_puts( &str, "hello" );
  string_puts( &str, ", world" );
  puts( str.contents );
  string_cleanup( &str );
}
```

Listing 1.16: Using `string`

Writing functions that take a pointer to a structure to manipulate it is what any object-oriented language does behind the curtain via an implicit "`this`" or "`self`" pointer. In C, you simply have to be explicit about the pointer. (You could rename `str` in all the examples to `this` if you wanted.) Similarly, in C++, an object's resources get cleaned-up automatically via a suitably defined "destructor." In C, you simply have to be explicit about calling cleanup functions.

1.10 Epilogue

This concludes the tour of C covering the core of the language: variables, functions, constants, loops, pointers, strings, arrays, and structures. Using these features, it's possible to build pretty much anything from Apache to Zlib. The next several chapters will fill in some features and details not covered in the tour.

At this point, you may be thinking that digressing on topics such as memory, pointers, and dynamic memory management in the *first* chapter seems surprisingly low-level. Modern languages are generally designed so that you don't need to think — or even know — about the details of how memory is organized or how data is stored in it. You're only supposed to write code that implements some semantics and such details are none of your business. In contrast, C's perspective is that such details *are* your business.[†]

You may also be wondering why C is this way. The answer is because *reality* is this way. Fundamentally, computers execute instructions, interpret sequences of bytes as particular data types like int, and access data via pointers. C was designed to be "close to the machine" to work with such details directly.[‡]

Even though modern languages often hide such details, they're dealing with them nonetheless behind the curtain. Indeed, in order for them to do what they do, some have their core components written in C. For example, you can't implement the Java Virtual Machine (JVM) in Java because a Java program needs a JVM to run. Similarly, you can't write the Python interpreter in Python.

Consequently, you will eventually *need* to understand such details to do anything non-trivial in C. But fear not: the details aren't that complicated.

> "This is your last chance. After this, there is no turning back. You take the blue pill: the story ends, you wake up in your bed, and believe whatever you want to believe. You take the red pill: you stay in Wonderland and I show you how deep the rabbit-hole goes."
> — Morpheus[§]

Exercises

1. The *strings* program in listing 1.4 (p.10) has a minor printing issue in that if the input ends with 4 or more printing characters not followed by a newline, then

---

[†] *The Descent to C*, Simon Tatham, 2013,
https://www.chiark.greenend.org.uk/~sgtatham/cdescent/

[‡] *The Development of the C Language*, Dennis M. Ritchie, *History of Programming Languages*, 2nd ed., ACM Press, New York, and Addison-Wesley, Reading, Mass, 1996.

[§] Laurence Fishburne (*Morpheus*), *The Matrix*, Lana Wachowski and Lilly Wachowski (directors), Warner Bros. and Village Roadshow Pictures, March 24, 1999.

the last string printed won't have a newline printed after it. Aesthetically, the output would look better if it did.

Modify the program so that a newline is always printed after 4 or more printing characters. Hint: you can use `str_len` to determine if a final newline needs to be printed after the `while` loop.

2. Even though `strlen` is part of C's standard library, it would be good to solidify your understanding of strings to write it yourself. Therefore, write a function:

    ```
    size_t strlen( char const *s );
    ```

    that returns the length of `s` (the number of non-null characters, if any, before the null character).

3. Write a function:

    ```
    size_t strnlen( char const *s, size_t n );
    ```

    that's similar to `strlen`, but returns L_n, the smaller of `n` and the length of `s`. To be efficient, your solution should not examine more than L_n characters, i.e., not call `strlen`.

4. Write a function:

    ```
    void string_putsn( struct string *str,
                       char const *s, size_t n );
    ```

    that puts at most `n` characters of `s` onto the end of `str`. The size of the reallocated memory should be `str->len` plus the smaller of `n` and the length of `s`. Hint: use your solution to the previous exercise as part of your solution to this exercise.

5. Write a function:

    ```
    void string_putc( struct string *str, char c );
    ```

    that puts `c` onto the end of `str`. Hint: use your solution to the previous exercise as part of your solution to this exercise.

6. Write a function:

    ```
    void string_paths( struct string *str,
                       char const *comp );
    ```

    that appends `comp`, a path component, ensuring exactly one / character separates it from the existing string, e.g., for a Unix path `"/a"` or `"/a/"` and component `"b"` or `"/b"`, the result would be `"/a/b"`. Hint: use your solutions to the previous exercises as part of your solution to this exercise.

Chapter 2
Comments, Names, and Types

Like many other programming languages, C is a typed language having distinct types for Boolean, character, integer, and floating-point numbers. Since C was designed to be "close to the machine," it has many variations of its types to suit particular situations. There are many detailed rules for conversions among types and also many ways to express literals for types.

Consequently, but necessarily, this chapter has a high information density. It's therefore recommended to skim it and refer back to it when necessary.

2.1 Comments

As first shown in listing 1.1 (p.6), there are two ways to include comments in C:

- Between /* and */ that may span multiple lines. Such comments cannot nest (but see §8.5).
- After // that spans until the end of the line.

Here's some advice for writing comments:

- Don't comment what the code already says, for example:

    ```
    ++i;                    // increment 'i'
    ```

    Such comments are pointless at best. Instead, say *why* something is being done:

    ```
    ++i;                    // ensure room for null character
    ```

- For files as a whole, include a comment stating what the purpose of the declarations contained within it have in common:

    ```
    // Declares a string type that grows when necessary
    // and functions for manipulating such strings.
    ```

- Include a copyright notice and license information.
- For functions:
    - Briefly state the purpose of the function.
    - For each parameter, if there are any preconditions, e.g., whether an argument can (or cannot) be nullptr — and what happens if it is.
    - For non-void functions, what the function returns under normal conditions and under error conditions (§9.6), if any. When returning a pointer, whether the caller is responsible for freeing it.
    - What related functions exist, if any.
- If code was based on code or algorithm in a book, cite it:

    ```
    // See "Introduction to Algorithms," 4th ed.,
    // 13.2, p. 336.
    ```

- If code was based on code online, include a URL:

    ```
    // From <https://gist.github.com/badocelot/5331587>
    ```

- Comment assumptions made and anything else non-obvious.
- If you update code, update its comments to match. Wrong comments are worse than no comments.

Unlike some other languages, C doesn't have a standard documentation comment format. However, Doxygen[†] has emerged as the de facto standard format and tool for documenting C (and C++) code. For example, the function mstrcat from listing 1.13 (p.21) might be documented using Doxygen as shown in listing 2.1.

```
/**
 * Concatenates \a s1 and \a s2 together into a new string.
 *
 * \param s1 The first string to concatenate; must not be
 * 'nullptr'.
 * \param s2 The second string to concatenate; must not be
 * 'nullptr'.
 * \return Returns a new string of \a s2 concatenated onto
 * \a s1.
 * The caller is responsible for freeing it.
 */
char* mstrcat( char const *s1, char const *s2 );
```

Listing 2.1: mstrcat documented using Doxygen

[†]https://www.doxygen.nl/

2.2 Names

The names of variables, constants, functions, and everything else (collectively, *identifiers*) have a few rules. An identifier:

1. Must start with a letter, underscore, or Unicode character from the `XID_Start`[†] class.
2. May continue with letters, underscores, digits, or Unicode characters from the `XID_Continue` class.
3. Can be of any length.
4. Considers upper case and lower case letters as distinct.
5. Must not be the same as a C keyword.
6. Must not begin with an underscore if it has *external linkage* (§4.3).
7. Must not begin with an underscore followed by either a capital letter or another underscore.

   ■ To evolve C, the C committee occasionally adds new keywords. The problem is that every new keyword has the potential to break existing programs because some may already use the same identifier. To help minimize this possibility, the committee decided that new keywords would generally start with an underscore followed by a capital letter (e.g., `_Bool`, §C.6), at least for a transition period to allow people time to update their programs. Such keywords may look odd, but it's better than breaking programs.

   Names that begin with double underscore are reserved for use by the implementation. □

8. If compatibility with C++ is desired (§13.4), must not contain a double underscore anywhere.

Generally, the names of most things are in all lower case, except the names of constants (§4.4), enumeration constants (§7), and macros (§8.3, §8.7) are in all upper case; underscores separate words.

■ This is another topic of insufferable debates that have raged for decades about which is the "one true style" for naming things. This book largely uses K&R's style. □

[†]*Properties for Lexical Classes for Identifiers*, Unicode Standard Annex #31, Unicode Identifiers and Syntax, table 2.

2.3 Namespaces

C also has a set of predefined *namespaces*: names in one namespace are distinct from names all other namespaces.

> ■ Aside from names in different namespaces being distinct, namespaces in C are nothing like namespaces in C++. Their respective standards both happen to use the term "namespaces." In C++, namespaces are explicitly named, e.g., std, you can create your own, and you explicitly put names into them. In C, namespaces have no name (ironically), are fixed, i.e., you can't create your own, and names are implicitly put into them based on the kind of name and context of its declaration.
>
> C++ has all of C's namespaces as well; it's just that the C++ standard doesn't call them "namespaces" or anything. □

The fixed namespaces in C are:

- **Attribute**: For attribute names (§4.9). Every attribute prefix also has its own namespace.
- **Member**: Every structure (§10) or union (§11) creates a namespace for all of its members.
- **Label**: For goto labels (§5.10).
- **Tag**: For all enumeration (§7), structure, and union names.
- **Ordinary**: For everything else: variable names, constant names (§4.4), function names (§9), typedef names (§2.6), and enumeration values (§7.5).

2.4 Scope

C also has a set of *scopes*:

- **File**: For all names declared within a file outside any function.
- **Block**: A compound statement (§5.2). Blocks can nest.
- **Function**: Every function creates a scope for its goto labels (§5.10).
- **Function Prototype**: Every function declaration creates a scope for its parameters (§9.1).

For an example of file scope, recall listing 1.3 (p.7) that declared BUF_SIZE:

```
constexpr size_t BUF_SIZE = 4096; // file scope

int main() {
  // ...
```

Variables can also be declared at file scope and is done typically when more than one function needs access to some shared information, for example:

2.5 Built-In Types

```
    bool is_testing;            // in testing mode?
```

Unlike local variables, all file-scope variables that are not explicitly initialized are automatically initialized to zero or equivalent. File-scope variables are also known as *global variables*. For listing 1.5 (p.12) repeated here in listing 2.2:

```
1  unsigned putubin( unsigned n ) {
2    if ( n == 0 ) {
3      putchar( '0' );
4      return 1;
5    }
6    unsigned digits = 0;
7    for ( unsigned bit = ~(~0u >> 1); bit != 0; bit >>= 1 ) {
8      bool const is_1 = (n & bit) != 0;
9      if ( is_1 || digits > 0 ) {
10       putchar( '0' + is_1 );
11       ++digits;
12     }
13   }
14   return digits;
15 }
```

Listing 2.2: Repeat of putubin to illustrate scope

- putubin (line 1) is in file scope.
- n (line 1) and digits (line 6) are in the block scope {} between lines 1–15. Even though n is declared before the { on line 1, it's "injected" into the subsequent block scope.
- bit (line 7) and is_1 (line 8) are in the block scope {} between lines 7–13. Even though bit is declared before the { on line 7, it's injected into the subsequent block scope.

2.5 Built-In Types

Table 2.1 shows the complete set of built-in types in C. The types bool, char, int, and _BitInt, comprise the *integer types*. The types above the line are used most often; the types below are used only in special circumstances. Each is covered in a subsequent section of this chapter.

2.5.1 Modifiers

In addition to the built-in types, there are *modifiers* for some of those types as shown in table 2.2.

Table 2.1: Built-in types

`bool`	Boolean (§2.5.2).
`char`	Single character (§2.5.3).
`int`	Signed integer (§2.5.4).
`float`	Single-precision floating-point (§2.5.6).
`double`	Double-precision floating-point (§2.5.6).
`_BitInt(`n`)`	Bit-precise integer (§2.5.5).
`_Decimal32`	32-bit decimal floating-point (§2.5.7).
`_Decimal64`	64-bit decimal floating-point (§2.5.7).
`_Decimal128`	128-bit decimal floating-point (§2.5.7).

Table 2.2: Modifiers

`signed`	Signed `char`, `int`, or `_BitInt`.
`unsigned`	Unsigned `char`, `int`, or `_BitInt`.
`short`	Short `int`.
`long`	Long `int` or `double`.
`long long`	Very long `int`.
`_Complex`	Complex `float`, `double`, or `long double` (§2.5.8).
`_Imaginary`	Imaginary `float`, `double`, or `long double` (§2.5.9).

Additionally, the modifiers `unsigned` and either `short` or `long` can be combined:

```
unsigned short      us;
unsigned long long  ull;
```

The modifier `signed` is generally useful only for `signed char` (§2.5.3) since signed is the default for integers (except §10.7). As a reminder, when at least one modifier is used, `int` is understood and typically omitted.

2.5.2 `bool`

As first shown in listing 1.5 (p.12), the type `bool` is used to store a "truth" value of either `true` or `false`. For historical reasons (§C.6), C considers *any* non-zero value "true" and only zero "false":

```
int  i = .5;        // i = 0 (truncates)
bool b = .5;        // b = true
```

Even though only one bit is needed to store either true or false, the size of a `bool` is invariably the same size as `char` because `char` is the smallest object that offers unique memory addresses.

2.5.3 char

The type char is used to store a single character, hence is generally synonymous with a *byte*.

■ In 1972 when C was created, the notion of what a *character* is was ASCII, hence C's char type is only capable of holding at best characters from American and western European character sets. Unicode wouldn't be invented for nearly another 20 years.

So as to remain backwards compatible, char is exactly the same today as it was in 1972. Eventually, both new character types and Unicode encodings would be invented and used in C. □

■ A byte is generally 8 bits, but some specialized computers use different values. The actual value for a given computer is provided by the CHAR_BIT constant defined in the limits.h standard header. □

Curiously, char has three versions:

char	Signed or unsigned character (implementation defined).
signed char	Signed character.
unsigned char	Unsigned character.

You should use char by default; signed char only when you need small, signed integers (rare, and int8_t is better, §2.7); and unsigned char when dealing with raw byte values (but uint8_t is better).

Literals for characters are of the form '*c*', that is a character enclosed by single quotation marks where *c* is any character, or an escaped character, one of \' (single quote), \" (double quote), \\ (backslash), \a (alert, aka, bell), \b (backspace), \f (form feed), \n (newline), \r (carriage return), \t (tab), \v (vertical tab), *ooo* (1–3 octal digits, 0–7), or \x*hh* (1–2 hexadecimal digits, 0–9, a–f, or A–F).

Literals for character strings are of the form "*c**", that is zero or more characters enclosed by double quotation marks where *c* is the same as for char literals.

For an example of character literals, a program that expands tab characters to their equivalent number of spaces based on tab-stops is shown in listing 2.3. While most of the program should be understandable by now, a few things need some explanation:

- Using len, line 9 calculates the number of spaces away the *next* tab-stop is, i.e., the number of spaces the current tab needs to expand into. The % is the *modulus* operator (§3.2).
- Line 10 use a particular feature of printf (§12.1.1) to print a specific number of spaces. The %s conversion specifier prints a string, here "", the empty string. Between the % and s is normally an integer that specifies a "field" width to print the string within: if the length of the string is less than that, it's padded with spaces. The * instead of an integer means to use the next int argument as the width, in this case, spaces, rather than a fixed number. Printing an empty string will pad it with spaces spaces.

```
 1  #include <stdio.h>
 2
 3  constexpr unsigned TAB_STOP = 8;    // chars per tab-stop
 4
 5  int main() {
 6    unsigned len = 0;                 // length of line so far
 7    for ( int c; (c = getchar()) != EOF; ) {
 8      if ( c == '\t' ) {
 9        unsigned const spaces = TAB_STOP - len % TAB_STOP;
10        printf( "%*s", spaces, "" );
11        len += spaces;
12        continue;
13      }
14      putchar( c );
15      if ( c == '\n' )
16        len = 0;
17      else
18        ++len;
19    }
20  }
```

Listing 2.3: Expand tabs to spaces

2.5.4 int

The type int is for storing integer values. As mentioned in §2.5.1, the modifiers short, long, or long long may be used in conjunction with unsigned.

Literals for integers are of form:

- d^+: decimal, where d starts with 1–9 and followed by zero or more of 0–9; or:
- 0bb^+ or 0Bb^+: binary, where b is one or more of 0–1; or:
- 0o^*: octal, where o is zero or more of 0–7; or:
- 0xh^+ or 0xh^+: hexadecimal, where h is one or more of 0–9, a–f, or A–F.

For example, 42 (decimal) can be alternatively written as 0b101010 (binary), 052 (octal), or 0x2A (hexadecimal). Additionally, ' (single quotes) may be interspersed as separators to aid readability.

Integer literals may optionally have suffixes, one of l or L for long, ll or LL for long long, or u or U for unsigned that may be combined with any of the others.

Examples of integer literals are: -40, 299'792'458, 0644, and 0xFFFFFFFFul.

2.5.5 _BitInt

The type _BitInt(n), where n is a positive constant integer expression, is for storing integer values having n bits — a *bit-precise integer*. Some examples:

2.5 Built-In Types

```
unsigned _BitInt(24)   rgb24;     // 24-bit RGB color
unsigned _BitInt(256)  sha256;    // SHA-256
```

The rules for _BitInt are:

- It may be either signed (the default) or unsigned.
- If signed, n includes the sign bit.
- Values are limited to the number of bits, n. For unsigned, values are modulo n:

```
unsigned _BitInt(3) x = 7;
++x;                         // x = 0, not 8
```

Without _BitInt, values would have to be constrained manually via masking (§3.8) that you could forget to do:

```
unsigned x = 7;
x = (x + 1) & 0b111;         // same, but more verbose
```

- The maximum bits for n is at least as many as for unsigned long long.
- _BitInt types do *not* participate in *integer promotions* (§2.13 #3, p.43).

_BitInt is also useful for *bit-fields* (§10.7).

Literals for _BitInt are the same as for integers (§2.5.4) except instead have the optional suffixes wb or WB for signed types and uwb or UWB for unsigned types.

2.5.6 float, double, and long double

The types float, double, and long double are for storing floating-point values.

■ Obviously, "float" comes from storing floating-point values. Perhaps less obviously, "double" comes from storing floating-point values with double the precision of float. The term "double precision" dates back to Fortran in the mid-1960s (as does "single precision").

Back then, when computers were a lot slower and memory was a lot more expensive, single precision was the default since it was faster than and half the storage of double precision. However, some calculations required extra precision despite the performance and storage penalties, hence double precision. You therefore used single precision by default unless you needed double precision. The single vs. double precision distinction has pervaded most every programming language since, including C.

These days, when performance is much better and memory is much cheaper, the situation has largely reversed in that you should generally use double by default unless you have storage constraints in which case you should use float. □

Literals for double have a *significand* optionally followed by an *exponent* optionally followed by a suffix:

- The significand is an optional + or -, followed by zero or more digits, optionally followed by a decimal point (.), optionally followed by a fractional part.
- The exponent is one of e, E, p, or P, optionally followed by a + or -, followed by one or more digits. Exponents using e or E are 10^n; exponents using p or P are 2^n.

Digit sequences may alternatively be specified in hexadecimal (start with 0x or 0X). Additionally, ' (single quotes) may be interspersed as separators to aid readability.

Examples of floating-point literals are: 42. (note the trailing .), 3.14, 1.21E9 (1.21×10^9), 6.626070150e-34 ($6.62607015 \times 10^{-34}$), and 0x1.2p3 (0x1.2 = 1.125 decimal $\times\, 2^3 = 9.0$).

Literals for float are the same as literals for double except with either a f or F suffix. Literals for long double are the same as literals for double except with either a l or L suffix.

2.5.7 _Decimal32, _Decimal64, and _Decimal128

The types _Decimal32, _Decimal64, and _Decimal128 (collectively, the *decimal-floating types*) are alternative floating-point types to float, double, and long double (collectively, the *standard-floating types*). Decimal-floating types are supported only if the __STDC_IEC_60559_DFP__ macro is predefined (§8.4).

Decimal-floating types are better for calculations involving money (dollars, euros, pounds, etc.) because they're not subject to the same rounding errors that the standard-floating types are. The standard-floating types are still better for general floating-point calculations.

Literals for the decimal-floating types are the same as for the standard-floating types except instead have the suffixes df or DF for _Decimal32, dd or DD for _Decimal64, and dl or DL for _Decimal128.

2.5.8 Complex Numbers

The _Complex modifier when used with one of float, double, or long double, is for storing complex numbers, that is floating-point numbers with real and imaginary parts. Complex numbers are generally used only for special applications in math or physics. Complex numbers are supported only if the __STDC_NO_COMPLEX__ macro is *not* predefined (§8.4).

The complex.h standard header defines math functions and macros (§8.3) for working with complex numbers. It also does:

```
#define complex _Complex
```

so you can use the more natural-looking `complex`.

For example, the function in listing 2.4 implements Euler's formula (where `I` is a constant defined in `complex.h` for the imaginary number i).

```
#include <complex.h>

double complex euler( double x ) {
  return cexp( I * x );
}
```

Listing 2.4: Example of complex numbers

2.5.9 Imaginary Numbers

The `_Imaginary` modifier when used with one of `float`, `double`, or `long double`, is for storing imaginary numbers, that is only the imaginary part of complex numbers (§2.5.8). Like complex numbers, imaginary numbers are generally used only for special applications in math or physics. Imaginary numbers are supported only if the `__STDC_NO_COMPLEX__` macro is *not* predefined (§8.4) *and* the `complex.h` standard header defines the macros `imaginary` (as a more natural-looking synonym for `_Imaginary`) and `_Imaginary_I` (for the imaginary number i).

2.6 typedef

C allows the creation of aliases to existing types via `typedef`. For example:

```
typedef unsigned short process_id;
process_id pid;
```

defines an alias called `process_id` that can subsequently be used anywhere the original type can be. Syntactically, a `typedef` declaration is exactly like a normal declaration except prefixed by `typedef`. Instead of declaring a variable *of* that type, it declares an alias *for* that type.

```
typedef char int32_buf[4];   // type: array 4 of char
int32_buf buf;               // variable: as if char buf[4]
```

Note that `typedef` does *not* create a distinct type. For example:

```
typedef unsigned short user_id;
user_id uid = pid;           // wrong, but legal
```

Even though process IDs and user IDs are conceptually different things, C allows assignment from one to the other without error or even warning because they're both aliases for `unsigned short`. In C, the only ways to create new, distinct types are via one of enumerations (§7), structures (§10), or unions (§11).

Despite this caveat, `typedef` declarations are useful for a number of reasons:

1. Even though the compiler doesn't care about alias names, a name like `user_id` documents to programmers what it's for.
2. Allow easy modification of the underlying type. If at some point you need to make `user_id` instead be an alias for `unsigned long`, you only have to change the `typedef` in one place rather than everywhere `unsigned short` was used for user IDs throughout your program.
3. Allow elimination of having to use `enum`, `struct`, or `union` before enumeration, structure, or union type names, respectively:

   ```
   typedef struct string string;
   string s;                    // don't need "struct" now
   ```

2.7 Fixed-Width Integer Types

In addition to the built-in types (§2.5), the C standard library also defines several fixed-width integer types having a specific number of bits in the `stdint.h` standard header shown in table 2.3. The fixed-width types should be used *only* if if you need to represent a value contained within a specific number of bits (§2.12).

Table 2.3: Fixed-width integer types

int8_t	signed 8-bit int.	uint8_t	unsigned 8-bit int.
int16_t	signed 16-bit int.	uint16_t	unsigned 16-bit int.
int32_t	signed 32-bit int.	uint32_t	unsigned 32-bit int.
int64_t	signed 64-bit int.	uint64_t	unsigned 64-bit int.
intmax_t	largest signed int.	uintmax_t	largest unsigned int.
intptr_t	pointer-sized signed int.	uintptr_t	pointer-sized unsigned int.

2.8 Unicode Character Types

The C standard library also defines other integer types specifically for either "wide" or Unicode characters shown in table 2.4 defined in the headers shown.

The type `char8_t` is used for storing an octet of a multi-byte Unicode character or string using the UTF-8 encoding. Literals for `char8_t` are the same as for `char` or strings (§2.5.3), but prefixed by `u8`:

```
constexpr char8_t SMILEY_FACE[] = u8"\xF0\x9F\x99\x82";
```

2.10 Numeric Limits   39

Table 2.4: Wide character types

char8_t	Unicode octet, UTF-8 encoding.	uchar.h
char16_t	Unicode character, UTF-16 encoding.	uchar.h
char32_t	Unicode character, UTF-32 encoding.	uchar.h
wchar_t	Wide character.	wchar.h

The types `char16_t` and `char32_t` are used for storing Unicode characters in the UTF-16 or UTF-32 encoding, respectively. Literals for `char16_t` are the same as for char or strings, but prefixed by u; literals for `char32_t` are prefixed by U.

The type `wchar_t` is an older type is used for storing "wide characters," that is characters beyond ASCII, but not necessarily Unicode. These days, most programs that work with Unicode do so using the UTF-8 encoding that works just fine with char; or one of `char8_t`, `char16_t`, or `char32_t`. However, programs for Microsoft Windows use `wchar_t` for Unicode. Literals for `wchar_t` are the same as for char or strings, but prefixed by L.

2.9 Other Standard Types

The C standard library also defines other types that you are likely to encounter as shown in table 2.5 defined in the headers shown.

Table 2.5: Other standard types

max_align_t	Maximum alignment type.	stddef.h
nullptr_t	Type of nullptr.	stddef.h
ptrdiff_t	Pointer difference.	stddef.h
size_t	Unsigned size in bytes.	stddef.h
ssize_t	Signed size in bytes.	stddef.h
time_t	Signed time relative to epoch.	time.h
wint_t	Integer corresponding to wchar_t.	wctype.h

■ An *epoch* is a fixed date and time (invariably midnight) used as a reference from which a computer measures the current date and time. For Unix systems (and others that implement the C standard library), that date is January 1, 1970, i.e., *Unix epoch*; for Microsoft Windows, that date is January 1, 1601, i.e., *Windows epoch*. □

2.10 Numeric Limits

The C standard library also defines constants for the minimum and maximum values for numeric types as shown in table 2.6 defined in the headers shown. See also INT_MAX_EXPR and INT_MIN_EXPR (p.295).

Table 2.6: Numeric limits

CHAR_MIN	CHAR_MAX	char	limits.h
SCHAR_MIN	SCHAR_MAX	signed char	limits.h
SHRT_MIN	SHRT_MAX	short	limits.h
INT_MIN	INT_MAX	int	limits.h
LONG_MIN	LONG_MAX	long	limits.h
LLONG_MIN	LLONG_MAX	long long	limits.h
UCHAR_MIN	UCHAR_MAX	unsigned char	limits.h
	USHRT_MAX	unsigned short	limits.h
	UINT_MAX	unsigned int	limits.h
	ULONG_MAX	unsigned long	limits.h
	ULLONG_MAX	unsigned long long	limits.h
INTMAX_MIN	INTMAX_MAX	intmax_t	stdint.h
	UINTMAX_MAX	uintmax_t	stdint.h
INTPTR_MIN	INTPTR_MAX	intptr_t	stdint.h
	UINTPTR_MAX	uintptr_t	stdint.h
PTRDIFF_MIN	PTRDIFF_MAX	ptrdiff_t	stdint.h
	SIZE_MAX	size_t	stdint.h
WCHAR_MIN	WCHAR_MAX	wchar_t	stdint.h
WINT_MIN	WINT_MAX	wint_t	stdint.h
FLT_MIN	FLT_MAX	float	float.h
DBL_MIN	DBL_MAX	double	float.h
LDBL_MIN	LDBL_MAX	long double	float.h

2.11 Signed Integer Overflow

Signed integer expressions can *overflow* (or *underflow*) when a value is larger (or smaller) than can be represented by a particular signed integer type resulting in undefined behavior (§15). A trivial example is:

```
int i = INT_MAX;
++i;                              // undefined behavior
```

A more subtle example is:

```
int abs( int n ) {
   return n < 0 ? -n : n;         // possibly UB
}
```

While it looks correct, the problem is that calling abs as written with a value of INT_MIN results in undefined behavior. Why? Because in two's complement arithmetic (that's typically the way signed integers are implemented), for any signed integer type T:

$$min(T) = -max(T) - 1$$

Assuming 32-bit integers, $max = 2^{32-1} - 1 = 2147483647$, hence $min = -2147483648$. The absolute value of $min = 2147483648$, but that's one greater than max which means it can't be represented by int. There is no perfect solution for this. The best you can do is to avoid the undefined behavior:

```
int abs( int n ) {
   return n < 0 ? -(unsigned)n : n;   // no UB
}
```

Casting (§3.14) to unsigned first eliminates the undefined behavior since overflow (and underflow) for unsigned integers is well-defined, specifically, a value will "wrap around," i.e., $max + 1 = 0$ and $0 - 1 = max$.

Unary - can be applied to unsigned types (§3.3). In the case of INT_MAX, abs returns −2147483648. Since it's negative, it's obviously wrong (again, there is no perfect solution), but at least it avoids the undefined behavior.

2.12 Choosing an Appropriate Integer Type

When Ritchie created C, he made int be the default type. The size (number of bits) of an int was deliberately not specified. Even when C was standardized, all that was guaranteed was a minimum size. The rationale was that the size of int should be the "natural" (most efficient) size for an integer on a given CPU.

If you needed only smaller signed integers and wanted to save a bit of space, Ritchie gave us short; or, if you needed bigger integers, he gave us long. (C99 gave us even bigger integers with long long.) If you only needed unsigned integers, you could include unsigned in a declaration. C99 also gave us specific-sized signed integer type aliases (e.g., int32_t) and unsigned type aliases (e.g., uint32_t).

However, in programming, negative integers (thus requiring a signed integer type) aren't needed most of the time. The length of strings, count of objects, size of objects, size of files etc., are all unsigned integers. Specific-sized type aliases are needed even less than signed integers.

A lot of C code uses integer types inappropriately. Such code can convey either underspecified or misleading information to programmers (including yourself in several months' time). It's best to choose the right integer type for the right purpose. Here are guidelines for choosing an integer type:

- When representing a count of bytes *in memory*, use the size_t standard type alias (§2.9). This is the type used by the C standard libraries, e.g., by memcpy, strlen, etc. (§B.2), so there's plenty of precedent.
- When representing either the size of or a position within a file *on disk*, use the off_t POSIX type alias (if available).

■ If you're dealing with very large files, on some Unix systems, you may need to compile with -D_FILE_OFFSET_BITS=64 command-line option (§8.3) to get a 64-bit version of off_t. □

- When representing a count of objects *in memory*, use size_t also. This is the type used by the C standard libraries, e.g., by fread (§12.4) and fwrite (§12.1).
- *Only* if you need to represent a value contained within a specific number of bits or you need to conform to a specific API, use one of the int8_t, int16_t, int32_t, or int64_t type aliases for signed types; or one of the uint8_t, uint16_t, uint32_t, or uint64_t type aliases for unsigned types.

The only times you typically need a fixed-size integer is when you "serialize" a value, e.g., write it to disk or send it over a socket. Using a fixed-size integer when you don't actually need a specific number of bits conveys misleading information to programmers.

Furthermore:

- When representing an integer value that *must* be the *exact* size of a pointer, use either the standard intptr_t or uintptr_t type alias.
- *Only if* you need negative values, use one of short, int, long, or long long with int being preferred unless you need either smaller or larger values.

Lastly:

- Otherwise use one of unsigned short, unsigned int, unsigned long, or unsigned long long similarly with unsigned int being preferred unless you need either smaller or larger values.

Choosing the right integer type conveys correct information to programmers. Preferring unsigned types eliminates run-time checks (because you don't have to check if a value of an unsigned type is < 0) and the possibility of undefined behavior (due to signed integer overflow).

One case where you need a signed integer type is when iterating from a positive number down to zero:

```
for ( int i = n; i >= 0; --i )   // 'i' needs to be signed
    // ...
```

If i were unsigned, i >= 0 would always be true. (See also the *tautological-type-limit-compare* warning, §18.7.1).

2.13 Type Conversions

When any operator (§3) has operands of different types, they are converted to a common type. Determining the common type involves a lot of detailed rules:

2.14 Epilogue   43

1. If both operands are floating-point types, their common type is the larger type.
2. Otherwise, if one operand is a floating-point type, the other is converted to it.
3. Otherwise, both operands are integer types. For each operand, integer *promotion* is first performed:

   - An operand of `char`, `short`, bit-field (§10.7), all either signed or unsigned, or enumeration (§7), is promoted to `int` if `int` can represent all the values of the original type or `unsigned int` if not.

4. Then, if both types are the same, that is the common type.
5. Otherwise, if their signedness is equal, but their sizes are not, the smaller type is converted to the larger type.
6. Otherwise, the operands have different signedness. If the signed type has a *rank* (table 2.7) less than or equal to the rank of the unsigned type, the operand with the signed type is converted to the unsigned type.

   Table 2.7: Integer ranks, high to low

6	`long long int`	`unsigned long long int`	
5	`long int`	`unsigned long int`	
4	`int`	`unsigned int`	
3	`short int`	`unsigned short int`	
2	`signed char`	`unsigned char`	`char`
1	`bool`		

7. Otherwise, the unsigned type has a rank less than that of the signed type. If the signed type can represent all the value of the unsigned type, the operand with the unsigned type is converted to the signed type.
8. Otherwise, both operands are converted to the unsigned version of the signed operand's type.

Despite the long list of rules, the upshot is that, generally, C does "the right thing." For every-day use, the rules can be simplified as:

- Integer types are converted to floating-point types when necessary.
- Smaller types are converted to larger types when necessary.

assuming you enable at least number-related warnings (§18.7.1).

2.14 Epilogue

Here's some key points about and some advice for comments:

- Comments are either between `/*` and `*/`, or after `//`.
- Don't comment *what* the code already says; do comment *why* the code does it.

- Comment files, functions (including their parameters, return value, and their pre- and post-conditions), citations, assumptions, anything non-obvious, and keep the comments up-to-date.

Here's some advice for naming things:

- Pick a naming style, such as "snake case" `like_this`, or "camel case" `likeThis OrThis`, and be consistent.
- With the exception of `for`-loop variables like `i`, give things meaningful names.

Here's some advice for types:

- Use the appropriate type for each situation. For integers, prefer unsigned types.
- Use `typedef` both to add meaning to types (e.g., `user_id`) and to make future changes easier.

Exercises

1. Write a program that does the reverse of the tabs-to-spaces program shown in listing 2.3 (p.34), that is converts sequences of `TAB_STOP` spaces to tabs. Fewer than `TAB_STOP` spaces should remain spaces.

    For example, given a sequence of 20 spaces, the first 16 should be converted to two tabs and the remaining four spaces should be left as-is.

2. Write a program that reads standard input and capitalizes the first letter of each word before printing it. Other text should be printed as-is.

    A "word" is defined as a sequence of one or more alphabetic characters at the beginning of the input or immediately following one of a space, tab `\t`, newline `\n`, left parentheses `(`, left bracket `[`, or left brace `{`. You will need the standard functions `strchr` (§B.2) and `toupper` (§B.1).

Chapter 3
Operators

C has a plethora of operators as shown in table 3.1. Operators are listed in precedence order from highest to lowest separated by horizontal lines. Operators in the same cell have the same precedence. An operator in a given cell will be bound more tightly to its operands than any operator in any cell below it. For example, *p++ is treated as *(p++) and not (*p)++ because ++ (*post-increment*, §3.4) is higher than * (*dereference*, §3.12). Despite the large number of precedence levels, the precedence of operators in expressions is generally what you'd expect (with the unfortunate exception of the *bitwise operators*, §3.8).

3.1 Associativity vs. Evaluation Order

Associativity has *only* to do with how expressions are parsed, for example:

```
s = a - b + c;      // left-to-right; as if: (a - b) + c
x = y = z;          // right-to-left; as if: x = (y = z)
```

Left-to-right or right-to-left associativity is *not* the same as left-to-right or right-to-left *evaluation*. In C, the order of evaluation is generally unspecified. For example:

```
s = f() - g() + h();    // parsed as: (f() - g()) + h()
```

Even though the value of f() - g() will be calculated first, then the value of h() added, the order in which the functions themselves are called is unspecified, e.g., h() could be called first. The values *could* be calculated like this:

```
h_val = h();
g_val = g();
f_val = f();
s = f_val - g_val + h_val;
```

Table 3.1: Operator precedence and associativity

`++ --`	Post-increment, post-decrement.	left-to-right
`( )`	Function-call.	
`[ ]`	Array-indexing.	
`.`	Structure and union member-access.	
`->`	Structure and union member-access via pointer.	
`++ --`	Pre-increment, pre-decrement.	right-to-left
`+ -`	Unary-plus, unary-minus.	
`! ~`	Logical-not, bitwise-not (aka, one's complement).	
`(type)`	Cast.	
`*`	Dereference.	
`&`	Address-of.	
`alignof`	Align-of.	
`sizeof`	Size-of.	
`* / %`	Multiplication, division, modulus.	left-to-right
`+ -`	Addition, subtraction.	
`<< >>`	Left-shift, right-shift.	
`< <=`	Less-than, less-than-or-equal-to.	
`> >=`	Greater-than, greater-than-or-equal-to.	
`== !=`	Equal-to, not-equal-to.	
`&`	Bitwise-and.	
`^`	Bitwise-exclusive-or.	
`|`	Bitwise-or.	
`&&`	Logical-and.	
`||`	Logical-or.	
`?:`	Conditional (aka, ternary).	right-to-left
`=`	Assign.	
`+= -=`	Assign with addition, subtraction.	
`*= /= %=`	Assign with multiply, divide, modulus.	
`<<= >>=`	Assign with left-shift, right-shift	
`&= |= ^=`	Assign with bitwise-and, or, exclusive-or.	
`,`	Comma	left-to-right

or any other permutation. Hence, you must not rely on multiple functions used in the same expression to be called in a specific order. The only operators that are guaranteed to have their operands evaluated in left-to-right order are: `&&` (*logical-and*, §3.6), `||` (*logical-or*, §3.6), `?:` (*conditional*, §3.7), and `,` (*comma*, §3.15).

3.2 Arithmetic Operators

The arithmetic operators are `+` (*addition*), `-` (*subtraction*), `*` (*multiplication*), `/` (*division*), and `%` (*modulus*). They may be applied to integer (§2.5), floating-point (§2.5.6,

§2.5.7, §2.5.8), or enumeration (§7) types — except % that is not for floating-point. (For floating-point modulus, the standard function `fmod` declared in `math.h` can be used instead.) The + and - operators may also be applied to pointer (§6.7) types.

Despite its plethora of operators, C doesn't have an *exponentiation* (aka, *to-the-power*) operator. While C does have a ^ operator, it's the *bitwise-exclusive-or* operator (§3.8). For floating-point types at least, the standard function `pow` declared in `math.h` can be used instead.

3.3 Unary Plus and Minus Operators

The + and - operators can also be used in unary form, e.g., `-i` to negate `i`. They may be applied to integer (§2.5), floating-point (§2.5.6, §2.5.7, §2.5.8), or enumeration (§7) types. The + is rarely used as unary plus since +*expr* is the same as *expr*. (But see §8.9.2 for a use.)

Perhaps surprisingly, - can be applied to expressions of unsigned integer types. It behaves as if the value were subtracted from 2^n where n is the number of bits comprising the type. Assuming 32-bit integers:

```
unsigned n = 42;
int a = -n;        // as if: (int)(2³² - 42 → 4294967254) → -42
```

because 4294967254 is `0b1111'1111'1111'1111'1111'1111'1101'0110` that, when interpreted as a 32-bit signed integer expressed in two's complement, is −42.

3.4 Increment and Decrement Operators

As first shown in §1.3, ++ and -- are the *increment* and *decrement* operators, respectively. They may be applied to integer (§2.5), enumeration (§7), or pointer (§6.7) types.

Both operators have pre- (e.g., `--i`) and post- forms (e.g., `i++`). The pre- form returns the *new* value after the operation whereas the post- form returns the *old* value before the operation. Neither form is more efficient than the other, so use whichever is needed in a particular case or preference.

Note that if these operators are used on the same variable more than once in the same expression, the result is even worse than implementation defined — it's undefined behavior (§15):

```
j = i++ + ++i;          // undefined behavior
f( i++, i++ );          // also undefined behavior
```

3.5 Relational Operators

The relational operators are == (*equal-to*), != (*not-equal-to*), < (*less-than*), <= (*less-than-or-equal-to*), > (*greater-than*), and >= (*greater-than-or-equal-to*). They may be applied to integer (§2.5), floating-point (§2.5.6, §2.5.7, §2.5.8), enumeration (§7), or pointer (§6.7) types.

Relational operators are binary operators and may not "chain." For example, to check whether i is between min and max requires two separate <= conjoined by &&:

```
if ( min <= i <= max )         // as if: (min <= i) <= max
if ( min <= i && i <= max )    // correct
```

The first condition tests whether the result of min $\leq$ i (either 0 or 1) is $\leq$ max.

3.6 Logical Operators

The logical operators are && (*logical-and*), || (*logical-or*), and ! (*logical-not*). They may be applied to integer (§2.5), floating-point (§2.5.6, §2.5.7, §2.5.8), enumeration (§7), or pointer (§6.7) types.

For && and ||, C guarantees left-to-right evaluation, not only left-to-right associativity. Additionally, && and || "short circuit," that is:

> *expr1* && *expr2* If *expr1* is false, *expr2* is not evaluated.
> *expr1* || *expr2* If *expr1* is true, *expr2* is not evaluated.

The precedence of && and || is very low so () are not needed. From listing 1.5 (p.12):

```
if ( is_1 || digits > 0 ) {    // is_1 || (digits > 0)
```

Of course you can (and should) add ( ) in complicated expressions to aid readability.

The ! converts either a false (or 0) value to true (or 1), or a true (non-zero) value to false. An idiom of !!*expr* (two ! in a row) converts a non-zero value to 1.

3.7 Conditional Operator

If you ever write code of the form:

```
if ( cond-expr )
  result = true-expr;
else
  result = false-expr;
```

3.8 Bitwise Operators

C provides a shorthand via the "?:" *conditional* (aka, *ternary*) operator:

cond-expr ? *true-expr* : *false-expr*

For example:

```
max = i > j ? i : j;          // maximum of i, j
```

Specifically, *cond-expr* is evaluated first: if true (non-zero), then (and only then) is *true-expr* evaluated and that is the result; otherwise, then (and only then) is *false-expr* evaluated and that is the result. C guarantees left-to-right evaluation. In particular, for an expression like:

```
r = x > y ? ++i : f();
```

C guarantees that i will be incremented only if x > y and f() called only if not (the same as if if-else were used).

The type of *cond-expr* may be integer (§2.5), floating-point (§2.5.6, §2.5.7, §2.5.8), enumeration (§7), or pointer (§6.7) type.

Note that an expression using ?: can be used anywhere, even inside another ?:. For example:

```
r = i < j ? -1 : i > j ? 1 : 0;
```

sets r to -1 if i < j, 1 if i > j, or 0 if i == j. Even though the precedence and associativity of ?: yield the correct result here, such expressions are clearer if you insert ():

```
r = i < j ? -1 : (i > j ? 1 : 0);    // same, but clearer
```

There can be cases where the precedence is *not* what you might expect, for example:

```
r = x + add_dx ? dx : 0;    // means: (x + add_dx) ? dx : 0
```

While the intent is to add dx and x only if add_dx is true, the reality is that, because + has a higher precedence than ?:, the result is dx if the sum of x and add_dx is true (non-zero). (A good compiler will warn you about the precedence here.) In such cases, () are necessary.

3.8 Bitwise Operators

The *bitwise* operators are of the form:

expr1	&	*expr2*	Bitwise-and.
expr1	|	*expr2*	Bitwise-or.
expr1	^	*expr2*	Bitwise-exclusive-or.
expr1	<<	*expr2*	Left-shift.
expr1	>>	*expr2*	Right-shift.
	~	*expr*	Bitwise-not (one's complement).

They may be applied to integer (§2.5) or enumeration (§7) types.

The & operator is used to "mask off" bits (force them to 0) or find the conjunction of two sets of bits (a bit in the result will be 1 only if the corresponding bit in both operands is 1). For example, to ensure c is 7-bit ASCII, we can mask off all but the lower 7 bits:

```
lower_7 = c & 0b0111'1111;         // ensure 7-bit ASCII
```

The | operator is used to force bits to 1 or find the disjunction of two sets of bits (a bit in the result will be 1 only if the corresponding bit in either operand is 1).

Unlike the && and || logical operators (§3.6) that short-circuit evaluation, both operands of & and | are always evaluated, but in an unspecified order. Additionally, the precedence of & and | is unfortunately too low, specifically lower than == and !=. This means that () are invariably needed. For example, from listing 1.5 (p.12):

```
bool const is_1 = (n & bit) != 0;  // () are needed here
```

■ The & and | bitwise operators are confusingly similar to the && and || logical operators. In B (the grandparent of C), the & and | operators performed both logical and bitwise operations depending on context. Ritchie believed this "overloading" was difficult to explain and use, so he introduced && and || for the logical operators.[†] □

The ^ operator is like | except that a bit in the result will be 1 only if the corresponding bit in either operand is 1, but not both.

As was first shown in listing 1.5 (p.12), the ~ operator is used to change 0 bits to 1 and vice versa. For another example, first consider a function rup that rounds a positive integer n up to some multiple m, e.g., rup(3,5) = 5, rup(5,5) = 5, rup(6,5) = 10, etc. It could be implemented as shown in listing 3.1.

```
size_t rup( size_t n, size_t m ) {
  size_t const remainder = n % m;
  return remainder == 0 ? n : n + m - remainder;
}
```

Listing 3.1: Round up to multiple

[†]*The Development of the C Language*, Dennis M. Ritchie, *History of Programming Languages*, 2nd ed., ACM Press, New York, and Addison-Wesley, Reading, Mass, 1996.

3.8 Bitwise Operators

If *m* is guaranteed to be a power of 2, an optimization is possible that avoids the use of % (a comparatively expensive operation) as shown in listing 3.2.

```
size_t rup2( size_t n, size_t m2 ) {
   return (n + m2 - 1) & ~(m2 - 1);
}
```

Listing 3.2: Round up to power of 2

To illustrate, let n = 5 (0b0101) and m2 = 8 (0b1000):

- The first parenthesized expression evaluates to 12 (0b1100).
- The second parenthesized expression evaluates to -7 or ~0b0111 or 0b1000.
- The final expression of 0b1100 & 0b1000 evaluates to 0b1000 or 8, the correct answer.

The << shifts a value one bit to the left with the new bit on the right becoming 0. It effectively multiplies by 2.

The >> shifts a value one bit to the right. The new bit on the left becomes 0 only for unsigned types. It effectively divides by 2. For signed types, whether the new bit becomes 0 or 1 is implementation defined, hence you should right-shift only unsigned types (unless you're writing code for a particular CPU where you know the behavior).

For an example, functions that swap the byte order of both 16- and 32-bit integers are shown in listing 3.3.

```
1  uint16_t swap16( uint16_t n ) {
2     return (uint16_t)((n >> 8) | (n << 8));
3  }
4
5  uint32_t swap32( uint32_t n ) {
6     return (uint32_t) swap16( (uint16_t)(n >> 16) )
7          | (uint32_t)(swap16( (uint16_t) n         ) << 16);
8  }
```

Listing 3.3: Functions to swap byte order

For explaining how these work, it's simpler to use values specified in hexadecimal.

- For swap16, let n be 0x0A'0B. On line 2, the n >> 8 makes a temporary value of 0x00'0A and the n << 8 makes a temporary value of 0x0B'00. The | then bitwise-ors the temporary values together to yield 0x0B'0A.
- For swap32, let n be 0x0A'0B'0C'0D. On line 6, the n >> 16 makes a temporary value of 0x00'00'0A'0B it then passes to swap16 to yield 0x00'00'0B'0A.

  On line 7, the (uint16_t)n "crams" the 32-bit value into 16 bits chopping off the high-order (left-most) 16 bits that makes a temporary value of 0x0C'0D it then passes to swap16 to yield 0x0D'0C that << 16 makes into 0x0D'0C'00'00.

  The | then bitwise-ors the temporary values together to yield 0x0D'0C'0B'0A.

3.9 Assignment Operators

The assignment operators are = (*assignment*), += (*increment-assign*), -= (*decrement-assign*), *= (*multiply-assign*), /= (*divide-assign*), %= (*modulus-assign*), <<= (*left-shift-assign*), >>= (*right-shift-assign*), &= (*bitwise-and-assign*), |= (*bitwise-or-assign*), and ^= (*bitwise-exclusive-or-assign*). The = operator works for any type including structures (§10) and unions (§11); it does not work for arrays (§6). The other assignment operators work for the same types their respective non-assignment counterparts work for.

Assignment operators yield expressions and associate right-to-left, so they may be "chained" to assign multiple variables to the same value:

```
x = y = 0;              // same as: x = (y = 0)
```

As shown in §1.4, for any variable *var* and assignment operator *op*, a statement of the form:

var op= expr;

is shorthand for:

var = var op (expr);

except *var* is evaluated only once.

3.10 Function Call Operator

The ( ) is the *function-call* operator and is of the form:

func-expr (arg-expr-list$_{opt}$)

where *func-expr* is either the name of any function or a pointer to function (§6.10) expression and *arg-expr-list* is a comma-separated list of expressions comprising the arguments corresponding to the number and types of the function's parameters (§9.2).

3.11 Array Indexing Operator

The [ ] is the *array-indexing* operator and is of the form:

expr [index-expr]

3.13 Member Access Operators

where *expr* can be of an array (§6) or pointer (§6.7) type and *index-expr* can be of any integer type (§2.5), the value of which specifies an element offset relative to *expr* (§6.3). Though rare, *index-expr* can be negative to access elements before *expr*. For example, consider:

```
char msg[] = "hello";
char *const end = msg + strlen( msg );
char last = end[-1];      // 'o'
```

where end is set to point to the end of the string at its terminating null character and indices are relative to it as shown in figure 3.1. Relative to end, -1 refers to the last character 'o'.

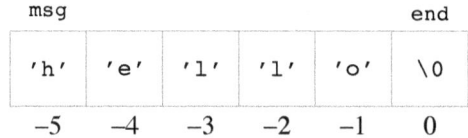

Fig. 3.1: Negative indexing

3.12 Address-of and Dereference Operators

As first shown in §1.6, & and * are the *address-of* and *dereference* operators, respectively. The address-of operator can be applied to any object or function (§6.10) to yield a pointer to it. The dereference operator can be applied to any pointer (except void*) to yield the object or function to which the pointer points.

3.13 Member Access Operators

As first shown in §1.9, the structure (§10) and union (§11) *member-access* operators are of the form:

expr.*member*   Accesses *member* of structure or union expression *expr*.
expr->*member*   Accesses *member* of structure or union via pointer *expr*.

where -> is syntactic sugar for:

expr->*member* ≡ (**expr*).*member*

3.14 Casting Operator

As first shown in listing 1.4 (p.10), an expression of the form:

   (*type*)*expr*

is a *cast* that converts the value of *expr* to *type*. There are several cases for casting:

1. To suppress a warning when converting a value of some type to a smaller type, e.g., int to char (as in listing 1.4, p.10, line 14).
2. To suppress a warning when converting a signed value to an unsigned type, e.g.:

    ```
    size_t pos = (size_t)-1;   // typical sentinel value
    ```

    Since size_t is an unsigned type, assigning a negative value to it will necessarily change its signedness. A compiler may warn you about this unless you use a cast. (In two's complement math, -1 would become the largest possible value for size_t.)

3. Converting an integer value to a floating-point type so an expression is evaluated using floating-point math. For example, assuming x and y are integer types, in:

    ```
    double c = (double)x / y;
    ```

    if the (double) were not there, the / would perform integer division truncating the value. The (double) "coerces" x to double so then the / operator will automatically convert y to double (§2.13 #2, p.43) and / will instead perform floating-point division. (It doesn't matter if y were cast instead: the result would be the same.)

4. Either to truncate or round a floating-point value to an integer type. For example:

    ```
    int round_half_up( double d ) {
      return (int)(d + .5);
    }
    ```

    returns d rounded (for a particular definition of round) to the nearest integer.

5. To discard the value of an expression by casting to void (§3.14.1).
6. To cast away const (§3.14.2).
7. To cast the underlying bits of a value to a type via a pointer (§3.14.3).

When using a cast, you're telling the compiler that you know what you're doing, so don't warn you (which means you really had better know what you're doing).

3.14.1 Casting to `void`

As a special case, any expression can also be cast to `void`. It tells both programmers and the compiler that the value of an expression is intentionally being discarded (so for the compiler, not to warn you). There are two cases for doing this:

1. To state that you don't need the value of an expression. See listing 16.1 (p.241) for an example.
2. In older code, to state that a function parameter is intentionally not being used and suppress a warning about it:

```
bool visit( void *node_data, void *user_data ) {
  (void)user_data;        // suppress "not used" warning
  // ...
```

In C23, you can simply omit the parameter's name (§9.2) in the definition.

3.14.2 Casting Away `const`

To "cast away `const`" means to remove the "const-ness" from what a pointer to `const` (first shown in §1.7) is pointing to by using a cast. Before getting to the cases where casting away `const` is OK, the one case that is *never* OK is casting away `const` to something that is *actually* constant with the intent of modifying it:

```
constexpr char MSG[] = "hello, world";
char *s = (char*)MSG;   // cast away const
*s = 'H';               // undefined behavior
```

Values that are either `constexpr` (§4.4) or `const` (§4.5) may actually be placed into a read-only memory segment. Attempting to modify such a value results in undefined behavior (§15), but likely will result in a *seg-fault* (§18.4).

It's *never* OK to cast away `const` to something that was declared `constexpr`; but there are cases where it's *sometimes* OK to cast away `const` to something that was declared `const`:

1. You want a variable to be immutable after being initialized and for the duration of its lifetime, but need to clean it up before the end of its lifetime.

```
char const *s = mstrcat( s1, s2 );
// ...
free( (char*)s );   // casting away const is OK here
```

2. You have a function that has a pointer to `const` parameter and returns the same, but you actually want to pass a pointer to non-`const` and get the same back. (For an example, see §19.3.)

3.14.3 Casting Pointers

It's possible and sometimes necessary to "reinterpret" the underlying bits comprising a value in memory as a type different from its declared type. For example, given:

```
char int32_buf[4];
*(int32_t*)int32_buf = 1941;
```

The (int32_t*) casts the address of the 4-byte char buffer int32_buf to be a pointer to uint32_t instead. The first * then dereferences that address and the = writes the bytes as if they really were a uint32_t. Such casts are platform specific — in this case, the *endianness* of the integer value.

■ *Endianness* refers to the order of the individual bytes in memory comprising a multi-byte value, usually an integer.[†] There are two dominant kinds of endianness:

- **Big-Endian**: When read from left-to-right, bytes comprising a value are in increasing addresses. (The "big end" of an integer is first in memory.)
- **Little-Endian**: When read from left-to-right, bytes comprising a value are in decreasing addresses. (The "little end" of an integer is first in memory.)

For example, the 4-byte decimal integer 123'456'789 stored in the memory range 0x1000–0x1003 would have the individual bytes stored in the order 0x07'5B'CD'15 when big-endian and 0x15'CD'5B'07 when little-endian. (While big-endian might seem more intuitive to humans, neither endianness is more "correct" than the other to CPUs.)

The word "endian" itself comes from *Gulliver's Travels*[‡] wherein conflict arose between two sects of Lilliputians: those who broke the shell of a boiled egg from the big end versus those who did so from the little end. The inconsequential nature of such a choice makes *endianness* apt for byte order. □

Such casts are necessary when either reading or writing data from or to disk or over a socket.

3.15 Comma Operator

The *comma* operator has form:

[†] *On Holy Wars and a Plea for Peace*, Danny Cohen, *Internet Experiment Note*, 137, April 1, 1980.
[‡] *A Voyage to Lilliput*, Jonathan Swift, *The Works of the Rev. Jonathan Swift*, 6(4), Oct. 28, 1726.

expr1, *expr2*

It evaluates *expr1* and discards the result; it then evaluates *expr2* and that is the result. C guarantees left-to-right evaluation. About the only place it's used is in the *next-expr* of a `for` statement (§5.6) when there is more than one *next-expr*:

```
for ( int i = 0, j = 0; i < m && j < n; ++i, ++j )
```

Commas separating declarations and function arguments are *not* the comma operator — they're simply ordinary commas. Above, only the last comma is the comma operator.

3.16 `sizeof` Operator

The `sizeof` operator has two forms:

    `sizeof` *expr*   Gets size of the type of *expr*.
    `sizeof(`*type*`)` Gets size of *type*.

Both forms return the size of their argument in bytes as a value of type `size_t` (§2.9).

■ Strictly speaking, they return the size as a multiple of `char` units since `sizeof(char)` is defined to be 1. □

Unlike most other operators, `sizeof` is a *compile-time operator*, that is, the compiler evaluates it at compile-time (except for VLAs, §6.14).

The `sizeof` operator is useful with `malloc` when you want to dynamically allocate objects other than `char`. For example, to allocate n `ints` and `strings`:

```
int *pi = malloc( n * sizeof(int) );
struct string *ps = malloc( n * sizeof(struct string) );
```

The `sizeof` operator is also useful to get the number of elements of a previously declared array:

```
char buf[ 4096 ];
// ...
size_t n = sizeof buf / sizeof buf[0];   // 4096
```

When applied to an array, `sizeof` returns the number of bytes of the *entire* array, hence the need to divide by the size of an element. If you don't want to have to remember when to use `()` with `sizeof`, you can simply always use `()`.

3.17 `alignof` Operator

The `alignof` operator is of the form:

> `alignof(`*type*`)`   Gets alignment of *type* in bytes.

It returns the minimum *alignment* for *type* in bytes as a value of type `size_t` (§2.9). Unlike most other operators, `alignof` is a *compile-time operator*, that is, the compiler evaluates it at compile-time.

Many CPU architectures require that objects be aligned in memory based on their type such that their address must be evenly divisible by their size. For example, an `int` on an x86–64 CPU is 32 bits (4 bytes) which means it can reside only at memory addresses evenly divisible by 4. (For an example use, see §6.13.)

3.18 Epilogue

Here are some key points about and some advice for operators:

- The = is *assignment* and the == is *equal-to*.
- The && is *logical-and* and the & is *bitwise-and*.
- The || is *logical-or* and the | is *bitwise-or*.
- Be mindful of operator precedence and associativity. When in doubt, insert ( ).
- Associativity is *not* the same as evaluation order.
- The only operators that are guaranteed to have their operands evaluated in left-to-right order are &&, ||, ?: (*conditional*), and , (*comma*); for all others, the order is unspecified, so don't rely on it.
- Only && and || "short circuit" (do not necessarily evaluate both operands).
- The precedence of & and | is too low so ( ) are invariably necessary.
- When casting, make sure you know what you're doing because the compiler assumes you do.
- When casting away `const`, make sure the object isn't *really* constant.
- When casting pointers among very different types, endianness might matter.

Exercises

1. Using the functions in listing 3.3 (p.51) as a starting point, write a function:

    ```
    uint64_t swap64( uint64_t n );
    ```

3.18 Epilogue

that swaps the byte order of a 64-bit integer to convert big-endian to little-endian or vice versa.

2. Assuming an unsigned integer value n has exactly one bit set b, e.g., 0b1000, write a function:

   unsigned bits_lt(unsigned n);

   that returns all and only the bits < b set, e.g., 0b0111.

3. Using your solution to the previous exercise, write a function:

   unsigned bits_le(unsigned n);

   that returns all and only the bits ≤ b set, e.g., 0b1111.

4. Using your solution to the previous exercise, write a function:

   unsigned bits_gt(unsigned n);

   that returns all and only the bits > b set, e.g., 0b1111111111110000. Your solution should work regardless of the number of bits comprising an integer.

5. Using your solution of any of the three previous exercises, write a function:

   unsigned bits_ge(unsigned n);

   that returns all and only the bits ≥ b set, e.g., 0b1111111111111000. Your solution should work regardless of the number of bits comprising an integer.

Chapter 4
Declarations

> *"I'm still uncertain about the language declaration syntax, where in declarations, syntax is used that mimics the use of the variables being declared. It is one of the things that draws strong criticism, but it has a certain logic to it."*
> — Dennis M. Ritchie

> *"I consider the C declarator syntax an experiment that failed."*
> — Bjarne Stroustrup

While we've seen many examples of declarations of constants and variables already, this chapter fills in the details. (Function declarations are deferred until §9.)

■ As part of designing a programming language, you generally need to design a separate syntax for declaring things (variables, constants, functions, etc.). The advantage of a separate syntax is that it's usually clear; the (slight) disadvantage is that a separate syntax doesn't tell you how to use the thing being declared. For example, to declare api as an array of pointers to integer in Pascal:

```
api: array[0..4] of ^integer;
```

That reads left-to-right and is crystal clear; but to *use* the variable in an expression, you'd write something like:

```
api[0]^ := 42;
```

Notice that:

- In the declaration, api and [are not adjacent (whereas in use they are).
- In the declaration, ^ is prefix (whereas in use it's postfix).

As the epigraph suggests, Ritchie took a different approach. To declare anything in C, you write the name of what you're declaring as if it were being used in an expression (part of the main syntax for the language) to yield a value of the base type that you prepend to the whole thing — the type of the "expression." Hence, the equivalent declaration of api in C is:

```
int *api[4];        // array of pointer to integer
```

That does *not* read left-to-right (nor right-to-left). Instead, api when used in an expression like *api[i] yields a value of an int (the type on the left). Though a bit strange, it does, as Ritchie noted, have a certain logic to it.

While such declarations may not seem that bad, once they get more complicated — and once things like `const` (§4.5) and function prototypes (§9.1) were added to C (neither of which existed in the original version of C) — declarations infamously get harder to read which is the reason behind Bjarne's comment. □

4.1 Multiple Declarations

In C, multiple things can be declared in the same declaration, so long as they have the same base type. For example:

```
char c, *s, buf[4], *fgets( char*, int, FILE* );
```

declares `c` as `char`, `s` as pointer to `char`, `buf` as array 4 of `char`, and `fgets` as function returning pointer to `char`.

■ You may encounter code that puts the `*` adjacent to the type in pointer declarations:

```
char* s;          // as opposed to: char *s
```

While such declarations work since the C compiler doesn't care about whitespace, the `*` still "binds" to the name, not the type. Hence:

```
char* s, t;       // s is pointer to char; t is char
```

declares `s` to be `char*` and `t` to be `char` — likely not what you meant. □

4.2 auto

When initializing a variable in its declaration from an expression, you ordinarily have to know what the type of the expression is in order to know what type to declare the variable as. For example, from listing 1.14 (p.24):

```
size_t const new_len = str->len + strlen( s );
```

you have to know that the type of `str->len` and `strlen` are `size_t` in order to know what type to declare `new_len` as. The thing is the compiler already knows what type that is. It would be nice to be able to say "declare `new_len` as whatever type the expression is." That's precisely what `auto` does, so you can instead do:

```
auto const new_len = str->len + strlen( s );
```

The advantages of `auto` are:

- You don't have to try to figure out the type of an initializing expression.
- If that type ever changes, you don't have to update the type of all variables initialized from an expression of that type.
- For pointers, preserves the "const-ness" of the pointed-to type. For example, if `pc` is of type `char*` and `pcc` is of type `char const*`, then:

```
auto p1 = pc;       // char *p1 = pc;
auto p2 = pcc;      // char const *p2 = pcc;
```

- It's useful for writing type-generic macros (§8.7).
- It's useful with `_Generic` (§19).

However, `auto` should *not* be used when a variable is being initialized by a literal:

```
auto count = 0;     // int -- need 0u for unsigned
auto c = '?';       // int -- char literals are int
```

In C:

- Unadorned integer literals are of type `int`, so if you want a type other than `int`, you need to use a suffix (§2.5.4) such as u for `unsigned`.
- Oddly, character literals are of type `int` and not `char` as you might expect.

Hence, use explicit types when initializing from a literal.

4.3 Storage Classes

In C, there are the concepts of *duration* and *linkage* of an object or function. A duration denotes when and for how long an object exists. There are three durations:

1. **Automatic**: exists only within blocks (§2.4). Objects declared within a block exist only within that block, that is they automatically come into existence upon their declaration and cease to exist at the end of the block (the `}`). For example, from listing 1.5 (p.12):

    ```
    unsigned putubin( unsigned n ) {
        // ...
        unsigned digits = 0;
    ```

    both function parameters (such as n) and local variables (such as `digits`) have automatic duration. (Even though n is declared before the `{`, it's "injected" into the subsequent block scope.)

2. **Static**: objects exist for the entire duration of the program (§9.9).
3. **Thread**: objects exist so long as their thread does (§14.7).

A linkage denotes where an object is visible. There are three types of linkage:

1. **External**: objects are visible to the entire program.
2. **Internal**: objects are visible only within a single .c file, hence it's like "private" for that file.
3. **None**: objects are visible only within their current scope. For example, all local variables have no linkage.

A *storage class* specifies both a duration and linkage.

4.3.1 auto

The auto keyword originally meant something completely different from what's described in §4.2. It originally meant "automatic storage duration." For example, from listing 1.5 (p.12):

```
unsigned putubin( unsigned n ) {
    // ...
    auto unsigned digits = 0;  // same as without "auto"
```

The local variable digits could have been declared with auto, but it would mean exactly the same thing as without it. It was used only if the programmer wanted to be explicit.

Which meaning auto has depends on whether there's a type specified in the declaration: if it's auto by itself, it deduces a type; if a type is also specified, it's the storage class. For example:

```
auto len = strlen( s );      // deduces type of size_t
auto unsigned digits = 0;    // unsigned; auto is redundant
```

Both because auto as a storage class is always redundant and has a new meaning, you therefore shouldn't use auto this way in any new C code.

■ If auto as a storage class is always redundant and its use as such could be confused with §4.2, why is it also a storage class? The auto keyword actually predates C. It first appeared in B (the grandparent of C) for use when declaring *automatic* variables (meaning "automatically created in the stack frame of the enclosing function").

B is a typeless language in that all variables are integers, so, for example, the following declared some variables in B:

```
auto a, b, c;
```

Since C is a typed language, to make migration of code from B to C easier, Ritchie:

4.3 Storage Classes

1. Adopted auto into C to be a storage class like static (§4.3.3).
2. Made int the default type (meaning if a type were omitted in a declaration, it was understood to be int).

Hence, the above declaration means the same thing in C as it does in B.

Since int requires typing one fewer character than typing auto, being explicit about int eventually became common. (In C99, int stopped being the default.) Hence there was no reason to specify auto explicitly in new code and its use faded away.

Eventually, C++11 repurposed auto to mean "automatically deduced type" where the type of the variable being declared is deduced based on the type of its initializer. As of C23, the repurposed auto of C++ was adopted into C (more or less, but mostly less). In C++, the original meaning of auto was dropped, but kept in C presumably out of an abundance of caution for backwards compatibility. □

4.3.2 extern

The extern storage class declares the name of an object that has external linkage defined elsewhere so that it can be used in the current scope. It's used in programs that have more than one .c file (§13). From the previous example where is_testing is defined at file scope in some .c file (§2.4, p.30), a declaration like:

extern bool is_testing;

in another .c file allows it to be used there as well. For any object, there can be any number of extern declarations, but only one definition (without extern).

You may encounter code that declares functions extern like:

extern char* mstrcat(**char const** *s1, **char const** *s2);

For non-inline functions (§9.10), external linkage is the default, so extern is redundant.

4.3.3 static

The static storage class makes a file-scope (§2.4) object or function (§9.8) have internal linkage. For example, a variable declared at file scope in a .c file like:

static unsigned obj_count;

is "private" to that file. Another .c file either in your own program or a library could have a static variable with the same name and the two variables would be distinct. Unless you want to make a file-scope variable "public," declare it static.

∎ The static keyword is the most over-used in C. It has three unrelated meanings:

- Internal linkage (this section).
- Static duration (§9.9).
- Non-null array syntax for parameters (§9.4.1).

C++ added even more unrelated meanings. □

4.3.4 register

The register storage class makes a variable have automatic duration and no linkage. It allows you to give the compiler a "hint" that a certain variable is used heavily within a function and would thereby likely benefit from being stored in a CPU register as opposed to ordinary memory. For example, the putubin function from listing 1.5 (p. 12) can be modified to use register as shown in listing 4.1.

```
unsigned putubin( register unsigned n ) {
    // ...
    for ( register unsigned bit = ~(~0u >> 1); bit != 0;
        bit >>= 1 ) {
    // ...
```

Listing 4.1: Function using register

Only parameters and local variables may be declared register. Note that it's *only* a hint that the compiler is free to ignore.

∎ Early C compilers had primitive optimizers, hence register was a way for you to help optimize your code by hand. Modern compilers have *much* better optimizers and can therefore decide for themselves which variables would benefit from being placed into registers. You are *very* unlikely to do a better job than a modern optimizer. You therefore shouldn't use register in any new C code. □

∎ C++ has gone even further: register is now only a reserved word stripped of meaning. C will likely eventually follow suit. □

4.4 constexpr

As a reminder, use `constexpr` to give names to things that otherwise would be magic values. The rules for `constexpr` are simple:

- It *must* be initialized in its declaration.
- The expression it's initialized with *must* be a *constant expression* calculated at compile-time involving only literals, enumeration values (§7.5), file-scope `const` values, or `constexpr` values.
- It can be used everywhere a literal can be.

4.5 const

As a reminder, use `const` to mark an object immutable after initialization. The rules for `const` are more complicated than those for `constexpr`:

- Like `constexpr`, it *must* be initialized in its declaration.
- Unlike `constexpr`, the expression it's initialized with can be any expression including one calculated at run-time, but only within a function; at file scope, the expression *must* be a constant expression.
- It can *not* be used everywhere a `constexpr` can be, specifically not as either a `case` value for a `switch` statement (§5.8) nor a dimension of an array (§6.1).

`const` is what's known as a *qualifier* because it "qualifies" some other type, e.g., not only `int`, but a *constant* `int`. C also has `_Atomic` (§17), `restrict` (§21), and `volatile` (§22) qualifiers.

The term *cv-qualified* is a shorthand for `const` and/or `volatile` qualified; the term *cvr-qualified* is a shorthand for `const`, and/or `volatile`, and/or `restrict` qualified.

4.6 typeof

Similar to `auto` (§4.2), C also has `typeof` that has two forms:

> **typeof**(*expr*)
> **typeof**(*type*)

For the first form, *expr* is not evaluated. Like `sizeof` (§3.16), `typeof` is a compile-time operator. It standardizes the long-existing `gcc` extension.[†] For example:

[†] *Referring to a Type with typeof*, Free Software Foundation, *Using the GNU Compiler Collection*, §6.7, 1988–2025, https://gcc.gnu.org/onlinedocs/gcc/Typeof.html

```
int x;              // int (obviously)
typeof(x) y;        // also int
```

■ If you know C++, typeof is like its decltype. Why isn't typeof called decltype in C also? (Or why isn't decltype in C++ called typeof?) The short answer is that C++ has references and C doesn't — and that affects the type deduced.[†] □

Since C has auto, why is typeof needed?

- Variables declared with typeof don't need initializers (§4.6.1).
- It can clarify complicated declarations (§4.6.2).
- It can be useful with _Generic (§19.6).

4.6.1 Declarations without Initializers

Using auto always requires an initializer since the compiler deduces the type of the object from the type of the initializer expression; using typeof does not:

```
double f();
auto x = f();       // double
typeof(f()) y;      // double, but without initializer
```

Depending on what you're doing, you may not want to initialize upon declaration, for example if a variable is initialized only conditionally or you need to defer initialization (§18.6.8). Of course you still can use an initializer with typeof if you want to guarantee a type based on something other than the initializer:

```
typeof(f()) y = g();   // type is what f() returns, not g()
```

4.6.2 Clarifying Complicated Declarations

The other way that typeof can be used is to clarify complicated declarations:

```
char *s1, *s2;          // both pointer to char
typeof(char*) t1, t2;   // same
```

Using typeof effectively provides an alternate declaration syntax that's more in line with other programming languages.

[†] *Not-so-magic — typeof for C*, JeanHeyd Meneide and Shepherd's Oasis LLC, *ISO/IEC JTC1/SC22/WG14: Programming Language — C*, N2927, §3.3, Feb. 2, 2022, https://www.open-std.org/jtc1/sc22/wg14/www/docs/n2927.htm

4.7 `typeof_unqual`

Similar to `typeof` (§4.6) is `typeof_unqual` that removes all top-level qualifiers (§4.5). Given the declarations at the top of listing 4.2, the differences between `typeof` and `typeof_unqual` are shown. For an example using `typeof_unqual`, see the listing for IS_SAME_TYPE (p.296).

```
extern int i;                     // int
extern int const ci;              // const int
extern int *pi;                   // pointer to int
extern int const *pci;            // pointer to const int
extern int *const cpi;            // const pointer to int
extern int const *const cpci;     // const pointer to const int

typeof         (i)     i2;        // int
typeof_unqual  (i)     i2u;       // int
typeof         (ci)    ci2;       // int const
typeof_unqual  (ci)    ci2u;      // int
typeof         (pi)    pi2;       // int *
typeof_unqual  (pci)   pci2u;     // int const*
typeof         (cpi)   cpi2;      // int *const
typeof_unqual  (cpi)   cpi2u;     // int *
typeof         (cpci)  cpci2;     // int const *const
typeof_unqual  (cpci)  cpci2u;    // int const *
```

Listing 4.2: Result of `typeof_unqual` on various types

4.8 `alignas`

The `alignas` specifier has two forms:

> `alignas(`*const-expr*`)` Aligns to *const-expr* bytes.
> `alignas(`*type*`)`   Aligns the same as *type*.

It *aligns* the memory for a variable to the specified number of bytes. The second form is shorthand for `alignas(alignof(`*type*`))` (§3.17). For example, the declaration of `int32_buf` (p.56) should be declared like:

> `alignas(int32_t) char int32_buf[ sizeof(int32_t) ];`

so it ensures that it's aligned the same as an `int` would be. For another example, see DECL_UNUSED (p.130).

4.9 Attributes

An *attribute* is an optional piece of additional information attached to most anything in C: a type, variable, statement, or function using the [[*attribute-list*]] syntax where *attribute-list* is a comma-separated list of *attribute*. In addition to the standard attributes given in the following sections, compiler vendors may offer their own attributes prefixed by *prefix*::, e.g., gnu::hot.

An attribute can be declared anywhere and either before or after a declaration. What it applies to depends on where it's declared. For example:

```
[[maybe_unused]] int a, b;         // applies to both
int x, y [[maybe_unused]], z;      // applies only to 'y'
```

4.9.1 deprecated

The deprecated attribute has two forms:

[[deprecated]]	Marks a name deprecated and warns when used.
[[deprecated("*reason*")]]	Same, but includes *reason* in warnings.

Marking a name with deprecated causes the compiler to print a warning whenever the name is used. For the second form, *reason* is included in the warning. The attribute allows you to provide a transition period while updating an API. For example, given a declaration like:

```
[[deprecated("use get_utoken")]]
char* get_token();
```

and a use like:

```
char *token = get_token();
```

would generate a warning like:

```
parser.c:42:13: warning: 'get_token' is deprecated:
    use get_utoken
```

4.9.2 fallthrough

This attribute is used only with the switch statement (§5.8). For an explanation and example, see listing 5.2 (p. 78).

4.9.3 maybe_unused

The compiler can warn you when one of a variable, `static` function (§9.8), or label (§5.10) is unused. (For `clang` and `gcc`, you need to specify the `-Wunused` command-line option.) Normally, this is a good thing, but sometimes you might want to keep unused variables or functions around in case you're currently unsure whether you need them. The `maybe_unused` attribute can be used to mark unused variables or functions so that the compiler won't warn you. For example:

```
[[maybe_unused]]
static bool dag_has_cycle( struct dag_node *node );
```

For another example, see §16.6 (p.245).

4.9.4 nodiscard

Some functions in the standard library return values that aren't needed most of the time. For example, `strcpy` (§B.2) is declared as:

```
char* strcpy( char *dst, char const *src );  // returns dst
```

It returns `dst` that generally isn't needed since you already have it. For such functions, it's OK simply to discard the return value. The compiler will never warn you for doing so.

Other functions, however, return values that are needed and therefore should not be discarded. Such functions can be marked with `nodiscard`. If the return value of such a function is discarded, the compiler will warn you. For example, from listing 1.13 (p.21), the function `mstrcat` should be marked `nodiscard` because it returns a pointer to newly allocated memory that, if discarded, would be a memory leak:

```
[[nodiscard]]
char* mstrcat( char const *s1, char const *s2 );
```

■ Admittedly, having to sprinkle `[[nodiscard]]` all over your programs is both tedious and verbose. Ideally, `nodiscard` would be the default and you'd have to specifically declare a function as, say, `[[okdiscard]]` to discard its return value without warning. Unfortunately, C didn't originally have `nodiscard` (or attributes at all) so you can't simply add an `okdiscard` attribute and make all other declarations `nodiscard` by default without causing warnings for every C program in existence. Hence, adding `nodiscard` to C was much less disruptive and better than not adding it. □

4.9.5 noreturn

The `noreturn` attribute should be used to mark functions that never return. For example, the standard function `exit` (§9.7.2) terminates a program as if it returned from `main`. It's declared as:

```
[[noreturn]] void exit( int status );
```

The reasons for marking a function `noreturn` include:

- It allows the compiler to warn you that code following a call to such a function will never be executed. (For `clang` and `gcc`, you need to specify the `-Wunreachable-code` command-line option.)
- It documents to programmers that it doesn't return.

A function marked `noreturn`:

- Must have a return type of `void`.
- Must never actually return. If it does, the result is undefined behavior (§15).

4.10 Epilogue

Here are some key points about and some advice for declarations:

- Multiple things may be declared in the same declarations. When doing so, remember that the `*` for pointers binds to the name, not the type.
- Use `auto` when declaring a variable that you are initializing in its declaration from an expression (but not a literal).
- Use `extern` to share global variables among multiple `.c` files.
- Use `static` to declare objects that are "private" to a file.
- Don't use `register`.
- Use `constexpr` to declare constants.
- Use `const` to mark objects immutable.
- Use attributes whenever possible.

Chapter 5
Statements

C code is fundamentally a series of *statements* where each generally performs some action. Many statements control the "flow" of execution of a program by conditionally executing some statements and not others, by looping, or unconditionally jumping to other statements. While we've seen most statement types already, this chapter will give the details of the complete set.

5.1 Expression Statement

An *expression statement* is any expression followed by a semicolon. As mentioned in §3.9, y = 0 is an expression that assigns 0 to y, but is still an expression having the value of zero that can be used anywhere an expression can be. Appending a semicolon makes it a statement.

5.2 Compound Statement

A *compound statement* (aka, *block*) is of the form:

  { *statement** }

that is, zero or more statements enclosed between {}. It can be used anywhere a single statement can be and can nest.

5.3 if-else

The basic version of the `if` statement is:

> **if** (*expr*)
>   *statement*

It executes *statement* only if *expr* is true. Reminder: in C, *any* non-zero value is considered `true` (§2.5.2).

> ■ Idiomatic C tends to rely on this. For example, if `count` is an `int` you'll often see code like:
>
> ```
> if ( count )         // means: if ( count != 0 )
> // ...
> ```
>
> Personally, I find that unclear since it *looks* like `count` *could* be `bool`. (Did we count anything? Was a count even performed?) Hence, you have to find the declaration for `count` to see if it's really `bool`. Being explicit with `!= 0` here makes it clearer that `count` is much more likely a numeric type. □

If *statement* needs to be multiple statements, they're enclosed between `{}`. The full version of the `if` statement adds an optional `else` clause:

> **if** (*expr*)
>   *if-true-statement*
> **else**
>   *if-false-statement*

Note that an `else` associates with the most recent `if`. For example, in:

```
if ( expr1 )
  if ( expr2 )
    // ...
else                   // indentation belies reality
  // ...
```

the `else` associates with *expr2* despite it being indented to match the `if` of *expr1*. To fix it, simply use `{}`:

```
if ( expr1 ) {
  if ( expr2 )
    // ...
}
else                   // {} make indentation match reality
  // ...
```

If either the `if` or `else` uses `{}`, it's also widely considered good style to make both use `{}`, i.e., omit `{}` *only* when there is an `if` having a single statement and no `else`, or *both* the `if` and `else` have single statements.

As shown in listing 1.4 (p. 10), a statement for an `else` can be another `if` statement. A sequence of `if-else-if` statements may "chain" up to some large implementation-defined limit.

```
if ( expr1 ) {
    // ...
} else if ( expr2 ) {
    // ...
} else if ( expr3 ) {
    // ...
```

5.4 while

The `while` statement is the simplest of the looping statements and is of the form:

```
while ( expr )
    statement
```

As long as *expr* remains true, it executes *statement* repeatedly. As with `if`, if *statement* needs to be multiple statements, they're enclosed between `{}`.

To write an "infinite loop," make *expr* be `true`:

```
while ( true )      // or, idiomatically: while (1)
    statement
```

Infinite loops can be broken out of via `break` (§5.7), `return` (§5.9), `goto` (§5.10), or `longjmp` (§20.4).

5.5 do-while

The `do-while` statement is a variation on `while` and is of the form:

```
do {
    body
} while ( expr );
```

Unlike `while`, `do-while` evaluates its condition at the end of the loop and so always executes its body at least once. As first shown in listing 1.3 (p. 7), it's occasionally useful, though in practice used much less frequently than either `while` or `for`.

Unlike either `while` or `for`, `do-while` is invariably used with `{}` even when there is only a single statement (otherwise the `while` looks like an ordinary one). It's also considered good style to put the `while` on the same line as the `}` so the `while` looks like the end of a `do-while` loop rather than the start of a `while` loop.

5.6 `for`

As first shown in listing 1.5 (p.12), the `for` statement is a generalization of a `while` statement and is of the form:

>   **for** (*init-expr*$_{opt}$; *cond-expr*$_{opt}$; *next-expr*$_{opt}$)
>   *statement*

where:

1. The *init-expr* performs any initialization once before the loop. Optionally, it can also declare the variables it's initializing. The scope of such variables are limited to the loop's body.
2. The *cond-expr* is the same as in a `while` statement.
3. The *next-expr* performs any steps necessary to go to the next iteration of the loop. It is performed after the last statement in the loop body or a `continue` (§5.7) statement.

A `for` statement is roughly equivalent to:

>   *init-expr*;
>   **while** (*cond-expr*) {
>   *statement*
>   *next-expr*;
>   }

but more concise. All expressions are optional, but the `;`s must remain. If *cond-expr* is omitted, it's equivalent to `true`, hence the following is another idiomatic way to write an infinite loop:

>   **for** (;;)   // infinite loop
>   *statement*

5.7 `break` and `continue`

The `break` statement simply breaks out of any loop or `switch` (§5.8) statement, for example:

>   **for** (;;) {
>   // ...
>   **if** (*cond-expr*)
>   **break**;
>   }

As first shown in listing 1.4 (p.10), the `continue` statement jumps back to the start of a loop. It's equivalent to a `goto` (§5.10) to a label at the end of the loop:

```
while-or-for ( ... ) {
  if ( cond-expr )
    goto next;      // equivalent to "continue"
  // ...
next:
  ;
}
```

5.8 switch

A `switch` statement is a multi-way `if` and is of the form:

```
switch ( cond-expr ) {
  case const-expr:
    statement*
  case const-expr:
    statement*
  // ...
  default:          // optional
    statement
}
```

A `switch` works as follows:

1. The *cond-expr* is evaluated.
2. Its value is then compared against a *const-expr*:

    - If it matches, the *statements* following the *const-expr* are executed.
    - Otherwise, if there is another *const-expr*, the value is compared against that in turn.

    The order in which the cases are tried is unspecified. It doesn't necessarily match the order in which the cases are declared. (The order shouldn't matter; if it does, use an `if-else` chain instead.)

3. If no *const-expr* matches:

    - If there is a `default` case, the *statements* following it are executed.
    - Otherwise, the control flow "falls out the bottom" of the `switch` without executing any statements.

    Note that a `default` case need not be last.

For example, the program that expands tabs to spaces from listing 2.3 (p. 34) rewritten using `switch` is shown in listing 5.1. For this program, whether you use `if-else` or `switch` is only a matter of preference. As the number of cases increases, `switch` is often preferable. Using `switch` with enumerations (§7.5.5) is particularly good.

```
#include <stdio.h>

constexpr unsigned TAB_STOP = 8;   // chars per tab-stop

int main() {
  unsigned len = 0;                // length of line so far
  while ( true ) {
    int const c = getchar();
    switch ( c ) {
      case EOF:
        return 0;
      case '\t':
        unsigned const spaces = TAB_STOP - len % TAB_STOP;
        printf( "%*s", spaces, "" );
        len += spaces;
        continue;
      case '\n':
        len = 0;
        break;
      default:
        ++len;
    }
    putchar( c );
  }
}
```

Listing 5.1: Expand tabs to spaces, version 2, using `switch`

A controversial feature of C is that, once a `case` matches and the statements following it start executing, execution "falls through" into to the subsequent `case` or `default`, if any, unless you explicitly `break`, `continue` (but only if inside a loop), `goto` (§5.10), `return` (§5.9), or `longjmp` (§20.4). In listing 5.1, if the `break` on line 19 were not there, then after matching `\n` on line 17 and setting `len = 0` on line 18, control would fall through into the `default` case and `++len` would occur — not what we want there.

You can request that the compiler warn you if you fall through. For `clang` and `gcc`, it's done via the `-Wimplicit-fallthrough` command-line option. Then if you really want to fall through, use a `fallthrough` attribute (§4.9.2) so the compiler won't warn you as shown in listing 5.2. If `goodness` is 2, the program will print very good.

```
switch ( goodness ) {
  case 2:
    printf( "very " );
    [[fallthrough]];   // fallthrough is intentional
  case 1:
    printf( "good" );
}
```

Listing 5.2: Use of `fallthrough` attribute

5.9 return

The `return` statement has two forms:

> `return;` Returns from a `void` function.
> `return` *expr*`;` Returns from a non-`void` function.

Both unconditionally return from a function immediately. For the second form, the type of *expr* should match the return-type of the function. If it's not an exact match, *expr* is automatically converted to match, if possible; if not, a cast (§3.14) can also be used. Note that `()` are *not* needed to enclose *expr*.

5.10 goto

The `goto` statement is of the form:

> **goto** *label*;
> // ...
> *label*: *statement*

where *label* is an identifier followed by a `:` preceding a statement. A `goto` unconditionally goes to the statement with the given label (that may be either before or after the `goto`). A `goto` is useful in a few situations:

- When going to shared error-handling code as first shown in listing 1.3 (p.7).
- When similarly going to shared cleanup code.
- When inside a nested loop, to break out of all loops.
- To break out of a loop from within a `switch` as shown in listing 5.3.

```
for ( int i = 0; i < n; ++i ) {
  switch ( s[i] ) {
    // ...
    case '?':
      goto done;   // break out of "switch" and "for"
  }
}
done:
  ;
```

Listing 5.3: `goto` out of a loop from within `switch`

A few notes about labels:

- Labels are local to functions, so labels with the same name may appear in multiple functions yet are distinct.
- That implies that you can't `goto` a label in a different function (but see §20).

- Label names are in their own namespace, so it's perfectly legal to have a label and a variable with the same name in the same function (though it's not recommended) as shown in listing 5.4.

```
bool error;          // variable ...
// ...
if ( error )
   goto error;
// ...
error:               // ... and label with same name
// ...
```

Listing 5.4: Label and variable with same name

5.11 Empty Statement (;)

The empty statement is simply a semicolon. It's useful as an empty body of a `while` (§5.4) or `for` (§5.6) statement. The sample implementation of the `strcpy` standard function (§B.2) from listing 1.11 (p.20) used an empty statement.

5.12 Epilogue

Here are some key points about and some advice for certain statements:

- For `if-else`:
  - Remember that `else` associates with the most recent `if`.
  - If either uses `{}`, make both use `{}`.
- For `do-while`, always use `{}` and place the `while` on the same line as the `}`.
- For `for`:
  - Remember that all expressions are optional, but the `;`s must remain.
  - Its *init-expr* may also declare a variable.
  - If its *cond-expr* is omitted, it's equivalent to `true`.
- When multiple constant expressions are being compared against, consider `switch`.
- For `switch`:
  - The order the cases are tried is unspecified.
  - By default, cases "fall through," so you'll typically need `break` statements between cases.
  - If falling through is intentional, use the `[[fallthrough]]` attribute.

5.12 Epilogue

- Use goto either to go to shared code or to break out of a loop when break is insufficient.

Exercises

1. Write a program that reads standard input and prints each word on a line by itself. A "word" is defined as a sequence of one or more alphanumeric characters. For example, given the line of text:

   ```
   C is quirky, flawed, and an enormous success.
   ```

   the program should print:

   ```
   C
   is
   quirky
   flawed
   and
   an
   enormous
   success
   ```

   Additional requirements:

   - The program must print only alphanumeric and newline characters.
   - The program must always print a newline after each word even if the input ends with an alphanumeric character.
   - The program must never print a blank line.
   - If no input is given, the program must not print anything.

   Hint: an optimal solution doesn't need to treat any of those requirements as special cases. You will need the standard function isalnum (§B.1).

Chapter 6
Arrays and Pointers

As first shown in listing 1.3 (p.7), an *array* is a contiguous set of objects in memory of the same type, e.g., array of char or array of int. As first described in §1.6, a *pointer* is an object that contains the memory address of some other object. Not described previously is the curious relationship between arrays and pointers in C that is unlike most other languages.

6.1 Array Declaration

An array is declared by appending [n] where n is a constant positive integer expression whose value is the size (number of elements) of the array. As first shown in listing 1.3 (p.7):

```
char buf[ BUF_SIZE ];
```

declares an array BUF_SIZE of char. In C, array elements are always 0 through $n-1$.

6.2 Array Initialization

As first shown in listing 1.4 (p.10), an array can be initialized to all zeros or equivalent via the = { } syntax:

```
char str_buf[ STRING_MIN ] = { };
```

Arrays can also be initialized with values. The following declarations are equivalent:

```
char msg1[6] = { 'h', 'e', 'l', 'l', 'o', '\0' };
char msg2[]  = { 'h', 'e', 'l', 'l', 'o', '\0' };
char msg3[]  = "hello";
```

The `msg1` array is initialized with explicit values. If the number of values is less than the size of the array, the remaining elements are initialized to zero or equivalent. If the number of explicit values equals the size of the array that you want, you can omit the size as was done for `msg2` and the compiler will count the elements for you. As a special case, arrays of `char` can be initialized with string literals as was done for `msg3`. Remember that string literals implicitly have a null character appended by the compiler.

Alternatively, you can use *designated initializers*, that is use a non-negative, constant integer index surrounded by `[ ]` and followed by `=` to initialize specific values:

```
int a[9] = { [3] = 1, [4] = 2, [5] = 3 };
```

The array has elements 3, 4, and 5 initialized to 1, 2, and 3, respectively, and the remaining elements are initialized to zero. Designated initializers can be given in any order.

6.3 Array Indexing

As first shown in listing 1.4 (p.10), an array element is accessed by appending `[i]` (§3.11) where i is an integer expression that specifies the offset of the desired element.

Unlike many other languages, C doesn't do *bounds checking*, meaning it doesn't check at run-time if i is within the "bounds" 0 to $n - 1$ where n is the declared size of the array. Accessing an element outside its bounds results in undefined behavior (§15).

■ Not doing bounds checking is an instance of the compiler assuming you know what you're doing. Bounds violations can be a source of bugs (§18.6.1).
   Why not do bounds checking? It takes time, especially in loops. Not doing bounds checking is another way C achieves its speed. In cases where you *know* the bounds are correct, why bother checking? □

6.4 Multidimensional Arrays

Like other programming languages, C supports multidimensional arrays (aka, matrices). Unlike some other languages, C uses one pair of `[ ]` per dimension. For example, to declare a 3 × 2 array of `double`:

```
double a2d[3][2];        // not: a2d[3,2]
```

6.4 Multidimensional Arrays

Conceptually, think of a 2D matrix as an array of arrays. In C, all the elements are allocated contiguously such that a2d[*i*][0] and a2d[*i*][1] are adjacent in memory for a given row *i* (*row-major order*) as shown in figure 6.1.

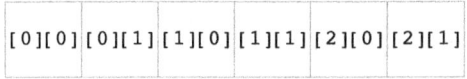

Fig. 6.1: Memory layout of a 3 × 2 array

Behind the curtain, memory is (always) one-dimensional as described in §1.5. To implement the syntactic sugar of two-dimensional arrays, the compiler actually does:

```
double *const a1d = &a2d[0][0];
a2d[i][j] = 0;           // really: a1d[ i * 2 + j ]
```

That is, to access a2d[*i*][*j*], the compiler multiplies *i* by the row size 2 then adds *j* and uses *that* as if it were the index into a one-dimensional array a1d.

Multidimensional arrays can be initialized similarly to one-dimensional arrays as shown in listing 6.1, lines 4–13.

```
1  #include <math.h>         // for sqrt()
2  #include <stdio.h>
3
4  constexpr double PLANET_AU[][2] = {
5     {  0.31,   0.47 },     // Mercury
6     {  0.72,   0.73 },     // Venus
7     {  0.98,   1.02 },     // Earth
8     {  1.38,   1.67 },     // Mars
9     {  4.95,   5.45 },     // Jupiter
10    {  9.01,  10.07 },     // Saturn
11    { 18.28,  20.09 },     // Uranus
12    { 29.80,  30.32 },     // Neptune
13 };
14
15 double orbital_period( unsigned p ) {
16    auto const a = (PLANET_AU[p][0] + PLANET_AU[p][1]) / 2;
17    return sqrt( a * a * a );
18 }
19
20 int main() {
21    for ( unsigned p = 0; p < 8; ++p ) {
22       auto const period = orbital_period( p );
23       if ( period < 1.0 )  // < 1 Earth year: print in days
24          printf( "%u %6.2fd\n", p, period * 365.25 );
25       else
26          printf( "%u %6.2fy\n", p, period );
27    }
28 }
```

Listing 6.1: Print orbital period of planets

PLANET_AU is an 8 × 2 array: one row per planet, each of which has two elements, perihelion and aphelion in Astronomical Units (AU). When initializing a multidimensional array, the left-most dimension can be omitted and the compiler will conveniently count the rows for you. Each row is enclosed between {} and separated by commas. (If you want to initialize all elements to non-zero values, you can omit the {} for the rows if you want. The compiler knows how many columns per row because it has to be specified explicitly.)

6.5 `void` Pointers

As stated in §1.6, pointers have types corresponding to the type of the objects to which they're pointing, e.g., pointer to `int`. Also stated, `void` is used instead of a return type when a function returns nothing.

In C, `void` is also used with pointers to get `void*` — a void pointer — a generic pointer that can point to any type. For example, the standard function `memmove` (§B.2) that copies n bytes from one area of memory to another is declared as:

```
void* memmove( void *dst, void const *src, size_t n );
```

A `void*` can never be dereferenced since `void` objects don't exist; hence, in order to access the object to which a `void*` points requires that it be cast to a specific type of pointer (§3.14.3), *then* dereferenced. As a special case, `void*` implicitly casts to or from any other type of pointer.

Since C doesn't have templates or generics, another use for `void*` is in data structures where the `void*` points to user-supplied data of any type. For example, a singly linked list structure might be declared as shown in listing 6.2.

```
struct slist {
  struct slist *next;
  void         *data;
};
```

Listing 6.2: Singly linked list structure with `void*` member

The `data` member allows you to store a pointer to anything you want. As an optimization to avoid dynamically allocating your data in addition to allocating an `slist` link, if the size of the data you want to store $\leq$ `sizeof(void*)`, you can cram your data *into* `data` directly via a cast (§3.14.1). For example, if `i` is an `int` you want to store, you can do:

```
head->data = (void*)i;    // cram int in
// ...
i = (int)head->data;      // pull int out
```

Remember, the compiler assumes you know what you're doing when using a cast.

6.6 Pointers to Pointers

Since pointers are objects like any other, pointers can also point to pointers, e.g., pointer to pointer to `int` or `int**`. There can be any number of `*`, but the number of pointer levels rarely exceeds two in practice.

Similar to the `swapi` function in listing 1.7 (p. 17), you can use a pointer to a pointer parameter to change the value of a pointer itself. For example, listing 6.3 implements the operations "push," "peek," and "pop" for an `slist`.

```
1   [[nodiscard]] struct slist* slist_push( struct slist *head,
2                                           void *data ) {
3     struct slist *const new_head =
4       malloc( sizeof(struct slist) );
5     new_head->next = head;
6     new_head->data = data;
7     return new_head;
8   }
9
10  [[nodiscard]] void* slist_peek( struct slist *head ) {
11    return head != nullptr ? head->data : nullptr;
12  }
13
14  [[nodiscard]] void* slist_pop( struct slist **phead ) {
15    auto const head = *phead;
16    if ( head == nullptr )
17      return nullptr;
18    *phead = head->next;
19    auto const data = head->data;
20    free( head );
21    return data;
22  }
```

Listing 6.3: Singly linked list functions

The functions `slist_push` and `slist_peek` are straightforward; `slist_pop` needs explanation:

- Line 14 declares `phead` as a pointer to an `slist*`, the current head of the list.
- Line 15 dereferences `phead` to get a copy of the head.
- Line 18 sets the original head to be `head->next` effectively popping the head off the list.
- Line 19 copies a pointer to the old head's `data`.
- Line 20 frees the old head's `slist` structure.
- Line 21 returns the old head's data.

6.7 Arrays and Pointers

There are a couple of quirky features of C when it comes to arrays and pointers:

1. The name of an array in an expression "decays" into a pointer to its first element. For example:

    ```
    int a[3];
    int *p = a;            // as if: p = &a[0]
    ```

2. The a[i] syntax is simply syntactic sugar for *(a+i). The compiler multiplies i × sizeof(int), then adds that to a (the address of its first element) to yield the address of the ith element, then dereferences *that* address. This means that [ ] does *no* bounds checking (§18.6.1).
3. Equivalently for any pointer p, *p can be written as p[0] which is the same as *(p+0). This means arithmetic can be done on pointers. More generally, *(p+i) is the element at the memory address p plus the offset of i × sizeof(*type*), which is the same as p[i]. This equivalence allows a one-dimensional array to be dynamically allocated and have the [ ] syntax still work:

    ```
    int *const p = malloc( 3 * sizeof(int) );
    // ...
    p[i] = 42;             // as if: *(p + i) = 42
    ```

While the syntactic sugar and equivalences are often convenient, the convenience comes at a price, specifically:

- There is no way to tell if a pointer points to a single object or multiple objects.
- Since the name of an array decays into a pointer in expressions, there is no way to tell how many elements an array has either (unless its declaration is in scope in which case you can use the sizeof operator, §3.16).

Both of these things mean it's too easy to attempt to access an object beyond what either a pointer points to or the number of elements in an array resulting in undefined behavior (§15) and bugs (§18.6.1), sometimes with serious consequences.

As a special case, it's perfectly OK for a pointer to point to one past the last element of an array. For example, given:

```
int buf[4];
int *const end = buf + 4; // one past last element is OK
```

it's OK to have end point to one past the last element of buf as shown in figure 6.2 for comparing against that enables code like this to be written:

```
for ( int *p = buf; p < end; ++p )
```

Of course, dereferencing such a pointer still results in undefined behavior.

6.9 Arrays of Pointers

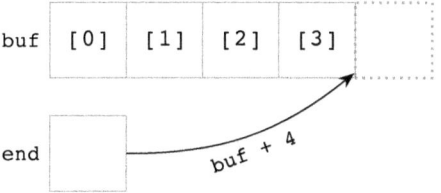

Fig. 6.2: Pointer to one past last array element is OK

6.8 Arrays vs. Pointers

Even though arrays and pointers work similarly, they are entirely different things. Given these two declarations:

```
char const   amsg[ ]  = "hello";
char const  *pmsg     = "hello";
```

they are in memory as shown in figure 6.3. The variable `amsg` is an array.

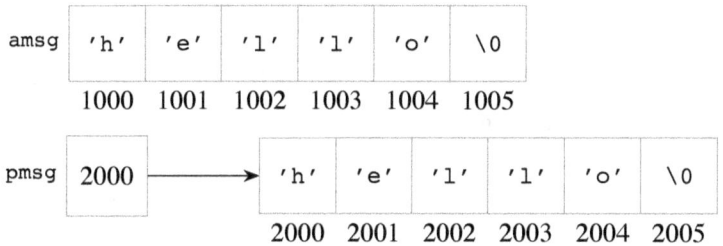

Fig. 6.3: Array vs. pointer

In memory, *only* the characters comprising `"hello"` exist. The total memory used is 6 bytes. When needed in an expression, the compiler uses the address of the array's first element, but it doesn't exist as a separate pointer object.

In contrast, `pmsg` is a pointer that points to the characters comprising `"hello"` somewhere else in memory. Assuming 64-bit pointers, the total memory used is 6 bytes for the string *plus* 8 bytes for the pointer for a total of 14 bytes. Another difference is that `pmsg` can be reassigned to point elsewhere whereas `amsg` can not.

6.9 Arrays of Pointers

Of course it's possible to have arrays of pointers, for example an array of pointers to `char` (strings):

```
char const *const COLORS[] = {
  "black", "white", "blue", "green", "red"
};
```

An array of strings could alternatively be declared as a true two-dimensional array:

```
char const COLORS_2D[][6] = {
  "black", "white", "blue", "green", "red"
};
```

but it's inconvenient because, although the compiler will count the number of rows for you, you'd have to specify the length of the longest string plus the terminating null character yourself (in this case, 6).

The other difference for `COLORS_2D` is that strings less than 6 characters would waste bytes, in this case, `"blue"` would waste 1 and `"red"` would waste 2, since the total space is always 30 bytes. On the other hand, while `COLORS` would require only exactly 27 bytes for the strings, it would also require 40 bytes for the pointers (assuming 64-bit pointers) for a total of 67 bytes.

That said, unless space is at a premium (such as it might be in embedded applications), using an array of pointers to strings is simply more convenient.

6.10 Pointers to Function

In addition to pointing to an object, a pointer can also point to a function because the compiled machine code for functions is in memory like objects are. Just as pointers to objects are typed, e.g., pointer to `int`, pointers to functions are also typed, e.g., pointer to function taking two `void` pointers to `const` as parameters and returning an `int`. For example, the standard function `qsort` that sorts an array is declared as:

```
void qsort( void *array, size_t n, size_t esize,
            int (*cmp_fn)( void const*, void const* ) );
```

where `array` points to the array of any type to be sorted, `n` is the number of elements, `esize` is the element size, and `cmp_fn` is a pointer to the function to use to perform comparisons of two elements i and j returning an integer $< 0, 0,$ or > 0 if `array[`i`]` is $<, =,$ or $>$ `array[`j`]`, respectively.

By using both `void*` and a pointer to function, `qsort` implements *only* the algorithm and has delegated element comparisons (that are independent of the algorithm) to the pointed-to function. Hence, a pointer to function is like an interface in either Go or Java or an abstract class in C++ having a single method — but without the interface or class envelope.

For the declaration of `cmp_fn` itself, the `()` are necessary because it would be a function returning a pointer to `int` without them. As noted in §4, declarations in C can get infamously complicated.

6.10 Pointers to Function

■ To help decipher complicated declarations, you can use `cdecl`[†] that can parse a C or C++ declaration (aka, "gibberish") and explain it in English:

```
cdecl> explain int (*cmp_fn)(void const*, void const*)
declare cmp_fn as pointer to function (pointer to
    const void, pointer to const void) returning
    integer
```

You can also type `declare` followed by a declaration in English and `cdecl` will print it in C or C++. □

For example, sorting the COLORS array would be done as shown in listing 6.4.

```
1  int strcmp_for_qsort( void const *ips, void const *jps ) {
2    return strcmp( *(char const**)ips, *(char const**)jps );
3  }
4
5  void sort_colors() {
6    qsort( COLORS, sizeof COLORS / sizeof COLORS[0],
7           sizeof COLORS[0], &strcmp_for_qsort );
8  }
```

Listing 6.4: Use `qsort` to sort an array of strings

- As shown in §3.16, the first `sizeof` on line 6 returns the total size of the array, the second returns the size of an individual element, and their quotient is the number of elements in the array.
- On line 7, the third `sizeof` returns the size of an individual element to sort and `strcmp_for_qsort` is the function to use to perform the comparisons of elements.
- When `qsort` calls a comparison function, it passes it two *pointers* to the elements to compare. Since COLORS is an array of `char const*`, `qsort` passes two *pointers* to `char const*`.

On line 2, each cast casts a `void const*` parameter (§3.14.3) to the `char const**` we know it to be. Each such pointer is then dereferenced via the leading `*` to yield actual pointers to the strings to be compared. Those are passed to the standard function `strcmp` (§B.2) that compares two strings returning an integer < 0, 0, or > 0 if the first string is <, =, or > the second string, respectively.

To call a function via pointer explicitly:

```
int cmp1 = (*cmp_fn)( s1, s2 );  // call via pointer
int cmp2 = cmp_fn( s1, s2 );     // same
```

For `cmp1`, the pointer to function `cmp_fn` is dereferenced via `*` (§3.12) to yield a function that is then called. The first set of `( )` are necessary otherwise it would instead be

---

[†] *cdecl: Composing and deciphering C (or C++) declarations or casts, aka "gibberish,"* Paul J. Lucas, https://github.com/paul-j-lucas/cdecl

calling a function named `cmp_fn` that returned a pointer that the `*` dereferenced. For `cmp2`, C allows you to elide the `(*...)` as a shorthand and call a pointer to function directly.

■ Personally, I prefer using the explicit `(*...)` form since it makes it clear that `cmp_fn` is a pointer to function and not a function named `cmp_fn`. □

6.11 Array Compound Literals

Listing 6.5 shows `str_is_any`, a function where the parameters are a string to find (the "needle") and an array of strings to compare against (the "haystack"). The convention here is that the last element of the array must be a null pointer to be a sentinel.

```
bool str_is_any( char const *needle,
                 char const *const haystack[] ) {
  for ( unsigned i = 0; haystack[i] != nullptr; ++i ) {
    if ( strcmp( needle, haystack[i] ) == 0 )
      return true;
  }
  return false;
}
```

Listing 6.5: Function to see if a string is among a set

You can call it like:

```
if ( str_is_any( answer, (char const*[])
                 { "true", "yes", nullptr } ) )
  // ...
```

Similar to a compound statement that is multiple statements enclosed by `{}` (§5.2), a *compound literal* for an array is multiple literals enclosed by `{}` prefixed by `(type[])` similar to a cast (§3.14) that specifies the type of the literals, in this case `char const*` for array of constant pointer to `char` (strings). A compound literal for an array allows you to specify an array "inline." Without compound literals, you'd need to use a separate array:

```
char const *const AFFIRM[] = { "true", "yes", nullptr };
if ( str_is_any( answer, AFFIRM ) )
  // ...
```

For a less verbose way to pass a compound literal for an array as an argument, see §8.12.

6.11.1 Compound Literal Lifetime and Storage Class

By default, the lifetime of a compound literal is the scope (§2.4) that encloses it. For example, as shown in listing 6.6, the scope of the compound literal on line 4 is limited to line 4.

```
1  void f( int const *a ) {
2    int *p;
3    if ( a == nullptr ) {
4      p = (int[]){ 0 };    // int[] exists only on this line
5    }
6    int n = p[0];          // undefined behavior
7    // ...
```

Listing 6.6: Compound literal lifetime

Outside of that scope, p becomes a *dangling pointer* (a pointer to an object that no longer exists), hence any attempt at access, such as on line 6, results in undefined behavior (§15).

The (*type*) for a compound literal may optionally include a storage class (§4.3), but only one of constexpr (§4.4), register (§4.3.4), static (§4.3.3), or thread_local (§14.7). To fix the lifetime in listing 6.6, you can either remove the {} on lines 3 and 5 (hence, the scope of the compound literal will be the entire function) or include static like:

```
p = (static int[]){ 0 };    // (int[]) exists forever
```

The caveat of using static is that the compound literal can then be initialized only with constants or literals at compile-time as opposed to arbitrary values at run-time.

6.12 Multidimensional Arrays vs. Pointers

Given these two declarations:

```
double a2d[3][2];     // array 3 x 2 of double
double *ap[3];        // array 3 of pointer to double
```

The variable a2d is in memory as was shown in figure 6.1, that is it has 6 double values comprising a true two-dimensional array. Assuming 64-bit doubles, the total memory used is 48 bytes.

In contrast, ap is an array of 3 pointers to double. Assuming 64-bit pointers, the total memory used is 24 bytes. If ap were initialized like this:

```
double *ap[3] = { a2d[0], a2d[2], a2d[4] };
```

then the expression ap[i][j] would refer to the same double as a2d[i][j] for all i and j. Even though ap is a one-dimensional array, the expression ap[i] gets the ith pointer to which the [j] can be applied via the $p[j]$ equivalence to $*(p+j)$ (§6.7 #3, p.88).

6.13 Dynamically Allocating 2D Arrays

As we saw in §6.7 #3 (p.88), a one-dimensional array can be dynamically allocated and have the [ ] syntax still work. But can the same be done for a two- or higher-dimensional array? The previous section hinted that the answer is "yes."

The trick is to allocate an array of i pointers where each pointer points at exactly the right element within an elements array. This would be like ap in the previous section. To be more efficient, the array of pointers and the array of elements can be allocated in one chunk of memory as shown in figure 6.4.

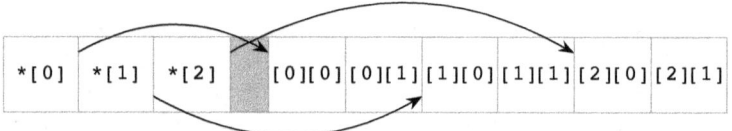

Fig. 6.4: Memory layout of a dynamically allocated 3 × 2 array

One slight caveat is shown as the shaded area between the row pointers and the elements. This is *padding* that may be necessary to ensure that the elements are properly aligned (§3.17). A function to allocate a 2D array is shown in listing 6.7.

```
 1  void** alloc2d( size_t esize, size_t align,
 2                  size_t r, size_t c ) {
 3    // ensure &elements[0][0] is suitably aligned
 4    auto const ptr_size = rup2( sizeof(void*) * r, align );
 5    auto const row_size = esize * c;
 6    // allocate the row pointers followed by the elements
 7    void **const rows = malloc( ptr_size + r * row_size );
 8    char *const elements = (char*)rows + ptr_size;
 9    for ( size_t i = 0; i < r; ++i )
10      rows[i] = &elements[ i * row_size ];
11    return rows;
12  }
```

Listing 6.7: Dynamically allocate $i \times j$ 2D array

- Lines 1–2 declare the parameters esize for the element size, align for the alignment, and r and c for the rows and columns of the 2D array to allocate. The function returns a pointer to the pointers. You'd use the function like:

6.13 Dynamically Allocating 2D Arrays

```
double **const a2d = (double**)
  alloc2d( sizeof(double), alignof(double), 3, 2 );
a2d[0][0] = 3.14;          // [i][j] syntax works
free( a2d );
```

The (double**) cast (§3.14.3) is necessary because, unlike void* that implicitly casts to any pointer type, void** does not.

- To ensure &elements[0][0] is suitably aligned, line 3 calculates the size of the pointers rounded up to align bytes so it includes any necessary padding using the rup2 function from listing 3.2 (p.51).
- Line 6 allocates rows that is a pointer to the entire chunk of memory containing both the array of pointers and the array of elements.
- Line 7 sets elements to point to the first element that is the address rows plus ptr_size that includes any necessary padding. The (char*) cast is necessary because arithmetic can't be done on void pointers because void objects don't exist, hence have no size.
- Lines 8–9 set rows[i] to point to the zeroth column of each row (the arrows in figure 6.4).

Not only does this need only one call to malloc, but also only one call to free. Had the array of elements been allocated separately from the array of pointers, another function of free2d would have been necessary to free both.

Another caveat is that, unlike a statically allocated 2D array, a dynamically allocated 2D array uses additional memory for the row pointers. Therefore whenever possible for an array with dimensions $i \times j$, make $i \leq j$ so you get the most elements per pointer. On the other hand, if you only need a triangular matrix, then it's possible to write a variant of alloc2d that allocates only i elements for row i. This will only use memory for $n(n+1)/2$ elements plus n pointers. For a triangular matrix where $n \geq 4$, this yields a memory savings.

If the cost of the additional row pointers is too much for your circumstances, you can eliminate them, but you have to sacrifice the use of the [][] syntax and write your own accessor function that does what the compiler does behind the curtain, something like:

```
void* a2d_ij( void *a2d, size_t esize, size_t c,
              size_t i, size_t j ) {
  return &((char*)a2d)[ (i * c + j) * esize ];
}
```

then use it like:

```
double *const a2d = malloc( sizeof(double) * 3 * 2 );
*(double*)a2d_ij( a2d, sizeof(double), 2, i, j ) = 3.14;
```

But that's pretty ugly. Like many other things in computer science, it's a trade-off.

6.14 Variable Length Arrays

Usually, all arrays have to be declared to be of a fixed length (known at compile-time). A *variable length array* ("VLA" for short) can be declared to be of a variable length (not known until run-time). For example, a function that prints a histogram for an array of integers is shown in listing 6.8.

```
1  void print_hist( unsigned nvals, unsigned const vals[],
2                   unsigned buckets, char marker ) {
3    unsigned hist[ buckets + 1 ] = { };
4    for ( unsigned i = 0; i < nvals; ++i ) {
5      if ( vals[i] <= buckets )
6        ++hist[ vals[i] ];
7    }
8    for ( unsigned b = 0; b <= buckets; ++b ) {
9      auto h = hist[ b ];
10     if ( h == 0 )
11       continue;
12     printf( "%3u: ", b );
13     while ( h-- > 0 )
14       putchar( marker );
15     putchar( '\n' );
16   }
17 }
```

Listing 6.8: Function using a VLA to print a histogram

The parameter `nvals` is the size of the array `vals` containing the values, `buckets` is the number of "buckets" the values should fall into, and `marker` is the character to print for the histogram. For example, to print a histogram of 25 student grades in the range 0–100 using '+':

```
print_hist( 25, grades, 100, '+' );
```

Line 3 declares `hist` as a VLA by using `buckets + 1` (a value not known until run-time) for its size rather than a constant expression.

While VLAs work and seem convenient, one serious caveat to VLAs is that, if the length is too big, it will *silently* overflow the stack resulting in undefined behavior (§15). Additionally, unlike `malloc` returning `nullptr` upon failure, there's no way to detect when a VLA overflows the stack. Hence, if the size can be "too big," your code has to guard against it:

```
constexpr unsigned HIST_BUCKETS_MAX = 1024;
// ...
if ( buckets > HIST_BUCKETS_MAX )
  // ... do something else ...
```

But if you know that `HIST_BUCKETS_MAX` is the maximum safe size, then you might as well simply declare `hist` to be of that size and not use a VLA.

Incidentally, you could do small size optimization as shown in listing 6.9.

```
void print_hist( unsigned nvals, unsigned const vals[],
                 unsigned buckets, char marker ) {
  unsigned hist[ HIST_BUCKETS_MAX + 1 ];
  unsigned *const phist = buckets <= HIST_BUCKETS_MAX ?
    hist : malloc( (buckets + 1) * sizeof(unsigned) );
  // ... use only "phist" to access array ...
  if ( phist != hist )
    free( phist );
}
```

Listing 6.9: Function using small size optimization to print a histogram

That is, if `buckets` isn't too big, use the (fixed sized) array on the stack; otherwise, use a dynamically sized array in the heap. This has the advantage of saving on the calls to `malloc` and `free` for "small" `buckets` yet still works for "large" `buckets`. But notice that a VLA is not being used.

Hence, the moral is: use VLAs *only* when you don't know the size at compile time but can *guarantee* that it won't be "too big." However, this is pretty much never true. In hindsight, VLAs, though they seem convenient at times, are problematic, so much so that C11 made VLAs an optional feature.

■ C++ never adopted VLAs from C. □

6.15 Epilogue

Here are some key points about and some advice for arrays and pointers:

- For any array declared as `a[n]`, the elements are always 0 through $n - 1$.
- Arrays may be initialized using the `= { }` syntax:
  - If empty, all elements are initialized to zero or equivalent.
  - If values are given, the size becomes optional: the compiler will count the number of values and use that for the size.
  - If the size is given, but the number of values is less than that, the remaining elements are initialized to zero or equivalent.
  - Designated initializers `[i] = v` can be used to initialize specific elements in any order.
  - Arrays of `char` may be initialized with string literals.
- When indexing an array, C doesn't do bounds checking so accessing an element outside its bounds results in undefined behavior (§15).
- Multidimensional arrays are arrays of arrays. C uses row-major order.
- `void` pointers are used as generic pointers that can point to any type, but never be dereferenced.
- Although arrays and pointers are very different things, they have a quirky relationship in C:

- The name of an array "decays" into a pointer to its first element.
- For an array, a[i] is simply syntactic sugar for *(a+i).
- For a pointer, *p can be written as p[0] which is the same as *(p+0). More generally, *(p+i) is the same as p[i].
- It's OK for a pointer to point to one past the last element of an array.

- Pointers to function can be used to allow one general function (such as qsort) to delegate specifics (such as comparisons) to another.
- Compound literals like (*type*[]){ ... } can be used to create arrays "inline."
- Multidimensional arrays can be simulated using arrays of pointers.
- Don't use VLAs (except as parameters, §9.4.3, §9.4.5).

Exercises

1. Write a function:

    ```
    int slist_cmp( struct slist const *i_list,
                   struct slist const *j_list,
                   int (*cmp_fn)(void const *i_data,
                                 void const *j_data) );
    ```

    to compare two lists using cmp_fn to compare the data at each pair of elements returning an integer $< 0, 0,$ or > 0 if i_list is $<, =,$ or $>$ j_list, respectively.

2. Write a function:

    ```
    struct slist* slist_dup( struct slist const *list,
                             void (*dup_fn)(void const*) );
    ```

    to duplicate list using dup_fn to duplicate the data at each element. Return a pointer to the head of the new list.

3. As mentioned in §6.13, if you need a triangular matrix, it's possible to write a variant of alloc2d that allocates only i elements for row i. Write a function:

    ```
    void** alloc_tri( size_t esize, size_t align,
                      size_t n );
    ```

    that allocates a triangular matrix of n rows, 0 ... n−1, where row i has $i + 1$ elements, e.g., row 0 has 1 element [0], row 1 has 2 elements [0] and [1], and so on. If n is 0, return nullptr.

4. Rather than have a single function print_hist (listing 6.8, p. 96) that both creates and prints a histogram, split it into two functions, the first:

6.15 Epilogue

```
unsigned* new_hist( unsigned nvals,
                    unsigned const vals[],
                    unsigned buckets );
```

that dynamically allocates a new histogram, fills in its values, and returns it; and the second, a new version of:

```
void print_hist( unsigned buckets,
                 unsigned const hist[],
                 char marker );
```

that prints the histogram returned by `new_hist`.

Chapter 7
Enumerations

As their simplest, *enumerations* are a small step up from either constants (§4.4) or object-like macros (§8.3). Suppose you want to define constants for a set of colors. Rather than doing something like:

```
constexpr unsigned COLOR_BLACK = 0;
constexpr unsigned COLOR_WHITE = 1;
constexpr unsigned COLOR_BLUE  = 2;
constexpr unsigned COLOR_GREEN = 3;
constexpr unsigned COLOR_RED   = 4;
```

you can instead do:

```
enum color {
  COLOR_BLACK,
  COLOR_WHITE,
  COLOR_BLUE,
  COLOR_GREEN,
  COLOR_RED,            // extra ',' here is OK
};
```

As a nicety, the compiler allows you to include a comma after the last value thus making it a tiny bit easier to add more values at the end. Once declared, you can then use `color` as a type and the enumerated constants as values:

```
enum color c = COLOR_BLACK;
```

The basic idea of enumerations is that you use them to express a set of related values.

7.1 Declarations

Formally, an enumeration declaration is of the form:

> **enum** *tag$_{opt}$* {
>   *enum-constants$_{opt}$*
> } *declarations$_{opt}$*;

that is the keyword `enum` optionally followed by a *tag* name followed by a set of one or more *enumeration constants* between {} optionally followed by declarations of the enumeration. An *enumeration constant* is at minimum simply an identifier.

In C, the names of enumerations, structures (§10), and unions (§11) are collectively put into a *tags* namespace (§2.3). To refer to an enumeration name, it must be preceded by `enum`:

```
enum color c;
```

If you forget to include it, you'll get an error:

```
color c;                // error: must use "enum" tag
```

Alternatively, you can use `typedef` (§2.6) to "inject" a tag name into the surrounding scope so you no longer need to use `enum`:

```
typedef enum color color;  // inject into surrounding scope
color c;                   // no "enum" needed now
```

As a second alternative, you can `typedef` an enumeration declaration directly:

```
typedef enum {             // or: typedef enum color {
  COLOR_BLACK,
  COLOR_WHITE,
  COLOR_BLUE,
  COLOR_GREEN,
  COLOR_RED,
} color;
```

7.2 Name Collisions

For the `color` enumeration, you might be wondering why verbose constant names were used. Why not more simply:

```
enum color { BLACK, WHITE, BLUE, GREEN, RED };
```

Unfortunately, despite appearances, enumeration constants aren't scoped, which means they're all "injected" into the surrounding scope.

If there were another enumeration like:

```
enum rb_color {        // Red-Black tree node color
    BLACK,             // error: redefinition of "BLACK"
    RED,               // error: redefinition of "RED"
};
```

you'd get redefinition errors. Hence, it's a good practice to name all constants of the same enumeration with a common prefix and hope they don't collide with other names elsewhere.

■ This problem was fixed in C++ with the addition of scoped enumerations, but that has yet to be adopted into C, if ever. □

7.3 Underlying Type

Every enumeration has an *underlying type*, that is the type that's actually used at the machine level to represent it. It's typically `int`, but can be any integer type big enough to hold the largest value of the enumeration. If you don't specify a type, the one used is implementation defined. In many cases, you don't care; but if you do, you can specify a fixed underlying type explicitly by following the name of the enumeration by a `:` and the underlying type such as:

```
enum color : unsigned char {
    // ...
```

This is useful if you want to guarantee a size smaller or larger than `int` and control its sign in expressions. An underlying type can be any integer or character type (signed or unsigned) or a `typedef` (§2.6) thereof.

7.4 Implicit Conversion

Enumeration constants and variables implicitly convert to values of their underlying type in expressions. Additionally, values of the underlying type also implicitly convert to enumerations. While these conversions can sometimes be convenient, they allow nonsensical code to be written with neither errors nor warnings:

```
enum color c = COLOR_BLACK + COLOR_WHITE * 2;   // ?
```

Fortunately, there are better uses for implicit conversion (§7.5.7).

7.5 Enumeration Constant Values

The values enumeration constants have are assigned by the compiler (by default) starting at zero and increasing by one for each constant. Often, you don't particularly care about what those values actually are. However, you can explicitly specify any values you want to all or only some constants. You can even specify negative values (unless you specified an unsigned underlying type). If omitted, the value of a constant is assigned by the compiler as the previous value plus one as shown in listing 7.1.

```
enum color {
  COLOR_NONE   = -1,
  COLOR_BLACK  = 0,
  COLOR_WHITE  = 1,
  COLOR_BLUE,            // value is 2 ...
  COLOR_GREEN,           // ... 3
  COLOR_RED,             // ... 4
};
```

Listing 7.1: Enumeration with explicit values

That said, you should not explicitly specify values unless:

- The values are "externally imposed" (§7.5.1) or otherwise have meaning; or:
- You need to "serialize" the values (§7.5.2) either to disk or over a socket; or:
- You are representing bit flags (§7.5.7).

7.5.1 Externally Imposed Values

Sometimes, enumeration values are externally imposed from the real world. For example, if you were writing software for a graphics terminal where the hardware uses specific values[†] for specific colors as shown in listing 7.2.

```
enum ansi_color {
  ANSI_FG_BLACK = 30, ANSI_FG_RED     = 31,
  ANSI_FG_GREEN = 32, ANSI_FG_YELLOW  = 33,
  ANSI_FG_BLUE  = 34, ANSI_FG_MAGENTA = 35,
  ANSI_FG_CYAN  = 36, ANSI_FG_WHITE   = 37,
};
```

Listing 7.2: Enumeration with externally imposed values

Thanks to implicit conversion to integer, you can use the values directly:

```
printf( "\33[%dm", ANSI_FG_RED ); // will print in red
```

[†] *Select Graphic Rendition*, Ecma International, *Control Functions For Coded Character Sets*, ECMA-48, 5th ed., June 1991.

7.5.2 Serializing Values

If you write values to disk (presumably to read them back at some later time), you want to ensure that, say, 3 will always correspond to COLOR_GREEN even if you add more colors. If the values weren't explicitly specified and you added a new color anywhere but at the end, the subsequent values would silently shift by 1 as shown in listing 7.3.

```
enum color {
  COLOR_BLACK,
  COLOR_WHITE,
  COLOR_YELLOW,  // New color is now 2.
  COLOR_BLUE,    // This used to be 2, but is now 3 ...
  COLOR_GREEN,   // ... and so on.
  COLOR_RED
};
```

Listing 7.3: Enumeration with new constant inserted

Of course you could have the policy always to add new values at the end, but that relies on programmers following the policy. If you specify values explicitly, the compiler can help you enforce unique values, but not in the way you might assume (§7.5.3).

Alternatively, you can serialize values as strings as shown in listing 7.4.

```
void print_color( color c ) {
  switch ( c ) {
    case COLOR_BLACK: fputs( "black", stdout ); return;
    case COLOR_WHITE: fputs( "white", stdout ); return;
    case COLOR_BLUE : fputs( "blue" , stdout ); return;
    case COLOR_GREEN: fputs( "green", stdout ); return;
    case COLOR_RED  : fputs( "red"  , stdout ); return;
  }
}
```

Listing 7.4: Serializing an enumeration value as a string

While serializing to text is more expensive, if you're serializing the rest of your data to a text format like JSON anyway, then it doesn't matter. The other advantage is that changes to the underlying values don't matter. (For another way to serialize values, see §8.9.)

7.5.3 Duplicate Values

It's perfectly legal to have two constants of the same enumeration with the same underlying value:

```
enum color {
  // ...
  COLOR_GREEN,
  COLOR_CHARTREUSE = COLOR_GREEN,
  // ...
};
```

They're synonyms. In this case, it's clearly intentional. However, it's possible to introduce synonyms by accident, especially in an enumeration with lots of explicitly supplied values. Since synonyms are legal, the compiler often can't help you detect accidental synonyms — until you `switch` on them since it's illegal to have more than one `case` with the same value as shown in listing 7.5.

```
switch ( c ) {
  // ...
  case COLOR_GREEN:
    // ...
    break;
  case COLOR_CHARTREUSE:  // error: duplicate case value
    // ...
```

Listing 7.5: `switch` on enumeration with duplicate value

7.5.4 "None" Values

If an enumeration can have a "default," "OK," "none," "not set," "'unspecified," or similar value, it should be declared first so:

1. It will get assigned the value of 0 by default by the compiler which is easily recognizable in a debugger.
2. File-scope (§2.4) enumeration variables will be initialized to it (0) automatically.

For example:

```
enum eol { EOL_UNSPECIFIED, EOL_UNIX, EOL_WINDOWS };
```

7.5.5 Checking Values

If you need to check an enumeration variable for one value, using an `if` is fine:

```
if ( file_eol == EOL_UNSPECIFIED )
  return;
```

But if you need to check for more than one value, you should always use a `switch` as shown in listing 7.6.

7.5 Enumeration Constant Values

```
switch ( file_eol ) {
  case EOL_WINDOWS:
    putchar( '\r' );
    [[fallthrough]];
  case EOL_UNIX:
  case EOL_UNSPECIFIED: // default to Unix-style
    putchar( '\n' );
    break;
}
```

Listing 7.6: Using `switch` for enumeration variable

Why? Because if you omit a `case` for a value, the compiler will warn you. This is extremely helpful if you add a new enumeration value: the compiler can tell you where you forgot to add a `case` to your `switch` statements.

You should avoid using `default` when switching on enumerations because it prevents the compiler from being able to warn you when you omit a `case` for a value. It's better to include a `case` for every value even if those cases do nothing.

7.5.6 "Count" Values

You may encounter code that adds a "count" value at the end as shown in listing 7.7.

```
enum color {
  COLOR_BLACK,
  COLOR_WHITE,
  COLOR_BLUE,
  COLOR_GREEN,
  COLOR_RED,
  NUM_COLOR              // = number of colors (here, 5)
};
```

Listing 7.7: Enumeration with "count" value at end

The intent is that the underlying integer value of NUM_COLOR will be the number of colors since the compiler will automatically assign 5 to it in this case which is the number of actual colors. This is then used to marginally simplify serialization to text by using the underlying value as an index into an array assuming the value of the first constant is 0) as shown in listing 7.8.

The caveat is that it adds a "pseudo color" value that you'd need to include as a `case` in every `switch` on color to prevent the compiler warning about the unhandled `case` even though the value will never match. (For a better way to count values, see §8.9.2.)

```
static char const *const COLORS[] = {
  "black", "white" "blue", "green", "red"
};

void print_color( color c ) {
  if ( c < NUM_COLOR )   // defensive check
    fputs( COLORS[ c ], stdout );
}
```

Listing 7.8: Serializing an enumeration with a "count"

7.5.7 Bit Flag Values

Another way to use enumerations is to declare a set of bit flags where each value is a unique power of 2 as shown in listing 7.9.

```
enum c_int_fmt {
  CIF_NONE     = 0,
  CIF_SHORT    = 1 << 0,
  CIF_INT      = 1 << 1,
  CIF_LONG     = 1 << 2,
  CIF_UNSIGNED = 1 << 3,
  CIF_CONST    = 1 << 4,
  CIF_STATIC   = 1 << 5,
};
```

Listing 7.9: Enumeration with bit-flag values

■ Rather than specify power-of-2 values explicitly, e.g., 0, 1, 2, 4, 8, etc., a common trick is to use `1 << n` where n is the nth bit from 0 to however many bits are needed and let the compiler do the calculation for you. □

You can then bitwise-or (§3.8) various flags together:

```
enum c_int_fmt fmt = CIF_CONST | CIF_UNSIGNED | CIF_INT;
```

This results in a value (`0b011010`) that isn't among the declared values — but that's perfectly legal. Debuggers are smart enough to notice this and print accordingly:

```
(gdb) p fmt
$1 = CIF_INT | CIF_UNSIGNED | CIF_CONST
```

You can also test for inclusion of particular bits as shown in listing 7.10.

```
if ( (fmt & CIF_STATIC) != CIF_NONE )
  puts( "static " );
if ( (fmt & CIF_CONST) != CIF_NONE )
  puts( "const " );
// ...
```

Listing 7.10: Testing for inclusion of bits in enumeration

Or test for sets of bits, for example, does `fmt` have two specific bits set:

```
if ( (fmt & (CIF_SHORT | CIF_LONG)) ==
      CIF_SHORT | CIF_LONG ) {
  goto illegal_format;
}
```

The caveat, of course, is that a `switch` on such an enumeration may not match any case. Despite that, enumerations are often used for bitwise flags. This is a case where implicit conversion to `int` is convenient because the bitwise operators "just work."

7.6 Epilogue

Here are some key points about and some advice for enumerations:

- Use enumerations *only* to specify a set of related values.
- Enumeration constant names are injected into the surrounding scope, so name them so they are unlikely to collide with others (typically with a common prefix).
- Use "none" constants when appropriate.
- Don't explicitly specify values unless necessary.
- Don't specify "count" values.
- Enumerations have an implementation defined underlying integer type. You can specify one explicitly, but do so only if necessary.
- Enumeration values implicitly convert to their underlying type.
- Use a `switch` statement when comparing an enumeration value against more than one constant.
- Avoid using `default` in `switch` statements on enumerations.
- Enumerations can be used for a set of related bit flag values.

Exercises

1. Write a function:

    ```
    enum color parse_color( char const *s );
    ```

    that does the inverse of `print_color` in listing 7.4 (p.105), that is parses a color name from the null-terminated string `s` and returns its corresponding enumeration value, e.g., parsing `"red"` would return `COLOR_RED`. If the value of `s` is not a known color name, return `(enum color)-1` instead.

2. Write a function:

    void `print_int_fmt(` **enum** `c_int_fmt fmt );`

    that prints the value of `fmt` as `gdb` does, this is, for all bits that are `1`, print their corresponding names separated by " | ".

Chapter 8
Preprocessor

One of C's quirks is that it has a separate *preprocessor* that's called by the C compiler to "preprocess" source files before compiling them — hence the name.

■ The reason C has a preprocessor unlike most other languages is that it seemed like a good idea at the time at Bell Labs due to the use of preprocessors in general such as m4 and the Troff suite of preprocessors. □

Modern C compilers have the preprocessor integrated, though there are often options to control it specifically as if it were still a separate program. For clang and gcc at least, the -E option causes a file only to be preprocessed that can often be illuminating as to what the preprocessor is doing. For Microsoft C, the option is /E.

8.1 Compilation Phases

Compilation happens in a number of *phases*, the first few of which are relevant to preprocessing:

1. Every escaped newline (a \ immediately followed by a newline) is deleted thereby splicing the lines together.
2. The sequence of individual characters comprising the text of a source file are coalesced into a sequence of *tokens*. For example, the sequence of characters ++i (two adjacent pluses followed by the letter i) are coalesced into the sequence of tokens *plus-plus* followed by the *identifier* i.
3. Preprocessing *directives* (§8.2) are performed and *macros* (§8.3, §8.7) are expanded. All preprocessing directives are then deleted.
4. Escaped character sequences are converted to the characters they represent, e.g., \n becomes a newline.
5. Adjacent string literals are concatenated, e.g., "A" "B" becomes "AB".

8.2 Language

The preprocessor has its own mini-language that is very different from C:

- A *directive* in the preprocessor corresponds to a statement in C. Directives are line-based and begin with # (that *must* be the first token on a line) and end with an end-of-line (on Unix systems, the newline character) — unless escaped via \ in which case a directive ends with the first unescaped newline.
- Following the # may be zero or more whitespace characters followed by a directive name, hence all the following are equivalent:

    ```
    #ifndef NDEBUG
    #   ifndef NDEBUG
        #ifndef NDEBUG
    ```

    ■ Some people, myself included, prefer the style where the # is always in the first column to make preprocessor lines stand out. □

- Other than the set of tokens that comprise C (identifiers, operators, punctuation, literals, comments), the preprocessor knows very little about C. In particular, it knows nothing about scope (§2.4).

8.3 Object-Like Macros

Object-like macros are the simplest: they replace a macro name with zero or more tokens comprising its replacement list wherever the name occurs (except within string literals).

To define an object-like macro, use the #define directive followed by the name of the macro followed by the set of tokens it should be replaced by. For example:

```
#define WS   " \n\t\r\f\v"
```

defines a WS macro that will be replaced by the given string literal wherever WS subsequently occurs in the source file.

Most compilers also allow you to define a macro via an option. For clang and gcc, the -D command-line option can be used to define a macro having an optional value via an argument of the form *name*[=*value*]. For Microsoft C, the option is /D. If *value* is omitted, it defaults to 1. For example:

```
$ cc -DDEBUG hello.c                    # as if: -DDEBUG=1
$ cc -DMSG='"hello, world"' hello.c     # shell needs '...'
```

■ Originally, C didn't have either enumerations (§7) or constexpr (§4.4), so object-like macros were the only way to give constants names. □

8.4 Predefined Macros

The preprocessor pre-defines several object-like macros shown in table 8.1. For `clang` and `gcc`, the `-std=`*version* command-line option sets what the current C (or C++) version is, e.g., `-std=c23`. For Microsoft C, the option is `/std:`*version*.

Table 8.1: Predefined macros

`__cplusplus`	The current C++ version expressed as an integer of the year of standardization plus a revision, e.g., `202302L` — defined only when compiling with a C++ compiler.
`__DATE__`	The local date in the form *"Mmm dd yyyy"*.
`__FILE__`	The current filename. (See also §8.10.)
`__LINE__`	The current line number. (See also §8.10.)
`__STDC__`	If `1`, compiling with a C compiler.
`__STDC_ENDIAN_BIG__`	Implementation defined value for big-endian.
`__STDC_ENDIAN_LITTLE__`	Implementation defined value for little-endian.
`__STDC_ENDIAN_NATIVE__`	Either of the above two values or some other value if the CPU's endianness is mixed.
`__STDC_IEC_60559_DFP__`	If not defined, the decimal floating-point types (§2.5.7) are *not* supported.
`__STDC_NO_ATOMICS__`	If `1`, the `_Atomic` keyword (§17) is *not* supported.
`__STDC_NO_COMPLEX__`	If `1`, complex types (§2.5.8) and the `complex.h` standard header are *not* supported.
`__STDC_NO_THREADS__`	If `1`, standard threads (§14) are *not* supported.
`__STDC_NO_VLA__`	If `1`, VLAs (§6.14) are *not* supported.
`__STDC_VERSION__`	The current C version expressed as an integer of the year of standardization plus a revision, e.g., `202311L` for C23 — defined only when compiling with a C compiler.
`__TIME__`	The local time in the form *"hh:mm:ss"*.

8.5 Conditional Compilation

Conditional compilation allows lines of code either to be passed through from the preprocessor to the compiler or filtered out depending on conditions.

The `#if` directive is of the form:

```
#if const-expr
// ...
#else          // optional
// ...
#endif
```

Only if *const-expr* is true, then the lines between `#if` and `#endif` (or `#else`, if present) are passed through to the compiler. Otherwise, if the optional `#else` is present, then the lines between it and `#endif` are passed through instead.

The *const-expr* can be *any* integer constant expression, may reference only names known to the preprocessor via either `#define` or either the -D (Unix) or /D (Microsoft) options, and may use any of C's operators (§3) except cast (§3.14). It can't reference C types, constants, variables, or functions. If *const-expr* references an object-like macro name that hasn't been defined, it's as if it were defined to 0.

In addition to `#if` and `#else`, there are few variants as shown in table 8.2.

Table 8.2: Preprocessor `#if` and `#else` directive variants

This ...	Is as if ...
`#ifdef` *name*	`#if defined` *name*
`#ifndef` *name*	`#if !defined` *name*
`#elif`	`#else #if`
`#elifdef`	`#else #ifdef`
`#elifndef`	`#else #ifndef`

The reason the variants exist is because you can't actually put multiple directives on the same line (but you could easily put them on the next line). The `#elif` variants don't offer any additional functionality; they only make their use a bit more concise.

Conditional compilation has a number of uses:

1. To write semi-portable code for various platforms. C compilers define many object-like macros so code can discriminate based on compiler (e.g., __GNUC__, __clang__, _MSC_VER), operating system vendor (e.g., __APPLE__, __linux__, _WIN32), CPU architecture (e.g., __aarch64__, __x86_64__), and many other things. For example, the following shows how to write code specific to various operating systems:

   ```
   #if __APPLE__
   // macOS-specific
   #elif __linux__
   // Linux-specific
   #elif _WIN32
   // Windows-specific
   #else
   // generic
   #endif
   ```

2. To enable or disable features based on a program's configuration options:

   ```
   #if ENABLE_TERM_SIZE
   // ...
   #endif /* ENABLE_TERM_SIZE */
   ```

3. To test for the availability of non-standard functions and falling back to doing something else if not available:

8.5 Conditional Compilation

```
#if HAVE_GETLINE
  static size_t cap;
  ssize_t const len = getline( &line, &cap, fin )
  if ( len == -1 )
    // ...
#else // fall back to using fgets
  char line[ LINE_CAP ];
  if ( fgets( line, sizeof line, fin ) == nullptr )
    // ...
#endif /* HAVE_GETLINE */
```

(The definition of a macro like HAVE_GETLINE requires using a build tool (§13.9) that can test the platform for the availability of functions.)

4. To try out new code to see if it works better without deleting the original code:

```
#if USE_NEW_CODE
// ... new code ...
#else
// ... original ...
#endif
```

Then either #define USE_NEW_CODE (or don't), or, on Unix systems, compile with a -DUSE_NEW_CODE command-line option (or don't).

5. Since /* ... */ comments (§2.1) don't nest, conditional compilation can "comment out" code regardless of comments it may contain by using #if 0:

```
#if 0
// ... code not compiled ...
#endif
```

6. For *include guards* (§13.1).

8.5.1 defined

The preprocessor has a defined built-in function that returns true only if the given macro name is defined. The only use for defined is if you want to distinguish between a macro not being defined from being defined to false:

```
#define N false
#if N                   // false
// ...
#endif
#if defined N           // true
// ...
#endif
```

8.5.2 __has_c_attribute

The preprocessor has a __has_c_attribute built-in function that returns true only if the given attribute (§4.9) is supported by the compiler. For example:

```
#if __has_c_attribute( gnu::hot )
# define ATTRIBUTE_HOT    [[gnu::hot]]
#else
# define ATTRIBUTE_HOT    /* nothing */
#endif
```

8.5.3 __has_include

The preprocessor has a __has_include built-in function that returns true only if the given header exists. For example:

```
#if __has_include( <readline/readline.h> )
# define WITH_READLINE   true
#endif
```

8.6 File Inclusion

The preprocessor has the #include directive in two forms:

> #include *<path>*   Includes *path* from a set of pre-defined system paths.
> #include *"path"*   Includes *path* relative to the current directory.

Both include the text from *path* verbatim into the current file then preprocessed recursively. Invariably, files included have a .h extension and are known as *header files* or simply *headers*. They contain macro, type, variable, and function declarations comprising an API.

- The <> form looks for the requested file from one of a set of pre-defined paths (the *include path*) and is largely used to include files from the C standard library or third-party libraries.
- The "" form looks for the requested file starting relative to the current directory first, then the include path, and is used to include files from your program.

There are compiler-specific ways to augment the include path. On Unix systems, this is done via the -I*path* command-line option of the compiler. For Microsoft C, the option is /I.

8.7 Function-Like Macros

Function-like macros can have zero or more parameters. For example, a common macro to get the number of elements of a statically allocated array is:

```
#define ARRAY_SIZE(ARRAY) \
    (sizeof(ARRAY) / sizeof(ARRAY[0]))
```

Unlike a C function, when defining a function-like macro, the (that follows the macro's name *must* be adjacent, i.e., not have any whitespace between them. (If there is whitespace between them, then it's an object-like macro where the first character of the replacement list is (.)

8.7.1 Parameters

Macro parameters, when used within the replacement list, invariably should be enclosed within parentheses. Additionally, if the replacement list is an expression, all of it should be enclosed within parentheses as well. For example:

```
#define MAX(X,Y)        ( (X) > (Y) ? (X) : (Y) )
```

Why? Because substitution can result in undesired operator precedence (§3). Suppose MAX were instead defined like:

```
#define BAD_MAX(X,Y)    X > Y ? X : Y
```

then called like:

```
int max = BAD_MAX( n & 0xFF, 8 );
```

The problem is the precedence of the operators is >, &, ?:, so it would be as if:

```
int max = n & ((0xFF > 8) ? n & 0xFF : 8);
```

that very likely isn't what you want.

8.7.2 Arguments

A macro argument can be *any* sequence of tokens, not only identifiers (like n) or valid expressions (like ++i), for example:

```
#define A_OR_B(A,OP,B)    ( (A) OP (B) ? (A) : (B) )
#define MAX(X,Y)          A_OR_B( (X), >, (Y) )
```

The > token is a perfectly valid preprocessor argument even though it would be a syntax error as an ordinary C function argument. Remember: the normal C rules do not apply to the preprocessor. Macros employing such "anything goes" arguments should generally be avoided.

Arguments that have side-effects (like ++i) should also be avoided since, depending on a macro's implementation, they may be evaluated more than once. For example, if ++i is passed to MAX, i may be incremented twice.

8.7.3 Variable Numbers of Arguments

Function-like macros can take a variable number of arguments (including zero). Such a macro is known as *variadic*. To declare such a macro, the last (or only) parameter is ... (an ellipsis). For example, given a fatal_error variadic function (§9.11) that prints an error message formatted in a printf-like way and exits with a status code, you might want to wrap that with an INTERNAL_ERROR() macro that includes the file and line whence the error came as shown in listing 8.1.

```
#define INTERNAL_ERROR(FORMAT, ...)                       \
    fatal_error( EXIT_INTERNAL,                           \
                 "%s:%d: internal error: " FORMAT,        \
                 __FILE__, __LINE__, __VA_ARGS__ )
```

Listing 8.1: Variadic INTERNAL_ERROR macro, version 1

The __VA_ARGS__ token expands into everything that was passed for the second (in this case) and subsequent arguments (if any) and the commas that separate them.

You may have noticed a possible problem with INTERNAL_ERROR, specifically this line:

```
__FILE__, __LINE__, __VA_ARGS__ )
```

What if the macro were called like:

```
INTERNAL_ERROR( "oops" );
```

passing zero additional arguments? Then __VA_ARGS__ would expand into nothing and the , after __LINE__ would cause a syntax error since C functions don't accept blank arguments. What's needed is a way to include the , in the expansion only if __VA_ARGS__ is not empty. That's precisely what __VA_OPT__ does. You can rewrite the macro using it as shown in listing 8.2. Tokens to include in the expansion are enclosed with ( ) immediately following __VA_OPT__.

```
#define INTERNAL_ERROR(FORMAT, ...)                    \
  fatal_error( EXIT_INTERNAL,                          \
               "%s:%d: internal error: " FORMAT,       \
               __FILE__, __LINE__                      \
               __VA_OPT__(,) __VA_ARGS__ )
```

Listing 8.2: Variadic `INTERNAL_ERROR` macro, version 2, with `__VA_OPT__`

8.7.4 Stringification

The preprocessor actually has two of its own operators. The first is (confusingly) # that "stringifies" its single argument:

```
#define STRINGIFY(X)      #X

STRINGIFY(a)              // results in: "a"
```

Specifically, # followed by a parameter name stringifies the set of tokens comprising the corresponding argument for that parameter. Note that:

- More than one token can comprise an argument.
- An argument's leading and trailing whitespace is eliminated.
- Intervening whitespace between an argument's tokens (if it has more than one) is collapsed to a single space.

For example:

```
STRINGIFY(a b)            // "a b"
STRINGIFY(  a b  )        // "a b"
STRINGIFY(a       b)      // "a b"
```

One place where stringification is typically used is with error-reporting macros to include the textual representation of a condition that was violated. For example, the `assert` macro (§16) is implemented something like:

```
#define assert(EXPR) ((EXPR) ? (void)0 : \
   __assert( __func__, __FILE__, __LINE__, #EXPR ))
```

For a use like:

```
assert( p != nullptr );
```

the literal text of `"p != nullptr"` is included in the error message as a string.

8.7.5 Concatenation

The second preprocessor operator is (confusingly, again) ## that concatenates (or pastes) its two arguments together:

```
#define PASTE(A,B)      A ## B

PASTE(x, y)             // results in: xy
```

Specifically, ## between two parameter names concatenates the set of tokens comprising the corresponding arguments for those parameters. Additionally, there can be multiple ## in a row:

```
#define PASTE3(A,B,C)   A ## B ## C
```

Arguments can be omitted resulting in empty arguments. For example:

```
PASTE(,)                // (nothing)
PASTE(x,)               // x
PASTE(,y)               // y
```

This is even true for one argument:

```
STRINGIFY()             // ""
```

8.7.6 # and ## Pitfalls

One curious (and often annoying) thing about arguments for either # or ## is that neither expands its arguments even when they're themselves macros. For example, the previous definition of PASTE can be insufficient:

```
PASTE(var_, __LINE__)   // results in: var___LINE__
```

What you want is a result like var_1941, that is the prefix var_ followed by the current line number. (Such names are typically used to help ensure unique names.) The problem is that, while PASTE expands its parameter B into the argument __LINE__, if the argument is itself a macro that ordinarily would expand (in this case, to the current line number), it won't be expanded.

To fix it (as with many other problems in software) requires an extra level of indirection:

8.7 Function-Like Macros

```
#define PASTE_HELPER(A,B)     A ## B
#define PASTE(A,B)            PASTE_HELPER(A,B)

PASTE(var_, __LINE__)         // var_1941
```

This fixes the problem because `__LINE__` will be expanded by `PASTE` (because it's not an argument of `##`) and then the result of that expansion (the current line number, here, 1941) will be passed to `PASTE_HELPER` that will simply concatenate it as-is. The same indirection fix should also be used with `STRINGIFY`:

```
#define STRINGIFY_HELPER(X)   #X
#define STRINGIFY(X)          STRINGIFY_HELPER(X)
```

■ Why does the preprocessor work this way, i.e., why do `#` and `##` not expand arguments that are macros? Because if it did expand them, then it would be impossible either to quote or paste arguments as-is.

For example, consider a macro that defines the C language version where `__LINE__` starts being supported:

```
#define LANG__LINE__          199409L
```

and a function `lang_is` that checks whether the current language is equal to or later than its argument:

```
if ( lang_is( LANG__LINE__ ) )
  // ...
```

Rather than having to type both `lang` and `LANG` which is redundant, you define a convenience macro like:

```
#define LANG_IS(X)            lang_is( LANG_ ## X )
```

and can now instead write:

```
if ( LANG_IS( __LINE__ ) )
  // ...
```

In this case, you want `LANG_IS` to paste `LANG_` and `__LINE__` together to get `LANG__LINE__` which is exactly what happens. If `##` expanded its arguments, you'd instead get something like `LANG_1941` which is not what you want in this case. □

8.8 Multiple Statements

When multiple statements comprise a macro, it's best to enclose them within a do-while loop (§5.5) as shown in listing 8.3.

```
#define INTERNAL_ERROR(FORMAT, ...)                    \
  do {                                                  \
    fprintf( stderr,                                    \
      "%s:%d: internal error: " FORMAT,                 \
      __FILE__, __LINE__ __VA_OPT__(,) __VA_ARGS__      \
    );                                                  \
    exit( EXIT_INTERNAL );                              \
  } while (0)
```

Listing 8.3: Macro using `do-while` to enclose multiple statements

Note that there is no ; after the `while` — that's supplied by the caller. Why use a do-while? If it were not part of the macro and it was used like:

```
if ( n < 0 )
  INTERNAL_ERROR( "n = %d", n );
```

then, when expanded, it would be as shown in listing 8.4.

```
if ( n < 0 )
  fprintf( stderr,
    "%s:%d: internal error: " "n = %d",
    "bad.c", 1941 , n
  );
  exit( EXIT_INTERNAL );
```

Listing 8.4: Macro expansion without `do-while`

Since no {} were used, only the `fprintf` is executed conditionally and the `exit` is always executed because it's a separate statement. Using a `do-while` will keep multiple statements grouped together as a compound statement and execute exactly once. (The compiler will optimize away the check for 0.)

8.9 X Macros

X macros aren't part of C, but they're a powerful technique to help write maintainable code. For example, when serializing enumerations (§7.5.2), having to remember to add a `case` to a `switch` whenever you add a new enumeration value is error-prone. Instead, you can use an X macro by first declaring a macro containing all of an enumeration's values as shown in listing 8.5.

Each value is given as an argument to x that itself will be a macro. (It's for this reason that X macros are also known as *higher-order macros*.) Next, declare a macro that, given a value, appends a comma:

8.9 X Macros

```
#define FOR_ALL_COLORS(X) \
  X(COLOR_BLACK)          \
  X(COLOR_WHITE)          \
  X(COLOR_BLUE)           \
  X(COLOR_GREEN)          \
  X(COLOR_RED)
```

Listing 8.5: Defining an X macro

```
#define VALUE_COMMA(V)                  V,
```

(The comma will separate values.) Finally, to declare the enumeration itself:

```
enum color {
  FOR_ALL_COLORS( VALUE_COMMA )
};
```

The trick is that you pass the name of some other macro for X that `FOR_ALL_COLORS` will expand for each value. In this case, the end result of all the macro expansion is a comma-separated list of values.

■ The X macros technique predates C by a few years and works in any language with a decent macro facility. □

■ Why are they called "X macros?" The reason is lost to time, but it's likely that they're simply named for the use of X to mean "placeholder." □

8.9.1 Serializing Enumeration Values

X macros can also be used to serialize enumeration values (§7.5.2). The trick is to pass a different macro for X, one that will generate a `case` and string literal for each value inside a `switch` as shown in listing 8.6.

```
#define CASE_VALUE_RETURN_STRING(V)     case V: return #V;

char const* color_string( color c ) {
  switch ( c ) {
    FOR_ALL_COLORS( CASE_VALUE_RETURN_STRING )
  }
}

void fput_color( color c, FILE *f ) {
  fputs( color_string( c ), f );
}
```

Listing 8.6: Serializing enumeration values with X macros

For a given value v, #v will cause the preprocessor to stringify it, e.g., COLOR_RED will become "COLOR_RED". If you can live with the serialized names exactly matching the values ("COLOR_RED" vs. "red"), X macros are a great technique.

8.9.2 Counting Enumeration Values

X macros can also be used to count the number of values of an enumeration rather than using "count" values (§7.5.6). For example:

```
#define PLUS_ONE(...)    +1

constexpr unsigned NUM_COLORS = FOR_ALL_COLORS( PLUS_ONE );
```

FOR_ALL_COLORS(PLUS_ONE) will expand to +1 for each value or +1 +1 +1 +1 +1 that the compiler will simply sum to get 5. As with all X macros, PLUS_ONE must take an argument (here, the enumeration value), but doesn't need it, hence the use of ... to indicate "don't care."

8.10 Filename and Line Information

The preprocessor has the #line directive in two forms:

#line *line*	Sets the current line number to *line*.
#line *line "filename"*	Same as above, but also sets the current filename to *filename*.

that affect the value of the __FILE__ and __LINE__ predefined macros (§8.4). It's typically used by programs that generate C source code such as lex[†] and yacc.[‡]

8.11 Errors and Warnings

The preprocessor has the directives:

#error *"message"*	Prints *message* and terminates.
#warning *"message"*	Prints *message* and continues.

[†] *Lex — A Lexical Analyzer Generator*, Michael E. Lesk and Eric Schmidt, *Computer Science Technical Report*, 39, Bell Laboratories, Murray Hill, New Jersey, July 21, 1975.

[‡] *Yacc: Yet Another Compiler Compiler*, Stephen C. Johnson, *Computer Science Technical Report*, 32, Bell Laboratories, Murray Hill, New Jersey, July 21, 1975.

to print either an error or warning message, respectively. In the case of `#error`, preprocessing (and thus compilation) is then terminated. For example:

```
#ifndef WITH_READLINE
#error "Don't include this unless WITH_READLINE defined."
#endif /* WITH_READLINE */
```

8.12 Not Expanding a Macro

A macro will not expand if either:

- It references itself (either directly or indirectly); or:
- A function-like macro is not followed by `(`. (See §19.3 for an example.)

From §6.11, calling `str_is_any` with a compound literal array is both verbose and error-prone (since you could forget to append `nullptr`). You can enlist the help of the preprocessor to solve both problems via a function-like macro (§8.7):

```
#define str_is_any(NEEDLE, ...) \
    str_is_any( (NEEDLE),       \
                (char const*[]){ __VA_ARGS__, nullptr } )
```

This defines a macro with the same name as the `str_is_any` function. When expanded, the preprocessor will encounter `str_is_any` again, but since it references itself, the `str_is_any` will *not* be expanded again avoiding infinite expansion.

The macro adds the boilerplate of both the array compound literal (§6.11) and the `nullptr` with the variadic arguments inserted for the array elements via `__VA_ARGS__` (§8.7.3). Given that, the function can be called much more simply like:

```
if ( str_is_any( answer, "true", "yes" ) )
    // ...
```

8.13 Paste Avoidance

As mentioned (§8.1), the preprocessor tokenizes the input. New (or different) tokens can only ever be created via `##` (§8.7.5). In all other cases where a new (or different) token would be created, the preprocessor inserts a space to avoid it. For example:

```
#define EMPTY          /* nothing */
#define AVOID1         -EMPTY-

AVOID1                 // - -, not --
```

Because `EMPTY` is defined to have zero tokens (comments don't count), when it's expanded into `AVOID1`, you'd think that nothing should be there — except the left - and right - would then come together and form `--` (a different token of the decrement operator, §3.4) so the preprocessor inserts a space between them to preserve the original, separate - tokens.

The preprocessor largely doesn't care whether it's preprocessing C or C++ code except when it comes to paste avoidance. For example:

```
#define AVOID2(X)      X*

AVOID2(->)             // in C  : ->*
AVOID2(->)             // in C++: -> *
```

The reason the results differ is because `->*` isn't an operator in C: it's simply the `->` and `*` operators next to each other. However, `->*` is a distinct operator in C++, so the preprocessor avoids pasting `->` and `*` together to form the different token of `->*` by inserting a space.

8.14 Undefining a Macro

The preprocessor has the `#undef` directive:

> `#undef` *name*   Undefines macro *name*.

It un-defines the previously defined macro *name*. (If *name* isn't defined, `#undef` does nothing.) Why would you ever want to *un*-define a macro?

- If you defined macros only for temporary use like those used for X macros (§8.9), it's a good practice to undefine them when you no longer need them:

    #undef CASE_VALUE_RETURN_STRING

- Some 3rd-party libraries define a macro having too-generic of a name that you don't use and that clashes with a macro you want to define for your own program:

    #undef VERSION

8.15 Embedding

The preprocessor has the `#embed` directive in two forms:

> `#embed <`*path*`>`   Embeds *path* from a set of pre-defined system paths.
> `#embed "`*path*`"`   Embeds *path* relative to the current directory.

that reads the raw bytes from *path* and converts them into a comma-separated list of integer literals corresponding to the binary values. The use of <> and "" matches #include (§8.6). Its purpose is to embed binary data into programs such as text, image, or sound files that programs will use in some way. For example:

```
constexpr unsigned char ALARM_SOUND[] = {
# embed "sounds/alarm.wav"
};
```

After preprocessing, it would be something like this:

```
constexpr unsigned char ALARM_SOUND[] = {
82, 73, 70, 70, ...
};
```

where the integer literals comprise the byte values of the file.

Additionally, #embed may have one or more trailing parameters from table 8.3.

Table 8.3: #embed parameters

if_empty(*tokens*)	Embeds *tokens* only if contents of *path* is empty.
limit(*n*)	Limits the number of objects to *n*, a constant expression.
prefix(*tokens*)	Inserts *tokens* before contents of *path* only if not empty.
suffix(*tokens*)	Appends *tokens* after contents of *path* only if not empty.

For example:

```
constexpr char ERROR_MSG[] = {
# embed "message.txt" if_empty( 'N', '/', 'A', '\n' )
, '\0'
};
```

8.16 Pragmas

The preprocessor has the #pragma directive in two forms:

#pragma *pragma-params*	Issues compiler-specific command.
_Pragma("*pragma-params*")	Same, but from within macro.

Pragmas are a way to issue compiler-specific commands. For example, using #pragma, listing 8.7 tells gcc to disable a specific warning for a particular block of code.

_Pragma does the same, but from within a macro. For example, using _Pragma, listing 8.8 tells gcc to disable a specific warning via a BEGIN / END pair of macros. Note that, for _Pragma, quotes must be escaped since *pragma-params* are given as a string literal.

A common non-standard pragma is #pragma once that's an alternative to using include guards (§13.1). It yielded faster compilation speeds because the preprocessor

```
#ifdef __GNUC__
# pragma GCC diagnostic push
# pragma GCC diagnostic ignored "-Wformat-nonliteral"
#endif /* __GNUC__ */

// ...

#ifdef __GNUC__
# pragma GCC diagnostic pop
#endif /* __GNUC__ */
```

Listing 8.7: #pragma example

```
#ifdef __GNUC__
#define NOWARN_UNINITIALIZED_BEGIN \
  _Pragma( "GCC diagnostic push" ) \
  _Pragma( "GCC diagnostic ignored \"-Wuninitialized\"" )

#define NOWARN_UNINITIALIZED_END \
  _Pragma( "GCC diagnostic pop" ) \
#else
#define NOWARN_UNINITIALIZED_BEGIN  /* nothing */
#define NOWARN_UNINITIALIZED_END    /* nothing */
#endif /* __GNUC__ */
```

Listing 8.8: _Pragma example

---

only checked filenames to determine whether a header was already included. Modern preprocessors implicitly do what #pragma once does with ordinary include guards, so #pragma once isn't really needed any more.

8.17 Useful Macros

Here's a collection of macros that are particularly useful in most any program. These macros work in either C or C++.

ARRAY_SIZE

Gets the number of elements of a statically allocated array (repeated here from §8.7):

```
#define ARRAY_SIZE(A)           (sizeof(A) / sizeof(A[0]))
```

See also IS_ARRAY_EXPR (p.290) for an improved ARRAY_SIZE.

8.17 Useful Macros

FLPRINTF

Calls either `fprintf` or `printf` with the file and line number prepended to the format string:

```
#define FLFPRINTF(FOUT, FORMAT, ...)                              \
    fprintf( (FOUT), "%s:%d: " FORMAT, __FILE__, __LINE__         \
             __VA_OPT__(,) __VA_ARGS__ )

#define FLFPRINTF(FORMAT, ...) \
    FLFPRINTF( stdout, FORMAT __VA_OPT__(,) __VA_ARGS__ )
```

These are useful when debugging (§18.1) so you know exactly what file and line a message was printed from.

BLOCK

Wraps multiple statements within a `do-while` loop:

```
#define BLOCK(...)             do { __VA_ARGS__ } while (0)
```

Using BLOCK is a bit less verbose than using `do-while` (§8.8). For example, listing 8.3 (p.122) is rewritten using BLOCK and FLFPRINTF as shown in listing 8.9.

```
#define INTERNAL_ERROR(FORMAT, ...)                      \
  BLOCK(                                                 \
    FLFPRINTF( stderr, "internal error: " FORMAT         \
               __VA_OPT__(,) __VA_ARGS__ );              \
    exit( EXIT_INTERNAL );                               \
  )
```

Listing 8.9: Macro using BLOCK to enclose multiple statements

NAME2

Concatenates two tokens together:

```
#define NAME2(A,B)             NAME2_HELPER(A,B)
#define NAME2_HELPER(A,B)      A ## B
```

For example, `NAME2(x,y)` will expand into `xy`.

■ It actually will concatenate *any* two tokens together, but concatenation is invariably used for identifiers. □

Why is this useful? See the next macro.

UNIQUE_NAME

Constructs a "unique" name:

```
#define UNIQUE_NAME(PREFIX) \
    NAME2(NAME2(PREFIX,_),__LINE__)
```

Well, unique *enough* for most cases. Specifically, it forms a unique name only for the line it's on. For example, UNIQUE_NAME(var) would expand into something like var_42.

Why is this useful? Having a unique name allows you to use the same macro multiple times in the same scope and not get "already declared" errors, or in nested scopes and not get "shadows" warnings. For an example, see the next macro.

DECL_UNUSED

Declares an unused member as an array of N objects of type T for use within a structure (§10.1):

```
#define DECL_UNUSED(T,N) \
    alignas(T) char UNIQUE_NAME(unused)[ sizeof(T) * (N) ]
```

The use of alignas (§4.8) ensures the char buffer is aligned to match a real object of type T.

Occasionally when declaring structures, you either need to conform to a particular memory layout such that some members are at specific offsets or the size of the structure includes reserved space for possible future additions. Typically, this is done by simply declaring "reserved" members of the right sizes. For example, Microsoft Windows' API declares the following structure in wdm.h where the Reserved member, according to the documentation, is "reserved for future use":

```
typedef struct _SCATTER_GATHER_LIST {
    ULONG                   NumberOfElements;
    ULONG_PTR               Reserved;
    SCATTER_GATHER_ELEMENT  Elements[];
} SCATTER_GATHER_LIST;
```

Some programmers sometimes "cheat" and use such members for their own purposes such as storing their additional data there. This hinders future considerations. If DECL_UNUSED were used instead, it would give the member an effectively "random" hidden name intentionally making it harder to use. For example:

```
DECL_UNUSED(ULONG_PTR,1);     // better than Reserved
```

For a more complete example, see listing 11.7 (p.174).

8.17 Useful Macros

OK_DISCARD

Explicitly marks a function such that it's OK to discard its return value:

```
#define OK_DISCARD              /* nothing */
```

For example, the putubin function from listing 1.5 (p.12) could be declared as:

```
OK_DISCARD unsigned putubin( unsigned n );
```

For functions not marked [[nodiscard]] (§4.9.4), discarding a function's return value is OK (at least as far as the compiler is concerned). If you're fastidious about declaring functions [[nodiscard]] (as you should be), marking a function where it's *actually* OK to discard its return value as OK_DISCARD both documents to programmers that this is so and reminds you that you didn't forget to mark it [[nodiscard]]. Since there is actually no attribute for this, a macro defined to nothing serving only as a visual cue is better than nothing.

STRLITLEN

Gets the length of a string literal:

```
#define STRLITLEN(S)            (ARRAY_SIZE(S) - 1)
```

Since string literals are only arrays of char, ARRAY_SIZE gets the size of the array then 1 is subtracted for the terminating null character. This macro is better than calling strlen on a string literal since this can be used in constant expressions whereas strlen can not. (See also IS_C_STR_EXPR, p.292, for an improved STRLITLEN.)

VA_ARGS_COUNT

Counts the number of variadic arguments (up to at most 10):

```
#define VA_ARGS_COUNT(...)             \
  ARG_11(__VA_ARGS__ __VA_OPT__(,)     \
         10, 9, 8, 7, 6, 5, 4, 3, 2, 1, 0)

#define ARG_11(_1,_2,_3,_4,_5,_6,_7,_8,_9,_10,_11,...) _11
```

- The ARG_11 macro always returns its 11th argument of at least 11 arguments. The _1, _2, ..., _10 are used only to discard the first 10 arguments. Remember that identifiers may start with _ (§2.2).

- The `VA_ARGS_COUNT` macro calls `ARGS_11` passing `__VA_ARGS__` followed by the numbers 10 ... 0. If the number of arguments comprising `__VA_ARGS__` is:
  0. Then `__VA_ARGS__` and `__VA_OPT__(,)` both expand into nothing and the 11 arguments of 10 ... 0 are passed to `ARG_11` that returns its 11th argument of 0.
  1. Then `__VA_ARGS__` expands into that argument, say `"A"`, followed by , (expanded from `__VA_OPT__(,)` since `__VA_ARGS__` is not empty) followed by 10 ... 0 comprising 12 arguments that are passed to `ARG_11` that returns its 11th argument of 1 because the 10 ... 0 was "shifted" right by `"A"`, so the 1 is now the 11th argument.
  2. And so on.

Note that these macros can be extended to support any maximum number of arguments. (See §9.11, p.150, for an example use.)

8.18 Epilogue

Here are some key points about and some advice for the preprocessor:

- The preprocessor "preprocesses" source files before they're compiled.
- A *directive* is to the preprocessor what a statement is to C.
- Directives are line-based and begin with # and end with an end-of-line unless escaped by a \.
- The `#define` directive is used to define either object-like or function-like macros.
- The preprocessor pre-defines several object-like macros that reflect the current compilation environment including macros for the current file, line, whether the compiler is C or C++, and whether certain language features are supported.
- The `#if` and related directives can be used to compile conditionally based on the compiler, operating system, CPU architecture, whether certain features are enabled or functions are available, and many other things.
- The `#include` directive is used for file inclusion.
- Function-like macros can have parameters, are similar to C functions, and are often useful to do things like reduce boilerplate code or hide ugly implementation details.
- Function-like macros can also take a variable number of arguments.
- The preprocessor has the operators of # (stringification) and ## (concatenation).

Exercises

1. Modify your solution of string_paths for exercise 1.6 (p.26) to use conditional compilation (§8.5) such that if it were compiled on Microsoft Windows, it would use Windows' directory separators of \ instead of Unix directory separators of /, e.g., for a Windows path "C:\a" or "C:\a\" and component "b" or "\b", the result would be "C:\a\b".

2. Write a function-like macro:

    ```
    #define ARRAY_END(ARRAY)                          /* ... */
    ```

    that returns a pointer to the "end" of an array ARRAY, i.e., one past the last element as shown in figure 6.2 (p.89). Given that macro, you could write code as shown below that would print 1 2 3.

    ```
    int const a[] = { 1, 2, 3 };
    for ( auto p = a; p < ARRAY_END(a); ++p )
      printf( "%d ", *p );
    puts( "" );
    ```

3. Using your solution to the previous exercise, write a function-like macro:

    ```
    #define FOREACH_ARRAY_ELEMENT(VAR,ARRAY)   /* ... */
    ```

    that could be used as a short-hand for iterating through an array like:

    ```
    FOREACH_ARRAY_ELEMENT( p, a )
      printf( "%d ", *p );
    ```

■ In addition to helping decipher complicated declarations, you can use cdecl (§6.10) to help develop and debug function-like macros since cdecl understands #define preprocessor directives and can expand them step-by-step so you can see what's going on. For example:

```
cdecl> #define NAME2_HELPER(A,B)    A ## B
cdecl> #define NAME2(A,B)           NAME2_HELPER(A,B)
cdecl> expand NAME2(var_, __LINE__)
NAME2(var_, __LINE__) => NAME2_HELPER(A,B)
| A => var_
| B => __LINE__
| | __LINE__ => 42
| B => 42
NAME2(var_, 42) => NAME2_HELPER(var_,42)
| NAME2_HELPER(var_, 42) => A ## B
| NAME2_HELPER(var_, 42) => var_ ## 42
| NAME2_HELPER(var_, 42) => var_42
NAME2(var_, 42) => var_42
```

□

Chapter 9
Functions

As stated in §1.4, except for the most trivial, programs in C are composed of multiple functions that allow a large, complicated program effectively to be decomposed into smaller, simpler mini-programs.

9.1 Declarations vs. Definitions

A function *declaration* is done via a *prototype*, that is a function's name and *signature*, that is its parameter types (if any), and return type (or void), but without a body. For example, from listing 13.6 (p.212), these are function declarations:

```
void string_puts( struct string *str, char const *s );
void string_cleanup( struct string *str );
```

The function string_puts has a signature of struct string*, char const* for its parameters and void instead of a return type. Parameter names are neither necessary for nor considered part of a signature (since the compiler needs only the types), but are sometimes included anyway for documentation as in listing 2.1 (p.28). Functions that have exactly the same parameters and return type have the same signature. A function must be at least declared before another function can use it. Function declarations are often put into .h files.

A function *definition* repeats its declaration, but also includes its body. Function definitions are put into .c files (mostly; see §9.10).

9.2 Parameters

Before discussing function parameters, the terms *parameter* and *argument* need proper definitions since those two are often (wrongly) used interchangeably:

- **Parameters**: The list of types of objects a function requires when called. (These are also known as *formal parameters*.)
- **Arguments**: Values copied *into* a function's parameters when called. (These are also known as *actual parameters*.)

Hence:

```
void swapi( int *pa, int *pb );    // pa, pb: parameters
swapi( &x, &y );                    // &x, &y: arguments
```

As first explained in §1.6, in C, all arguments are passed *by value*, that is they are copied into their respective parameters. If you want to change the value of the original (not the copy), the parameter needs to be a pointer.

In definitions, names for unused parameters may be omitted. Why would you have a function with a parameter that you don't use? In some cases, a function's signature needs to conform to a specific API.

In older code, you may see declarations and definitions like:

```
pid_t getpid( void );              // means: zero parameters
```

where void is *not* declaring an unnamed parameter of type void (since void objects don't exist), but instead is declaring that the function has zero parameters (§C.13).

9.3 No Overloading

Unlike C++, functions in C can't be *overloaded*, that is have more than one function with the same name, but different signatures.

■ This is why many similar functions in the C standard library have similar names, but with additional letters tacked on, e.g., sqrtf and sqrtl in addition to sqrt. (But see §19.) □

9.4 "Array" Parameters

Array syntax can be used to declare function parameters. For example, a declaration for a function that prints an array of n integers as comma-separated values might be:

```
void print_csi( size_t n, int const vals[] );
```

Since it can be called with an array of any size, vals is declared with only [ ] and no size; hence the need for n that gives the size.

9.4 "Array" Parameters

Another quirky feature of C is that the use of [ ] for function parameters is just syntactic sugar since the compiler rewrites such parameters as pointers. It's as if you declared the function as:

```
void print_csi( size_t n, int const *vals );   // reality
```

In fact, you can do so explicitly with no change in meaning. Hence, despite appearances, array parameters don't exist in C.

■ Array syntax for parameters in C is a "living fossil" of how pointers are declared in New B (the parent of C).[†] □

As mentioned in §6.7, the name of an array in an expression "decays" into a pointer to its first element. This happens for function argument expressions just the same.

In the definition of print_csi shown in listing 9.1, either array syntax of [ ] or pointer syntax of * can be used *regardless* of which was used in the declaration. This works because, as also mentioned in §6.7, the a[i] syntax is just syntactic sugar for *(a+i). Use whichever syntax is easier for a particular case or preference.

```
void print_csi( size_t n, int const *vals ) {
  if ( n == 0 )
    return;
  printf( "%d", vals[0] );
  for ( size_t i = 1; i < n; ++i )
    printf( ", %d", vals[i] );
}
```

Listing 9.1: print_csi

The only potential benefit of using array syntax for parameters is that it conveys to programmers that vals is presumed to be a pointer to *at least* one int rather than *exactly* one int. But it's only a presumption and not a guarantee since you can call such a function with nullptr:

```
print_csi( 0, nullptr );         // "vals" will be nullptr
```

Note that even if you were to change the signature to print an array of, say, exactly 10 ints:

```
void print_csi_10( int const vals[10] );   // int *vals
```

it wouldn't change anything since the compiler *still* rewrites such parameters as pointers discarding any size in the process. The only potential benefit of including the 10 is that, again, it conveys to programmers that vals is presumed to be an array of 10 ints.

[†]*The Development of the C Language*, Dennis M. Ritchie, *History of Programming Languages*, 2nd ed., ACM Press, New York, and Addison-Wesley, Reading, Mass, 1996.

9.4.1 Non-Null Array Syntax for Parameters

You can specify that an "array" function parameter can not be `nullptr` and must be of a minimum size, for example:

```
void print_csi_10( int const vals[static 10] );
```

That means "declare `vals` as a pointer for which `nullptr` can not be given as an argument and must point to at least 10 constant `int`s." If you try to pass either `nullptr` or an array that has fewer than 10 `int`s, the compiler will warn you.

■ This marks another overloading of the `static` keyword in C since this `static` has nothing to do with either linkage (§4.3.3) or duration (§9.9). □

■ C++ never adopted this syntax from C. □

9.4.2 Qualified Array Syntax for Parameters

To drive home that parameters declared with array syntax really are pointers, you can *change* them:

```
int ra[10];                  // real array

void f( int pa[] ) {         // int *pa
    ++ra;                    // error (as expected)
    ++pa;                    // OK (surprisingly)
```

You can also qualify the rewritten pointer:

```
void f( int pa[const] ) {    // int *const pa
    ++pa;                    // error now
```

In addition to `const`, you can also qualify the pointer with `_Atomic` (§17), `restrict` (§21), and `volatile` (§22). Note that neither of these:

```
void f( int const pa[] );    // pointer to const int
void f( const int pa[] );    // same
```

is the same thing: the `const` *outside* the `[ ]` refers to the `int` and not `pa`.

■ Why doesn't the compiler convert parameters with array syntax to pointers to `const`? Because `const` didn't exist when Ritchie invented C and retroactively making such pointers be `const` when `const` was added to C would have broken programs. □

■ C++ never adopted this syntax from C either. □

9.4 "Array" Parameters						139

9.4.3 Variable Length Array Syntax for Parameters

You can also use VLA (§6.14) syntax for parameters:

```
void print_csi( size_t n, int const vals[n] );
```

That is, the size of the "array" is given by an integer parameter that precedes it. Note that vals is *still* a pointer. Despite having the size information at run-time, sizeof(vals) will *still* return the size of the pointer. Hence, this "feature" serves only to document to programmers that n is the presumed size of the "array."

9.4.4 Multidimensional Array Syntax for Parameters

Array syntax can also be used for parameters for multidimensional arrays (§6.4):

```
void f( int a[10][20] );    // int (*a)[20]
```

The quirk where the compiler rewrites array syntax for a function parameter as a pointer happens *only* for the first (left-most) dimension; the remaining dimension(s) keep their "array-ness." Hence, a is a pointer to a real array of 20 ints. Note that the parentheses shown in the comment are necessary: without them, it would be an array of 20 pointers to int.

Pointers to array don't often occur in C programs since the name of an array "decays" into a pointer to its first element (§6.7). In most cases, that's good enough even though the size information is lost. But a pointer to an array retains the array's size as part of the type, so assignments between pointers to arrays of different size are warned about:

```
int (*p3)[3];           // pointer to array 3 of int
int (*p5)[5];           // pointer to array 5 of int
p5 = p3;                // warning: incompatible pointers
```

In particular, given:

```
int a[10];
int *pi = a;            // pointer to int (via decay)
int (*pa)[10] = &a;     // pointer to array 10 of int
```

both pi and pa point to the same location in memory (here, &a[0]), but a "pointer to array" is an entirely different thing from a pointer that results from array decay. For pi, the compiler "forgets" the size of the array to which it points; for pa, it "remembers" the size.

Part of the reason pointers to array aren't used much is because it's clunky to access array elements since you have to dereference the pointer first:

```
    int e1 = (*p3)[1];        // must dereference p3 first
```

But you can dereference the pointer once into another pointer then use *that* pointer:

```
    int *p = *p3;
    int e1 = p[1];            // same as: (*p3)[1]
```

9.4.5 Multidimensional VLA Parameters

Multidimensional array syntax for parameters can be used for VLAs. For example, a declaration for a function that prints a matrix of $m \times n$ integers as rows of comma-separated values might be:

```
    void print_mcsi( size_t m, size_t n, int vals[m][n] );
```

The compiler rewrites *only* the first dimension as a pointer, so the above is really:

```
    void print_mcsi( size_t m, size_t n,
                    int const (*vals)[n] );
```

hence `vals` is a pointer to a VLA of `n` `int`s. In this case, the VLA is actually a useful feature since the `n` allows the compiler to know the length of each row of the array. Additionally, `sizeof` (the first one below) once again becomes a run-time operator:

```
    size_t size = sizeof *vals / sizeof **vals;  // size = n
```

Unlike VLAs in general, VLAs used for function parameters are safe since the actual arrays passed to the function can be (and often are) normal arrays:

```
    int matrix[10][20] = { /* ... */ };
    print_mcsi( 10, 20, matrix );
```

There's no new VLA being created at run-time here, so it can't overflow the stack.

When *declaring* (as opposed to defining) functions, C allows you to omit the parameter names; however, if you do that, then there's no name to specify the size of a VLA; but C has a special syntax for this case:

```
    void print_mcsi( size_t, size_t, int const[][] );     // err
    void print_mcsi( size_t, size_t, int const[*][*] );   // OK
```

That is, use `*` to denote a VLA of an unnamed size. Since the first dimension is always converted to a pointer, the `*` is needed only starting with the *second* dimension:

```
    void print_mcsi( size_t, size_t, int const[][*] );    // same
```

Hence, you never need `*` when using single dimension array syntax.

9.4.6 Array Syntax for Parameters Pitfalls

Using array syntax for function parameters can lead to code that looks correct, but isn't. For example, given:

```
void print_csi_10( int const vals[10] ) { // int *vals
  for ( size_t i = 0; i < sizeof vals / sizeof vals[0];
        ++i ) {
    // ...
```

Using `sizeof` (§3.16) to calculate the number of elements in the array, the intention here is to iterate over all the elements of the array. But, despite the `sizeof` expression being correct for an array, `vals` is *still* a pointer; so `sizeof` here will get the size of a *pointer* (likely 8) divided by the size of an `int` (likely 4) and the entire array won't be iterated over. Fortunately, most compilers will warn about this.

This is a reason against using array syntax for parameters: such parameters look like arrays, but aren't.

9.5 Return Values

Functions can return enumerations (§7), structures (§10), or unions (§11) like any other type. Unlike some languages, C can return at most one value from a function. But structures can be created and used as return types when more than one value needs to be returned.

For example, consider a function `ht_insert` that attempts to insert data into a *hash table* (§25.1). It returns a pointer to either a new entry containing the inserted data or an existing entry containing the existing data. To distinguish those two cases, it also needs to return an `inserted` flag that's `true` only if the data was inserted. A structure to contain both an entry and a flag is shown in listing 9.2.

```
struct ht_insert_rv {           // insert return value
  struct ht_entry *entry;       // existing or inserted entry
  bool            inserted;     // entry inserted?
};

struct ht_insert_rv ht_insert( struct hash_table *ht,
                               void const *key,
                               size_t value_size ) {
  // ...
  return (struct ht_insert_rv){
    .entry = entry, .inserted = true
  };
}
```

Listing 9.2: Function returning a structure

You might think that returning structures is inefficient because the entire structure would need to be copied twice: once from the stack frame of a function to a temporary variable, and a second time from the temporary to the destination variable in the caller's stack frame. But the compiler can perform *return value optimization* (RVO) by rewriting the function to take a pointer to the destination variable that the function can write to directly without using a temporary as shown in listing 9.3.

```
void ht_insert( struct ht_insert_rv *rv,
                struct hash_table *ht,
                void *key, size_t value_size ) {
  // ...
  *rv = (struct ht_insert_rv){
    .entry = entry, .inserted = true
  };
}

void caller() {
  struct ht_insert_rv rv;
  ht_insert( &rv, ht, key, sizeof(int) );
  // ...
```

Listing 9.3: Function "returning" a structure via RVO

9.6 Error Handling

C doesn't have exceptions (but see §27), nor is there a standard way to communicate errors from functions to their callers. But there are several ways that are typically used in practice:

- If the function returns `bool`, it returns `false` on error.
- If the function returns `int`, it returns `-1` (or some other invalid value) on error.
- If the function returns a pointer, it returns `nullptr` on error.
- The function can return an error flag or code as part of a structure similar to listing 9.2 (p.141).
- If the function returns `void`, it can print an error message to a file (§12.2).
- If the error is fatal (meaning there's no easy way to recover and continue), the function can print an error message and call either `exit` (§9.7.2) or `abort` to dump core (§18.4).

In any case, the standard global variable `errno` declared in `errno.h` may also be set to a standard error code (also declared in `errno.h`) if one is applicable. If none of the standard error codes is applicable, you can use your own global variable to be set to a custom error code. (See also §14.7.)

Regardless of which method is used to communicate errors, the documentation for the function should specify how errors, if any, are handled.

9.7 `main`

As first shown in §1.1, a C program begins execution in a function named `main`. Additionally, `main` serves as the "interface" between the "outside" (typically, the operating system) and your program via arguments and its return value.

9.7.1 Declaration and Parameters

In addition to `main` being declared with no parameters, it may alternatively be declared with two specific parameters for passing arguments to it from the "outside" (on Unix systems, another process, typically a shell). For example, the program in listing 9.4, if executed from a shell, will print each of its arguments, if any, preceded by its index as shown in run 9.1.

```
int main( int argc, char const *const argv[] ) {
  for ( int i = 0; i < argc; ++i )
    printf( "%d %s\n", i, argv[i] );
}
```

Listing 9.4: `main` with parameters that prints its arguments

```
$ cc -o args args.c
$ ./args hello, world
0 args
1 hello,
2 world
```

Run Output 9.1: `args` output

The parameter `argc` is the *argument count* and `argv` is an "array" of *argument values* where `argv[0]` is the executable's pathname, `argv[1]` is the first argument, `argv[argc-1]` is the last argument, and `argv[argc]` is guaranteed to be `nullptr`. (You can name the parameters anything you want, but "argc" and "argv" are conventional.)

■ On non-Unix systems, it's implementation defined as to what the values of `argv` correspond to, if anything. □

Alternatively, `main` may be declared as:

```
int main( int argc, char const *const *argv ) {
```

That is, `argv` may be declared as a pointer (which it really is) to pointers rather than an "array" of pointers (§9.4). In this and the original declaration, `const` is optional, but recommended.

The executable's filename being in `argv[0]` allows a program to alter its behavior based on the name. For example, `cdecl` (§6.10) starts in C++ mode if the basename of `argv[0]` is `c++decl`.

9.7.2 Return Value and Exit Status

As mentioned in §1.1, `main` *must* return `int` (§2.5.4) whose value indicates the status, either the success or failure, of the program. By convention, zero means "success" and any non-zero value means "failure" where the value is often a code for the type of failure. As a special case, returning a value from `main` is optional. If omitted, it's equivalent to returning zero (success).

When `main` returns, it calls the standard function `exit` that terminates the program. Alternatively, you can call `exit` yourself at any time. It's for this reason that a program's return value is also known as its *exit status*.

Except for zero, there are no other standard values for exit codes. However, the standard does define `EXIT_SUCCESS` as a synonym for zero and `EXIT_FAILURE` for any failure, though its specific value is implementation defined. Some programs that search for things (like *grep*(1)) return 1 meaning they ran successfully, but there were no matches.

> ■ BSD-derived systems have the `sysexits.h` header that defines 15 or so values for various errors. Unfortunately, it's not standard, choosing an appropriate exit value can often be non-obvious, and their use has been deprecated in new programs since 2020. □

For your own programs, you can use any values you like. A minimal approach is simply to return either 1 or `EXIT_FAILURE` for any error. If you want to use specific values for specific errors, you can use an enumeration (§7) as shown in listing 9.5. Even though an exit status is an `int`, values should be constrained to be in the range -128–127.

```
enum {
  EXIT_USAGE = 1, // command-line usage error
  EXIT_CONFIG,    // configuration file error
  EXIT_NOFILE,    // no such file
  EXIT_DATAERR,   // invalid data
  EXIT_IO,        // I/O error
  EXIT_NOPERM,    // insufficient permission
  EXIT_INTERNAL,  // internal error (bug)
  // ...
};
```

Listing 9.5: Possible exit status codes for your program

9.8 Static Functions

A function declared `static` gives it internal linkage (§4.3), that is it will be "private" to the `.c` file it's defined in. Within a `.c` file, `static` functions are used as private "helper" functions to other functions. For example, if `print_mcsi` were the only public function, we could still have `print_csi` as a helper function for `print_mcsi` by declaring it `static` as shown in listing 9.6. Decomposing a larger function into a few smaller functions is a good practice since each is more readily understandable.

```
static void print_csi( size_t n, int const vals[n] ) {
  if ( n == 0 )
    return;
  printf( "%d", vals[0] );
  for ( size_t i = 1; i < n; ++i )
    printf( ", %d", vals[i] );
}
void print_mcsi( size_t m, size_t n,
                 int const vals[m][n] ) {
  for ( size_t j = 0; j < m; ++j ) {
    print_csi( n, vals[j] );
    putchar( '\n' );
  }
}
```

Listing 9.6: A `static` helper function

9.9 Static Local Variables

A variable declared `static` inside a function gives it static duration (§4.3), that is it will be initialized to zero or equivalent and exist for the entire duration of the program. For example, the function shown in listing 9.7 will return a new value for every call.

```
unsigned long get_new_id() {
  static unsigned long next_id;
  return ++next_id;
}
```

Listing 9.7: Function with `static` local variable

The declaration of `next_id` could have been at file scope (§2.4) and have the same behavior. Inside the function, the variable is "private" to the function. It's a good practice to make objects as private as possible.

■ This marks yet another overloading of the `static` keyword in C since this `static` has nothing to do with either linkage (§4.3.3) or non-null array syntax for parameters (§9.4.1). □

9.9.1 __func__

The identifier `__func__` is implicitly declared by the compiler immediately following the { of each function definition as if it did:

```
static char const __func__[] = "function-name";
```

For example, the following function would print `hello_world` when called:

```
void hello_world() {
  puts( __func__ );
}
```

9.10 Inline Functions

The `inline` keyword can prefix a function definition such as:

```
inline int maxi( int a, int b ) {
  return a > b ? a : b;
}
```

It allows you to give the compiler a "hint" that certain functions are called frequently and would thereby likely benefit from being *inlined*.

A function that has been inlined has had its code expanded at every point it's been called rather than performing the normal function-call mechanism of:

- Saving CPU registers.
- Either assigning argument values to registers or pushing them onto the stack.
- Executing a "call" assembly language instruction.
- Returning from the function.
- Restoring CPU registers or popping the stack.

For *very* small functions, inlining can yield a performance gain. But like most everything else, there are trade-offs.

9.10.1 Differences from Macros

Inline functions are like (and meant to replace many uses of) function-like macros (§8.7). Generally, this is a good thing because inline functions *are* functions and have full function semantics rather than mere text substitution done by the preprocessor that doesn't understand C.

A naively equivalent macro to the `maxi` function is:

```
#define MAXI(A,B)    A > B ? A : B   /* bad implementation */
```

that has the following problems:

- Expanded arguments, e.g., `MAXI(n & 0xFF, 8)`, can result in the wrong operator precedence.

9.10 Inline Functions

- Arguments with side effects, e.g., `MAXI(n++, 8)`, can have multiple side effects.
- There's no type-checking of the arguments at definition.
- Errors are often verbose and hard to read.

Additionally, a macro can modify its arguments (that often is not what you want). Inline functions have none of these problems yet can yield the same performance benefit. Use inline functions instead of function-like macros whenever possible.

9.10.2 Only a Hint

As mentioned, specifying `inline` is only a "hint" to the compiler that the program overall might benefit in performance from the function being inlined. The compiler is free to ignore the hint. Why? Because there are cases when it's either not a good idea or impossible. A function is either not inlined or typically not inlined when any one of the following is true:

- The function is "too big."
- You call the function via a pointer-to-function (§6.10).
- The function is recursive.
- The function has a loop.

There may be other reasons. It's all highly dependent on the function, its arguments, the compiler, and whatever options are given to it.

If the compiler either can't or chooses not to inline a function, it does not warn you that it hasn't done so (by default). Some compilers, e.g., `gcc`, have a `-Winline` option that will warn you and give you the reason why a function wasn't inlined.

Specifying `inline` is similar to specifying `register` (§4.3.4) — they're both only hints.

9.10.3 When (and When Not) to Inline

For most functions, the bulk of the cost of executing the function is in the function's body, not in the function-call mechanism. Hence, in order for a function to be a good candidate for inlining, it generally has to be:

- Small enough so that the cost of the function-call mechanism dominates.
- Used in places where performance actually matters, e.g., in tight loops.

When in doubt, profile your code (§18.9). Using `inline` is not a magic "make me faster" keyword. Additionally, over-use of `inline` can lead to code bloat that additionally makes the performance of your program worse overall.[†]

Functions that are often good candidates for inlining include:

- "One-liners" such as "getters" and "setters."
- Simple wrappers around calls to other functions that supply specific values for arguments or do casts (§3.14).

An ideal inline function *both* increases performance and decreases code size.

One caveat for any inline function is that if its definition changes, it will require recompiling all code that uses it.

9.10.4 Inline Definition

In order for the compiler to be able to inline a function, it has to be able to "see" its definition (not only its declaration) in every `.c` file it's used in exactly like a macro. Hence, an inline function *must* be defined in a header file.

Normally, a function, like everything else, must have exactly one definition by adhering to the *one definition rule* (ODR). However, since the definition of an inline function is "seen" in multiple `.c` files, the ODR is suspended for that function.

It is possible to have different definitions for inline functions having the same name, but this results in undefined behavior (§15) since the compiler has no way to check that every definition is the same.

In addition to defining a function `inline` in a header, you additionally *must* explicitly tell the compiler into what `.o` file to put the one definition in the event the compiler is either unable or unwilling to inline a function via `extern inline`. For example, in *exactly one* `.c` file, you would declare a function like:

```
extern inline int maxi( int, int );
```

That tells the compiler to put the one definition for `maxi` into its `.o` file.

■ This is an overloading of the `extern` keyword in C since this `extern` has nothing to do with linkage (§4.3.2). □

Alternatively, you can define an inline function `static` in the header:

```
static inline maxi( int a, int b ) {
  return a > b ? a : b;
}
```

[†]*The Inline Disease*, Linus Torvalds, et al, *Linux kernel coding style*, §15, https://www.kernel.org/doc/html/latest/process/coding-style.html

If you do this, then:

- You do not have to declare a function `extern inline` anywhere.
- However, if the compiler doesn't inline a function, it will generate a definition in every .c file it's included into again leading to code bloat.
- If the function has any `static` local variables (§9.9), every definition will have distinct copies (that likely isn't what you want).

9.11 Variadic Functions

Most of the functions shown take a specific number of arguments. However, one in particular, `printf` (§12.1.1), is *variadic* meaning it takes a varying number of arguments. C allows you to write your own variadic functions.

■ Originally, C had no way for you to write your own variadic functions portably. When function prototypes were adopted from C++ into C, it included syntax for declaring variadic functions. □

For example, a function that sums n additional arguments is shown in listing 9.8.

```
#include <stdarg.h>

int vnsum( unsigned n, ... ) {
   va_list args;
   va_start( args );
   int sum = 0;
   while ( n-- > 0 )
      sum += va_arg( args, int );
   va_end( args );
   return sum;
}
```

Listing 9.8: Variadic function to sum n integers

- Line 1 includes the `stdarg.h` standard header that defines types, functions, and macros (that all start with "va_") for working with variadic arguments.
- To declare a variadic function, the last (or only) parameter is ... (an ellipsis) as is done on line 3.
- Line 4 declares `args` of type `va_list` to access the variadic arguments.
- Line 5 calls `va_start` to start iterating over the variadic arguments.
- Line 8 calls `va_arg` passing `args` and the presumed type of the next variadic argument; it returns the value of that argument.
- Line 9 calls `va_end` to end iterating over the variadic arguments.

Then you can call it like:

```
int r = vnsum( 3, 1, 2, 5 );   // r = 8
```

Note that *we* are using the explicit parameter to specify how many arguments follow as our own convention here. The compiler does not infer any meaning from the explicit parameter. It's only an ordinary parameter.

To make the count implicit (so you either can't forget it or get it wrong), you can use the preprocessor and the VA_ARGS_COUNT macro (p.131):

```
#define vsum(...) \
   vnsum( VA_ARGS_COUNT( __VA_ARGS__ ), __VA_ARGS__ )
```

For another example, listing 9.9 shows an implementation of vstr_is_any, a variadic version of str_is_any from listing 6.5 (p.92). In this version, the arguments are terminated by a null pointer as a sentinel.

```
bool vstr_is_any( char const *needle, ... ) {
  va_list args;
  va_start( args );
  bool found = false;
  do {
    char const *const hay = va_arg( args, char* );
    if ( hay == nullptr )
      break;
    found = strcmp( needle, hay ) == 0;
  } while ( !found );
  va_end( args );
  return found;
}
```

Listing 9.9: Variadic function to see if a string is among a set

It can be called like:

```
if ( vstr_is_any( pet, "cat", "dog", "bird", nullptr ) )
```

To make the nullptr implicit (so you can't forget it), you can use the preprocessor to append it:

```
#define vstr_is_any(NEEDLE, ...) \
   vstr_is_any( (NEEDLE), __VA_ARGS__, nullptr )
```

The original, non-variadic str_is_any is a much better implementation due to the pitfalls of variadic functions.

9.11.1 Variadic Pitfalls

Variadic arguments have several serious pitfalls:

9.11 Variadic Functions

- Notwithstanding the VA_ARGS_COUNT macro, there is no standard way to know how many arguments were given. (Attempting to access more arguments than were given results in undefined behavior (§15); but accessing fewer is OK.)
- There is no way to require that any argument be of a specific type nor is there any way to require that all the arguments be of the same type.
- There is no way to know for certain what the type of any argument actually is.
- Because there is no type information, only default argument conversions occur:
  - char, signed char, unsigned char, short, and unsigned short are promoted to either int or unsigned int as appropriate.
  - float is promoted to double.
  - An array "decays" into a pointer to its first element (§6.7).
  - A function name is converted to a pointer to that function (§6.10).
- The ... must always be last.
- When iterating over arguments via va_arg, the given type *must* match the actual type. If it doesn't, the result is undefined behavior.

Hence, the top two problems when implementing a variadic function are:

1. Knowing either the number of arguments or when to stop iterating over them.
2. Knowing their types.

The vnsum implementation "solves" the first problem by using an explicit parameter to specify how many arguments follow. However, if you were to do (without the VA_ARGS_COUNT macro):

```
int r = vnsum( 3, 1, 2 );      // said 3, but only 2
```

that is specify that there are 3 arguments that follow but there are fewer, the result would be undefined behavior. Even if you use the VA_ARGS_COUNT macro, vnsum can still only *assume* the provided arguments are of type int. If you were to do:

```
int r = vsum( 1, 2.7, 5 );     // double, not int
```

that is provide a value of type double (or any other type) where int is expected, the result would be undefined behavior.

The vstr_is_any function "solves" the first problem by using a sentinel so it doesn't care how many arguments there are. But similar to vnsum, it still can only *assume* the provided arguments are strings and that the last argument is nullptr. If either of those are false, the result would be undefined behavior.

The standard printf function (§12.1.1) "solves" both problems by using the one required argument as the format for what to print: each % within the format is a conversion specifier and has a one-to-one correspondence with an argument. For example, given:

```
printf( "x=%d, y=%d\n", x, y );
```

the `printf` implementation scans the format string looking for `%` characters. Upon encountering one, it fetches the next variadic argument's value via `va_arg` using the type specified by the character(s) that follow the `%`, e.g., `%d` specifies `int` (and prints it in decimal).

However, as with `vnsum`, if you either provide fewer arguments than specifiers or the type of a specifier and its associated argument don't match the result would be — you guessed it — undefined behavior. Fortunately, modern compilers have specific knowledge about `printf` and so can warn when either the number of types or arguments don't match the format string. For your own functions, however, you're generally on your own to get it right.

Given all their pitfalls, are variadic functions a good idea? Not really. Their use was a clever hack stemming from C originally not caring about function arguments at all (§C.13), so functions like `printf` and `scanf` (§12.4.1) took advantage of this. Even the introduction of `stdarg.h` did only the minimum amount to make implementing variadic functions *portable*, but not *good*.

Should you write your own variadic functions? Generally, no. However, there is one use for implementing your own variadic functions.

9.11.2 Calling Other Variadic Functions

In a large program that prints many messages, it would be helpful if you could know what line of code printed a given message so you can determine the state of the program at the time the message was printed. For example, in a program like `cdecl` (§6.10), if you get:

```
c++decl> explain int &*p
                     ^
13: error: pointer to reference is illegal; did you mean "*&"?
```

you might want to know where in the source code that message was printed from. In many cases, you can simply `grep` for the text of the message, but only if the message text appears literally in the code — which isn't the case for this message.

`cdecl` has a *debug* option that, among other things, prints the source code location whence an error message came:

```
13: error: [c_ast_check.c:2170] pointer to reference is
    illegal ...
```

The way this is implemented is that there's an `fl_print_error` variadic function that's a wrapper around `fprintf` that takes additional file and line arguments whence it was called. A (slightly simplified) implementation is shown in listing 9.10.

- The functions `printf` and `fprintf` have `vprintf` and `vfprintf` counterparts that take a `va_list` parameter:

9.12 Epilogue

```
 1  void fl_print_error( char const *file, int line,
 2                       char const *format, ... ) {
 3    fprintf( stderr, "error: " );
 4    if ( opt_cdecl_debug != CDECL_DEBUG_NO )
 5      fprintf( stderr, "[%s:%d] ", file, line );
 6    va_list args;
 7    va_start( args );
 8    vfprintf( stderr, format, args );
 9    va_end( args );
10  }
11
12  #define print_error(FORMAT,...) \
13    fl_print_error(__FILE__, __LINE__, (FORMAT), __VA_ARGS__)
```

Listing 9.10: Simplified `fl_print_error` implementation

```
int vprintf( const char *format, va_list args );
int vfprintf( FILE *file, const char *format,
              va_list args );
```

They allow your variadic function to pass along its variadic arguments. Line 8 calls `vfprintf` passing `args`.

- Lines 12–13 define a macro that hides the passing of __FILE__ and __LINE__.

A `va_list` parameter allows one variadic function to pass its variable arguments to another.

9.12 Epilogue

Here are some key points about and some advice for functions:

- Make functions relatively small and do one thing. Decompose larger functions into smaller, simpler functions.
- Functions can't be overloaded.
- For function parameters:
  - All arguments are passed by value, i.e., copied. Modifying an argument's value affects only its copy. To affect the original, use a pointer.
  - Despite appearances, array parameters don't exist in C. They "decay" to pointers. Despite this, "array" parameters can be useful to indicate that one or more values may be given.
  - VLA syntax can be used and, for multidimensional arrays, it's actually useful for the row size.
- A function can return one value of any type including enumerations, structures, or unions; or none using `void`.

- A function that returns either success or failure typically returns one of `false`, `-1`, or `nullptr` for failure.
- A function declared `static` is "private" to the `.c` file it's defined in.
- A local variable declared `static` will be initialized to zero or equivalent and exist for the entire duration of the program.
- A function can be declared `inline` and defined in a header file. Inline functions, if used judiciously, can yield performance gains. Generally, only *very small* functions are good candidates for inlining.
- Variadic functions in C are basically a hack. Given their serious pitfalls, you generally should not write your own unless it's a wrapper around another variadic function.
- A program must have exactly one function named `main` that:
  - May have either zero parameters, or two parameters, `argc` (argument count) and `argv` (argument values), for command-line arguments (on a Unix system) where `argv[0]` is the executable's pathname, `argv[1]` is the first argument, `argv[argc-1]` is the last argument, and `argv[argc]` is guaranteed to be `nullptr`.
  - Must return `int` where zero indicates success and any non-zero value indicates failure to the operating system. As a special case, an omitted return value is equivalent to returning zero.

Exercises

1. Using your solution for `new_hist` and `print_hist` for exercise 6.4 (p. 98) as a starting point, write a program that, given a line of text as command-line arguments, prints a histogram of only the letters comprising the text. Uppercase letters should be converted to and counted as lowercase. For example:

    ```
    $ ./alphahist C is quirky, flawed, and an enormous success.
    ```

    should print:

    ```
    a: +++
    c: +++
    d: ++
    e: +++
    f: +
    i: ++
    k: +
    l: +
    m: +
    n: +++
    o: ++
    q: +
    ```

9.12 Epilogue

```
r: ++
s: +++++
u: +++
w: +
y: +
```

You will need the `isalpha` and `tolower` functions (§B.1).

Chapter 10
Structures

A *structure* is one object of (potentially) many types whose data is related such as a string's contents and length as shown in §1.9.

The closest analog in other languages would be a *class* except a structure has all members "public," no "constructors" (automatic initialization), no "destructors" (automatic cleanup), and no "methods." You can write such functions, but you have to be explicit about calling them.

10.1 Definition

Formally, a structure definition is of the form:

>   **struct** *tag$_{opt}$* {
>   *members$_{opt}$*
>   } *declarations$_{opt}$*;

that is the keyword `struct` optionally followed by a *tag* name followed by a set of zero or more *members* optionally followed by declarations of the structure. Members are in their own namespace specific to their structure, so different structures can have members with the same name.

> ■ You may eventually notice that many structures in the C standard library are named such that they are prefixed by a common abbreviation. For example, all the members of the `tm` structure (listing B.1, p.367) are prefixed by "`tm_`."
>
> You might think that this was simply a style idiosyncrasy of the original Unix authors. It turns out that early C compilers had only a single, global symbol table, so they added prefixes to members to avoid name collisions. Once C compilers improved, this style faded away.
>
> However, the style persists in a few places, e.g., the Solaris' internal style guide still recommends this style to this day, even in new code:

> *Systematic prefix conventions for ... structure or union member names can be useful.*

though it doesn't elaborate as to *why*. Having common prefixes does make member names easily `grep`-able. □

As with enumerations (§7), the names of structures are put into a *tags* namespace (§2.3). To refer to a structure name, it must be preceded by `struct`. If you forget to include it, you'll get an error:

```
string str;             // error: must use "struct" tag
```

Alternatively, you can use `typedef` (§2.6) to "inject" a tag name into the surrounding scope so you no longer need to use `struct`:

```
typedef struct string string;  // inject string into scope
string str;                    // no "struct" needed now
```

As a second alternative, you can `typedef` a structure declaration directly:

```
typedef struct {        // or: typedef struct string {
  char    *contents;
  size_t  len;
} string;
```

10.2 No Nesting

To the surprise of some (especially those who know C++), even though you can nest the declaration of a structure inside another, it's not meaningful in C. For example, consider the declaration shown in listing 10.1.

```
struct geo_loc {
  struct coord {        // warning: doesn't declare anything
    int deg, min;
    float sec;
  };
  struct coord lat, lng;
};

struct coord c;         // OK (surprisingly)
```

Listing 10.1: Structure nesting belies reality

Even though its perfectly legal C, it's deceptive because `coord` is *not* "inside" `geo_loc`. As far as the compiler is concerned, it's as if `coord` were declared at file scope (§2.4) which is how the declaration of `c` is also legal.

The compiler may also warn you that the declaration of `coord` doesn't declare anything. What it means is that, while it does declare the `coord` structure, it doesn't

10.3 Initialization

declare any `geo_loc` members *of* `coord`. Had you declared the structures as shown in listing 10.2, then the compiler wouldn't have warned you (but `coord` would still be as if it were declared at file scope just the same).

```
struct geo_loc {
  struct coord {
    int deg, min;
    float sec;
  } lat, lng;         // members of struct coord
};
```

Listing 10.2: Structure nesting belies reality, version 2

Even so, declaring nested structures in C is confusing — don't do it.

10.3 Initialization

As first shown in §1.9, a structure can be initialized in its declaration using {} where the order of the values corresponds to the order that the members were declared:

```
struct string str = { "hello", 5 };
```

If the {} are empty, then all members are initialized to zero or equivalent. Alternatively, you can use *designated initializers*, that is use the member names preceded by . (dot) and followed by =:

```
struct string str = { .contents = "hello", .len = 5 };
```

Designated initializers can be given in any order.

For another example, let's rewrite listing 6.1 (p.85) to use an array of structure rather than a two-dimensional array as shown in listing 10.3.

- Lines 1–3 add a `planet` structure containing `perihelion_au` and `aphelion_au` as members.
- Lines 5–14 define `PLANET` as an array of `planet` rather than a two-dimensional array of AUs. Conveniently, the syntax for initializing this array of structures hasn't changed from initializing the two-dimensional array shown in listing 6.1.
- Line 17 uses `perihelion_au` and `aphelion_au` that is more readily understandable than the way it was in listing 6.1 since we're referring to data by name rather than the numbers of `[0]` and `[1]`.
- Line 23 uses pointer arithmetic directly rather than the slightly more verbose equivalent of `&PLANET[p]` (§6.7).

While multidimensional arrays have their uses, if the dimensions are semantically different (in this case, one is perihelion and the other is aphelion), it's often better to use an array of structure instead since:

```
 1  struct planet {
 2    double perihelion_au, aphelion_au;
 3  };
 4
 5  constexpr struct planet PLANET[] = {
 6    {  0.31,  0.47 },    // Mercury
 7    {  0.72,  0.73 },    // Venus
 8    {  0.98,  1.02 },    // Earth
 9    {  1.38,  1.67 },    // Mars
10    {  4.95,  5.45 },    // Jupiter
11    {  9.01, 10.07 },    // Saturn
12    { 18.28, 20.09 },    // Uranus
13    { 29.80, 30.32 },    // Neptune
14  };
15
16  double orbital_period( struct planet const *p ) {
17    auto const a = (p->perihelion_au + p->aphelion_au) / 2;
18    return sqrt( a * a * a );
19  }
20
21  int main() {
22    for ( unsigned p = 0; p < 8; ++p ) {
23      auto const period = orbital_period( PLANET + p );
24      if ( period < 1.0 )  // < 1 Earth year: print in days
25        printf( "%u %6.2fd\n", p, period * 365.25 );
26      else
27        printf( "%u %6.2fy\n", p, period );
28    }
29  }
```

Listing 10.3: Print orbital period of planets, version 2, using structures

- The code more clearly speaks for itself rather than having to comment that `[0]` is perihelion and `[1]` is aphelion as in listing 6.1.
- Having an array of structure uses the same amount of memory and is as efficient as a two-dimensional array. (In this case, both are stored in memory in *exactly* the same way.)
- The structure allows more members to be added easily (e.g., diameter, mass, etc.), but this code wouldn't need to be changed at all.

10.4 Structure Compound Literals

Consider the structure shown in listing 10.4 and a function to compare two `user` objects by name. (For simplicity here, we'll stipulate that `last` and `first` will never be `nullptr` and instead be the empty string `""` for no entry.) Suppose we want to search a linked list from listing 6.2 (p.86) of `user`. Let's add a generic function to do that as shown in listing 10.5.

10.4 Structure Compound Literals

```
struct user {
  char         *last;
  char         mi;
  char         *first;
  unsigned short uid;
};

int user_cmp( struct user const *u1,
              struct user const *u2 ) {
  int cmp;
  if ( (cmp = strcmp( u1->last, u2->last )) != 0 )
    return cmp;
  if ( (cmp = strcmp( u1->first, u2->first )) != 0 )
    return cmp;
  return (int)u1->mi - (int)u2->mi;
}
```

Listing 10.4: User structure and comparison function

```
1  typedef bool (*slist_pred_fn)( void const *list_data,
2                                 void const *pred_data );
3
4  struct slist* slist_find( struct slist *list,
5                            slist_pred_fn pred_fn,
6                            void const *pred_data ) {
7    while ( list != nullptr &&
8            !(*pred_fn)( list->data, pred_data ) ) {
9      list = list->next;
10   }
11   return list;
12 }
```

Listing 10.5: Function to search a singly linked list

- Lines 1–2 define a type for a *predicate* function that `slist_find` will call for each list item until the predicate returns `true`.
- Lines 4–6 declare `slist_find` that takes a list to search, a predicate function, and `pred_data` that's additional data passed to the predicate.

You can then call it as shown in listing 10.6.

```
1  bool user_name_equal( struct user const *i_user,
2                        struct user const *j_user ) {
3    return user_cmp( i_user, j_user ) == 0;
4  }
5
6  struct user* find_root( struct slist *user_list ) {
7    struct slist *found = slist_find( user_list,
8                           (slist_pred_fn)&user_name_equal,
9                           &(struct user){ .last = "root" } );
10   // ...
```

Listing 10.6: Function using a structure compound literal

- Lines 1–4 define a predicate function that returns `true` if two user's names are equal.
- Lines 7–9 call `slist_find` passing a list, the `user_name_equal` predicate, and the address of a structure compound literal setting `last` to `"root"`.

Similar to compound literals for arrays (§6.11), a compound literal for a structure is zero or more literals or designated initializers for members enclosed by `{}` prefixed by (*type*) that specifies the type of the structure. Omitted members are initialized to zero or equivalent. A compound literal for a structure allows you to specify a structure "inline" and even take its address.

The lifetime of and storage classes for structure compound literals are the same as for array compound literals (§6.11.1).

10.5 Padding

Assuming pointers are 64-bits, how many bytes is the `user` structure in listing 10.4? The answer is 32 bytes because of *padding* or "holes" in the structure as shown in listing 10.7:

```
struct user {                       // Storage      Padding
    char              *last;        // 1000-1007
    char              mi;           // 1008         1009-1015
    char              *first;       // 1016-1023
    unsigned short    uid;          // 1024-1025    1026-1031
};
```

Listing 10.7: User structure with padding shown

- `first` has to be aligned at a memory address divisible by its size. Since `mi` takes only a single byte, the space between 1009–1015 is padding.
- Similarly, `uid` takes two bytes, so the space between 1026–1031 is padding.

Why is there padding at the end? Consider an array of `user`, `u`. Since array elements are contiguous in memory, `u[1]` immediately follows `u[0]`, hence `u[1].last` has be be aligned exactly like `u[0].last` which means its address can *not* be 1026, but instead must be 1032, hence padding is added at the end.

Padding in structures can be reduced by sorting the members by descending size. For comparison, the structure shown in listing 10.8 is only 24 bytes.

10.6 Flexible Array Members

The last member of a structure with more than one named member may be a *flexible array member* (not to be confused with a VLA, §6.14), that is an array of an

10.6 Flexible Array Members

```
struct user_v2 {               // Storage      Padding
  char             *last;      // 1000-1007
  char             *first;     // 1008-1015
  unsigned short   uid;        // 1016-1017
  char             mi;         // 1018         1019-1023
};
```

Listing 10.8: User structure, version 2, members sorted descending by size

---

unspecified size. For example, an *intrusive* singly linked structure might be declared as shown in listing 10.9.

```
struct islist {
  struct islist *next;
  alignas(max_align_t) char data[];
};
```

Listing 10.9: Intrusive singly linked list structure

Typically, a structure with a flexible array member serves as a "header" for a larger region of memory, perhaps containing a binary file read from disk. It's usually up to your code to somehow remember how big the array is. (This can, of course, be stored in a member that precedes the array in the structure.)

In this case, unlike the slist structure shown in listing 6.2 (p. 86), the user-supplied data is stored with the list node rather than as a pointer to it (hence, intrusive). The alignas (§4.8) max_align_t (§2.9) is necessary to ensure that whatever data is stored there is suitably aligned.

Generally, intrusive data structures have the following advantages:

+ No separate memory allocation for the data is needed.
+ No extra space is needed for the pointer to the data.
+ Accessing the data is faster since it's most likely on the same *cache line* as the node itself.

> ■ When data is read from memory, it's actually read into cache memory first under the reasonable assumption that data accessed once will likely be accessed again shortly. Additionally, rather than reading only a single byte, an entire chunk — a *cache line* — of memory is read that contains not only the sought after byte, but the surrounding bytes as well under the also reasonable assumption that nearby data will likely be accessed shortly. (This is why arrays are faster than linked lists and intrusive data structures are faster than pointers to data.) The size of cache lines vary by CPU, but are typically one of 32, 64, or 128 bytes. □

Intrusive data structures also have the following disadvantages:

− If you already have a pointer to the data, inserting it requires that the data be copied in, not simply copying the pointer.

– Keeping the data when deleting a list node requires that the data be copied out rather than simply getting a pointer to it.

Like many other things in computer science, it's a trade-off. But it's your trade-off to make for your circumstance rather than be stuck with whatever trade-offs the implementers made when programming in a language that provides lists either built-in or part of its standard library.

Listing 10.10 reimplements the functions for the operations "push," "peek," and "pop" as shown in listing 6.3 (p.87), but for `islist`.

```
[[nodiscard]]
struct islist* islist_push( struct islist *head,
                            size_t size ) {
  struct islist *const new_head =
    malloc( sizeof(struct islist) + size );
  new_head->next = head;
  return new_head;
}

[[nodiscard]] void* islist_peek( struct islist *head ) {
  return head != nullptr ? head->data : nullptr;
}

void islist_pop( struct islist **phead ) {
  auto const head = *phead;
  if ( head == nullptr )
    return;
  *phead = head->next;
  free( head );
}
```

Listing 10.10: Intrusive singly linked list functions

- Line 3 declares `islist_push` to take the `size` of the data rather than the data itself that is then included in the call to `malloc` on line 5. Inserting the data requires an extra step, for example:

  ```
  struct islist *list = islist_push(nullptr, sizeof(int));
  *(int*)islist_peek( list ) = 1941;
  ```

- Lines 10–12 declare `islist_peek` that's exactly the same as `slist_peek` from listing 6.3.
- Lines 14–20 declares `islist_pop` to return `void` instead of `void*` since it can't return a pointer to the data after it's been deleted. If you want the data before popping it, you have to peek it first:

  ```
  int i = *(int*)islist_peek( list )
  islist_pop( &list );
  ```

Some additional points about structures with a flexible array member:

10.7 Bit-Fields

1. Such structures can be either on the stack or a member of another structure, but the array will have no size. Attempting to access the array would result in undefined behavior (§15). To have an accessible array, such structures have to be allocated on the heap.
2. Assignments among such structures do *not* copy the array (because the compiler has no idea how big it is):

    ```
    struct islist *list1, *list2;
    // ...
    *list2 = *list1;        // copies only "next" member
    ```

3. When `sizeof` is applied to such a structure, it's as if the array isn't there (except there *may* be some additional padding).
4. C++ hasn't (yet) adopted flexible array members from C.[†]

10.7 Bit-Fields

A *bit-field* is a structure member that takes up only a specified number of bits. It's specified by following a member declaration by a `:` followed by a non-negative integer number of bits.

One use for bit-fields is instead of using bit-flag values for enumerations (§7.5.7). For example, the enumeration `c_int_fmt` from listing 7.9 (p.108) can be rewritten to use bit-fields as shown in listing 10.11 where each `bool` takes up only 1 bit rather than the typical 8.

```
struct c_int_fmt {
  bool cif_short    : 1;
  bool cif_int      : 1;
  bool cif_long     : 1;
  bool cif_unsigned : 1;
  bool cif_const    : 1;
  bool cif_static   : 1;
};
```

Listing 10.11: Structure with bit-field members

The caveat is that the compiler sometimes has to generate several more assembly language instructions to manipulate a bit-field. For example, consider code that temporarily sets `fmt->cif_const` to `true` then back such as:

[†] *I got you, FAM — Flexible Array Members for C++*, JeanHeyd Meneide, Arvid Gerstmann, and Nicole Mazzuca, ISO/IEC JTC1/SC22/WG21: Programming Language — C++, Oct. 19, 2018, https://www.open-std.org/jtc1/sc22/wg21/docs/papers/2018/p1039r0.html

```
bool const old_const = fmt->cif_const;
fmt->cif_const = true;
// ...
fmt->cif_const = old_const;
```

The compiler would generate assembly instructions that includes shifts and a mask (§3.8) necessary to extract only the bit for `cif_const` as if the code were (assuming a big-endian CPU):

```
bool const old_const = (fmt->cif_const >> 3) & 1;
// ...
fmt->cif_const |= old_const << 3;
```

For example, if `*fmt` were `0b1001'1000`, setting `old_const` would require a shift to yield `0b0001'0011` and a mask to yield `0b0000'0001`. Hence, the compiler would generate code that does what you would have done manually if using bit-flags for enumerations. In this particular case, copying the entire structure likely would generate fewer assembly instructions because copying a byte as-is doesn't require shifts or masks:

```
struct c_int_fmt const old_fmt = *fmt;
// ...
*fmt = old_fmt;
```

A few notes about bit-fields:

- The type must be one of `bool`, `unsigned int`, `signed int`, `int`, `_BitInt(n)`, or `unsigned _BitInt(n)`.
- Plain `int` when used for a bit-field does *not* imply `signed` as it normally does. Instead, it's implementation defined whether it's signed or unsigned like `char`.
- The number of bits specified must be ≤ the number of bits comprising the type.
- The endianness (§3.14.3) of the bits is implementation defined.
- Whether bit-fields may straddle a word boundary is implementation defined.
- Accessing more than one bit-field of the same structure concurrently in a multi-threaded program results in a data race (§14) and thus undefined behavior (§15).
- If the member name is omitted, the bits are used for padding. If the number of bits is 0, it means the *next* bit-field member will start at a word boundary.

The other use for bit-fields is when you have to conform to a memory layout for specific hardware or a protocol. For example, listing 10.12 shows the layout for the R6000 CPU physical page number structure. Line 3 shows an example of a padding bit-field.

10.8 Epilogue

```
struct r6000_ppn {      // MIPS R6000 CPU Physical Page Number
    unsigned pfn         : 22; // Page Frame Number
    int                  : 3;  // unused
    unsigned cca         : 3;  // Cache Coherency Algorithm
    bool     nonreachable: 1;
    bool     dirty       : 1;
    bool     valid       : 1;
    bool     global      : 1;
};
```

Listing 10.12: R6000 CPU physical page number structure memory layout

10.8 Epilogue

Here are some key points about and some advice for structures:

- Use structures to group related data into a single object.
- Don't nest structure declarations.
- A structure variable can be initialized in its declaration using the = { } syntax optionally with designated initializers.
- Compound literals like (*type*){ ... } (where *type* is a structure type) can be used to create structures "inline."
- To minimize padding between members, sort members by descending size.
- The last named member of a structure may be a flexible array member that's useful for storing data of an arbitrary or varying size.
- Structure members can be bit-fields, but don't use them unless there's a specific reason for doing so.

Exercises

1. Modify your solution of slist_cmp for exercise 6.1 (p.98) to work with islist shown in listing 10.9 (p.163):

   ```
   int islist_cmp( struct islist const *i_list,
                   struct islist const *j_list,
                   int (*cmp_fn)( void const *i_data,
                                  void const *j_data ) );
   ```

2. Modify your solution of slist_dup for exercise 6.2 (p.98) to work with islist shown in listing 10.9 (p.163):

   ```
   struct islist* islist_dup( struct islist const *list,
                              void (*dup_fn)( void const* ) );
   ```

3. Modify your solution of print_int_fmt for exercise 7.2 (p.109) to work with the version of c_int_fmt shown in listing 10.11 (p.165):

   void print_int_fmt(**struct** c_int_fmt **const** *fmt);

Chapter 11
Unions

A *union* is syntactically like a structure (§10), but is used to store data for any *one* of its members at any *one* time. For example:

```
union value {
  long    i;
  double  f;
  char    c;
  char    *s;
};

union value v;
v.i = 1941;             // value is now 1941
v.c = 'a';              // value is now 'a' (no more 1941)

union value *pv = &v;
pv->s = malloc(6);      // -> works too
strcpy( pv->s, "hello" );
```

All members have the *same* offset. The size of a union is the size of its largest member. A common use for a union would be in a compiler or interpreter where a token is any one of a character literal, integer literal, floating-point literal, string literal, identifier, operator, etc. It would be wasteful to use a structure since only one member would ever have a value.

11.1 Definition

Formally, a union definition is of the form:

> **union** *tag$_{opt}$* {
>   *members$_{opt}$*
> } *declarations$_{opt}$*;

that is the keyword `union` optionally followed by a *tag* name followed by a set of zero or more *members* optionally followed by declarations of the union. As with structures (§10), members are in their own namespace specific to their union, so different unions can have members with the same name. Additionally, the names of unions are put into a *tags* namespace (§2.3). To refer to a union name, it must be preceded by `union`. If you forget to include it, you'll get an error:

```
value v;                    // error: must use "union" tag
```

Alternatively, you can use `typedef` (§2.6) to "inject" a tag name into the surrounding scope so you no longer need to use `union`:

```
typedef union value value;  // inject value into scope
value v;                    // no "union" needed now
```

As a second alternative, you can `typedef` a union declaration directly:

```
typedef union {             // or: typedef union value {
  long    i;
  double  f;
  char    c;
  char   *s;
} value;
```

11.2 Initialization

Since all members of a union have the same offset, their order mostly doesn't matter — except that the first member is the one that is initialized when an initializer list is used so the value given must be the same type:

```
union value v = { 1941 };   // as if: v.i = 1941
```

Alternatively, you can use a designated initializer to specify a member:

```
union value v = { .c = 'a' };
```

11.3 Union Compound Literals

Similar to compound literals for structures (§10.4), a compound literal for a union is a literal or designated initializers for a member enclosed by {} prefixed by (*type*) that specifies the type of the union. A compound literal for a union allows you to specify a union "inline" and even take its address.

The lifetime of and storage classes for union compound literals are the same as for structure compound literals (§6.11.1).

11.4 Which Member?

One obvious problem with a union is, after you store a value in a particular member, how do you later remember which member that was? With a union by itself, you generally can't. You need some other variable to "remember" the member you last stored a value in. Often, this is done using an enumeration (§7) and a structure as shown in listing 11.1.

```
enum token_kind {
  TOKEN_NONE,
  TOKEN_INT,
  TOKEN_FLOAT,
  TOKEN_CHAR,
  TOKEN_STR
};

struct token {
  enum token_kind kind;
  union {
    int     i;
    double  f;
    char    c;
    char   *s;
  };
};
```

Listing 11.1: Structure with anonymous union

Given that, you'd do something like:

```
struct token t = { .kind = TOKEN_CHAR, .c = 'a' };
```

When a union is used inside a structure, it's often made an *anonymous* union, that is a union without a name. In this case, the union members behave as if they're direct members of their enclosing structure except they all have the same offset.

11.5 Type Punning

Type punning is a technique to read or write an object as if it were of a type other than what it was declared as. Since this circumvents the type system, you really have to know what you're doing. In C (but not C++), a `union` can be used for type punning. For example, listing 11.2 shows a way to get the value of a 32-bit integer with the high and low order 16-bit halves swapped.

The union members `u32` and `u16[2]` "overlay" each other allowing you to read and write a `uint32_t` as if it were a 2-element array of `uint16_t`. (You could alternatively write a version that used `uint8_t[4]` and reverse the entire byte order depending on your particular need.)

```
uint32_t swap16of32( uint32_t n ) {
  union {
    uint32_t u32;
    uint16_t u16[2];
  } u = { n };
  auto const t16 = u.u16[0];
  u.u16[0] = u.u16[1];
  u.u16[1] = t16;
  return u.u32;
}
```

Listing 11.2: Swap 16-bit halves of 32-bit integer

You can also use unions to do type punning of unrelated types, for example `int32_t` and `float` allowing you to access the sign, exponent, and mantissa individually. (However, this is CPU-dependent.)

11.6 Restricted Class Hierarchies

Another use for unions is to implement class hierarchies in C, but only "restricted" class hierarchies. A restricted class hierarchy is one used only to implement a solution to a problem where all the classes are known. Users are not permitted to extend the hierarchy via derivation.

■ This can be partially achieved via `final` in C++ or fully achieved via `sealed` in Java or Kotlin. □

Of course C doesn't have either classes or inheritance, but restricted class hierarchies can be implemented via a union of structures.

The token example shown previously is a simple example of this: all the kinds of tokens are known and there's one member in the union to hold the data for each kind. But what if there's more than one member per kind?

For a larger example, consider `cdecl` first mentioned in §6.10:

```
cdecl> explain int *const (*p)[4]
declare p as pointer to array 4 of constant pointer to
    integer
```

During parsing, `cdecl` creates an *abstract syntax tree* (AST) of nodes where each node contains information for a particular kind of declaration. The previous declaration could be represented as an AST as shown in listing 11.3 (expressed in JSON5).

For this example, consider a subset of the kinds of AST nodes in a C++ declaration (to keep the example shorter) as shown in listing 11.4. Listing 11.5 declares some structures to contain the information needed for each AST node kind. Notice that, of the AST structures declared thus far, there are similarities, specifically:

1. Each node points to another and the pointer is declared first.

11.6 Restricted Class Hierarchies

```
{
  name: "p",
  kind: "pointer",
  pointer: {
    to: {
      kind: "array",
      array: {
        size: 4,
        of: {
          kind: "pointer",
          type: "const",
          pointer: {
            to: {
              kind: "built-in type",
              type: "int" } } } } } } }
```

Listing 11.3: AST in JSON5 for `int *const (*p)[4]`

```
typedef enum {
  K_BUILTIN,                    // e.g., int
  K_CLASS_STRUCT_UNION,
  K_ARRAY,
  K_ENUM,
  K_POINTER,
  K_TYPEDEF,
  K_FUNCTION,
  K_OPERATOR,
  // ...
} c_ast_kind_t;
```

Listing 11.4: `c_ast_kind` declaration

---

2. Functions and operators both have return types and parameter lists and the parameter lists are declared second.
3. For nodes that have bit-field widths, the width is alternatively declared second.

The fact that the same members in different structures are at the same offset is convenient because it means that code that, say, iterates over the parameters of a function will also work for the parameters of an operator. Having noticed this, we can make an effort to keep the same members in any remaining structures at the same offsets. For example, the information for K_BUILTIN could be declared as shown in listing 11.6 because that's all the information that's needed for a built-in type. But then the `bit_width` member wouldn't be at the same offset as the same member in either `c_enum_ast` or `c_typedef_ast`. To fix that so code that accesses `bit_width` can do so for any type that has it, we need to insert an unused `c_ast_t` pointer using the DECL_UNUSED macro (p.130) as shown in listing 11.7.

If you think inserting unused members might waste space, remember that, once all these structures are put into the same union, the union will be the size of the largest member; hence, inserting unused members doesn't waste space.

We can apply the same fix for `c_csu_ast` so `csu_name` is at the same offset as `enum_name` in `c_enum_ast` as shown in listing 11.8.

```
struct c_array_ast {
  c_ast_t            *of_ast;           // array of ...
  unsigned           size;
};

struct c_enum_ast {
  c_ast_t            *of_ast;           // fixed type?
  unsigned           bit_width;         // width when > 0
  char const         *enum_name;        // enum name
};

struct c_function_ast {
  c_ast_t            *ret_ast;          // return type
  c_ast_list_t       param_ast_list;    // parameters
};

struct c_operator_ast {
  c_ast_t            *ret_ast;          // return type
  c_ast_list_t       param_ast_list;    // parameters
  c_operator_t const *operator;         // operator info
};

struct c_ptr_ref_ast {
  c_ast_t            *to_ast;           // ptr/ref to ...
};

struct c_typedef_ast {
  c_ast_t const      *for_ast;          // typedef for ...
  unsigned           bit_width;         // width when > 0
};
```

Listing 11.5: cdecl AST node kind structures

```
struct c_builtin_ast {
  unsigned bit_width;                   // width when > 0
};
```

Listing 11.6: Structure for built-in type, version 1

```
struct c_builtin_ast {
  DECL_UNUSED(c_ast_t*,1);              // instead of for/to_ast
  unsigned bit_width;                   // width when > 0
};
```

Listing 11.7: Structure for built-in type, version 2, with reserved space

```
struct c_csu_ast {
  DECL_UNUSED(c_ast_t*,1);              // instead of for/to
  DECL_UNUSED(unsigned,1);              // instead of bit_width
  char const *csu_name;
};
```

Listing 11.8: Structure for class, structure, or union with reserved space

11.6 Restricted Class Hierarchies

Given all those declarations, we can now put them all inside an anonymous union inside a structure for an AST node as shown in listing 11.9.

```c
struct c_ast {
  c_ast_kind_t kind;
  char const   *name;
  c_type_t     type;
  // ...

  union {
    struct c_array_ast     array;
    struct c_builtin_ast   builtin;
    struct c_csu_ast       csu;
    struct c_enum_ast      enum_;
    struct c_function_ast  func;
    struct c_operator_ast  oper;
    struct c_ptr_ref_ast   ptr_ref;
    struct c_typedef_ast   tdef;
    // ...
  };
};
```

Listing 11.9: Structure using union for restricted class hierarchy

In a programming language that has inheritance, `c_array_ast`, `c_builtin_ast`, etc., would be derived from `c_ast`; using this technique in C, they've been "absorbed" into `c_ast`. Some example code using `c_ast` is shown in listing 11.10.

```c
static void c_ast_visitor_english( c_ast_t const *ast ) {
  // ...
  switch ( ast->kind ) {
    case K_ARRAY:
      c_array_ast_english( ast->array );
      break;
    case K_BUILTIN:
      c_builtin_ast_english( ast->builtin );
      break;
    // ...
  }
}
```

Listing 11.10: Using an AST node

After switching on `ast->kind`, each union member is accessed as if it were "derived" from a common base class.

11.6.1 Safeguards

One problem with this approach is that, if you modify any of the structures, you might inadvertently change the offset of some member so that it no longer is at the same offset as the same member in another structure. One way to guard against this is via the `offsetof` macro declared in `stddef.h` standard header and `static_assert` (§16.5) as shown in listing 11.11. Now you'll get a compile-time error if any of the offsets change inadvertently.

```
static_assert(
  offsetof( c_operator_ast_t, param_ast_list ) ==
  offsetof( c_function_ast_t, param_ast_list ),
  "offsetof param_ast_list in c_operator_ast_t !=
    c_function_ast_t"
);

static_assert(
  offsetof( c_csu_ast_t, csu_name ) ==
  offsetof( c_enum_ast_t, enum_name ),
  "offsetof csu_name != offsetof enum_name"
);

// ... more for other members ....
```

Listing 11.11: Use `static_assert` to safeguard restricted class hierarchies

11.7 Epilogue

Here are some key points about and some advice for unions:

- A union is for storing data for any *one* member at any *one* time.
- A union variable can be initialized in its declaration using the = { } syntax optionally with designated initializers.
- Compound literals like *(type)* { ... } (where *type* is a union type) can be used to create unions "inline."
- Unions can be used for type punning. Don't forget about endianness (§3.14.3).
- Unions can be used to implement restricted class hierarchies.

Exercises

1. Write a function:

    ```
    void token_cleanup( struct token *t );
    ```

    that cleans-up a `token` (listing 11.1, p.171): if its kind is `TOKEN_STR`, frees the `s` member.

2. Write a function:

    ```
    uint64_t swap32of64( uint64_t n );
    ```

    similar to `swap16of32` from listing 11.2 (p.172) that gets value of a 64-bit integer with the high and low order 32-bit halves swapped.

Chapter 12
Input, Output, and Files

As mentioned in §1.1, C has no built-in input/output (I/O) facilities. Instead, they're provided by C's standard library, chiefly via the standard `FILE` type and functions that have a `FILE*` as a parameter.

As mentioned in the preface, POSIX extends the C standard library with additional functions. Such functions are are tagged with "[POSIX]" in this chapter.

12.1 Output

Program output goes to *standard output* by default. On Unix systems, standard output goes to a terminal's display by default. The global variable `stdout` declared in `stdio.h` is the pre-opened `FILE` for standard output. Also declared are functions for printing output:

    `int fprintf(FILE *file, char const *fmt, ...)`
        Prints formatted (§12.1.1) to `file`. Returns the number of characters printed on success or a negative value on failure.

    `int fputc(char c, FILE *file)`
        Prints character `c` to `file`. Returns `c` on success or `EOF` on error.

    `int fputs(char const *s, FILE *file)`
        Prints string `s` to `file`. Returns a non-negative integer on success or `EOF` on failure.

    `int putc(char c, FILE *file)`
        Macro version of `fputc`. Returns `c` on success or `EOF` on error.

    `int putchar(char c)`
        Equivalent to `putc(c, stdout)`.

    `int puts(char const *s)`
        Equivalent to `printf("%s\n", s)`. Returns a non-negative integer on success or `EOF` on failure.

```
int printf(char const *fmt, ...)
```
Prints formatted (§12.1.1) to standard output. Returns the number of characters printed on success or a negative value on failure.

```
int vprintf(char const *fmt, va_list args)
```
Prints variadic `args` (§9.11) formatted. Returns the number of characters printed on success or a negative value on failure.

```
int vfprintf(FILE *file, char const *fmt, va_list args)
```
Prints variadic `args` formatted to `file`. Returns the number of characters printed on success or a negative value on failure.

```
int vsnprintf(char const *buf, size_t n, char const *fmt,
              va_list args)
```
Prints variadic `args` formatted to `buf` of size `n`. Returns the number of characters printed on success or a negative value on failure.

```
size_t fwrite(char const *buf, size_t size, size_t n,
              FILE *file)
```
Writes `n` objects, each `size` bytes, from `buf` to `file`. Returns `n` (the number of objects, not bytes) on success or less than `n` on failure.

If any function fails, it sets the global variable `errno` to indicate the error.

The global variable `stderr` declared in `stdio.h` is the pre-opened `FILE` for *standard error* — a second output file specifically for error messages. On Unix systems, standard error also goes to a terminal's display by default. Hence, to print an error message, either of these can be done:

```
fputs( "oops\n", stderr );
fprintf( stderr, "usage: %s [infile [outfile]]\n", prog );
```

■ Personally, I think that's too verbose. For my own programs, I define the following macros as shorthands:

```
#define EPUTC(C)      fputc( (C), stderr )
#define EPUTS(S)      fputs( (S), stderr )
#define EPRINTF(...)  fprintf( stderr, __VA_ARGS__ )
```

and use them consistently. □

■ In a Unix shell, you can redirect standard error independently from standard output with 2>:

$ *command* > output.txt 2> errors.txt

See §12.2.5 regarding the 2. □

12.1.1 Formatted Printing

The standard function `printf` and related functions all use a *format* string that is composed of zero or more *directives* where a directive is either:

- A sequence of ordinary characters (not containing `%`) that are copied verbatim to the output.
- A sequence of characters containing one or more *conversion specifications* starting with `%` of the form:

    %[*flags*][*width*][.[*precision*]][*size*]*specifier*

Each specification results in fetching zero or more subsequent arguments. The type of each argument (after default argument conversions, §9.11.1) *must* correspond with the type given by its associated conversion specifier. Some compilers will warn you (§18.7) if the two disagree.

The components comprising a conversion specification are:

- *flags*: Zero or more of:

#	Print in "alternate form."
0	Left-pad with 0s.
-	Left-align.
(space)	Space before positive number.
+	Always print sign.
'	Insert thousands separators for `diu` or integer part for `fF`.

- *width*: A digit string specifying the minimum field width. If the converted value has fewer characters, it will be padded with spaces (or 0s if the 0 flag was given) on the left (or right if the - flag was given) to fill out the field width.
- *precision*: A . (decimal point) followed by an optional digit string. (If omitted, *precision* is taken as zero.) For the following specifiers, *precision* means:

bBdiouwxX	Minimum number of digits to print.
aAeEfF	Number of digits to print after the decimal point.
gG	Maximum number of significant digits.
s	Maximum number of characters to be printed.

- *size*: The size of the argument (similar to §2.5.1) and precedes a specifier in table 12.1 (p. 183). The following modifiers are valid for the specifiers shown and expect an argument of the given type:

	di	bBouxX	n
h	short	unsigned short	unsigned short*
hh	signed char	unsigned char	unsigned char*
j	intmax_t	uintmax_t	intmax_t*
l	long	unsigned long	unsigned long*
ll	long long	unsigned long long	unsigned long long*
t	ptrdiff_t	ptrdiff_t	ptrdiff_t*
wN	int$N$_t	uint$N$_t	int$N$_t*
z	ssize_t	size_t	size_t*

The wN specifies an integer with a specific width N, e.g., int32_t.

	aAeEfFgG	c	s
l	double	wint_t	wchar_t*
L	long double		
H	_Decimal32		
D	_Decimal64		
DD	_Decimal128		

- **specifier**: The type of the argument and how to print it is shown in table 12.1.
  Notes:

    1. If *precision* is omitted, it defaults to 6; if 0, no decimal point is printed.

Additional notes:

- A *width*, *precision*, or both may be *. The next int argument specifies its value. For example, from listing 2.3 (p.34), the following prints spaces spaces:

    ```
    printf( "%*s", spaces, "" );
    ```

- A negative *width* specifies left-alignment; a negative *precision* is ignored.

Some example conversion specifications are: %ld (long, decimal), %#llX (unsigned long long, hexadecimal, with 0X and A-F), %zu (size_t, decimal), %5.1f (double, 5 characters total, 1 after the decimal point), %.2E (double, 2 digits after the decimal point, with E, a sign, and a 2-digit exponent). For %s using the string "hello, world" (12 characters), some example conversion specifications and the resulting output (including >...< to highlight widths) are:

```
>%s<        >hello, world<
>%10s<      >hello, world<
>%.10s<     >hello, wor<
>%-15s<     >hello, world   <
>%15.10s<   >hello, wor<
>%-15.10s<  >hello, wor     <
```

Table 12.1: `printf` conversion specifiers

aA	double	Floating-point in the form [-]0xh.h^*p±d where there is one digit before the decimal point and *precision* digits after it. The exponent is a + or - followed by a decimal number for an exponent of 2. For A, uses 0X, A-F, and P instead. Also note 1.
bB	unsigned	For b, unsigned binary integer. If the # flag is specified, 0b is prepended. For B, uses 0B instead.
c	int	Character.
di	int	Signed decimal integer where *precision* (if any) specifies the minimum number of digits to print. If the converted value has fewer digits, it's padded on the left with zeros.
eE	double	Floating-point in the form [-]d.d^*e±dd where there is one digit before the decimal point and *precision* digits after it. For E, uses E instead for the exponent that always contains at least two digits. Also note 1.
fF	double	Floating-point in the form [-]d^*.d^* where *precision* specifies the number of digits after the decimal point. Also note 1.
gG	double	Similar to e or f (for g) or E or F (for G). Specifier e is used if the exponent from its conversion < −4 or ≥ *precision*. Trailing zeros are removed from the fractional part of the result. A decimal point is printed only if followed by at least one digit. The *precision* specifies the number of significant digits. If omitted, defaults to 6; if 0, it's treated as 1.
n	int*	The number of characters written so far is stored into the int* (or pointer type specified by *size*) pointed to by the argument.
o	unsigned	Unsigned octal integer. If the # flag is specified, increases *precision* by 1 to force a leading 0 to be printed.
p	void*	Pointer as a hexadecimal integer as if %#x or %#lx were given.
s	char*	String.
u	unsigned	Unsigned decimal integer.
xX	unsigned	For x, unsigned hexadecimal integer using a-f. If the # flag is specified, 0x is prepended. For X, uses 0X and A-F instead.
%		Literal %.

12.2 Files

While reading from standard input and writing to standard output is sufficient for many smaller programs, larger programs often need to read from multiple or write to specific named files on disk.

■ A *filesystem* (FS) is the way bytes are organized to comprise files and directories on a "storage device." Storage devices include spinning hard disks (HDDs), solid-state disks (SDDs), RAM disks, DVDs, and (going way back) floppy disks. Typically, "disk" is used to mean any of them.

There are many filesystems: APFS (macOS), Ext4 (Linux), NFS (Network), NTFS (Microsoft Windows), ZFS (Unix), and many others, each with its own advantages or niche. The term "filesystem" is often interchangeably with "disk." □

We can modify the copy-file program from listing 1.3 (p. 7) to accept optional command-line arguments (§9.7.1) of a pathname to copy from and another to copy to as shown in listing 12.1.

```
26  int main( int argc, char const *const argv[] ) {
27    if ( --argc > 2 )
28      usage( argv[0] );
29
30    char   buf[ BUF_SIZE ];
31    size_t bytes;
32    FILE   *fin = stdin, *fout = stdout;
33
34    if ( argc > 0 ) {
35      fin = check_open( argv[1], "r" );
36      if ( argc > 1 )
37        fout = check_open( argv[2], "w" );
38    }
39
40    errno = 0;
41    do {
42      bytes = fread( buf, 1, BUF_SIZE, fin );
43      if ( ferror( fin ) )
44        break;
45      if ( fwrite( buf, 1, bytes, fout ) < bytes )
46        break;
47    } while ( bytes == BUF_SIZE );
48
49    fclose( fin );
50    fclose( fout );
51    if ( errno != 0 )
52      perror_exit();
53  }
```

Listing 12.1: Copy file, version 4, using files

- Line 27 first decrements argc so its value is more intuitive. (Recall from §9.7.1 that the argument count is inclusive of the program's name, so the number of actual arguments is one less.) If it's > 2, calls usage that prints a usage message and exits:

```
[[noreturn]] static void usage( char const *prog ) {
  fprintf( stderr,
           "usage: %s [infile [outfile]]\n", prog );
  exit( 1 );
}
```

12.2 Files

If invoked incorrectly, it's customary for Unix programs to print a usage message in the format shown, that is "`usage: `" followed by the program's name, followed by a synopsis of its arguments using an EBNF-like notation.[†]

- Line 32 introduces two new variables `fin` and `fout` that are initialized to `stdin` and `stdout`, respectively, for a default.
- Lines 34–35 check to see if there's at least one argument: if so, `argv[1]` is the path of the file to read from that we pass to `check_open` to open it:

```
18  static FILE* check_open( char const *path,
19                           char const *mode ) {
20    FILE *const f = fopen( path, mode );
21    if ( f == nullptr )
22      perror_exit();
23    return f;
24  }
```

- Line 20 calls the standard function `fopen` that "opens" a file in the given *mode* (§12.2.1) where `"r"` means for reading. If it returns `nullptr`, it means an error occurred, so call `perror_exit` to print an error message and exit:

```
[[noreturn]] static void perror_exit() {
  perror( "copy" );
  exit( 2 );
}
```

- Lines 36–37 check to see if there are 2 arguments: if so, `argv[2]` is the path of the file to write to that we pass to `check_open` to open it this time with the mode `"w"` for writing.
- Line 40 sets the global variable `errno` to 0 (no error) to ensure it's zero since functions that set it upon error do *not* set it to zero first.
- Lines 41–47 are basically unchanged from the previous version of the program except that it is now reading from `fin` and writing to `fout`.
- Lines 49–50 close the files by calling the standard function `fclose`. Even though all files are closed automatically upon normal program termination, you should explicitly close every file opened as soon as you no longer need it.

By default, files are *fully buffered* meaning data "written" to a file is accumulated in an internal buffer until some implementation defined capacity is reached, *then* actually written — *flushed* — to minimize slow writes to disk. The last chunk of data to be "written" won't actually be written to disk until the file is closed since it likely didn't fill the buffer to capacity. If your program were to terminate abnormally via a crash before closing open files, data could be lost.

[†]*Extended BNF — A generic base standard*, R. S. Scowen, *Software Engineering Standards Symposium*, 1993.

Closing `fout` might fail attempting to flush its buffer. While `fclose` returns `EOF` upon error, we don't need to check it explicitly since it will also set `errno` upon error that we do check for.

- Line 51 checks `errno` to see if an error occurred: if so, calls `perror_exit`.

12.2.1 Open Modes

An *open mode* is one or more of the characters shown in table 12.2.

Table 12.2: File open modes

r	Open for reading from the beginning of the file. Fails if the file doesn't exist.
w	Open for writing to the beginning of the file. Creates the file if needed.
a	Open for writing to the end of the file ("append"). Creates the file if needed.
+	May follow one of rwa that opens the file for both reading and writing.
x	May follow w or w+ that causes the open to fail if the file already exists ("exclusive").
b	May follow one of rwa+ that opens the file in "binary" mode, i.e., bytes are read and written verbatim. On Unix systems, this is ignored; on Microsoft Windows, suppresses line-ending conversions.

12.2.2 File Information

You can get information about a file via these functions declared in the `sys/stat.h` standard header:

int fstat(int fd, struct stat *s)
   [POSIX] Gets file information for the file descriptor (§12.2.5) `fd` into `*s`.

int lstat(char const *path, struct stat *s)
   [POSIX] Gets file information for `path` into `*s`. If `path` is that of a symbolic link, gets information about the link whereas `stat` gets information about the file linked to.

int stat(char const *path, struct stat *s)
   [POSIX] Gets file information for `path` into `*s`.

All functions return 0 on success or −1 on failure. If any function fails, it sets the global variable `errno` to indicate the error.

The members of the `stat` structure are shown in listing 12.2. (There are other esoteric members as well.) The members of the `timespec` structure are shown in listing B.2 (p. 367). The value of the `st_mode` member indicates the type of file as given by the object-like macros shown in listing 12.3.

12.2 Files

```
struct stat {
  mode_t          st_mode;   // file mode
  nlink_t         st_nlink;  // number of hard links
  uid_t           st_uid;    // user ID
  gid_t           st_gid;    // group ID
  off_t           st_size;   // file size (bytes)
  struct timespec st_atime;  // last access time
  struct timespec st_mtime;  // last modification time
  struct timespec st_ctime;  // last status change time
  // ...
};
```

Listing 12.2: Members of `stat` structure

```
#define S_IFIFO  0010000   // FIFO (named pipe)
#define S_IFCHR  0020000   // character special
#define S_IFDIR  0040000   // directory
#define S_IFBLK  0060000   // block special
#define S_IFREG  0100000   // regular
#define S_IFLNK  0120000   // symbolic link
#define S_IFSOCK 0140000   // socket
```

Listing 12.3: Values for `st_mode`

However, don't use those macros directly; instead use the function-like macros shown in table 12.3.

Table 12.3: Macros for obtaining file type

S_ISBLK(MODE)	Block device?
S_ISCHR(MODE)	Character device?
S_ISDIR(MODE)	Directory?
S_ISFIFO(MODE)	FIFO (named pipe)?
S_ISLNK(MODE)	Symbolic link?
S_ISREG(MODE)	Regular file?
S_ISSOCK(MODE)	Unix domain socket?

An example use of `lstat` that print's a file's information is shown in listing 12.4.

12.2.3 File State

Every FILE object also maintains a "state" of its internal buffer and whether either EOF has been encountered or an error has occurred. The following functions involve a file's state:

```
void clearerr(FILE *file)
```
    Clears both the end-of-file and error states.

```
#include <sys/stat.h>    // for lstat(2)

static char const* mode_str( mode_t mode ) {
  if ( S_ISREG ( mode ) ) return "file";
  if ( S_ISDIR ( mode ) ) return "directory";
  if ( S_ISLNK ( mode ) ) return "link";
  if ( S_ISBLK ( mode ) ) return "block";
  if ( S_ISCHR ( mode ) ) return "character";
  if ( S_ISFIFO( mode ) ) return "named pipe";
  if ( S_ISSOCK( mode ) ) return "socket";
  return "unknown";
}

int main( int argc, char const *const argv[] ) {
  if ( --argc != 1 )
    usage( argv[0] );
  struct stat st;
  if ( lstat( argv[1], &st ) == -1 )
    perror_exit( argv[0] );
  printf( "%s %s %llu\n", argv[1], mode_str( st.st_mode ),
          (unsigned long long)st.st_size );
}
```

Listing 12.4: Example use of lstat that prints a file's information

---

int feof(FILE *file)
Returns non-zero only if file has encountered EOF.

int ferror(FILE *file)
Returns non-zero only if an error occurred using file.

int fflush(FILE *file)
Flushes the internal buffer of file to disk. If file is nullptr, flushes all open files. Returns 0 on success or −1 on error. If it fails, sets the global variable errno to indicate the error.

12.2.4 File Position

When reading or writing a file, there's a current *position* — an offset from the beginning of the file — that the next byte will either be read from or written to that advances automatically. The following functions either get or set the current position to an arbitrary offset:

long ftell(FILE *file)
Returns the current file position on success or −1 on failure.

int fseek(FILE *file, long *offset, int whence)
Sets the current file position to offset relative to whence, one of SEEK_SET

(beginning of file), SEEK_CUR (current position), or SEEK_END (end of file). Returns 0 on success or −1 on failure.

void rewind(FILE *file)
Equivalent to fseek(file, 0, SEEK_SET).

If any function fails, it sets the global variable errno to indicate the error.

12.2.5 Low-Level File I/O

On Unix systems, there's a lower-level set of I/O functions, a subset of which is:

int open(char const *path, int flags, ...)
[POSIX] Opens path using flags. Returns a non-negative file descriptor on success or −1 on failure.

ssize_t read(int fd, char const *buf, size_t size)
[POSIX] Reads size bytes from file descriptor fd into buf. Returns the number of bytes read on success or −1 on failure.

ssize_t write(int fd, char const *buf, size_t size)
[POSIX] Writes size bytes to file descriptor fd from buf. Returns the number of bytes written on success or −1 on failure.

int close(int fd)
[POSIX] Closes file descriptor fd. Returns 0 on success or −1 on failure.

If any function fails, it sets the global variable errno to indicate the error.

A *file descriptor* (fd) is an ornate name for simply an int that Unix associates with an open file. By default, stdin is fd 0, stdout is fd 1, and stderr is fd 2. Each also has the constants STDIN_FILENO, STDOUT_FILENO, and STDERR_FILENO defined in unistd.h.

■ Why are there two sets of functions? These functions are actually *system calls*. A system call is a core function provided by an operating system that implements only basic functionality. For example, there are no system call counterparts for getchar, getline, or putchar; read, and write don't do buffering. Such functionality is provided by the C standard library.

Calling a system call is usually more expensive than calling an ordinary function because it requires a privilege escalation to switch from *user mode* to *kernel mode* in order to access kernel-owned memory or other resources, then a privilege de-escalation upon return. (That's why fread and fwrite do buffering: to minimize system calls.)

Generally, you should avoid using system calls because your programs will be more portable to other Unix (or non-Unix) systems that may not provide the same system calls. In contrast, the C standard library provides the same and easier-to-use API regardless of the operating system. However, system calls typically offer finer-grained control than their standard library counterparts or offer functionality not provided by the standard library. □

You can convert between a `FILE*` and a file descriptor via the functions:

`FILE* fdopen(int fd, char const *mode)`
[POSIX] Returns a `FILE*` for file descriptor `fd` on success or `nullptr` on failure. The `mode` is from table 12.2 (p.186) and must be compatible with the mode what was used when the file was opened (presumably using `open`).

`int fileno(FILE *file)`
[POSIX] Returns the underlying file descriptor for the given `file`.

If any function fails, it also sets the global variable `errno` to indicate the error.

Hence, you can use `FILE*` most of the time, and file descriptors only when you have to.

12.2.6 Memory as a File

You can also "open" a chunk of memory and treat it as if it were a (nameless) file via a `FILE*` by using either of these functions:

`FILE* fmemopen(char *buf, size_t size, char const *mode)`
[POSIX] Opens `buf` of `size` as a `FILE`. The `buf` pointer can either point to an existing buffer of `size` or be `nullptr` in which case a buffer of `size` bytes will both automatically be allocated initially and deallocated when the file is closed. Returns a non-null `FILE*` on success or `nullptr` on error. The `mode` is from table 12.2 (p.186).

Even though `mode` can be `w` for writing, the capacity of `buf` is fixed at `size`. Consequently, `fmemopen` is useful only for reading. This is useful if you need to use an API that uses `FILE*`, but you want to use memory instead, perhaps a string read from either the terminal or a socket.

`FILE* open_memstream(char **pbuf, size_t *psize)`
[POSIX] Opens `*pbuf` for writing only. The buffer is both allocated and grows automatically. A null character is maintained at the end of the buffer. This byte is not included in the value written to `*psize`. Returns a non-null `FILE*` on success or `nullptr` on error. After closing the file, the buffer must be freed. The function is typically used as shown in listing 12.5.

If either function fails, it sets the global variable `errno` to indicate the error.

12.2 Files

```
char *buf;
size_t size;
FILE *const file = open_memstream( &buf, &size );
// ... write to file ...
fclose( file );
// ... do something with buf ...
free( buf );
```

Listing 12.5: Typical use of `open_memstream`

12.2.7 A File as Memory

Conversely, you can open a file and treat it as it it were an in-memory buffer via the functions declared in the `sys/mman.h` header:

`void* mmap(void *addr, size_t size, int prot, int flags, int fd, off_t off)`
  [POSIX] "Maps" `size` bytes at offset `off` of a file descriptor `fd` to memory returning a pointer to it on success or `nullptr` on error.

`int munmap(void *addr, size_t size)`
  [POSIX] "Unmaps" the memory at `addr` previously returned by `mmap` of `size`. Returns 0 on success or −1 on error.

If either function fails, it sets the global variable `errno` to indicate the error.

These are useful if you need to use an API that uses pointers, but you want to use a `FILE*` instead. A file mapped with `mmap` *must* be unmapped with `munmap`.

■ This section is provided only so you're aware that such functions exist in case you might need to use them. The details of `mmap`, in particular the `prot` and `flags` arguments, are beyond the scope of this book, but readily available in the *mmap*(2) manual page on most Unix systems or online. □

12.2.8 Deletion

To delete either a file or directory:

`int remove(char const *path)`
  Deletes the file (last) component of `path`. Returns 0 on success or −1 on failure.

If it fails, it sets the global variable `errno` to indicate the error. When deleting a directory, it must be empty.

■ On many filesystems (§12.2), a file can be "linked" to from more than one directory, hence it's literally in multiple directories simultaneously. Deleting a file is done via a path to it where the next-to-last component of the path is a directory (of possibly many) that has a link to the file. Deleting a file "unlinks" it only from *that* directory. If other directories have a link to the file, then it still exists. A file isn't actually deleted until the last link is.

Opening a file creates an in-memory link to it that counts exactly the same as a directory link. On Unix systems, the number of directory links can fall to zero by deletion, but the file will continue to exist as long as at least one program has the file open. On Microsoft Windows, a file may not be deleted while it's open. □

12.2.9 Temporary Files

Sometimes you need a file to write data to temporarily and read it back at some later time. You don't care about the name of the file, only that it's unique. Additionally, you want to ensure that it's automatically deleted upon program termination.

FILE* tmpfile()
Creates a file having a unique, unspecified name, opens it with mode w+ (§12.2.1), "unlinks" it (§12.2.8) so it will be automatically deleted upon close, and returns a pointer to it on success or nullptr on failure.

On Unix systems, the file is created in the directory given by the value of the TMPDIR environment variable (§12.4.4); if unset, defaults to /tmp.

If the function fails, it sets the global variable errno to indicate the error.

12.3 Directories

In addition to opening and reading files, you can also open and read directories to get the list of files in them.

DIR* opendir(char const *path)
[POSIX] Opens path that refers to a directory for reading and returns a pointer to a directory structure DIR on success or nullptr on failure.

struct dirent* readdir(DIR *dir)
[POSIX] Reads the next directory entry from dir and returns a pointer to a dirent ("directory entry") structure or nullptr if either there are no more entries or on failure.

int closedir(DIR *dir)
[POSIX] Closes file directory dir. Returns 0 on success or −1 on failure.

12.3 Directories

If any function fails, it sets the global variable `errno` to indicate the error. A program to print the names of the files in the current directory is shown in listing 12.6.

```c
#include <dirent.h>

static bool is_dot_or_dot_dot( char const *path ) {
  return path[0] == '.' && (path[1] == '\0' ||
         (path[1] == '.' &&  path[2] == '\0'));
}

int main( int, char const *const argv[] ) {
  DIR *const dir = opendir( "." );
  if ( dir == nullptr ) {
    fprintf( stderr, "%s: could not open\n", argv[0] );
    exit( 1 );
  }
  for ( struct dirent const *ent;
        (ent = readdir( dir )) != nullptr; ) {
    if ( !is_dot_or_dot_dot( ent->d_name ) )
      puts( ent->d_name );
  }
  closedir( dir );
}
```

Listing 12.6: Reading a directory

- Line 1 includes the `dirent.h` standard header where types and functions for working with directories are declared.
- Line 9 calls `opendir` to open the directory given by the path argument returning a pointer to a `DIR` object for the directory. On Unix systems, "." means "the current directory" and ".." means "the parent directory."
- Lines 14–18 loop as long as `readdir` doesn't return `nullptr`, i.e., there is another entry. The `dirent` structure contains information about the entry:

```c
struct dirent {
  char d_name[N];   // entry name
  // ...
};
```

The only member that's guaranteed to exist on all Unix systems is `d_name`, the directory entry's name. Its maximum size N is implementation defined.

The order that directory entries are returned is implementation defined; hence, if you wanted to print them sorted, you'd have to read them into an array first, sort the array, then print them.

- Line 16 calls `is_dot_or_dot_dot` to check if the entry's name is either "." or ".." (the current or parent directory) and prints the entry's name only if neither.
- Lines 3–6 define the `is_dot_or_dot_dot` function that checks at most the first 3 characters of `path`. Alternatively, the function could have made two calls to `strcmp`, but this implementation is more efficient.

12.4 Input

Program input comes from *standard input* by default. On Unix systems, standard input comes from the terminal's keyboard by default. The global variable `stdin` declared in `stdio.h` is the pre-opened `FILE` for standard input. Also declared are functions for reading input:

int fgetc(FILE *file)
Gets the next character from `file`. Returns the character or `EOF` on either end-of-file or error.

int getc(FILE *file)
Macro version of `fgetc`.

int getchar()
Same as `getc(stdin)`.

int scanf(char const *fmt, ...)
Scans formatted (§12.4.1). Returns `EOF` only if the end-of-file is encountered before any conversions. Otherwise returns the number of variables assigned. If fewer than specified, it means the input didn't match the format.

int fscanf(FILE *file, char const *fmt, ...)
Scans formatted from `file`.

int vscanf(char const *fmt, va_list args)
Scans variadic `args` (§9.11) formatted.

int vfscanf(FILE *file, char const *fmt, va_list args)
Scans variadic `args` formatted from `file`.

int vsscanf(char const *str, char const *fmt, va_list args)
Scans variadic `args` formatted from string `str`.

size_t fread(void *buf, size_t size, size_t n, FILE* file)
Reads n objects, each `size` bytes, into `buf` from `file`. Returns the number of objects (not bytes) read.

To distinguish `EOF` from error, you can use the functions from §12.2.3. If any function fails, it sets the global variable `errno` to indicate the error.

12.4.1 Formatted Reading

The standard function `scanf` along with its related functions are similar to `printf` (§12.1.1) and its related functions except in reverse — that is, instead of converting values to string representations for printing, string representations of values are converted to values of specific types. All use a *format* string that is composed of zero or more *directives* where a directive is either:

12.4 Input

- A sequence of ordinary characters (not containing %) that are read and matched verbatim except that white space (e.g., spaces, tabs, and newlines) will match *any* amount of whitespace, including none, from the input.
- A sequence of characters containing one or more *conversion specifications* starting with % of the form:

   %[*width*][*size*]*specifier*

Each specification results in fetching zero or one subsequent pointer arguments to store the converted values into. The type of each pointer argument *must* correspond with the type given by its associated conversion specifier. (Some compilers will warn you if the two disagree.)

The components comprising a conversion specification are:

- *width*: A digit string specifying the maximum field width.
- *size*: Specifies the size of the argument (similar to §2.5.1) and precedes a specifier. The following size modifiers are valid for specifiers shown and expect an argument of the given type:

	bBdinouxX	aAeEfFgG	cs
*			
h	short*		
hh	char*		
H		_Decimal32*	
D		_Decimal64*	
DD		_Decimal128*	
j	intmax_t*		
l	long*	double*	wchar_t*
ll	long long*		
L		long double*	
t	ptrdiff_t*		
w*N*	int*N*_t*		
z	size_t*		

The * causes the conversion to happen just the same, but the converted value is discarded and no pointer argument is used nor value stored. The w*N* specifies a pointer to an integer with a specific width N, e.g., int32_t (§2.7).

- *specifier*: The type of the argument to scan and type of pointer to store the converted value into is shown in table 12.4.
   Notes:
   1. The usual skipping of leading white space is suppressed.
   2. Scanning stops at a white-space character or when *width* (if any) is reached, whichever occurs first.

3. The array must be large enough to hold the entire sequence and the terminating null character.

Table 12.4: scanf conversion specifiers

aAeFfGg	float*	Floating-point number.
c	char*	Sequence of *width* characters (default of 1). Also notes 1, 3.
C	wchar_t*	Same as lc.
d	int*	Signed decimal integer.
i	int*	Signed decimal integer. If the integer begins with 0, it's in octal; 0b or 0B, it's in binary; 0x or 0X, it's in hexadecimal.
n	int*	No conversion. Instead, the number of characters parsed so far is stored into the pointed-to int.
o	unsigned*	Unsigned octal integer.
p	void*	Pointer value as if printed by %p for printf (§12.1.1).
s	char*	Sequence of non-white-space characters. Also notes 2, 3.
u	unsigned*	Unsigned decimal integer.
xX	unsigned*	Unsigned hexadecimal integer.
[	char*	Begins a set of characters to match one or more of and ends with the] character. If the first character after [is ^, then the set of characters to match is all *but* the given set. To include] in the set, make it the first character after [or ^. To include a range of characters, place - between the first and last character in the range. To include -, make it the last character before]. The string ends when a character not in (or, with ^, in) the set is encountered or *width* (if any) is reached, whichever occurs first. Also notes 1, 3. For example, [^]0-9-] means "everything except], 0-9, and -."
%		Literal %.

The scanf and related functions return the number of successful conversions or EOF.

For an example using fscanf, let's rewrite listing 10.3 (p. 160) to add a function to read the planetary data from a FILE as shown in listing 12.7 rather than hard-code it into the program.

Despite its seeming convenience, scanf and related functions aren't generally suitable for production-quality programs because of lack of sufficient error handling. For example, if the fscanf in listing 12.7 returns fewer than 2 converted values, you have no idea why a value wasn't converted whereas a production-quality program would likely print only the invalid value and highlight specifically which character was the invalid one.

12.4 Input

```
void read_planet_data( FILE *f ) {
  for ( unsigned p = 0; p < 8; ++p ) {
    if ( fscanf( f, "%lf,%lf\n",
                 &PLANET[p].perihelion_au,
                 &PLANET[p].aphelion_au ) != 2 ) {
      fprintf( stderr, "data error for planet %u\n", p );
      exit( 1 );
    }
  }
}
```

Listing 12.7: Read planet data from FILE using fscanf

12.4.2 String-to-Number Conversion

Although not strictly I/O-related, functions that convert strings to numbers are relevant since reading input often involves reading strings of characters and converting them to numbers to do better error handling instead of using scanf and related functions. Declared in the stdlib.h standard header, the standard string-to-number conversion functions are:

long strtol(char const *str, char **pend, int base)
    Converts string to long.
long long strtoll(char const *str, char **pend, int base)
    Converts string to long long.
intmax_t strtoimax(char const *str, char **pend, int base)
    Converts string to intmax_t.
unsigned long strtoul(char const *str, char **pend, int base)
    Converts string to unsigned long.
**unsigned long long strtoull(char const *str, char **pend,
                              int base)**
    Converts string to unsigned long long.
uintmax_t strtoumax(char const *str, char **pend, int base)
    Converts string to uintmax_t.
float strtof(char const *str, char **pend)
    Converts string to float.
double strtod(char const *str, char **pend)
    Converts string to double.
long double strtold(char const *str, char **pend)
    Converts string to long double.

- For all functions, if the string is empty, returns zero and sets errno to EINVAL.
- Otherwise, there may be leading white space that's ignored, followed by an optional + or -, followed by the digits comprising the number.

- For functions that have a pend parameter, if it's not nullptr, the functions store the address of the first invalid character in str into *pend. If there were no digits at all, the functions store str into *pend. (Hence, if *str is not '\0', but **pend is '\0' on return, the entire string was valid.)
- For the functions that have a base parameter, it specifies the base of the number to parse, typically one of 2 (binary), 8 (octal), 10 (decimal), or 16 (hexadecimal). If base is 0, then the base will be determined by the first one or two characters of str: if 0b or 0B, binary; if 0x or 0X, hexadecimal; if 0, octal; if 1–9, decimal.
- If the converted value is either less than the minimum or greater than the maximum value for the type, then either the minimum or maximum value for the type, respectively, is returned instead and the global variable errno is set to ERANGE.

For example, the code in listing 12.8 attempts to convert the string s into a long integer, checks for errors, and, if an invalid character is encountered, prints the value of s with a ^ under the offending character.

```
1   long check_strtol( char const *s ) {
2     char *end;
3     errno = 0;
4     auto const n = strtol( s, &end, 10 );
5     if ( errno == EINVAL )
6       fprintf( stderr, "\"%s\": invalid string\n", s );
7     else if ( errno == ERANGE )
8       fprintf( stderr, "\"%s\": range error\n", s );
9     else if ( *end != '\0' )
10      fprintf( stderr, "%s\n%*s^\n", s, (int)(end - s), "" );
11    return n;
12  }
```

Listing 12.8: Calling strtol and checking for errors

The format string on line 10 can be broken down into: %s\n prints the string s followed by a newline; %*s repeats the feature of printf to print a specific number of spaces shown in listing 2.3 (p. 34), in this case the difference end - s is the offset of the offending character; and ^\n that prints a literal ^ and newline.

12.4.3 Line Reading

The functions that read entire lines are:

char* fgets(char const *buf, int buf_size, FILE *file)
Reads at most buf_size−1 characters into buf from file. Reading stops short upon encountering a newline, EOF, or error. The newline, if any, is kept. Returns buf on success or nullptr upon either EOF or error.

12.4 Input

```
ssize_t getdelim(char **pline, size_t *pcap, int delim,
                 FILE *file)
```
[POSIX] Reads a line delimited by `delim` into `*pline` of capacity `*pcap` from `file`. The `delim` character is kept. Returns the number of characters written or −1 upon encountering EOF or error.

Initially, `*pline` may either be a pointer to a `malloc`'d buffer or `nullptr` and `*pcap` its capacity. In either case, `getdelim` will automatically grow the buffer as needed by calling `realloc` and updating both `*pline` and `*pcap`.

```
char* getline(char **pline, size_t *pcap, FILE *file)
```
[POSIX] Same as `getdelim` with `'\n'` for `delim`.

To distinguish EOF from error, you can use the functions from §12.2.3. If any function fails, it sets the global variable `errno` to indicate the error.

For an example using `fgets`, let's rewrite listing 12.7 (p.197) to read the planetary data from a FILE using it as shown in listing 12.9.

```
 1  double parse_double( char const **ps,
 2                       char const *term_chars ) {
 3    char *end;
 4    errno = 0;
 5    auto const n = strtod( *ps, &end );
 6    if ( errno == ERANGE ) {
 7      fprintf( stderr, "\"%s\": value out of range\n", *ps );
 8      exit( 3 );
 9    }
10    if ( strchr( term_chars, *end ) == nullptr ) {
11      fprintf( stderr, "'%c': invalid character\n", *end );
12      exit( 4 );
13    }
14    *ps = *end == '\0' ? end : end + 1;
15    return n;
16  }
17
18  void read_planet_data( FILE *f ) {
19    char line[128];
20    for ( unsigned p = 0; p < 8; ++p ) {
21      char const *s = fgets( line, sizeof line, f );
22      if ( s == nullptr ) {
23        if ( ferror( f ) ) {
24          perror( "orbits" );
25          exit( 2 );
26        }
27        break;
28      }
29      PLANET[p].perihelion_au = parse_double( &s, ",\n" );
30      PLANET[p].aphelion_au   = parse_double( &s, ",\n" );
31    }
32  }
```

Listing 12.9: Read planet data from FILE using `fgets`

- Line 19 declares `line`, a buffer to read a line of characters into. The size is arbitrary, but is more than big enough for this program.
- Lines 21–23 call `fgets` that returns a pointer to the line read or `nullptr` upon either `EOF` or error.
- Lines 29–30 call `parse_double` passing a pointer to `s` and a set of characters that are acceptable to terminate the conversion, in this case, either a comma (that separates perihelion and aphelion on a line) or a newline (that separates lines).
- Lines 1–16 expand upon listing 12.8 (p. 198) to parse a `double` from a string.
- Line 10 calls the standard function `strchr` (§B.2) that returns a pointer to a character in `term_chars` that `*end` matches or `nullptr` if none. In this case, either the aforementioned comma or newline.
- If it's *not* one of those, lines 11–12 print an error message including the offending character and exits.
- Line 14 updates `*ps` so that it points to the first character *after* the character that terminated the conversion (unless it's the null character) so the next time `parse_double` is called, it'll start parsing at the correct place for the *next* number. For example, the first time `parse_double` is called for a line, it will update `*ps` to point to the character after the comma.

Compared to listing 12.7 (p. 197) that uses `fscanf` (9 lines), the `fgets` version (31 lines) requires over 3 times as much code. While it's more involved, it does a better job of error reporting, something that users of programs appreciate. Doing a better job of *anything* invariably requires more code.

We could have used `getline` instead of `fgets`, but the problem with `getline` is that it grows the line buffer as needed automatically. While convenient, it's vulnerable to attack because a malicious user could input a multi-gigabyte file with no newline in it: `getline` would keep calling `realloc` to make the line bigger and it will eventually fail. One of the foundational rules of programming is: *never trust your input*.[†]

12.4.4 Environment Variables

On most systems, there are *environment variables*: a set of key-value pairs containing configuration settings. On Unix systems, environment variables include `HOME` (user's home directory), `PATH` (set of directories containing executable programs), `TMPDIR` (directory for temporary files), and many others. You are also free to create your own. Environment variables can be read by your programs as another way to input information in addition to either command-line options or files.

[†] *How One Bad CrowdStrike Update Crashed the World's Computers*, Lily Hay Newman, Matt Burgess, and Andy Greenberg, *Wired*, July 19, 2024.

```
char* getenv(char const *name)
```
Returns the value of the environment variable having name or nullptr if no such variable exists.

If the function fails, it sets the global variable errno to indicate the error.

12.5 Epilogue

Here are some key points about and some advice for input, output, and files:

- C has no built-in input/output (I/O) facilities. Instead, they're provided by C's standard library.
- POSIX extends the C standard library with additional functions.
- Use standard C library functions instead of system calls whenever possible.
- In addition to stdout (standard output), there's also stderr (standard error) for print error messages to.
- When opening and reading files, you should always check for errors and print informative error messages.
- Avoid using scanf for production-quality programs. It's better to read text files a line at a time and parse them individually.
- Environment variables offer another way to input information to your programs.

Exercises

1. The perror_exit function (p. 185) is somewhat lacking in that, when called from check_open, it doesn't print the filename that had the error.
   To print the filename, modify perror_exit to have the signature:

   ```
   [[noreturn]]
   static void perror_exit( char const *what );
   ```

   that prints to standard error as before and if what is:

   - Not nullptr, prints "copy: " as before, followed by what, followed by a colon and the error message that perror would have printed.
   - nullptr, calls perror as before.

   With this modification, *what* the error message is about will be printed, e.g., check_open can pass path. You will need the standard function strerror (§B.2) that you can pass errno to.

2. Modify listing 12.4 (p. 188) to print a file's size using units, one of bytes (B), kilobytes (KB), megabytes (MB), or gigabytes (GB) depending on its size.

3. Combine listings 12.4 (p.188) and 12.6 (p.193) to print a file's name, type, and size for every file in the current directory.
4. Modify your solution to the previous exercise to use a *width* in a `printf` conversion specification (§12.1.1) so that a file's name, type, and size are printed in aligned columns.
5. Listing 12.9 (p.199) includes the line:

   21   **char const** *s = fgets(line, **sizeof** line, f);

   A problem with this is that if the length of a line > `sizeof line`−1, the line is too long and `line` will not end with a newline.

   Modify listing 12.9 to check for this case and print an error message and exit if encountered.

Chapter 13
Program Organization

For all but the most trivial programs, a typical C program is composed of several source (.c) files and header (.h) files. For example, the source files of ad[†] are:

```
ad.c      color.h    match.c    options.h     unicode.c  util.h
ad.h      dump.c     match.h    pjl_config.h  unicode.h
color.c   dump_c.c   options.c  reverse.c     util.c
```

Often, .c and .h files come in pairs where the .c implements some functionality and the .h provides the "public" API for using it. All the functions comprising a program are spread among pairs of files with each pair specializing in some particular aspect of the program. One or more pairs roughly approximates a "module" in other languages. For example, color.c contains the definitions of functions for printing text in color to a terminal and its corresponding color.h contains their declarations so that other files may #include it to use those functions.

13.1 Include Guards

Compared to a proper module facility, #include (§8.6) is rather simple because it includes the full text of a header file as-is. In C, it's an error to declare enumerations (§7), structures (§10), or unions (§11) more than once, even if the declarations are identical. Given that, you can get "redefinition errors" when a header containing a declaration is included more than once. For example, color.h contains the declaration:

```
enum color_when { // ...
```

[†] *ad: ASCII or UTF-8 file dump that can also search for and highlight strings or numbers*, Paul J. Lucas, https://github.com/paul-j-lucas/ad

It's included by options.h and ad.c that *also* includes it:

```
options.h  ← color.h
ad.c       ← color.h, options.h
```

Given that, the declaration for color_when would be seen twice and be an error. To fix this, an *include guard* should be used in every header file. It has the form:

```
#ifndef name
#define name
// ... declarations ...
#endif
```

That is, all the declarations should be between an #ifndef *name*, #define *name*, ... #endif sequence where *name* is a unique name within a program. Generally, making the names be the name of the file prefixed by the name of the program is sufficient. A properly included-guarded color.h is shown in listing 13.1.

```
#ifndef ad_color_H
#define ad_color_H

enum color_when { // ...

#endif /* ad_color_H */
```

Listing 13.1: A properly include-guarded color.h

■ Putting comments after #endif isn't necessary, of course, but it's generally considered good style to repeat the condition used in the #ifndef, #ifdef, or #if. □

Assuming ad.c contains:

```
#include "color.h"
#include "options.h"
```

when it's being compiled, the following happens:

1. The preprocessor opens ad.c and starts processing text, line by line.
2. It encounters #include "color.h", so it opens that file and begins processing:
   a. It encounters #ifndef ad_color_H: since ad_color_H hasn't been defined, it continues processing text.
   b. It encounters #define ad_color_H and defines that name. (That it's defined to *nothing* doesn't matter; what matters is that the name itself is defined.)
   c. It then continues processing text passing it through verbatim to the compiler.
   d. It encounters the #endif corresponding to the #ifndef and reaches the end-of-file.

3. Returning to ad.c, it encounters #include "options.h", so it opens that file and begins processing:

   a. It encounters #include "color.h", so it opens that file and begins processing it.
   b. It again encounters #ifndef ad_color_H: this time since ad_color_H has been defined, it continues processing text, but discards it instead.
   c. It encounters the #endif corresponding to the #ifndef and reaches the end-of-file.
   d. Returning to options.h, it processes the rest of that file.

4. Returning to ad.c, it processes the rest of that file.

13.2 Opaque Types

As an alternative to putting structure definitions in headers, you can put only declarations; the definitions are put into .c files. For example, instead of defining the entire string structure, only *declare* that string *is* a structure:

```
struct string;     // "string" is a struct (no details)
```

This is known as an *opaque type* (aka, *incomplete type*). C allows pointers to such structures exactly the same as pointers to those that are defined since all pointers are the same size (on modern computers). The advantages of opaque types include:

+ Prevents programmers from "cheating" by accessing members they shouldn't, i.e., undocumented members or members documented as private. If programmers cheat, making changes to members can break programs.
+ Adding or removing members does not require that any dependent code be recompiled thereby providing *binary compatibility*. This is especially important for libraries since it allows updated versions to be "drop-in" replacements for older versions.
+ That means fewer dependencies between files that translates into both fewer and faster recompilations.

The disadvantages of opaque types include:

− All objects of an opaque type in user code must be dynamically allocated and deallocated that is less efficient than objects on the stack.
− Doing anything with an opaque type requires using non-inline functions that are slower than either simply accessing members directly or using inline functions (§9.10).

13.3 Self Sufficient Headers

Before continuing, what it means for a header file to be *self-sufficient* needs to be defined:

- **Self-sufficient header**: a header where if it were included by itself into a .c file, that file would compile without errors (specifically, without "undeclared" errors).

For example, a trivial program like:

```
#include "color.h"
int main() { }
```

will compile without errors only if color.h is self-sufficient.

13.3.1 Including Headers in a Header

Typically, a header file will need to include other header files because the declarations make use of other declarations in those other header files. Within a header file:

- Include other local headers first (with ""), if any, followed by standard headers (with <>), if any.

For example, color.h has its includes like:

```
#include "config.h"  // Good: include local headers ...
#include "util.h"

#include <stdio.h>   // ... before standard headers.
// ...
```

Why put local headers first? Because this helps ensure that every header file is self-sufficient. For example, if you put standard headers first like:

```
#include <stdio.h>   // Bad: include of standard headers ...
#include "util.h"    // ... before local headers.
```

then it's possible for declarations in util.h to use declarations in stdio.h by "accident" without util.h itself including stdio.h. This will continue to work indefinitely, but if at some point you no longer need stdio.h in color.h and so delete its #include, then you'll get "undeclared" errors in util.h. Up until this time, you'll never have noticed that util.h isn't self-sufficient. Once you notice, it's easily fixed, but it's better to avoid the problem in the first place by always including local headers before standard headers.

13.3.2 Include Everything Necessary

Within a header file:

- You *must* include every other header it needs to be self-sufficient.

Never force users of your header to have to include some other header(s) before yours in order to compile without errors.

> ■ BSD-derived operating systems have historically tended to violate this guideline. The rationale for doing so is that it's an alternate way to help maximize compilation speed. It does this by forcing *you* to be a "human include guard." For example:
>
> ```
> #include <sys/types.h>
> #include <pwd.h>        // needs <sys/types.h>
> #include <unistd.h>     // needs <sys/types.h> too
> ```
>
> Rather than pwd.h and unistd.h each including sys/types.h, both rely on *you* to do the include yourself.
>
> How does that help? It eliminates the step whereby the preprocessor has to open types.h, read the file, encounter the include guard, and omit the rest of the contents if the guard has been seen before (as would be the case for unistd.h).
>
> While it does help, the price is that it forces users to have to remember to include files manually that can lead to having unnecessary includes that slow down compilation. For example, if at some point you removed the includes for pwd.h and unistd.h, that might result in types.h no longer being needed, but you might forget to remove it.
>
> Like many other things in computer science, it's a trade-off. BSD-derived systems have been moving away from this practice and making headers self-sufficient. □

13.3.3 Interdependencies

Larger programs typically contain many type definitions, specifically structure definitions (§10). Sometimes those definitions contain interdependencies. Consider listing 13.2 showing two headers, c_alignas.h and c_ast.h, each declaring its own structure.

The c_alignas structure contains a c_ast*, so c_alignas.h would need to include c_ast.h. The c_ast structure contains a c_alignas*, so c_ast.h would need to include c_alignas.h. They can't successfully include each other.

One common way to break the interdependency is to create a third header like types.h that contains only structure *declarations* as shown in listing 13.3. Such declarations state that c_alignas and c_ast *are* structures and allow pointers to

```
struct c_alignas {              // declared in c_alignas.h
  // ...
  struct c_ast    *type_ast;    // aligned as this type
};

struct c_ast {                  // declared in c_ast.h
  struct c_alignas *align;      // alignment, if any
  // ...
};
```

Listing 13.2: Interdepenent headers

```
// types.h
struct c_alignas;
struct c_ast;
// ...
```

Listing 13.3: "Types" header to break header interdependencies

them to be used, but the definitions aren't important now and will be defined later. While similar to opaque types (§13.2), they're only temporarily opaque since the definitions are still in headers.

13.4 Cooperating with C++

Libraries written in C are often used by C++ programs, so header files for such libraries are included by both C and C++ programs. C++ has the concept of *language linkage* that is specified by a variant of extern (§4.3.2) having two forms:

   extern "C" *declaration*   Gives *declaration* C linkage.
   extern "C" { *declarations$_{opt}$* } Gives *declarations* C linkage.

Declarations marked extern "C" have "C linkage."

■ Producing executables for C programs involves using several programs comprising a *toolchain* in sequence:

   preprocessor → compiler → assembler → linker → a.out

A *linker* is a program that takes one or more .o files and the C standard and other libraries and "links" them together into a single executable file — a.out by default.

Traditional Unix linkers have only a single namespace. Since C++ supports function overloading, the compiler has to "mangle" every function's name to encode its signature (§9.1) to yield a unique name. Mangling algorithms are implementation defined, but are along the lines of:

```
void foo( );            // _Z3foov
void foo( int );        // _Z3fooi
```

The prefix "_Z" marks the start of a mangled name followed by the length of the function's name followed by the name followed by an encoding of its parameter types, here "v" for void and "i" for int.

Since C doesn't support function overloading (§9.3), mangling isn't necessary. A function foo( ) in C is simply foo. For a C++ compiler to be able to compile and link with C code, there needs to be a way to turn off mangling while compiling C declarations in header files (since the compiler doesn't know they're C and not C++ declarations). That's what extern "C" does.

In C++, "C" and "C++" are the only standard language linkages (though you never need to use "C++" explicitly since that's the default). Additional language linkages are implementation defined. For example, IBM's XL C/C++ compiler also supports "COBOL", "FORTRAN", and "PLI". □

Since extern "C" is C++ only, such declarations have to be seen only when compiling with a C++ compiler. The preprocessor can be used to check whether __cplusplus (§8.4) is defined and declare an EXTERN_C macro appropriately as shown in listing 13.4. The EXTERN_C macro can then be used on a declaration-by-declaration basis.

```
#ifdef __cplusplus
# define EXTERN_C extern "C"   // compiling with C++
#else
# define EXTERN_C /* nothing */ // compiling with C
#endif /* __cplusplus */

EXTERN_C void string_puts( struct string *str,
                           char const *s );
EXTERN_C void string_cleanup( struct string *str );
```

Listing 13.4: Using extern "C" via a macro

Alternatively, and more commonly because it's simpler, the preprocessor can be used to "wrap" the entire contents of a header file with extern "C" { ... } as shown in listing 13.5.

13.5 Including Headers in a .c File

For a .c file, all the guidelines for including headers in a header file also apply, but with one tweak for including local headers:

- For a given .c file, e.g., color.c, include its matching header, color.h, first.

Why? Two reasons:

```
#ifdef __cplusplus
extern "C" {
#endif /* __cplusplus */

void string_puts( struct string *str, char const *s );
void string_cleanup( struct string *str );

#ifdef __cplusplus
} // extern "C"
#endif /* __cplusplus */
```

Listing 13.5: Using `extern "C" { ... }` conditionally

1. It helps ensure the header is self-sufficient.
2. It ensures the function declarations in a `.h` match their definitions in a `.c` file. Calling functions via mismatched signatures results in undefined behavior (§15).

13.6 Initialization and Clean-Up

If your `.c` file requires that some initialization is done prior to use, you can define an "init" function and document that it must be called first. Similarly, if your `.c` file requires that some cleanup is done prior to normal program termination, you can define a "cleanup" function and document that it be called last.

■ C doesn't have a standard naming convention for such functions, but naming them *module*`_init` and *module*`_cleanup` is what I do for my own programs. □

C does offer a mechanism for registering functions that are called automatically upon normal program termination after `exit` is called via the standard function `atexit` declared in `stdlib.h`:

```
int atexit( void (*function)() );
```

That is, you pass `atexit` a pointer to a function (§6.10) having neither parameters nor a return value. The best place to call `atexit` is from an init function:

```
void colors_init() {
  atexit( &colors_cleanup );
  // ...
```

Any function can call `atexit` to register a cleanup function, but no cleanup function should be registered more than once. The number of times `atexit` may be called is implementation defined, but guaranteed to be at least 32. Upon normal program termination, registered functions are called in reverse order of registration. A registered function can do any necessary cleanup, but if it encounters an unrecoverable error, it *must not* call `exit`; instead, it should call `_Exit`.

C also offers an alternate way to terminate a program via:

[[**noreturn**]] **void** quick_exit(**int** status);

The difference between it and exit is that quick_exit does slightly less cleanup than exit. The intent is to provide a way for a program to exit quickly perhaps in response to a signal (§18.5).

Correspondingly, C offers a way to register functions that are called automatically upon quick_exit being called via the standard function at_quick_exit:

int at_quick_exit(**void** (*function)());

Functions registered with at_quick_exit should perform only the bare minimum of cleanup and do so quickly. The specific differences between it and exit are:

- Functions registered with at_quick_exit are *not* called automatically upon normal program termination; instead, quick_exit must be called explicitly.
- Similarly, functions registered with atexit are *not* called automatically upon calling quick_exit.
- If a cleanup function should be called upon either normal program termination or quick_exit, it can be registered with both atexit and at_quick_exit.

Advice: use atexit by default unless you have a reason to use at_quick_exit.

13.7 Header Example

A complete, self-sufficient wlc_string.h header file for the string structure and associated functions given in §1.9 is shown in listing 13.6. (It's not named simply string.h so it's not confused with the string.h standard header.)

- Lines 1, 2, and 22 comprise the header's include guard (§13.1).
- In order to be self-sufficient, line 4 includes stddef.h, a standard header that defines size_t (among other things) used on line 12.
  It's a good practice to add a comment at the end of a #include line saying what you're including the header *for*. (When a file includes lots of headers, it can be easy to forget.)
- Lines 15–16 declare the functions provided for the string structure.
- Lines 6–8 and 18–20 ensure the functions have C linkage (§13.4) when compiled with a C++ compiler.

The corresponding wlc_string.c file would simply #include it followed by the function definitions:

```
#include "wlc_string.h"
// ... definitions of functions ...
```

```
1  #ifndef wlc_string_H
2  #define wlc_string_H
3
4  #include <stddef.h> /* for size_t */
5
6  #ifdef __cplusplus
7  extern "C" {
8  #endif /* __cplusplus */
9
10 struct string {
11   char   *contents; // pointer to actual contents
12   size_t len;       // length (not including null at end)
13 };
14
15 void string_puts( struct string *str, char const *s );
16 void string_cleanup( struct string *str );
17
18 #ifdef __cplusplus
19 } // extern "C"
20 #endif /* __cplusplus */
21
22 #endif /* wlc_string_H */
```

Listing 13.6: `wlc_string.h` header

13.8 File Organization

Unlike some modern languages, C has no requirements for how files are organized in directories. Small programs typically have all their files in a single directory; medium-sized programs typically have their files organized by type (source files, test files, documentation files, etc.). For example, the files of ad are organized as shown in table 13.1. This organization of files and directories is typical for open-source programs.

Table 13.1: File and directory organization

AUTHORS	Doxyfile	NEWS	configure.ac	man/
COPYING	INSTALL	README.md	lib/	src/
ChangeLog	Makefile.am	bootstrap	m4/	test/

- **AUTHORS**: List of authors and their major contributions.
- **COPYING**: The software license file.
- **ChangeLog**: List of changes to other files by date and author.
- **Doxyfile**: Doxygen (§2.1) configuration file.
- **INSTALL**: Instructions for compiling and installing the program.
- **Makefile.am**: automake[†] (part of Autotools) configuration file.

[†]https://www.gnu.org/software/automake/

- **NEWS**: Description of user-visible changes.
- **README.md**: Description of the program, examples of use, specific compilation or installation instructions, and anything else of interest, i.e., anything the user should read beforehand.
- **bootstrap**: Shell script to "bootstrap" building the program.
- **configure.ac**: autoconf[†] (part of Autotools) configuration file.
- **lib/**: Directory containing source code for 3rd-party libraries the program requires, if any.
- **m4/**: Directory containing automake macros.
- **man/**: Directory containing program documentation (manual pages).
- **src/**: Directory containing source code of the program.
- **test/**: Directory containing test files.

Within src, small to medium-sized programs typically have all their .c and .h files in the same directory; larger programs typically further divide files into subdirectories by "subsystem," where each subsystem focuses on one aspect of the program. For example, a compiler might be broken down into subsystems like: lexer, parser, symtable, codegen, optimizer, and util.

13.9 Build Tools

Unlike some modern languages, C has no official build tools beyond the compiler and linker, specifically tools for building sets of files comprising any non-trivial C program. You *could* always simply do something like:

```
$ cc -o ad *.c          # works, but inefficient
```

that would compile all the .c files and link them into an executable named ad, but that would recompile *all* files needlessly every time you recompiled. If you change some files, you ideally want to recompile those files and *only* those other files that depend on (via #include, §8.6) the ones you changed.

The oldest build tool is Make. To use it, you create a Makefile containing both lists of dependencies (which files depend on which other files) and list of commands needed to build files when the file on which they depend have changed (have a later time-stamp), e.g., how to build a .o file from a .c file.

In addition to Make, there's also Ninja. Both are "low-level" build tools. There are also several "higher-level" build tools like Autotools, CMake, GN, Meson, and others, that are easier to use, cross-platform, have more capabilities, or a combination, that generate one or more of Make, Microsoft Visual Studio C, Ninja, or Xcode files as output. The details of any of the low- or high-level build tools are beyond

---
[†]https://www.gnu.org/software/autoconf/

the scope of this book — entire other books and web sites have been written about them.

Alternatively, you can use an IDE like CLion, Code::Blocks, Eclipse, Microsoft Visual Studio C, Xcode, and others, that handle the building for you.

■ For my own projects (including this book written using LaTeX), I use Autotools as my build tool (to build not only the PDF for the book, but all of the larger C examples to ensure they compile and pass tests so I know they're correct) and `vim` as my editor. But I've been programming a long time, so I'm likely set in my ways. Don't let my choices bias yours. □

13.10 Epilogue

Here are some key points about and some advice for organizing your programs:

- Split your program into "modules" where each specializes in some aspect of your program.
- Use include guards.
- Make all your headers be self sufficient.
- Include your own headers before standard headers.
- If you have mutually dependent headers, use a "types" header to break the dependency cycle.
- Use `extern "C"` if your headers can also be used in a C++ program.
- Consider using opaque types if you need any of their advantages and can live with their disadvantages.
- Consider using `atexit` or `at_quick_exit` for module clean-up.

Chapter 14
Multithreading

Operating systems, with the exception of those for early home computers, are able to run multiple programs, aka, processes, simultaneously. Each process runs independently and concurrently, typically on its own CPU (in multi-CPU systems) and has its own memory space meaning that one process can't access the memory of another (by default). In turn, processes are able to run multiple *threads* concurrently where each thread is typically running a different function (or the same function, but on different data) independently at any given time for improved throughput thus performance.

Every process starts out having only one thread, aka, is *single-threaded*, known as either "thread 1" or the "main thread." Any thread can create or "spawn" new threads at which point the process becomes *multithreaded*. Eventually, after the work threads were doing has completed, they must be *joined* prior to program termination. This is illustrated in figure 14.1.

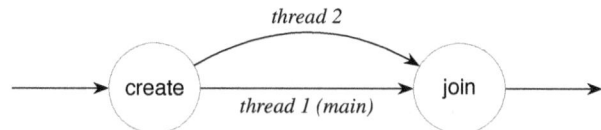

Fig. 14.1: Creating and joining a thread

■ In the late 1960s, early 1970s, programs (running on computers such as the PDP-7 and later the PDP-11) were:

- Single-threaded. (While nascent "threads" appeared in 1966, POSIX threads didn't appear until 1995.)
- Executed sequentially. (That is, machine code instructions generated by compilers were executed one at a time and in the same order as the original statements in your program were written.)
- Running in flat (non-hierarchical) memory. (CPU caches didn't exist until the late 1970s and didn't go mainstream until 1993 with the Intel Pentium.)

While CPU performance was increasing rapidly, memory performance lagged. By as early as the late 1980s, processor performance was already an order of magnitude faster than memory. In order not to have overall performance constrained by memory, CPU designers had to employ mitigation tactics of:

- Memory caching.
- Instruction parallelization.
- Speculative execution.
- Multiple CPUs/cores.

All of these tactics are done entirely by the hardware. You as the programmer have no way either to know or really influence what's going on behind the curtain. Additionally, compiler implementers also employ their own mitigation tactics of:

- Constant folding.
- Copy elision.
- Statement hoisting.
- Instruction scheduling.
- Loop unrolling.
- ... and many more.

The compiler is free to do any optimization so long as it makes no change to the *observable behavior* of your program.

As long as your program has only a single thread, you can remain blissfully unaware of either the hardware or compiler tactics being employed. But once you have multiple threads, you must become acutely aware of what's going on behind the curtain. □

Because different threads are typically running different functions, each may take a different amount of time and so reach the "finish line" in an order that's different than either expected or in different runs of the same program. This is known as a *race condition* that results in undefined behavior (§15).

Unlike processes, all threads share the same memory space. While efficient, one serious pitfall is that a *data race*, a kind of race condition, can occur when multiple threads share the same memory, say of a variable. Mechanisms to prevent data races must be used consistently to prevent subtle bugs that are often hard to reproduce. A variable or function is said to be *thread-safe* only if accessing the variable or calling the function from multiple threads concurrently will not cause a data race.

C supports writing multithreaded programs, specifically by providing mechanisms to create and join threads, and to access data in thread-safe ways.

■ Originally, C didn't support multithreading at all. As mentioned, POSIX threads, aka, *pthreads* ("pea-threads"), didn't appear until 1995 in the form of a library. Pthreads is widely available on any Unix system and even Microsoft Windows ports exist.

Sixteen years after pthreads was introduced, C11 finally added standard library support for threads via the `threads.h` header with the following caveats:

- Threads are an optional feature. If the `__STDC_NO_THREADS__` macro (§8.4) is pre-defined to be 1, then standard threads are *not* supported. Consequently, pthreads is more likely to be supported than standard threads.
- Standard threads offer only a small subset of the functionality provided by pthreads. If your program needs only that subset, then the choice of which threads you use can be a matter of availability or preference. More complex multithreaded programs or those that need wide portability may require pthreads.

Because of its smaller API, this chapter uses standard threads. Entire other books have been written about pthreads.[†] Fortunately, except for one small difference of the standard thread's start function returning `int` whereas pthreads' returns `void*`, the two APIs are otherwise entirely compatible and translated easily from standard to pthreads. □

14.1 Creating and Joining Threads

A small example program that creates and joins a thread is shown in listing 14.1.

```
1  static int print_msg( void *thread_data ) {
2    char const *const msg = thread_data;
3    fputs( msg, stdout );
4    return 0;
5  }
6
7  int main() {
8    thrd_t t;
9    thrd_create( &t, &print_msg, (void*)"hello, world\n" );
10   // ...
11   thrd_join( t, /*pretval=*/nullptr );
12 }
```

Listing 14.1: Creating and joining a thread

- Line 8 declares an object of type `thrd_t`, an opaque type for a "handle" object to a thread.
- Line 9 creates a thread by calling `thrd_create` passing `&t`, where to deposit the thread's handle, `&print_msg`, the address of the *start function* the thread will

---

[†]*Programming with POSIX Threads*, David R. Butenhof, Addison-Wesley, Reading, Massachusetts, 1993.

start execution in, and an optional pointer to arbitrary data passed to the function, here a message to print. The cast is necessary to cast away `const` (§3.14.2) since string literals are `char const*`.

Upon successful return, the thread is created and starts execution *immediately* in the given function.

- Line 11 calls `thrd_join` to join the thread:
  - If the thread's function has already returned, `thrd_join` returns immediately.
  - Otherwise `thrd_join` will wait indefinitely for the function to return.

  `thrd_join` takes an optional `int*` for where to store the return value of the thread's start function.
- Meanwhile, `print_msg` starts executing on line 2 by converting `thread_data` to `char*`, the message to print on line 3.
- Line 4 returns an integer as the thread's return value. Unlike `main` (§9.7), the value 0 has no significance to the operating system. The value is stored at the address given by `thrd_join`'s second argument (if not `nullptr`). When a thread's start function returns, the thread terminates and awaits to be joined (if not detached, §14.2).

Alternatively, you can terminate a thread at any time from any function by calling `thrd_exit` passing an integer for the thread's return value as if it had been returned by the thread's start function.

14.2 Detaching Threads

By default, every thread created *must* be joined. Failure to join threads will result in a "thread leak." Eventually, resources for creating new threads will be exhausted. Alternatively, a thread can be *detached* meaning that when it terminates, its resources will be cleaned-up automatically. A thread can be detached by calling:

    thrd_detach(*thread*);

on *thread* any time after its creation (typically, shortly after) by either the creating thread (as above) or the created thread by doing:

    thrd_detach(thrd_current());

Once a thread has been detached, it can't be joined. Detaching threads has the following caveats:

- It's impossible to get the return value of a thread's start function.
- It's harder to know when the thread has terminated.

And one serious pitfall:

- It's possible for the main thread to terminate (thus terminating the program) out from under the detached thread that may still be running leading to undefined behavior (§15).

While the caveats can be ignored, the pitfall can't. There are other ways for the main thread to wait for detached threads to terminate, but then the threads might as well not have been detached in the first place.

14.3 "Atomic"

When doing multithreaded programming, you'll hear the term *atomic* used. What, exactly, is meant by "atomic" anyway? There are three related, but distinct, meanings:

1. A value operation (read or write) completes with no possible intervening operation by another thread, e.g., writing single-byte values on any CPU, or 16- or 32-bit values on a 32-bit CPU, or 64-bit values on a 64-bit CPU.
2. An updated value is visible to every CPU.
3. Multiple value operations complete with no possible intervening operation by another thread, e.g., updating A and B *together* ("transactional").

"Atomic" always means #1; it usually also means #2; or all three.

14.3.1 A Bad Example

Consider the code shown in listing 14.2 where the main thread creates another. Both threads run so long as shutdown remains false. To shut down, the main thread sets shutdown to true. In response, both while loops will exit and the main thread will join the other thread. Unfortunately, the code is wrong.

■ More unfortunately, I've seen such code in production. □

It's wrong because shutdown is shared among multiple threads improperly. Some programmers mistakenly think along the lines of:

> It's only a bool, a single byte, so of **course** it's thread-safe because you can't read or write **half** a byte, so it must be atomic.

The problem is that, while that's actually true, it's insufficient. A bool is atomic *only* by meaning #1; it's *not* atomic by meaning #2. That is, just because a bool is updated by one thread does *not* mean that updated value is *visible* to other threads (running on other CPUs).

```c
bool shutdown;

static int worker_main( void* ) {
  while ( !shutdown ) {
    // ...
  }
  return 0;
}

int main() {
  thrd_t t;
  thrd_create( &t, &worker_main, nullptr );

  while ( !shutdown ) {
    // ...
    if ( cond-expr )
      shutdown = true;
  }
  thrd_join( t, nullptr );
}
```

Listing 14.2: A bad example

■ Even though all modern CPUs implement cache coherency, registers among CPUs are *not* coherent (by design). Often, values are copied from the cache into a register in order to be operated on, e.g., decremented. Additionally, even a simple statement like `--count` may be compiled into several assembly language instructions. For example, the optimized assembly for ARMv8 looks something like:

```
adrp   x8, count       ; x8 = &count
ldr    w9, [x8]        ; w9 = *x8
sub    w9, w9, #1      ; w9 = w9 - 1
str    w9, [x8]        ; *x8 = w9
```

If another thread updates `count` after the `ldr` (load into register) but before the `str` (store from register) completes, then that value will be overwritten by the `str`. □

■ I've also seen code where programmers knew they had to do something to make such code thread-safe. Unfortunately, that something was:

```c
bool volatile shutdown;   // Thread-safe now?   No!
```

That is, they inserted `volatile` (§22) because they kind-of understand what it does, but not what it's *for*. The use of `volatile` to attempt to make something thread-safe is *always* wrong in C. □

14.4 Mutexes

One thread-safe way to share data among threads is to ensure that all accesses are *mutually exclusive* meaning that only one thread is allowed access at a time — others must wait their turn. A *mutex* (a portmanteau of "mutual exclusion") is an object that is used to coordinate access.

To access shared data, a thread first *locks* a mutex ("holds the lock"), then accesses the data, and finally *unlocks* the mutex. A mutex enables data accesses to be atomic (all meanings). One way to fix the bad example shown in listing 14.2 is by using a mutex as shown in listing 14.3.

```
 1  bool   shutdown;
 2  mtx_t shutdown_mtx;
 3
 4  static bool load_bool_mtx( bool *src, mtx_t *mtx ) {
 5    mtx_lock( mtx );
 6    bool const value = *src;
 7    mtx_unlock( mtx );
 8    return value;
 9  }
10
11  static void store_bool_mtx( bool *dst, bool value,
12                              mtx_t *mtx ) {
13    mtx_lock( mtx );
14    *dst = value;
15    mtx_unlock( mtx );
16  }
17
18  static int worker_thread( void* ) {
19    while ( !load_bool_mtx( &shutdown, &shutdown_mtx ) ) {
20      // ...
21    }
22    return 0;
23  }
24
25  int main() {
26    mtx_init( &shutdown_mtx, mtx_plain );
27    thrd_t t;
28    thrd_create( &t, &worker_thread, nullptr );
29
30    while ( !load_bool_mtx( &shutdown, &shutdown_mtx ) ) {
31      // ...
32      if ( cond-expr )
33        store_bool_mtx( &shutdown, true, &shutdown_mtx );
34    }
35    thrd_join( t, nullptr );
36    mtx_destroy( &shutdown_mtx );
37  }
```

Listing 14.3: The bad example, fixed using a mutex

- Line 2 declares `shutdown_mtx` to be a mutex to *guard* accesses to `shutdown`.
- Line 26 initializes `shutdown_mtx` using the standard function `mtx_init` before its first use. The `mtx_plain` specifies that the mutex is to be of the "plain" type.
- Rather than read `shutdown` directly, lines 19 and 30 call `load_bool_mtx` to read it using `shutdown_mtx`.
- Lines 4–9 declare `load_bool_mtx`, a useful function to read the value of a `bool` guarded by a mutex by first locking it, copying the data, and unlocking it.
- Similarly, rather than assign to `shutdown` directly, line 33 calls `store_bool_mtx` to write it using `shutdown_mtx`.
- Lines 11–16 declare `store_bool_mtx`, a useful function to write the value of a `bool` guarded by a mutex by first locking it, writing the data, and unlocking it.
- Line 36 destroys `shutdown_mtx` using the standard function `mtx_destroy`. All mutexes must be destroyed when no longer needed.

For another way to fix the bad example, see listing 17.2 (p.248).

■ In programs like the one shown in listing 14.3 where only one thread ever writes to a variable like `shutdown` and all other threads only ever read it, the readers block each other unnecessarily because locking a `mtx_t` blocks *all* accesses.

Pthreads has another kind of mutex, a *read-write lock*, where threads can request either a read-only lock that allows any number of threads to read the variable concurrently without blocking each other, or a read-write lock that allows only one thread exclusive access to the variable. In cases where a variable is read frequently but updated infrequently, read-write locks are better. Unfortunately, standard threads don't yet implement read-write locks. □

For another example, thread-safe versions of the `slist` functions from listing 6.3 (p.87) are shown in listing 14.4. The code is virtually the same as before except that calls to `mtx_lock` and `mtx_unlock` were inserted where necessary and almost doesn't need explanation.

- In `slist_push_mtx`, `mtx_lock` was *not* inserted at the very start of the function on line 3 because the code on lines 3–4 can (and should) be done without holding the lock. Line 6 locks the mutex only when absolutely necessary, i.e., when we need to read and update *phead.
- Similarly in `slist_pop_mtx`, `mtx_unlock` was *not* inserted immediately before the last return on line 33 because the code on lines 31–32 can (and should) be done without holding the lock. Line 30 unlocks the mutex as soon as possible, i.e., after *phead has been updated.

You might be wondering why thread-safe versions of the functions are needed at all: why not simply lock a mutex before calling any one of the original functions and unlock it after? While that would work, it wouldn't be as efficient since the locks would be held longer than necessary. By implementing separate thread-safe

14.4 Mutexes

```cpp
void slist_push_mtx( struct slist **phead, void *data,
                     mtx_t *mtx ) {
  struct slist *const new_head =
    malloc( sizeof(struct slist) );
  new_head->data = data;
  mtx_lock( mtx );
  new_head->next = *phead;
  *phead = new_head;
  mtx_unlock( mtx );
}

[[nodiscard]] void* slist_peek_mtx( struct slist *head,
                                    mtx_t *mtx ) {
  mtx_lock( mtx );
  auto *const data = head != nullptr ?
    head->data : nullptr;
  mtx_unlock( mtx );
  return data;
}

[[nodiscard]] void* slist_pop_mtx( struct slist **phead,
                                   mtx_t *mtx ) {
  mtx_lock( mtx );
  auto const head = *phead;
  if ( head == nullptr ) {
    mtx_unlock( mtx );
    return nullptr;
  }
  *phead = head->next;
  mtx_unlock( mtx );
  auto const data = head->data;
  free( head );
  return data;
}
```

Listing 14.4: Thread-safe versions of `slist` functions

functions, we can lock and unlock a mutex at exactly the right points to minimize the time the lock is held.

In general, but especially for high-performance code, keep the following in mind about mutexes:

> *"I've often joked that instead of picking up Dijkstra's cute acronym, we should have called the basic synchronization object "the bottleneck." Bottlenecks are useful at times, sometimes indispensable — but they're never **good**. At best, they're a necessary evil. Anything, **anything** that encourages anyone to overuse them, to hold them too long, is bad."*
> — David R. Butenhof[†]

[†]"Re: recursive mutexes," David R. Butenhof, `comp.programming.threads`, May 17, 2005.

14.4.1 Timed Mutexes

In addition to `mtx_lock`, there's also `mtx_timedlock` that will only wait until a time in the future to lock a mutex. If it can't lock the mutex by then, it'll return `thrd_timeout`. A caveat is that the mutex *must* be initialized with `mtx_timed` that specifies the "timed" type. For example, code to create a timed mutex and try to lock it for at most 10 seconds is shown in listing 14.5.

```
mtx_t mtx;
mtx_init( &mtx, mtx_timed );            // must use mtx_timed
// ...
struct timespec timeout;
timespec_get( &timeout, TIME_UTC );     // get current time
timeout.tv_sec += 10;                   // seconds from now

auto const rv = mtx_timedlock( &mtx, &timeout );
if ( rv == thrd_timeout )
    // ... do something else ...
```

Listing 14.5: Using `mtx_timedlock`

To get the current time, use the standard function `timespec_get` (§B.3).

14.4.2 Deadlocks

A *deadlock* typically occurs when threads need to lock more than one mutex at the same time, but do so in a different order from each other as shown in table 14.1.

Table 14.1: Deadlock

Time	Thread 1	Thread 2
t_1	`mtx_lock( mtx1 );`	`mtx_lock( mtx2 );`
t_2	`mtx_lock( mtx2 );`	`mtx_lock( mtx1 );`

At time t_1, thread 1 locks `mtx1` and thread 2 locks `mtx2`. At time t_2, thread 1 attempts to lock `mtx2`, but it's already been locked by thread 2, so it waits. Meanwhile, thread 2 attempts to lock `mtx1`, but it's already been locked by thread 1, so it waits. The result is that both threads wait forever — deadlock.

Different data guarded by different mutexes won't be a problem if the data are truly independent, i.e., if no code will ever need to access them simultaneously. Where the data are not independent, there are common ways to avoid deadlock:

1. Use a fixed locking order, i.e., *always* lock `mtx1` first and `mtx2` second. Some situations have a natural order, e.g., a thread-safe linked list would have a mutex for the list as a whole and might have a mutex for each element. You'd naturally always lock the list's mutex first followed by an element's mutex. In cases where there's no natural order, you can simply create an arbitrary one.

14.4 Mutexes

2. Use `mtx_lock` for the first mutex and `mtx_trylock` for additional mutexes. Using `mtx_trylock`, attempting to lock a locked mutex will return `thrd_busy`. If any are locked, unlock them all and try again.

For #2, we can write `mtx_lockall` as shown in listing 14.6.

```
int mtx_lockall( size_t n, mtx_t *mtx[n] ) {
  if ( n == 0 )
    return thrd_success;
  int status = thrd_success;
  do {
    if ( mtx_lock( mtx[0] ) == thrd_error )
      break;
    for ( size_t n_lock = 1; n_lock < n; ++n_lock ) {
      status = mtx_trylock( mtx[n_lock] );
      if ( status != thrd_success ) {
        while ( n_lock > 0 ) {
          if ( mtx_unlock( mtx[--n_lock] ) == thrd_error )
            status = thrd_error;
        }
        goto try_again;
      }
    }
    return thrd_success;

try_again:
    thrd_yield();
  } while ( status != thrd_error );
  return thrd_error;
}
```

Listing 14.6: `mtx_lockall` implementation

- Lines 6–7 attempt to lock the first mutex: if an error occurs, abort; if it's locked, simply wait.
- Otherwise, lines 8–17 attempt to lock the remaining mutexes:
  - Line 9 calls `mtx_trylock` instead of `mtx_lock`: if it's anything other than `thrd_success`, unlock all the mutexes we've locked so far and try the whole thing again (unless it's `thrd_error`).
  - If we get to line 18, it means all mutexes were locked without error and we can return `thrd_success`.
- Before trying again, line 21 calls `thrd_yield` to "yield" the CPU to other threads to give them a chance to progress and hopefully unlock mutexes they've locked before we retry.

To make `mtx_lockall` easier to use, we can enlist the help of the preprocessor:

```
#define mtx_lockall(...)                                    \
    mtx_lockall( VA_ARGS_COUNT( __VA_ARGS__ ),               \
                 (mtx_t*[]){ __VA_ARGS__ } )
```

This macro uses the `VA_ARGS_COUNT` macro (p.131) to count the number of variadic arguments (§8.7.3) and constructs a compound array literal (§6.11) of the arguments for the `mtx_lockall` function. The upshot is that `mtx_lockall` can be called with a comma separated list of mutexes:

```
mtx_lockall( &mtx1, &mtx2 );
```

14.4.3 Recursive Mutexes

By default, mutexes initialized with either `mtx_plain` or `mtx_timed` are *not* recursive — meaning if a thread locks a mutex it's already locked, the thread will deadlock. A *recursive mutex* is one that allows it to be locked more than once by the same thread. To create a recursive mutex, bitwise-or `mtx_recursive` into the second argument of `mtx_init`:

```
mtx_init( &m, mtx_plain | mtx_recursive );
```

While recursive mutexes may sound like a good idea even to the point where perhaps you're wondering why mutexes aren't recursive by default, it's not:

> *"The biggest of all the big problems with recursive mutexes is that they encourage you to completely lose track of your locking scheme and scope. This is deadly. Evil. It's the "thread eater." You hold locks for the absolutely shortest possible time. Period. Always. If you're calling something with a lock held simply because you don't know it's held, or because you don't know whether the callee needs the mutex, then you're holding it too long. You're aiming a shotgun at your application and pulling the trigger. You presumably started using threads to get concurrency; but you've just **prevented** concurrency."*
> — David R. Butenhof[†]

14.5 Condition Variables

A typical use for multithreaded programs is a more elaborate version of listing 14.3 (p.221), specifically one thread creating one or more "worker" (aka, "consumer")

[†]"Re: recursive mutexes," David R. Butenhof, `comp.programming.threads`, May 17, 2005.

14.5 Condition Variables

threads to work concurrently. If the work isn't constant, there needs to be a way for the original (aka, "producer") thread to communicate to the consumer threads that new work is available. One way to do this would be for the consumer threads to check a global `work_avail` flag repeatedly as shown in listing 14.7.

```
static int consumer_main( void* ) {
  while ( !load_bool_mtx( &shutdown, &shutdown_mtx ) ) {
    for ( bool work_copy = false; !work_copy;
         thrd_yield() ) {
      mtx_lock( &work_avail_mtx );
      work_copy = work_avail;
      mtx_unlock( &work_avail_mtx );
    }
    // ... do work ...
```

Listing 14.7: Any work?

The problem with this is that all the consumer threads are spiking the CPUs repeatedly checking the flag. This is known as a *spin lock* because the CPU is "spinning its wheels." There are uses for spin locks (§17.3.3), but this isn't one of them. What we want here is a way for the consumer threads to sit idle until work becomes available. This is precisely what *condition variables* are for.

A condition variable allows one or more threads to sit idle waiting for some "condition" to be "signaled." Another thread can then "signal" one or more of the waiting threads and they can proceed. An example is shown in listing 14.8.

```
1  static bool  work_avail;
2  static cnd_t work_avail_cnd;
3  static mtx_t work_avail_mtx;
4
5  static int consumer_main( void* ) {
6    while ( !load_bool_mtx( &shutdown, &shutdown_mtx ) ) {
7      mtx_lock( &work_avail_mtx );
8      while ( !work_avail )
9        cnd_wait( &work_avail_cnd, &work_avail_mtx );
10     work_avail = false;
11     mtx_unlock( &work_avail_mtx );
12     // ... do work ...
13   }
14   return 0;
15 }
```

Listing 14.8: Condition variable example, consumer thread perspective

- Lines 1–3 declare `work_avail` to indicate whether work is available, a mutex to guard it, and a condition variable for waiting for and signaling when work is available.

Though not shown in the listing, condition variables must be initialized and destroyed similarly to a mutex via:

```
cnd_init( &work_avail_cnd );
// ...
cnd_destroy( &work_avail_cnd );
```

- Line 7 locks `work_avail_mtx` first before checking `work_avail` on line 8.
- If there is no work available:
  - Line 9 calls `cnd_wait` that implicitly unlocks the mutex and waits indefinitely for the condition variable to be signaled.
  - When `cnd_wait` returns, it implicitly re-locks the mutex and we loop back to line 8 to check `work_avail` again.
- Otherwise, there is work available and we can proceed.
- Line 10 sets `work_avail` to `false` since this thread will do the current batch of work.
- Line 11 unlocks the mutex to allow the producer thread to signal to the consumer threads that there is more work.

Why does `cnd_wait` unlock the mutex prior to waiting only to re-lock it upon return? Code that signals the conditional variable from the producer thread is shown in listing 14.9.

```
 1  static int producer_main( void* ) {
 2    while ( !load_bool_mtx( &shutdown, &shutdown_mtx ) ) {
 3      // ... prepare work ...
 4      mtx_lock( &work_avail_mtx );
 5      work_avail = true;
 6      cnd_signal( &work_avail_cnd );
 7      mtx_unlock( &work_avail_mtx );
 8    }
 9    return 0;
10  }
```

Listing 14.9: Condition variable example, producer thread perspective

- In order to set `work_avail` to `true` on line 5, the thread *must* hold the lock — which means no consumer thread can hold the lock while waiting. If it did, the result would be a deadlock.
- Line 6 calls `cnd_signal` to signal one of the waiting consumer threads. (Which thread it sends the signal to is arbitrary since it doesn't matter.)
- Line 7 unlocks the mutex so the consumer thread's `cnd_wait` can re-lock it.

In addition to `cnd_signal` that signals one thread arbitrarily, there is also the function `cnd_broadcast` that signals all waiting threads.

Why is line 8 in listing 14.8 a `while` and not an `if`? Two reasons:

1. If `cnd_broadcast` were used, it's possible that by the time a particular consumer thread checks `work_avail`, other threads will have already grabbed all the work and so `work_avail` will be `false`.

2. Due to intricacies in some thread implementations, it's possible that `cnd_wait` can receive a "spurious" signal and wake up even when no work is available.

Hence, you should *always* use `while` when checking a condition.

14.5.1 Timed Condition Variables

In addition to `cnd_wait`, there's also `cnd_timedwait` that will only wait until a time in the future for a condition to be signaled. If the condition hasn't been signaled by then, it'll return `thrd_timeout`. For example, code to wait for at most 10 seconds is shown in listing 14.10.

```
while ( !work_avail ) {
  struct timespec timeout;
  timespec_get( &timeout, TIME_UTC );  // get current time
  timeout.tv_sec += 10;                // seconds from now
  auto const rv = cnd_timedwait( &word_avail_cond,
                                 &work_avail_mtx,
                                 &timeout );
  if ( rv == thrd_timeout )
    // ... do something else ...
```

Listing 14.10: Using `cnd_timedwait`

14.6 Doing Something Once

Occasionally, you need to do some initialization at most once. In a single threaded program, a simple `bool` will work as shown in listing 14.11.

```
struct logger* logger() {
  static struct logger instance;
  static bool init;
  if ( !init ) {
    // ... initialize instance ...
    init = true;
  }
  return &instance;
}
```

Listing 14.11: Initializing once in a single threaded program

In a multithreaded program, you have to guarantee that any thread that calls `logger` either won't initialize `instance` more than once or start to use it before initialization has completed. A simple `bool` (or even an `_Atomic bool`, §17) is insufficient.

One way to fix this is by doing all initialization before spawning any threads. However, sometimes you want to initialize objects only when necessary that may be after spawning them. Another way to fix this is by using `call_once` as shown in listing 14.12.

```
1  static struct logger logger_instance;
2
3  static void logger_init() {
4    // ... initialize logger_instance ...
5  }
6
7  struct logger* logger() {
8    static once_flag init = ONCE_FLAG_INIT;
9    call_once( &init, &logger_init );
10   return &logger_instance;
11 }
```

Listing 14.12: Initializing once in a multithreaded program

- Line 8 declares a variable of type `once_flag` that *must* be initialized with `ONCE_FLAG_INIT`. In order to call a function at most once, the `once_flag` variable used must be the *same* once for that function, hence the use of `static` (§9.9) exactly as for the `bool` in listing 14.11.
- Line 9 calls the standard function `call_once` that takes pointers to the `once_flag` to use and the function to call once.

14.7 `thread_local`

A variable declared `thread_local` has a distinct instance per thread. It can be used only either at file or block scope (§2.4); if used at block scope, it must also explicitly be declared either `extern` (§4.3.2) or `static` (§4.3.3).

Thread-local variables automatically come into existence when a thread is created and cease to exist when a thread terminates. One use for `thread_local` is to have a global variable to communicate error codes like `errno` (§9.6) per thread:

```
thread_local int error_code;
```

Or to keep a linked list of active `try` blocks per thread (listing 27.2, p.352):

```
static thread_local
struct cx_impl_try_block *cx_impl_try_block_head;
```

One caveat is that there's no way to clean up `thread_local` variables automatically when a thread terminates. Hence, dynamically allocated memory pointed to by `thread_local` pointers must be freed explicitly.

14.8 Thread-Specific Storage

An alternative to `thread_local` is thread-specific storage as shown in listing 14.13.

```
1  static tss_t buf_tss;
2
3  static int thread_main( void* ) {
4    tss_set( buf_tss, malloc( 1024 ) );
5    // ...
6    return 0;
7  }
8
9  int main() {
10   // ...
11   if ( tss_create( &buf_tss, &free ) != thrd_success ) {
12     FLFPRINTF( stderr, "tss_create failed\n" );
13     return 0;
14   }
15   // ... create & join threads ...
16   tss_delete( buf_tss );
17 }
```

Listing 14.13: Thread-specific storage example

- Line 1 declares a global variable of type `tss_t`.
- In the main thread, line 11 calls `tss_create` to create a thread-specific storage "key" and store it in `buf_tss`. The key's value is initialized to `nullptr`.
  Optionally, the second argument can be a pointer to a "destructor" function (§6.10) that is called automatically upon thread termination to clean up the pointed-to data. In this case, we simply passed the address of the standard function `free`, though you can pass a pointer to any function that takes a `void*` and returns nothing (`void`).
- Like mutexes and condition variables, thread-specific keys must also be destroyed, hence the call to `tss_delete` on line 16.
- Within the thread's start function (or any function called from the thread's start function), `tss_set` can be called as it is on line 4 to set the value of the thread-specific key's data to point to any data, in this case a 1K buffer.
  Even though all threads share the same key, in this case `buf_tss`, each thread has a distinct pointer to the key's value.

To get the value of thread-specific data, call `tss_get`, for example:

```
char *const buf = tss_get( buf_tss );
```

The value returned is specific to the thread that called it.

14.9 Epilogue

Here are some key points about and some advice for multithreading:

- Always join every thread you create. Don't detach threads.
- Even single-byte types like `bool` are *not* atomic in the sense that matters.
- Even simple operations like increment or decrement are *not* atomic in any sense. The compiler may generate several assembly language instructions for even a trivial C statement that, together, are *not* atomic.
- Do *not* think for one second that `volatile` has anything to do with thread-safety.
- To make accessing variables thread-safe, use mutexes.
- Always lock a mutex only for the shortest time possible.
- To avoid a deadlock, don't lock more than one mutex at a time on the same thread. But if you must, always lock them in the same order and unlock them in the reverse order.
- Even if available, don't use recursive mutexes.
- Use condition variables to communicate among threads.
- Always uses a `while` when checking a condition.
- If you need to do something exactly once, use `call_once`.
- If you need to have different data per thread, use `thread_local`. If you need that data automatically cleaned-up, use thread-specific storage.

Exercises

1. Write a function:

    ```
    int mtx_unlockall( size_t n, mtx_t *mtx[n] );
    ```

    that's the opposite of `mtx_lockall` from listing 14.6 (p. 225), i.e., it unlocks all the mutexes in the `mtx` array and returns `thrd_success` only if all mutexes were unlocked successfully or `thrd_error` if one or more mutexes could not be unlocked.

2. Since `mtx_timedlock` requires an absolute time, write a function:

    ```
    int mtx_durtimedlock( mtx_t *mtx,
                          struct timespec const *duration );
    ```

    that takes a duration and returns the same values as `mtx_timedlock`.

Part II
Selected Topics

Part II covers several additional advanced or obscure parts of C that aren't explained well elsewhere, if at all:

15. **Undefined Behavior**: Covers what undefined behavior is, why it exists, and how optimization can make it worse.
16. **Assertions**: Covers the `assert` macro for aiding in writing bug-free programs, a sample implementation, assertions vs. errors and exceptions, use in production code, adding a message, and `static_assert`.
17. **`_Atomic`**: Covers the `_Atomic` keyword as an alternative to a mutex, atomic library functions, memory barriers, compare-and-swap, lock-free operations, the "ABA Problem," versioned pointers, and false sharing.
18. **Debugging**: Covers debugging programs, printing values, how optimization affects debugging, core dumps, signals, common bugs, warnings, profiling, and a case study of a particularly bizarre bug and how it was fixed.
19. **`_Generic`**: Covers the `_Generic` keyword, its motivation, using it to do `const` overloading, static `if`, and implement type traits.
20. **`setjmp` and `longjmp`**: Covers the `setjmp` and `longjmp` standard functions for doing non-local `goto`s and their relationship to `volatile` variables.
21. **`restrict`**: Covers the `restrict` keyword, the problem it solves, pitfalls, and when to use it.
22. **`volatile`**: Covers the `volatile` keyword, optimization suppression, signal handling, use with `setjmp`, and wrong uses.

Chapter 15
Undefined Behavior

Prior to the first C standard in 1989, there were two "flavors" of C:

- **Unportable C**: a step up from assembly language used to program operating systems using any technique that worked for the particular hardware.
- **Semi-portable C**: use of `#ifdef` (§8.5) made many programs "semi-portable" so they'd compile and run the same on all the hardware and operating systems considered.

As C's popularity grew, it was becoming clear that a standard was needed. While K&R was *the* definitive description of C for over a decade, it was insufficiently precise to be a standard. For a standard, you ideally want it to specify precisely what happens in every circumstance for every aspect of a language.

However, by the mid-1980s, there were many unportable and semi-portable programs that *worked*. The problem was that doing X on computer 1 with compiler 1 yielded result R_1 whereas doing X on computer 2 with compiler 2 yielded result R_2 and their respective programs *relied* on those results. A standard would ordinarily have to mandate that only one of either result R_1 or R_2 was correct. Updated standard-conforming compilers would have broken many programs.

To not do this, the concepts of *implementation defined behavior*, *unspecified behavior*, and *undefined behavior* were invented as part of the standard to serve as "escape hatches" to allow many working programs to continue to work with standard-conforming compilers. While this may not seem completely satisfying, definitively stating that X is one of implementation defined, unspecified, or undefined is an improvement over stating nothing at all about X.

The differences between the three somewhat related "bad" behaviors in C are explained in the *comp.lang.c FAQ*, question 11.33:[†]

- **Implementation defined behavior**: The implementation *must* pick some behavior, it *must* be consistent, and it *must* be documented.

[†] *comp.lang.c Frequently Asked Questions*, Steve Summit, Jan. 1995, https://c-faq.com/ansi/undef.html

- **Unspecified behavior**: Like implementation defined, except it need not be documented.
- **Undefined behavior**: *Anything at all can happen.* The program may execute incorrectly (either crash or silently generate incorrect results), or it may fortuitously do exactly what the programmer intended.

An example of unspecified behavior is:

```
new_offset = ftell( f ) + fread( buf, 1, n, f );
```

■ This is unspecified behavior because, as mentioned in §3.1, the order in which the operands of + are evaluated (left, then right; or right, then left) is not specified by the C standard. □

While implementation defined and unspecified behaviors are bad, at least they're consistent for the same expression (using the same platform, compiler, and compiler options). Undefined behavior is *worse* in that:

- Different runs of the same executable can produce different results!
- The same run of an executable can produce different results at different times!

C lists hundreds of things that result in undefined behavior. Examples of the common ones, most of which have been mentioned in this book, include:

- Signed integer overflow and underflow (§2.11).
- Object is referred to outside of its lifetime.
- Dereferencing a pointer to an object that no longer exists (§6.11.1).
- Reading from an uninitialized object (§18.6.8).
- Addition and subtraction of pointers of unrelated arrays.
- Indexing beyond the end of an array (§18.6.1).
- Modifying a `const` object (§3.14.2).
- Data races (§14).
- Anything not explicitly listed as one of defined behavior, implementation defined behavior, or unspecified behavior is undefined behavior!

15.1 Implications and Example

But what are the implications of undefined behavior? The compiler is allowed to assume undefined behavior *never* happens, hence all programs are valid. This allows the compiler to generate very efficient code, especially in tight loops. (This is the *only* good thing about undefined behavior.)

15.2 Two Parts to Undefined Behavior

A simple example that can result in undefined behavior is:

```
bool no_overflow( int x ) {
  return x+1 > x;
}
```

■ Normally, you'd never write silly code like this; but such code can sometimes happen from macro expansion, so the compiler should do a good job of optimizing it. □

The compiler will unsurprisingly create the following optimized x86–64 assembly:

```
no_overflow:
    mov    eax, 1    ; return true
    ret
```

because x+1 is *always* > x — or it is in pure math. But computer math has limited precision, so there are two possible cases:

1. `x != INT_MAX`: Behavior of + is well-defined; must return `true`.
2. `x == INT_MAX`: Behavior of + is undefined; can do anything.

The compiler is allowed to assume that case 2 never happens. Why? Because the only reason for considering that case would be if the compiler could check for and do something about it such as rewrite the code as if it were:

```
return x != INT_MAX && x+1 > x; // compiler doesn't do this
```

But that would be inserting a check you didn't ask for; and it would be less efficient for the majority of cases. Programmers write in C typically for performance, so inserting such code would be antithetical.

15.2 Two Parts to Undefined Behavior

There are actually two parts to undefined behavior:

1. Actually performing undefined behavior at run-time; examples:
   - Dereferencing a null pointer.
   - Indexing beyond the end of an array.
2. The compiler being allowed to assume undefined behavior never happens (a false premise) allows it to generate sometimes surprising code. In logic, if you accept a false premise, you can draw any conclusion. For example:
   - If the streets are wet, it has rained recently. (False premise.)
   - The streets are wet.

- Therefore, it has rained recently. (Conclusion: logically valid, but wrong.)

It's the second part that causes the most surprise. For another example, consider the code in listing 15.1.

```
extern int table[4];

bool exists_in_table( int v ) {
  for ( int i = 0; i <= 4; ++i ) {
    if ( table[i] == v )
      return true;
  }
  return false;
}
```

Listing 15.1: Undefined behavior example

The compiler will surprisingly generate the following optimized x86–64 assembly:

```
exists_in_table:
  mov    eax, 1    ; return true
  ret
```

How is that possible? Where did the `for` loop and `if` go? The problem stems from the fact that the code has a bug. (Did you notice it?) The bug is `i <= 4` *should* be `i < 4`. Even so, how does the compiler generate `return true`? The "rationale" is:

1. The first four times through the loop, the function might return `true`.
2. If `i` were `4`, the code would perform undefined behavior (by attempting to access an element beyond the end of the array).
3. The compiler is allowed to assume undefined behavior never happens (all programs are valid); therefore:
   - The variable `i` can "never" be `4`. (False premise.)
   - Implies we *must* have found a match when `i < 4`.
   - Therefore, we can always return `true`. (Conclusion: logically valid, but wrong.)

This is *not* a compiler bug. Given the choice between assuming the programmer wrote a valid program versus an invalid program, we've told the compiler to choose the former — and it optimizes accordingly.

15.3 Optimization Can Make Things Worse

Consider the function in listing 15.2. Line 2 is dead code. (Presumably, the function used to do something with `old_v`, but the code was rewritten and this line was left in by mistake. These kinds of things happen in the real world.) You'd think such

15.4 Undefined Behavior in Other Languages

```
void assign_not_null( int *p, int v ) {
  int old_v = *p;
  if ( p == nullptr )
    return;
  *p = v;
}
```

Listing 15.2: Optimization example, unoptimized

---

dead code would be harmless, but, depending on what optimizations the compiler performs — and in what order — this can cause undefined behavior.

Assume there are at least two optimizations that the compiler performs:

1. **Dead Code Elimination**: code that isn't used is eliminated.
2. **Redundant Null Check Elimination**: if the compiler can deduce that a given pointer can't possibly be null on a given line, it eliminates the `if` check for null.

Assume the compiler does the optimizations in the above order. It therefore would:

1. Eliminate line 2 because `old_v` is not used.
2. Do nothing else since the `if` on line 3 is a necessary check before the `*p = v` on line 4 and so can't be eliminated.

So far, so good. But what if the compiler does the optimizations in the reverse order? It then instead would:

1. Knowing that dereferencing a null pointer is undefined behavior and being allowed to assume that undefined behavior never happens, it means that:
    - If the code gets to the `if`, the `*p` on the previous line *must* have succeeded.
    - That means `p` is never null.
    - Therefore, the null check is unnecessary and so the `if` can be eliminated.
2. Now it performs dead code elimination and eliminates line 2.

The resulting code would be as shown in listing 15.3. It's logically valid, but *wrong*.

```
void assign_not_null( int *p, int v ) {
  *p = v;
}
```

Listing 15.3: Optimization example, optimized

15.4 Undefined Behavior in Other Languages

At this point, you might be wondering whether undefined behavior exists in other languages. Other than C++ that inherits all of C's undefined behavior (and adds some of its own), the answer is generally "no" — with two exceptions:

1. If a language provides a mechanism to perform "unsafe" operations, those typically can perform undefined behavior.
2. Data races (§14) are *always* undefined behavior.

   ■ Ada has a similar, but weaker concept of *bounded errors*. □

But for languages with always-defined behavior, the price paid is in performance:

- Always initializing variables.
- Always checking array indices.
- Garbage collection.
- Etc.

15.5 Epilogue

Here are some key points about and some advice for undefined behavior:

- The concepts of implementation defined, unspecified, and undefined behavior, were a way to standardize C without breaking existing programs.
- Undefined behavior means *anything is possible*.
- The compiler is allowed to assume that undefined behavior never happens. This allows the compiler to generate very efficient, but sometimes surprising code.
- Optimization can make the consequences of undefined behavior worse.

   ■ To drive home that undefined behavior means *anything is possible*, John Woods posted the following in the Usenet newsgroup comp.lang.c:

   ```
   From: John F. Woods
   Newsgroups: comp.lang.c
   Date: Feb 25, 1992, 11:51:52 AM

   > * Undefined behavior -- behavior, upon use of a
   > nonportable or erroneous program construct, ... for
   > which the standard imposes no requirements.  Permissible
   > undefined behavior ranges from ignoring the situation
   > completely with unpredictable results, to having demons
   > fly out of your nose.

   In short, you can't use sizeof() on a structure whose
   elements haven't been defined, and if you do, demons may
   fly out of your nose.

   OK, OK; so the Standard doesn't *ACTUALLY* mention demons
   or noses. Not as such, anyway.
   ```

   Someone else followed up coining the term "nasal demons" that stuck. □

Chapter 16
Assertions

The `assert` macro, part of the C standard library defined in `assert.h`, has been around since the early days of C as a mechanism to aid in writing less buggy code. It allows you to "assert" that some condition *must* be true in order to continue. If not, the program will print an error message (including the assertion that was violated and the source file and line of the `assert`), calls the standard function `abort` that terminates the program, and typically provides a core dump (§18.4) as a debugging aid. Conditions include preconditions, postconditions, and invariants for implementing design by contract.

16.1 Sample Implementation

To demystify `assert`, a basic implementation is shown in listing 16.1.

```
 1  #ifndef NDEBUG
 2  # define assert(EXPR) (                                  \
 3      (EXPR) ? (void)0 : (                                 \
 4        printf( "%s:%d: failed assertion '%s'\n",          \
 5          __FILE__, __LINE__, #EXPR                        \
 6        ),                                                 \
 7        abort()                                            \
 8      ))
 9  #else
10  # define assert(EXPR)    ((void)0)
11  #endif /* NDEBUG */
```

Listing 16.1: Sample `assert` implementation

- The first thing to notice on line 1 is that `assert` is defined only if the macro NDEBUG is *not* defined. The consequence is that if you include `assert.h` and do nothing else, assertions will be enabled, that is they will actually assert what you are asserting.

But if you define NDEBUG (the value doesn't matter), then assert is defined to a do-nothing expression and assertions will be disabled ("No Debug"), that is they will not do anything at all. You *might* want to do this for production code (§16.3).

- Line 3 tests EXPR:
  - If true (non-zero), the result is simply 0. (The (void) discards the value.)
  - If false, an error message is printed containing the file and line (§8.4) of the assert plus the stringified (§8.7.4) EXPR.
- Line 6 uses the comma operator (§3.15) as a trick to cram both the printf and abort statements into a single expression.

While this sample implementation uses a macro, any implementation invariably will since it needs to obtain the file and line number of the assert as well as the stringification of the expression — things only the preprocessor can give. While some implementations use a function to call printf and abort instead, they call a function only if the check fails; the check itself needs to be fast via inlining.

16.2 Assertions vs. Errors and Exceptions

Errors, exceptions, and assertions are related in that they're all used to catch and report an invalid state; but they're for different purposes:

- Errors are for conceivable invalid states, but there may be a way to recover and continue.
- Exceptions are for errors that are "exceptional" (in the "unlikely" sense, not in the "outstanding" sense), but there still may be a way to recover and continue.

In C++ having exceptions, the line between errors and exceptions can sometimes get blurry. For example, if you attempt to open a file that doesn't exist, should that be an error or exception? It's debatable. (Since C doesn't have exceptions, that debate can be deferred to another time.)

Assertions, however, are only for inconceivable[†] states that should "never" happen — but if one does anyway, it means there's a bug and either:

1. While there may be a way to recover and continue, it's better to crash and produce a core dump (§18.4) as an aid to debug and fix the bug; or:
2. There's no way to recover, so you have no choice but to crash.

Case 2 typically happens in a function that's at the bottom of the call stack and there's no way to report the error, to return the error all the way up the call stack (but see

---

[†] Wallace Shawn (*Vizzini*), *The Princess Bride*, Rob Reiner (director), Act III Communications and Buttercup Films, Sep. 25, 1987.

§20), or, even if you could, the caller wouldn't know how to handle the error. In such a case, it's better to crash in a controlled way rather than have the program limp along possibly doing irreparable damage, e.g., overwriting data in a file with garbage, before possibly crashing anyway and possibly far from where the assertion was violated making debugging harder.

A simple example of using `assert` to ensure we don't write beyond the end of an array (§18.6.1) used to implement a fixed-size stack is shown in listing 16.2.

```
static unsigned lineno_stack[64];
static int      lineno_stack_top = -1;

void lineno_stack_push( unsigned lineno ) {
  ++lineno_stack_top;
  assert( lineno_stack_top < ARRAY_SIZE( lineno_stack ) );
  lineno_stack[ lineno_stack_top ] = lineno;
}
```

Listing 16.2: Example use of `assert`

16.3 Disabling Assertions in Production Code

As mentioned, if NDEBUG is defined, then assertions are *disabled* — and you might want to do this for production code. The arguments for disabling assertions include:

1. They take a small, but non-zero amount of time to perform the checks that can add up, especially in hot code.
2. Assertion failures are typically caught by unit tests.
3. Having your program crash generally results in unhappy customers.
4. An attacker has found a way to put your program into an invalid state failing an assertion and causing it to crash that can result in a denial-of-service attack.

The arguments against disabling assertions include:

1. Since the time to perform the checks is small, it's likely small enough to be negligible. The way to know for sure is to profile your program (§18.9). If your `assert` checks are inconsequential, then you can leave them enabled.
2. While assertion failures are typically caught by unit tests, passing a test suite can never prove that no bugs exist, so better to leave assertions enabled to detect invalid states.
3. Having your program not crash but yield incorrect results (that customers may not even realize are incorrect) or cause lasting damage also generally results in unhappy customers and can be even worse for your reputation.
4. You should *never* use assertions to validate any input anyway (§16.6).

■ Personally, I think assertions should be left enabled. If you want to disable assertions only in hot code, you can use `assert` there and define NDEBUG, but then define your own macro similar to the sample implementation in listing 16.1 (p.241) that is unaffected by NDEBUG and use it everywhere else:

```
#define always_assert(EXPR)    /* ... */
```

Still: disabling any assertions means you're running a higher risk of uncaught bugs and possibly damage to both data and your reputation. □

16.4 Adding a Message

Sometimes you might want to include an additional string in the error message produced by assert. Unfortunately the assert macro can not optionally take a string to add to the error message, but there is a commonly used trick to work around this:

```
assert( (expr) && "message" );
```

That is put the message after a && operator (§3.6): the string literal decays into a char* that is not nullptr, hence is always true thus will be discarded (in terms of the value of the expression, but still included in the error message) and the result will be the value of *expr*.

16.5 Static Assertions

In addition to assert that performs checks at run-time, there is also static_assert that performs checks at compile-time. Unlike assert that's a macro, static_assert is a keyword. It has two forms where *expr* must be a constant expression and *message* must be a string literal since it's evaluated at compile-time:

```
static_assert(expr)             Asserts that expr is true.
static_assert(expr,message)     Same, but prints message if expr is false.
```

A static_assert is legal anywhere a declaration is. Use static_assert to:

- Ensure assumptions about the platform your program requires are actually true, for example, that pointers are 64 bits if your program doesn't support 32-bit platforms:

```
static_assert( sizeof(void*) == 8,
               "64-bit pointers required" );
```

- Ensure offsets of structure members are what your program requires. See listing 11.11 (p.176) for an example.

- Ensure macro arguments are of a specific type. See listing 19.11 (p.291) for an example.

Being able to use `static_assert` in an expression would also be useful. To do so, the trick is to realize that `static_assert` can be used inside a structure declaration that's an argument to `sizeof` that makes the whole thing an expression:

```
#define STATIC_ASSERT_EXPR(EXPR,MSG) \
  (!!sizeof(struct { static_assert((EXPR), MSG); int i; }))
```

If EXPR is true, `sizeof` will return non-zero that `!!` (§3.6) will convert to 1; if EXPR is false, then you'll get a compile-time error that the assertion failed. (The `int` is there only so the structure isn't empty.)

16.6 Epilogue

Here are some key points about and some advice for assertions:

- Use `assert` to check for invalid conditions and abort your program in a controlled way.
- Ensure that assertions do not cause side-effects:

    ```
    assert( --count > 0 );              // No!
    ```

    Why not? Because if assertions are disabled, the statement doesn't happen at all. In some cases, you might need to add a variable only to assert on:

    ```
    bool const colors_ok = colors_parse();
    assert( colors_ok );
    ```

    Doing so, however, can cause "unused variable" warnings when assertions are disabled. To fix that, add the `maybe_unused` attribute (§4.9.3):

    ```
    [[maybe_unused]] bool const colors_ok = colors_parse();
    assert( colors_ok );
    ```

- Do *not* use assertions to validate input from a human (e.g., via keyboard), machine (e.g., via socket), or file — even trusted humans, machines, or files. Your program should not crash because a human made a typo or you received or read corrupted or otherwise unexpected data.
- In `assert` conditions, you should not use `&&` to conjoin unrelated expressions:

    ```
    assert( n > 0 && n < N_MAX );        // OK
    assert( n > 0 && p != nullptr );     // Meh
    ```

Why not? Because for the second `assert`, you won't know which assertion failed: was $n \leq 0$ or p `== nullptr`? Separate assertions should be used instead:

```
assert( n > 0 );                    // Better
assert( p != nullptr );
```

- To include a message in an assertion, use the `&&` *"message"* trick.
- Keep assertions enabled in production code.
- Use `static_assert` to check for required conditions at compile-time.

Chapter 17
`_Atomic`

C has the `_Atomic` keyword that has two forms:

    `_Atomic` *type*   Atomic qualifier.
    `_Atomic(`*type*`)`   Atomic specifier.

The qualifier form can be included in a declaration of any type (except arrays and functions) and may be used like any other qualifier of `const` (§4.5), `volatile` (§22), or `restrict` (§21). Listing 17.1 shows some example declarations.

```
_Atomic int ai;              // atomic int
int _Atomic ia;              // same

int _Atomic *pai;            // pointer to atomic int
int *_Atomic api;            // atomic pointer to normal int
int _Atomic *_Atomic apai;   // atomic pointer to atomic int

int _Atomic const *pcai;     // pointer to const atomic int
// ...
```

Listing 17.1: Example `_Atomic` declarations

The specifier form is for compatibility with C++23 that defines the following macro in the `stdatomic.h` standard header:

```
#if __cplusplus >= 202302L   // C++23 or later?
# define _Atomic(T)          std::atomic<T>
#endif
```

In either form, an `_Atomic` variable is "atomic" in meanings #1 and #2 (§14.3), specifically the increment and decrement operators (§3.4) as well as the assignment operators (§3.9) that work on an object of type `T` will also work on an object of type `_Atomic T` except do so atomically. Other differences are that the size, alignment, or both for `_Atomic T` may be different than for `T`.

Even though _Atomic may be applied to structure (§10) and union (§11) types, it's not useful since accessing a member of either results in undefined behavior (§15).

The _Atomic keyword and the stdatomic.h standard header are supported only if the __STDC_NO_ATOMICS__ macro is *not* predefined (§8.4).

17.1 Alternative to a Mutex

Another way to fix the bad example shown in listing 14.2 (p. 220) is by using an _Atomic variable as shown in listing 17.2.

```
 1  bool _Atomic shutdown;   // Thread-safe now?  Yes!
 2
 3  static int worker_thread( void* ) {
 4    while ( !shutdown ) {
 5      // ...
 6    }
 7    return 0;
 8  }
 9
10  int main() {
11    thrd_t t;
12    thrd_create( &t, &worker_thread, nullptr );
13
14    while ( !shutdown ) {
15      // ...
16      if ( cond-expr )
17        shutdown = true;
18    }
19    thrd_join( t, nullptr );
20  }
```

Listing 17.2: The bad example, fixed using _Atomic

This version is almost exactly the same as the bad example except for the addition of _Atomic. This version is a much simpler fix than the one using a mutex shown in listing 14.3 (p. 221).

In general, when sharing independent variables among threads, _Atomic is not only simpler, but more efficient than locking, unlocking, and potentially waiting for a mutex. If you need to be "atomic" in meaning #3 ("transactional," §14.3), e.g., you need to read or write more than one variable atomically, then you need a mutex.

17.2 Atomic Functions

The following functions are _Generic (§19) in that they accept any _Atomic-qualified object of type A, e.g., _Atomic int; T is the non-_Atomic version of A,

17.2 Atomic Functions

e.g., `int`. Functions that are not named with `_explicit` use the memory-order-seq-cst memory order (§17.3.1); functions with `_explicit` use the given memory order. (Memory orders are covered in the next section; `volatile` is covered in §22. The `volatile` is part of the functions' signatures only so they will also work with `volatile` variables. You can safely ignore it here.)

```
T atomic_load(A const volatile *pv);
T atomic_load_explicit(A const volatile *pv, memory_order m);
```
Atomically loads and returns the value of `*pv`.
```
void atomic_store(A volatile *pv, T new);
void atomic_store_explicit(A volatile *pv, T new,
                           memory_order m);
```
Atomically stores `new` into `*pv`.
```
T atomic_exchange(A volatile *pv, T new);
T atomic_exchange_explicit(A volatile *pv, T new,
                           memory_order m);
```
Atomically stores `new` into `*pv` and returns its old value.
```
T atomic_fetch_add(A volatile *pv, T arg)
T atomic_fetch_add_explicit(A volatile *pv,
                            T arg, memory_order m);
```
Atomically adds `arg` to `*pv` and returns its old value.
```
T atomic_fetch_sub(A volatile *pv, T arg)
T atomic_fetch_sub_explicit(A volatile *pv, T arg,
                            memory_order m);
```
Atomically subtracts `arg` from `*pv` and returns its old value.
```
T atomic_fetch_and(A volatile *pv, T arg)
T atomic_fetch_and_explicit(A volatile *pv, T arg,
                            memory_order m);
```
Atomically bitwise-ands `arg` with `*pv` and returns its old value.
```
T atomic_fetch_or(A volatile *pv, T arg)
T atomic_fetch_or_explicit(A volatile *pv, T arg,
                           memory_order m);
```
Atomically bitwise-ors `arg` with `*pv` and returns its old value.
```
T atomic_fetch_xor(A volatile *pv, T arg)
T atomic_fetch_xor_explicit(A volatile *pv, T arg,
                            memory_order m);
```
Atomically bitwise-exclusive-ors `arg` with `*pv` and returns its old value.

Functions that are not named with `_explicit` are equivalent to their operator counterparts, e.g.:

```
atomic_fetch_add( &v, 1 );   // equivalent to: v++
```

except the old value of `v` is returned instead of the new value.

■ While using the normal C operators instead of the verbose functions might be convenient, I always use the functions to make it obvious that the variable being manipulated is `_Atomic`. □

17.3 Memory Barriers

Atomic (by any meaning) is *not* enough to ensure thread-safety because the order of memory operations does not necessarily match the order of statements in a program. Why not? Because the hardware, the compiler, or both, may reorder memory operations to improve performance. Not making a change to the observable behavior (§14) applies only from the perspective of a single thread.

Memory barriers (aka, "memory fences") help ensure thread-safety by selectively prohibiting reordering of memory operations across the barrier. They also provide some synchronization among threads. C provides the `memory_order` enumeration containing six memory order values explained in the following sections.

The sometimes confusing thing about memory barriers is that they're about controlling the order of operations relative to each other, *not* the operations themselves.

17.3.1 `memory_order_seq_cst`

Sequential consistency is the safest memory order which is why it's the default. It's also the least performant because it establishes a global constraint (bottleneck) of memory ordering across all threads. In specific cases, the constraint can be relaxed to make the code be more performant.

■ Writing thread-safe code even with ordinary mutexes is hard to get right, even for experts. Writing thread-safe code using atomics with memory orders other than sequential consistency is even harder! Before considering them, you should:

- Remember that using efficient algorithms matters far more than locking technique. For example, an $n\ lg(n)$ algorithm with slower mutexes will still very likely be more performant than an n^2 algorithm using `_Atomic`.
- Profile your code (§18.9) to see if it's spending too much time either locking or waiting for locks. (Remember: results are CPU-dependent!)
- Only if locking and waiting for those locks takes a significant percentage of time, then consider the following techniques.

Bugs caused by improper use of memory ordering are hard to reproduce and hard to debug. □

17.3.2 `memory_order_relaxed`

Relaxed is the most basic and least safe memory order in that it does not guarantee operation order or synchronization, but still guarantees modification order. For example, given the following ordinary code running in a single thread where x = y = 0 to start:

```
int r = y;           // r = 0
x = r;               // x = 0
int s = x;           // s = 0
y = 4;               // y = 4
```

then r = s = 0 and y = 4 — no surprises there. However, doing the same thing running in two threads using relaxed:

```
// thread 1
r = atomic_load_explicit( &y, memory_order_relaxed );  // 1A
atomic_store_explicit( &x, r, memory_order_relaxed );  // 1B
// thread 2
s = atomic_load_explicit( &x, memory_order_relaxed );  // 2A
atomic_store_explicit( &y, 4, memory_order_relaxed );  // 2B
```

can result in y = r = x = s = 4 because, even though the statement order in thread 1 is 1A, 1B, and in thread 2 is 2A, 2B, it's possible that the *memory order* is 2B, 1A, 1B, 2A. What good is that? For *independent* variables, eliminating the global constraint (bottleneck) of memory ordering improves performance. A practical use for relaxed is incrementing reference counts.

Suppose we want to implement a reference-counted shared object such that when the last pointer to the object goes away, the object is automatically freed. Types for this are shown in listing 17.3.

```
1  struct shrd_obj;
2  typedef void (*shrd_free_fn)( struct shrd_obj* );
3
4  struct shrd_obj {
5    size_t _Atomic            ref_cnt;
6    shrd_free_fn              free_fn;
7    alignas(max_align_t) char data[];
8  };
```

Listing 17.3: Shared object types

- Line 1 simply forward-declares `shrd_obj` so that it can be used to declare `shrd_free_fn` on line 2, a function to call to free the object when the reference count gets decremented to zero.
- Lines 4–8 declare `shrd_obj` that contains `ref_cnt`, an `_Atomic` reference count, `free_fn`, and `data` as a flexible array member (§10.6) for the object as was done for `islist` in listing 10.9 (p.163).

To create a new `shrd_obj`, the function `shrd_new` is shown in listing 17.4.

```
1  struct shrd_obj* shrd_new( size_t data_size,
2                             shrd_free_fn free_fn ) {
3    struct shrd_obj *const so =
4      malloc( sizeof(struct shrd_obj) + data_size );
5    atomic_init( &so->ref_cnt, 1 );
6    so->free_fn = free_fn;
7    return so;
8  }
```

Listing 17.4: Shared object creation

- Lines 1–2 declare the function to take the size of the data to allocate additional space for and an optional `shrd_free_fn` to clean up the object when the reference count falls to zero.
- `_Atomic` objects at either file or block scope (§2.4), can be initialized by ordinary assignment; `_Atomic` objects that are dynamically allocated *must* be initialized via the standard function `atomic_init` as is done on line 5.

We can now implement incrementing the reference count as shown in listing 17.5.

```
inline struct shrd_obj* shrd_inc( struct shrd_obj *so ) {
  atomic_fetch_add_explicit( &so->ref_cnt, 1,
                             memory_order_relaxed );
  return so;
}
```

Listing 17.5: Shared object reference count increment

At this point, you might ask something along the lines of:

If there's no synchronization, how can this possibly work? Couldn't thread 1 increment the value from n to $n+1$ and thread 2 also increment the value from n to $n+1$?

The answer is "no" for two reasons:

1. Each increment is *still* atomic (by meanings #1 and #2) so each thread always sees the latest value. What relaxed does is allow the hardware to reorder *other* operations having nothing to do with `ref_cnt` either before or after its increment to improve overall performance, not the performance of `ref_cnt` specifically.
2. When updating the value and *not* using it in an expression, then use of relaxed is safe. For example, using the value in an expression for an `if` is *not* safe.

An example of when relaxed is *not* safe is when decrementing reference counts (§17.3.5).

Now that you hopefully understand relaxed you should *never* use it — unless you can *prove* your use of it is correct and it actually significantly improves performance via profiling (§18.9). Use of relaxed in the general case is hard to get right.

17.3.3 `memory_order_acquire` and `memory_order_release`

Acquire and release memory orders are safer than relaxed and are typically used in pairs:

- **Release** (used with `_store`) is used to "publish" information: no memory accesses can be reordered after.
- **Acquire** (used with `_load`) is used to "subscribe" to information: no memory accesses can be reordered before.

For example, given the following declarations:

```
struct islist *work_list; // listing 10.9, p. 163
bool _Atomic  work_avail;
```

a producer thread can prepare work by doing, say:

```
work_list = islist_push( work_list, sizeof(char*) );
*(char**)islist_peek( work_list ) = path;
atomic_store_explicit( &work_avail, true,
                       memory_order_release );
```

The shared data (`work_list`) neither needs to be `_Atomic` nor guarded by a mutex. This is particularly useful for data that can't be made `_Atomic` and for functions that can't be retrofitted to use a mutex. You can also prepare any amount of data, then "publish" all of it simultaneously. What the "no memory accesses can be reordered after" means is that no memory accesses done before the release in your code can be reordered after it by the hardware, i.e., you won't signal that data is ready before it actually is.

Meanwhile, a consumer thread can wait for and receive work by doing:

```
while ( !atomic_load_explicit( &work_avail,
                               memory_order_acquire ) )
    ; // wait
char *const path = *(char**)islist_peek( work_list );
```

that is, the consumer thread repeatedly checks `work_avail` until it becomes `true`. What the "no memory accesses can be reordered before" means is that no memory accesses done after the acquire in your code can be reordered before it by the hardware i.e., you won't access data before it's ready.

Yes, what the consumer is doing is another instance of a spin lock first mentioned in §14.5. Spin locks are useful when the work is continuous and when the waits are short — shorter than the time it would take to lock and unlock a mutex.

17.3.4 `memory_order_consume`

Consume is a special case of acquire that allows operations to be dependency-ordered that can be more performant on *weakly-ordered* CPUs.

> ■ A weakly-ordered CPU (a weak memory model) is one where one core can see values change in memory in a different order than another core wrote them as is what happens via relaxed (§17.3.2). Weakly-ordered CPUs include those from Apple (e.g., A and M Series), ARM (e.g., Neoverse Series), and IBM (e.g., PowerPC); but not Intel (e.g., x86).
>
> Weakly-ordered CPUs are simpler to design, implement, use less power (important for mobile applications), and allow for a higher degree of parallelism (performance) because independent memory operations are unconstrained by a total ordering. The caveat is that the burden of ensuring memory operations are correct shifts to the programmer.
>
> In contrast, a strongly-ordered CPU (a strong memory model) is one where every core sees values change in memory in the same order that another core wrote them. Strongly-ordered CPUs include those from Intel (e.g., x86). The advantage (for programmers) is that the burden of ensuring memory operations are correct shifts to the CPU designer. □

From the previous example:

```
struct islist *work_list;  // listing 10.9, p. 163
bool _Atomic  work_avail;
```

There's no actual dependency between `work_list` and `work_avail` other than what's in our minds — which the compiler has no way to know. To create an actual dependency that the compiler can use to keep things in dependency order, we can use the following declaration for `work_avail` instead:

```
struct islist *_Atomic work_avail;
```

Using that, a producer thread can prepare work by doing:

```
work_list = islist_push( work_list, sizeof(char*) );
*(char**)islist_peek( work_list ) = path;
atomic_store_explicit( &work_avail, work_list,
                    memory_order_release );
```

and a consumer thread can wait for and receive work by doing:

```
while ( !atomic_load_explicit( &work_avail,
                            memory_order_consume ) )
    ; // wait
char *const path = *(char**)islist_peek( work_avail );
```

Now, we've created an actual dependency using a pointer and a pointed-to value in that the value of the pointer must be loaded before the pointer can be dereferenced. The compiler can preserve this order without using the less performant acquire.

17.3.5 `memory_order_acq_rel`

As mentioned in §17.3.2, relaxed is *not* safe is when decrementing reference counts. Instead, acquire-release is needed to perform a *read-modify-write* operation atomically (all meanings). For example, to decrement the reference count of a `shrd_obj` from listing 17.3 (p.251), the function `shrd_dec` is shown in listing 17.6.

```
bool shrd_dec( struct shrd_obj *so ) {
  if ( atomic_fetch_sub_explicit( &so->ref_cnt, 1,
        memory_order_acq_rel ) == 1 ) {
    if ( so->free_fn != nullptr )
      (*so->free_fn)( so );
    return true;
  }
  return false;
}
```

Listing 17.6: Shared object reference count decrement

- Lines 2–3 decrement `ref_cnt` and return its old value: if that value is 1, it means `so` was the last pointer pointing to the `shrd_obj`, so it should be freed.

17.4 Compare and Swap

Compare-and-swap (CAS), as its name suggests, is both a compare *and* a swap operation done together atomically (all meanings). Conceptually, it's implemented as shown in listing 17.7 except done atomically (where A is any `_Atomic` type and T is the non-atomic version of A).

```
bool compare_and_swap( A *obj, T *expected, T desired ) {
  if ( memcmp( obj, expected, sizeof(T) ) == 0 ) {
    memcpy( obj, &desired, sizeof(T) );
    return true;
  }
  memcpy( expected, obj, sizeof(T) );
  return false;
}
```

Listing 17.7: Conceptual implementation of compare-and-swap

The idea is that you check the value of an `_Atomic` variable and:

- If it's the value you expect, then (and only then) set it to the desired value; or:

- If it's *not* the value you expect, it means some other thread changed the value, so do nothing. (You are free to reattempt setting the value.)

Like the functions in §17.2, the actual functions are `_Generic` (§19) in that they accept any `_Atomic`-qualified object of type `A`; `T` is the non-`_Atomic` version of `A`. Functions that are not named with `_explicit` use the sequential consistency memory order (§17.3.1); functions with `_explicit` use the given memory orders.

```
bool atomic_compare_exchange_strong(A volatile *pv,
                                    T *expected, T want);
bool atomic_compare_exchange_strong_explicit(A volatile *pv,
                                    T *expected, T want,
                                    memory_order succ,
                                    memory_order fail);
```

Compares `*pv` with `*expected`: if they're equal, does `*pv = want` (performs a read-modify-write operation) and returns `true`; otherwise, does `*expected = *pv` (performs a load operation) and returns `false` — all atomically (all meanings).

For the `_explicit` version, `succ` is used for the memory order in the success case and `fail` is used for the failure case.

```
bool atomic_compare_exchange_weak(A volatile *pv, T *expected,
                                    T want);
bool atomic_compare_exchange_weak_explicit(A volatile *pv,
                                    T *expected, T want,
                                    memory_order succ,
                                    memory_order fail);
```

Same as the `strong` versions except that, similarly to `cnd_wait` (§14.5), weak versions can spuriously fail, that is act as if `*pv != *expected` and return `false` even if they're equal.

■ Why is the concept known as "compare-and-swap" yet the functions are named "compare-exchange?" There was no deliberate decision for the names not to match. Some assembly languages, e.g., Intel, have xchg and cmpxchg instructions, so there is precedent there for "exchange." Additionally, `std::swap` in the C++ standard library:

```
std::swap( x, y );  // auto t = x; x = y; y = t;
```

replaces each object with the contents of the other and there is no return value. In contrast, `std::exchange`:

```
auto x0 = std::exchange( x, y );
// auto x0 = x; x = y; return x0;
```

17.4 Compare and Swap

replaces only x with y, does *not* replace y with x, and returns the old value of x. Hence, the semantics of the compare-exchange functions are closer to exchange than swap. □

Conceptually, the compare-exchange functions are implemented as shown in listing 17.8.

```
enum cas_result {
  CAS_EQUAL, CAS_NOT_EQUAL, CAS_SPURIOUS_FAILURE
};

enum cas_result cas_weak_impl( A *pv, T *expected,
                               T want );

inline bool atomic_compare_exchange_weak( A *pv,
                                          T *expected,
                                          T want ) {
  return cas_weak_impl( pv, expected, want ) == CAS_EQUAL;
}

bool atomic_compare_exchange_strong( A *pv, T *expected,
                                     T want ) {
  enum cas_result cr;
  do {
    cr = cas_weak_impl( pv, expected, want );
  } while ( cr == CAS_SPURIOUS_FAILURE );
  return cr == CAS_EQUAL;
}
```

Listing 17.8: Conceptual implementation of weak and strong CAS

Assume there's only `cas_weak_impl` that implements a weak version of CAS:

- Lines 8–12 implement `atomic_compare_exchange_weak`, a simple wrapper around `cas_weak_impl`.
- Lines 14–21 implement `atomic_compare_exchange_strong` that's simply a wrapper around `cas_weak_impl` with a loop that filters out spurious failures. The important thing to remember here is that there's a loop.

Given that, the benefits of `atomic_compare_exchange_weak` include:

+ Spurious failures tend not to happen all that often.
+ When your code is using a loop anyway, the weak version will yield better performance on weakly-ordered CPUs and no worse on strongly-ordered CPUs.
+ Detects the *ABA Problem* (on weakly-ordered CPUs; §17.6).

So then why does `atomic_compare_exchange_strong` exist?

- If you have a loop *only* to filter out spurious failures, don't: use the strong version because it conceptually uses a loop internally as shown in listing 17.8.
- But if you have a loop anyway, use the weak version.

- However, if handling spurious failures is expensive (for example, if you have to discard and reinitialize a new object), use the strong version.
- But the strong version doesn't detect the ABA Problem.

17.5 Lock-Free Operations

One of the primary uses for CAS is that it allows you to implement *lock-free* operations on data structures.

> ■ Operations fall into two broad categories: *blocking* and *non-blocking*. The former can occur when attempting to lock a mutex that's already locked, for example.
>
> Non-blocking also has two categories: *lock-free* and *wait-free*. Intuitively, lock-free operations never lock a mutex. Using _Atomic and the appropriate memory orders, data can still be shared in a thread-safe way. Lock-free operations are generally more performant than blocking ones. However, while you won't have to lock, you may still have to wait (as we'll see). □

For example, a lock-free version of islist_push from listing 10.10 (p. 164) is shown in listing 17.9.

```
1  void islist_lfpush( struct islist *_Atomic *plist,
2                      size_t size ) {
3    struct islist *const new_head =
4      malloc( sizeof(struct islist) + size );
5    new_head->next =
6      atomic_load_explicit( plist, memory_order_relaxed );
7
8    while ( !atomic_compare_exchange_weak_explicit( plist,
9              &new_head->next, new_head,
10             memory_order_release, memory_order_relaxed ) );
11 }
```

Listing 17.9: Singly linked list lock-free push

- The function's signature on line 1 has changed: it now takes a pointer to an _Atomic pointer to the head of the list so that it can be updated atomically.
- Lines 5–6 set new_head->next to the old head value.
- Lines 8–10 try to update *plist (the current head):
  - If it's still equal to new_head->next (the original value of *plist), update *plist to point to new_head.
  - If it's not equal, it means another thread sneaked in and updated *plist to point to different new node, so do nothing and reattempt. (Note that new_head->next has been updated to be the updated *plist pointing to the different node.)

- Lines 6 and 10 (in the failure case) can use memory-order-relaxed because *new_head is an object pointed to only by this function, i.e., it's not (yet) shared with any other thread, so there's no issue with thread-safety.
- Line 10 *must* at least use memory-order-release to ensure that the write to the next pointer can't be reordered after the update to *plist.

17.6 The "ABA Problem"

Suppose thread 1 performs the following steps:

1. Read a memory location: the value is "A".
2. Do some work.
3. Read the same memory location again: the value is still "A".
4. Compare the original and recent values: they're equal.
5. Conclusion: nothing has changed.

The problem is suppose thread 2 performs the following steps while thread 1 is doing its step 2:

1. Write "B" to the same memory location.
2. Do some work.
3. Write "A" to the same memory location.

By the time thread 1 does its step 3, it reads "A" and believes nothing has changed — even though it has. You might now ask:

If the value of "A" is the same, why does it matter?

The answer is: sometimes it doesn't — but sometimes it does. This is known as the *ABA Problem*.

Consider the islist_lfpush function from listing 17.9 (p. 258). Figure 17.1 illustrates the steps comprising a push.

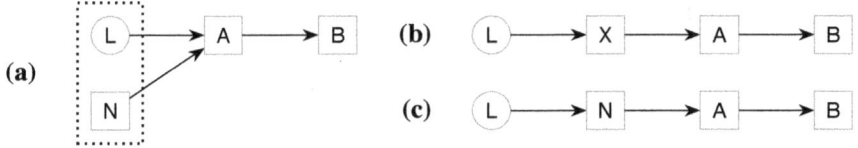

Fig. 17.1: ABA analysis of singly linked list lock-free push

State (a) shows shows the initial conditions where A and B are nodes on the list, *plist (L) points to A, and new_head (N) has its next also point to A. The dotted box contains *plist (L) and new_head->next that are being compared. State

(c) shows the desired final state where *plist (L) points to new_head (N) and new_head->next points to A.

But what if another thread sneaks in before the while loop is entered, pushes a new node X shown by state (b), then immediately pops it? Both *plist (L) and new_head->next still point to A, so *plist will be set to new_head — which is correct. In this case, the ABA Problem isn't actually a problem.

Now consider a lock-free version of islist_pop from listing 10.10 (p. 164) as shown in listing 17.10.

```
1  struct islist*
2  islist_lfpop( struct islist *_Atomic *plist ) {
3    struct islist *head =
4      atomic_load_explicit( plist, memory_order_relaxed );
5
6    while ( head != nullptr &&
7            !atomic_compare_exchange_weak_explicit( plist,
8              &head, head->next, memory_order_release,
9              memory_order_relaxed ) );
10
11   return head;
12 }
```

Listing 17.10: Singly linked list lock-free pop, version 1

- Lines 3–4 load the current head of the list.
- Line 5 checks head for nullptr meaning the list is empty that will cause the loop either never to be entered (if the list was empty initially) or exit if becomes empty (if another thread popped the last element).
- Line 7–9 try to update *plist (the current head):
  - If it's still equal to head (the original value of *plist), update *plist to point to head->next.
  - If it's not equal, it means another thread sneaked in and updated *plist to point to different node (via either pushing or popping), so do nothing and reattempt. (Note that head->next has been updated to be the updated *plist, the current head.)

Figure 17.2 illustrates the steps comprising a pop.

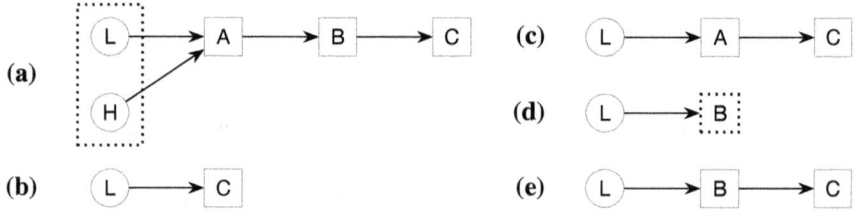

Fig. 17.2: ABA analysis of singly linked list lock-free pop

17.7 Versioned Pointers

State (a) shows shows the initial conditions where A, B, and C are nodes on the list, *plist (L) points to A, and head (H) also points to A. The dotted box contains *plist (L) and head (H) that are being compared. State (e) shows the desired final state where *plist (L) points to B.

But what if another thread sneaks in before the while loop is entered, pops A and B shown by state (b), then pushes A shown by state (c)? Both *plist (L) and head (H) still point to A, so *plist will be set to head->next — which is wrong!

Why? Originally, head pointed to A whose next pointed to B, hence head->next (the desired argument in the compare) is B. But B was popped in (b), so we'll end up in state (d) with *plist (L) being a dangling pointer to B. In this case, the ABA Problem is really a problem! (It wasn't a problem for islist_lfpush because the desired value of new_head could never become stale since new_head isn't shared.)

Even worse, there's no easy fix for this. In this case, the problem is that part of the desired value expression (here, head->next) can change. Detecting ABA Problems is hard, even for experts. Now what? There are a few choices:

1. Give up and use a mutex (§14.4).
2. Implement *versioned pointers* (§17.7).
3. Implement *hazard pointers*.[†]

17.7 Versioned Pointers

A *versioned pointer* is a pointer plus a "version number" where every time the value of the pointer changes, the version number is incremented, something like:

```
struct vers_ptr {
    void      *ptr;      // pointer to object
    uintptr_t vers;      // version number
};
```

The type of vers is uintptr_t (§2.7) so it's the same size as a pointer. Assuming 64-bit pointers, the size of vers_ptr would be 16 bytes. Modern CPUs support 16-byte atomic CAS, e.g., as Intel does with its cmpxchg16b instruction. We can then use a vers_ptr to write a lock-free islist_lfpop as shown in listing 17.11.

- Line 1 defines a convenience macro to declare a versioned pointer having a ptr of type T* rather than void* to eliminate casting.
- Line 3 uses VERS_PTR to typedef islist_vptr that will always be used to point to the head of a list.

[†] *Lock-Free Data Structures with Hazard Pointers*, Andrei Alexandrescu and Maged Michael, *Dr. Dobb's*, Dec. 1, 2004,
https://www.drdobbs.com/lock-free-data-structures-with-hazard-po/184401890

```
#define VERS_PTR(T)    struct { T *ptr; uintptr_t vers; }

typedef VERS_PTR(struct islist) islist_vptr;

struct islist* islist_lfpop( islist_vptr _Atomic *plist ) {
  islist_vptr head =
    atomic_load_explicit( plist, memory_order_relaxed );

  while ( head.ptr != nullptr ) {
    islist_vptr const new_next =
      { head.ptr->next, head.vers + 1 };
    if ( atomic_compare_exchange_weak_explicit( plist,
            &head, new_next, memory_order_release,
            memory_order_relaxed ) )
      break;
  }

  return head.ptr;
}
```

Listing 17.11: Singly linked list lock-free pop, version 2

- The function's signature on line 5 has changed: it now takes a pointer to a vers_ptr rather than an ordinary pointer to the head of the list.
- Lines 6–7 load the current head of the list. Unlike before, head is a versioned pointer.
- Line 10–11 constructs new_next, what we want the head's updated next versioned pointer to be. Notice that new_next's vers is one more than before.
- Lines 12-14 try to update *plist (the current head):
  - If it's still equal to head (the original value of *plist), update *plist to be new_next. Even though both *plist (L) and head (H) still point to A as before in figure 17.2(a), they won't compare equal because the respective values of vers in *plist and head are different.
  - If it's not equal, it means another thread sneaked in and updated *plist to point to either a different node or the same node but with a different next pointer (via either pushing or popping), so do nothing and reattempt. (Note that head has been updated to be the updated *plist, the current head.)

17.8 False Sharing

As mentioned in §10.6, when data is read from memory, rather than reading only a single byte, an entire chunk — a cache line — of memory is read that contains not only the sought after byte, but the surrounding bytes as well. For code that exhibits locality of reference, the chunking yields a performance gain. However, in some cases, it can yield a performance loss. Consider a lock-free linked list that contains both head and tail pointers:

```
struct lf_islist {
  struct islist *_Atomic head, *_Atomic tail;
};
```

Assume that your code has one thread pushing items onto the tail of the list (repeatedly updating `tail`) and a second thread popping items from the head of the list (repeatedly updating `head`). With `lf_islist` defined as it is, `head` and `tail` will very likely reside on the same cache line. This means updating one will invalidate the entire cache line adding otherwise unnecessary contention for the other. This is known as *false sharing*.

To eliminate false sharing, you want `head` and `tail` to reside on different cache lines so updating one doesn't affect the other. You can achieve that by using `alignas` (§4.8) as shown in listing 17.12.

```
 1  #if defined(__aarch64__) || defined(__powerpc__)
 2    constexpr unsigned CACHE_LINE_SIZE = 128;
 3  #elif // ... other CPU architectures ...
 4    // ...
 5  #else
 6    constexpr unsigned CACHE_LINE_SIZE = 64;
 7  #endif
 8
 9  struct lf_islist {
10    alignas(CACHE_LINE_SIZE) struct islist *_Atomic head,
11                                           *_Atomic tail;
12  };
```

Listing 17.12: Using `alignas` to eliminate false sharing

- Lines 1–7 define `CACHE_LINE_SIZE` in bytes using conditional compilation (§8.5) based on object-like macros defined for the CPU by the compiler. Aside from a few exceptions, the cache line size for most modern CPUs is 64 bytes so that's a reasonable default to use on line 6 if none of the `#if`s match.
- Lines 10–11 use `alignas` to align both `head` and `tail` to be on cache-line-size boundaries by intentionally introducing padding (§10.5). This wastes a little bit of memory, but ensures that `head` and `tail` reside on different cache lines and eliminates false sharing between them.

17.9 Epilogue

Here are some key points about and some advice for `_Atomic`:

- `_Atomic` is syntactically a qualifier like `const`, like `volatile`, and `restrict`.
- For pointers, the pointer, the object pointed to, or both, can be `_Atomic`.
- In some cases, `_Atomic` can be used as an alternative to a mutex.

- Deciding whether to use _Atomic instead of a mutex is a choice between a possible performance gain and simpler and relatively safer code. Like many other things in computer science, it's a trade-off. But it's your trade-off to make for your circumstances rather than be stuck with whatever trade-offs the implementers made when programming in a language that provides data structures either built-in or part of its standard library.
- Your algorithm matters far more than the choice between _Atomic and a mutex.
- Thread-safety in general and using _Atomic with memory barriers specifically is very hard to get right, even for experts.
- Before using _Atomic, profile your code (§18.9) to see if it's spending too much time either locking or waiting for locks.
- Be aware of the ABA Problem. Versioned pointers are a technique to solve it.
- Be aware of false sharing.

Use wisely.

Exercises

1. Using listing 17.9 (p.258) as a starting point, write an updated islist_lfpush that uses vers_ptr like islist_lfpop does in listing 17.11 (p.262).

Chapter 18
Debugging

Inevitably, you're going to have to debug your program. The top two ways to do so are to:

1. Temporarily add statements to print values of interest.
2. Use a debugger such as either gdb[†] or lldb[‡] (on Unix systems) or the one that's bundled with an IDE.

The first is relatively straightforward; the second requires that you learn some debugger commands or application. There are times, however, when neither method works. Fortunately, there are other tools available. In §18.8, a case study for a bizarre bug and how it was diagnosed and fixed is presented.

18.1 Printing Values

When temporarily adding statements to print values of interest, you should print to standard error rather than standard output because standard error is generally *unbuffered* meaning all output is printed immediately rather than being buffered before printing whereas standard output is generally *buffered*. If debugging a crash and you're printing to standard output, it's possible that your program will crash before values of interest are printed.

Additionally, if your program prints to both standard output and standard error, the output can become unsynchronized due to the difference in buffering. If available on your system, the stdbuf command can change the buffering of standard output for your program by running:

```
$ stdbuf -o0 command
```

[†] https://www.sourceware.org/gdb/
[‡] https://lldb.llvm.org/

If `stdbuf` isn't available on your system, you can add the following line of code in your `main` function before you print anything that will make standard output unbuffered:

```
setvbuf( stdout, nullptr, _IONBF, 0 );
```

18.2 Debug Information

Debug information consists of the names of functions and variables, and a mapping from assembly language instructions back to their corresponding C source files and line. While names are meaningful and line number mappings are useful to programmers, they're unnecessary for compiled programs. All that's needed are memory addresses of functions to call or variables to access. Consequently, when a C compiler generates an executable, it doesn't contain any debug information by default.

To use a debugger, having debug information is extremely helpful. Both `clang` and `gcc` accept the `-g` command-line option to generate debug information in the executable. For Microsoft C, the option is `/DEBUG`. The caveat is that your program will be bigger both on disk and in memory (but usually not problematically so).

18.3 Optimization

A compiler typically does not perform a simple translation from C statements to sets of assembly language instructions. It also performs many kinds of optimization resulting in assembly code that can be very different from what you might expect a direct translation from C statements to be, or in a different order, or eliminated completely ("optimized out"). This can confound using a debugger to step through the execution of a program because the assembly instructions don't cleanly map back to C statements.

Both `clang` and `gcc` accept the `-O0` ("oh zero") command-line option to set the optimization level to zero, i.e., no optimization. For Microsoft C, the option is `/Od` ("oh dee"). Therefore before debugging, it's *much* better if you recompile your program with optimization disabled. The caveat is that your program will typically run slower.

18.4 Core Dumps

A *core dump* is a file containing a snapshot of memory of a program when execution caused a serious error. A core dump usefully contains the entire stack frames of your program including both local variables and heap memory. Core dump files can be read by debuggers so you can see exactly where a program crashed (file and line), go up the call stack, and print the values of variables or memory.

> ■ The name *core dump* comes from magnetic-core memory, aka, *core*, the leading type of RAM until the 1970s. A core is a very small (roughly .5mm) ferrite ring that, via the direction of an induced magnetic field, stored either a 0 or 1. Hence, a core dump was literally a dump of the state of core memory. Even though core memory has long since been obsoleted, the term *core dump* persists. □

On Microsoft Windows, the equivalent is a *minidump*, a file ending with a .dmp extension.

18.5 Signals

On Unix systems, when certain errors occur during the execution of a program, the operating system sends the program a *signal* interrupting it. (Signals are assigned integers and are defined in the signal.h standard header.) Some signals trigger a core dump by default. The ones you're most likely to encounter are:

- **SIGABRT** (abort): Caused because either a program explicitly called abort or it was called by a violated assert (§16).
- **SIGBUS** (bus error): A *bus* is a communication system among components of a computer. A *system bus* is the bus between the CPUs and main memory. Some CPUs can access memory for types (§2.5) only at addresses that are suitably aligned (§4.8).
  A *bus error* occurs when an attempt is made to access either a nonexistent memory address or a type via an unaligned address.
- **SIGILL** (illegal instruction): At the lowest level, a program is a sequence of byte values where each corresponds to a CPU *opcode* that is a CPU instruction. (For example, on an x86–64 CPU, c6 is the opcode for the 8-bit mov instruction.) When a CPU is executing a program, it reads a value for an opcode, then executes it. Afterwards, it simply proceeds to the next byte in memory to read the next opcode.
  An *illegal instruction error* occurs when a CPU reads a value that doesn't correspond to an opcode. This can happen if a program calls a function via pointer (§6.10), but the pointer points to somewhere in memory that doesn't contain opcodes.
- **SIGSEGV** (segmentation violation, aka, "segmentation fault" or "seg-fault"): A segmentation fault occurs when a program attempts to access a memory address that it doesn't have permission to access.

18.6 Common Bugs

There are types of bugs that happen more frequently than others. Some have already been discussed: data races (§14), thread leaks (§14.2), and undefined behavior (§15). In this section, additional bugs you are likely to encounter are presented.

18.6.1 Array Bounds

As mentioned in §6.3, accessing an element of an array outside its bounds results in undefined behavior (§15). If you're lucky, you'll get a segmentation fault (§18.5) followed by a core dump (§18.4); if you're unlucky, your program may appear to work correctly — some of the time.

For example, given the code shown in listing 18.1, the use of <= rather than < when iterating through arrays is invariably wrong.

```
bool rv = false;
char buf[1024];

for ( unsigned i = 0; i <= 1024; ++i )   // should be <
    buf[i] = /* ... */;
// ...
return rv;                    // may return random value
```

Listing 18.1: Array bounds violation

In this case, when `i` is 1024, assigning a value to `buf[i]` *may* overwrite `rv` if it's located in memory immediately after `buf` in the function's stack frame. (The order in which local variables are laid out in memory is implementation defined.) The value of `rv` *may* become `true` if `buf[1024]` is odd and `false` if even. The function would appear to return `true` randomly.

18.6.2 Buffer Overflow

A *buffer overflow* is kind of an array bounds violation, but is usually caused differently, typically by calling a function that writes beyond the end of a buffer rather than you doing so explicitly via an array index. Standard functions that can do this far too easily include `scanf` (§12.4.1), `strcat` (§B.2), and `strcpy` because they don't have the capacity of the buffer as a parameter.

In production-quality programs, `scanf` with strings shouldn't be used; the non-standard but common safer functions `strlcat` and `strlcpy` should be used instead of `strcat` and `strcpy`, respectively. Even safer functions like `memcpy` (§B.2) can cause a buffer overflow if you get the capacity of the buffer wrong. Whenever using a buffer, always know its capacity.

18.6.3 Double Free

A *double free* bug is when you `free` memory via a pointer, then attempt to `free` the *same* memory again. This typically happens because either:

1. You call `free` on the *same* pointer more than once, e.g., an error occurred, so your error-path code freed an object, but then your normal-path code also freed the same object.
   As an alternative, after freeing an object, you can set its pointer to `nullptr`. Calling `free` on a `nullptr` is guaranteed to do nothing.
2. You have two or more *owning pointers* to an object and `free` was called on more than one. (An *owning pointer* is a pointer that you decided "owns" the object to which it points. Before disposing of such a pointer, you must `free` the owned object.) For any object, there should only ever be at most one owning pointer (or use a shared pointer like in listing 17.3, p.251).

18.6.4 Null Pointer Dereference

A *null pointer dereference* is simply an attempt to dereference a pointer whose value is `nullptr`. As to *why* it's null when you're assuming it shouldn't be, there can be any number of reasons ranging from you never setting it to a non-null value or resetting it to a null value. Generally, it's one of the simplest bugs to diagnose and fix (except when it isn't — see §18.8).

18.6.5 Off-by-One

The array bounds error (§18.6.1) is a particular case of the more general *off-by-one* error where a calculated value is either one less or one more than it should be. Such miscalculations often occur when dealing with either strings or buffers. For an example, recall the `mstrcat` function from listing 1.13 (p.21) that contains the line:

```
char *const s12 = malloc( s1_len + strlen( s2 ) + 1 );
```

A common mistake is to forget the + 1 for the terminating null character.

18.6.6 Use After Free

A *use-after-free* bug is when you `free` a pointer to an object, then attempt to dereference the pointer to the (now non-existent) object.

Recalling the slist structure from listing 6.2 (p.86), consider a function to free an entire slist as shown in listing 18.2.

```
void slist_free( struct slist *list,
                 void (*free_fn)(void*) ) {
  for ( ; list != nullptr; list = list->next ) {
    (*free_fn)( list->data );
    free( list );
  }
}
```

Listing 18.2: Function to free an entire list (the wrong way)

While it may look correct, the problem is that the free frees the slist object pointed to by list, but then reads list->next that no longer exists. Since this results in undefined behavior (§15), the function may even work *some* of the time.

18.6.7 Memory Leak

As first mentioned in §1.8, a *memory leak* occurs when the value of a pointer to allocated memory is somehow lost thus making it impossible to pass to free. Repeated leaks will eventually exhaust memory.

Recall the token structure from listing 11.1 (p.171). Since the s member is a pointer to a dynamically allocated string, then, if t1 and t2 are variables of token, simply assigning one to the other like:

```
t1 = t2;                  // overwrites t1.s leaking it
```

will overwrite t1.s leaking it. What's needed for this and any other structure that contains an owning pointer is a function to copy it as shown in listing 18.3.

```
void token_cpy( struct token *dst,
                struct token const *src ) {
  if ( dst == src )
    return;
  if ( dst->kind == TOKEN_STR )
    free( dst->s );
  if ( src->kind == TOKEN_STR ) {
    *dst = (struct token){
      .kind = TOKEN_STR, .s = strdup( src->s )
    };
  } else {
    memcpy( dst, src, sizeof *dst );
  }
}
```

Listing 18.3: Function to copy a token containing an owning pointer

18.6 Common Bugs

- Lines 3–4 check for self-copying, e.g., `t1 = t1`, and do nothing. While you'd never intentionally write code like that, you should still guard against it.
- Lines 5–6 check if `*dst` is a token for a string: if so, frees the string.
- Lines 7–10 check if `*src` is a token for a string: if so, copies the string using the standard function `strdup` (§B.2).
- Otherwise, line 12 simply uses `memcpy` (§B.2) to copy `*src`.

18.6.8 Uninitialized Variable

As first mentioned in §1.3, attempting to read from an uninitialized variable results in undefined behavior (§15). One way to avoid this would be always to initialize variables when declared "just in case." The pitfall is that doing so can cause a different bug. How? Consider the code in listing 18.4.

```
1  int x_min = 0, x_max = 0;
2  int y_min = 0, y_max = 0;
3  // ...
4  x_min = MIN( x1, x2 );
5  y_min = MIN( y1, y2 );
6  x_max = MAX( x1, x2 );
7  x_max = MAX( y1, y2 );
8  draw_rect( x_min, y_min, x_max, y_max );
```

Listing 18.4: Initializing "just in case" pitfall

This code will compile without warning despite the bug. (Did you notice it?) The bug is the `x_max` on line 7 is a typo: it should be `y_max`. It goes unnoticed because the compiler has no way to know it's a typo. Because `y_max` was initialized on line 2, the code is "fine" as far as the compiler is concerned. Had you left all of `x_min`, `x_max`, `y_min`, and `y_max` uninitialized in their declarations, the compiler could have warned you with the `-Wuninitialized` command-line option (§18.7.1):

```
rect.c:8:34: warning: 'y_max' uninitialized when used here
       8 |    draw_rect( x_min, y_min, x_max, y_max );
         |                                    ^~~~~
```

and you'd have realized you made a typo. In this case, the better solution would have been to declare and assign the variables together on the same lines, but there are cases where you do need to pre-declare variables. In such cases, it's sometimes better *not* to initialize "just in case."

18.7 Warnings

The best way to avoid debugging is not to put bugs into your programs in the first place. By default, most compilers automatically give some warnings, but not all. By enabling more warnings, the compiler can help you catch bugs before committing your code.

■ If warnings are so helpful, why aren't they errors instead? Because sometimes you *really* want to do something and you know what you're doing. Then why aren't all warnings at least enabled by default? Because some warnings are quite pedantic; others are considered pedantic by some programmers. Recall that part of C's philosophy includes "trust the programmer," hence many warnings are disabled by default, but are available and can be enabled if desired. □

18.7.1 Recommended Warnings

In the warnings that follow, not all are supported by all compilers. They're a union of those supported by both `clang` and `gcc`. Warnings are invariably specified via build tools, not manually on the command-line. During an initial "configure" step, the compiler is probed to see which warning command-line options it accepts. Microsoft C has equivalent warnings, but they're specified by number, e.g., `C4018`.

-Wall
Enables "all" warnings that many users think are a good idea. (You should enable this.)

-Wcast-align
Warn when a pointer is cast to a type that has a stricter alignment. For example, warn if a `char*` is cast to an `int*` on CPUs where integers must be aligned (§3.17) only at two- or four-byte boundaries.

-Wcomma
Warn about possible misuses of the comma operator (§3.15). For example, although it's legal to combine multiple expressions into a single statement using the comma operator:

```
x = -1, y = 0;          // same as: x = -1; y = 0;
```

it's a bad practice because it's confusing to many programmers. The only exceptions are either the *init-expr* or the *next-expr* in a `for` loop (§5.6).

-Wconditional-uninitialized
Warn when a variable may be uninitialized when used on a certain code path as shown in listing 18.4 (p.271) if `y_max` were not initialized.

18.7 Warnings

-Wconversion

Warn when an implicit conversion may alter a value, e.g.:

```
unsigned n = -1;         // better: n = (unsigned)-1
```

To suppress such warnings, use a cast (§3.14).

-Wduplicate-enum

Warn when an enumeration constant (§7) has been implicitly assigned a value that another constant has been assigned. For example:

```
enum color {
  COLOR_BLACK, COLOR_WHITE,   // COLOR_WHITE = 1
  COLOR_NONE = COLOR_BLACK,
  COLOR_GREEN, COLOR_RED      // COLOR_GREEN = 1
};
```

will generate a warning that COLOR_GREEN has been implicitly assigned the value 1 that COLOR_WHITE already has. When using implicit enumeration values, it's best to declare duplicate values (§7.5.3) at the end.

-Wenum-enum-conversion

Warn when two or more constants from different enumerations (§7) are used in the same expression.

-Wextra

Enables even more warnings than -Wall. (You should enable this.)

-Wfloat-equal

Warn if floating-point values are compared for equality or inequality. Many floating-point values can't be accurately represented using finite precision, e.g., 10/3 or π: there will always be imprecision due to either truncation or rounding. (This is true for computers in general, not only C.) Consequently, it's a bad idea to compare the result of a floating-point calculation for either equality or inequality. For example, summing an array of floating-point values and seeing whether they sum to zero:

```
bool sum_to_zero( size_t n, double const v[n] ) {
  double sum = 0.0;
  for ( size_t i = 0; i < n; ++i )
    sum += v[i];
  return sum == 0.0;        // will hardly ever work
}
```

If sum ends up being 0.00000001 or even less, it will *not* compare equal to zero because it's not *exactly* zero. For floating-point equality, you generally need to compare against ε that is some very small number such that when sum $< \varepsilon$, it's "close enough" to zero to be considered "zero."

-Wfor-loop-analysis

Warn if a variable is either incremented or decremented in one of the for expressions and in the loop's body, or used in the loop condition expression but not modified in the body. For example:

```
for ( size_t i = 0; i < n; ++i ) {
  // ...
  ++i;              // warning: incremented above also
}
```

-Wformat-nonliteral

Warn if the format string to either `printf` (§12.1.1), `scanf` (§12.4.1), or one of their variants, is not a string literal. Generally, the format string should always be a string literal since the number of `%` in it specify the number and types of expected arguments that follow. Any mismatch results in undefined behavior (§15).

-Wformat-signedness

Warn if the format string to either `printf` (§12.1.1), `scanf` (§12.4.1), or one of their variants, contains a specification where its sign does not agree with that of its corresponding variable, e.g., the specifier is `%d`, but the variable is `unsigned`.

-Wformat-type-confusion

Similar to `-Wformat-signedness`, but warn when the type of the specification does not agree with that of its corresponding variable, e.g., the specifier is `%s`, but the variable is `int`.

-Wimplicit-fallthrough

Warn when the `case` of a `switch` (§5.8) "falls through" into to the subsequent `case` or `default` without the `[[fallthrough]]` attribute (§4.9.2).

-Wlogical-op-parentheses

Warn when `&&` is used within `||` expressions. For example (assuming all variables are `bool`):

```
if ( a || b && c || d )    // a || (b && c) || d
```

Because `&&` has a higher precedence than `||` (table 3.1, p.46), the `&&` binds more tightly. Assuming you didn't mean that, adding parentheses fixes it:

```
if ( (a || b) && (c || d) )
```

If you *really* meant the original, then add parentheses both to suppress the warning and for clarity:

```
if ( a || (b && c) || d ) // addition of () clarifies
```

-Wshadow

Warn whenever a variable or type declaration in an inner scope "shadows" (has the same name as) another variable, parameter, or type in an outer scope. For example:

```
static unsigned count;

void f() {
    unsigned count = 0;    // legal, but a bad practice
```

It's a bad practice to have multiple things with the same name since it can lead to confusion and consequently bugs.

-Wshift-sign-overflow
Warn when shifting a signed integer and the sign bit becomes negative.

-Wsometimes-uninitialized
Warn when a variable is sometimes used before being initialized, e.g., when a condition is true or false, or a loop is entered or exited. For example:

```
int min;
if ( i < j )
    min = i;
printf( "%d\n", min );    // sometimes uninitialized
```

-Wtautological-type-limit-compare
Warn if the result of a comparison is always either true or false. For example, if n is unsigned, then the following is always true:

```
if ( n >= 0 )              // always true for unsigned n
```

-Wuninitialized
Warn when a variable is used before being initialized.

-Wunreachable-code
Warn when lines of code are unreachable. Typically, it's because one of break or continue (§5.7), goto (§5.10), return (§5.9), or longjmp (§20.4) is performed unconditionally beforehand.

-Wunused
Warn if a variable, function (§9), function parameter (§9.2), or label (§5.10) is unused. While unused variables are generally harmless, if one has a name similar to another such as y_max is to x_max in listing 18.4 (p.271), it can mean you made a typo and aren't using a variable you should be.

As mentioned in §16.6, variables can sometimes be unused when disabling assertions. To suppress warnings for such variables, add the maybe_unused attribute (p.245).

-Wwrite-strings
Warn when assigning a string literal to a variable of type char*. Since const (§4.5) wasn't originally part of C, the type of a string literal is char* and not char const*. Since it's not const, the following will compile without warning yet result in undefined behavior (§15):

```
char *s = "hello, world";
*s = 'H';                    // undefined behavior
```

The `-Wwrite-strings` command-line option changes the type of string literals to `char const*` so assigning a string literal to a variable of type `char*` will generate a warning.

Generally, there are no other consequences, but it does affect the type deduced for the controlling expression of `_Generic` (§19.1) for string literals. This is one reason why the definition of the `IS_C_STR_EXPR` macro (p.292) has both `char*` and `char const*`.

-Wzero-as-null-pointer-constant
  Warn if `0` is used as the null pointer instead of `nullptr` (§C.15).

18.7.2 Disabling Warnings

Even though enabling warnings is a good idea, occasionally you might need to disable a particular warning for a block of code because you *really* want to do something despite the warning. For example, as mentioned for the `-Wformat-nonliteral` warning, the format string for `printf` and its variants should always be a string literal. One exception is when wrapping the function with another variadic function (9.11.2). In such a case, you want to pass the format string argument along verbatim.

Using pragmas (§8.16), you can disable a warning for a block of code, then re-enable it afterwards. However, you want to re-enable it only if it was enabled in the first place. Both `clang` and `gcc`[†] maintain a set of enabled warnings. Using additional pragmas, you can "push" the current set onto an internal stack, disable a warning for a block of code, then pop the stack to restore the previous set of enabled warnings as shown in listing 18.5.

18.8 The Curious Case of the Disappearing `if`

In June, 2022, I discovered a test-case that crashed `cdecl` first mentioned in §6.10:

```
c++decl> explain int operator new(size_t)
Assertion failed: (ast != NULL), c_ast_unpointer_qual,
    file c_ast_util.c, line 404.
abort (core dumped)
```

[†]*Diagnostic Pragmas*, Free Software Foundation, *Using the GNU Compiler Collection*, §6.67.13, 1988–2025, https://gcc.gnu.org/onlinedocs/gcc/Diagnostic-Pragmas.html

18.8 The Curious Case of the Disappearing if

```
#pragma GCC diagnostic push
#pragma GCC diagnostic ignored "-Wformat-nonliteral"

[[noreturn]] void fatal_error( int status,
                               char const *format, ... ) {
  fprintf( stderr, "%s: ", prog_name );
  va_list args;
  va_start( args );
  vfprintf( stderr, format, args );
  va_end( args );
  exit( status );
}

#pragma GCC diagnostic pop
```

Listing 18.5: Temporarily disabling a warning

■ cdecl parses declarations and constructs an *abstract syntax tree* (AST) that is traversed to check for semantic errors. Note that cdecl is written in C11, not C23, hence its use of NULL rather than nullptr (§C.15). □

The crash was strange for a couple of reasons that I knew initially. The test:

- Crashed *only* when cdecl is compiled using clang 14.0.5.
- Did *not* crash when compiled with various versions of gcc on any platform.

The Code

The code with line 404 is shown in listing 18.6.

```
396  static c_ast_t const*
397  c_ast_unpointer_qual( c_ast_t const *ast,
398                       c_tid_t *qual_stids ) {
399    ast = c_ast_untypedef( ast );
400    if ( ast->kind != K_POINTER )
401      return NULL;
402
403    ast = ast->as.ptr_ref.to_ast;
404    assert( ast != NULL );
405    assert( qual_stids != NULL );
406    *qual_stids = ast->type.stids & TS_ANY_QUALIFIER;
407    // ...
408    return c_ast_untypedef( ast );
409  }
```

Listing 18.6: c_ast_unpointer_qual

The function c_ast_unpointer_qual takes pointer to an AST node and, if it represents a pointer in a C declaration, "un-pointers" it to obtain the pointed-to AST node. It also gets the qualifiers, e.g., const, of the pointed-to AST node.

The first `assert` on line 404 fails which means `ast` is `NULL` which means `as.ptr_ref.to_ast` is `NULL`. That means `to_ast` wasn't set when the AST was being constructed in the parser — or so I thought.

Using a Debugger

First, I tried to use a debugger to set a breakpoint a few lines up. Unfortunately, the line I wanted was "optimized out" by the compiler, so I tried setting a breakpoint nearby. Unfortunately again, the value of `ast` had been optimized out. I recompiled with `-O0`, but then the program *didn't* crash — a *heisenbug*!

> ■ A *heisenbug* is a software bug that either disappears or alters behavior when you attempt to debug it. The term is a portmanteau of *Werner Heisenberg*, the physicist famous for his *uncertainty principle* (that states there is a limit to the precision certain pairs of physical properties, such as position and momentum, can be known simultaneously), and *bug*.[†]
>
> Unfortunately, the uncertainty principle is often confused with the related *observer effect* (where the act of measuring a system can't be made without affecting the system). In programming, it's the observer effect you'll occasionally run into, not the uncertainty principle.
>
> Heisenbugs happen typically because when you recompile with no optimization, the generated code is just sufficiently different so as not to cause the bug to manifest (though it's still there). □

I set a breakpoint in the function that calls `c_ast_unpointer_qual` (which I learned from the backtrace) and it's `c_ast_is_ptr_to_tid_any` shown in listing 18.7.

```
1  c_ast_t const* c_ast_is_ptr_to_tid_any( c_ast_t const *ast,
2                                          c_tid_t tids ) {
3    c_tid_t qual_stids;
4    ast = c_ast_unpointer_qual( ast, &qual_stids );
5    return c_ast_is_tid_any_qual_impl( ast, tids,
6                                       qual_stids );
7  }
```

Listing 18.7: `c_ast_is_ptr_to_tid_any`

This time, the debugger stopped at the breakpoint and I discovered the AST node is for the built-in type (`K_BUILTIN`) of `int` (the declared return type of operator new) and in particular it's *not* `K_POINTER`. That means the `if` on line 400 in listing 18.6 (p.277) *should* have evaluated to `true`, the function *should* have returned `NULL`, and, most importantly, *should not* have even executed line 404. It's as if the `if` disappeared.

[†]*A Conversation with Bruce Lindsay: Designing for failure may be the key to success*, Steve Bourne, *ACM Queue*, 2(8), Nov. 2004, pp. 22–33.

18.8 The Curious Case of the Disappearing `if`

Memory Checkers and Sanitizers

My next step was to try `valgrind`[†] — nothing useful. I also tried `clang`'s address[‡] and undefined behavior[§] sanitizers — also nothing useful. Now what?

Older `clang` Versions

The failing test didn't crash previously using `clang`. (The problem is that, while I do run my full suite of unit tests using `gcc` every time I change the source code, I don't also do it every time using `clang`.) So I started downloading older and older versions of `clang` and trying them out. I finally found out that the crash didn't happen using `clang` 13.0.1 and started happening using `clang` 14.0.0. Although highly unlikely in a compiler as mature as `clang`, it is possible that I found an optimizer bug.

Viewing the Object Code

So then I thought to look at the generated x86–84 assembly code using `objdump`:

```
$ objdump -gSMintel --no-show-raw-insn \
    --symbolize-operands c_ast_util.o
```

Looking at the output for `c_ast_is_ptr_to_tid_any`, I discovered that the compiler inlined the call to `c_ast_unpointer_qual`, but that the `if` was there:

```
; if ( ast->kind != K_POINTER )
    cmp     eax, 256
    jne     <L3>
```

I then recompiled using `clang` 14.0.0 and dumped again: this time, that `if` was *not* there! The likelihood that I found an optimizer bug increased.

Static Analysis

I had started to file a bug against `clang` when I came across `scan-build` and tried it. It flagged undefined behavior (§15) in `c_ast_is_ptr_to_tid_any` (listing 18.7,

---

[†]https://valgrind.org/
[‡]https://clang.llvm.org/docs/AddressSanitizer.html
[§]https://clang.llvm.org/docs/UndefinedBehaviorSanitizer.html

p.278). Specifically, `qual_stids` can be passed to `c_ast_is_tid_any_qual_impl` uninitialized on line 6 since `c_ast_unpointer_qual` doesn't always set it. However, I didn't think it mattered because:

1. The only way `qual_stids` remains uninitialized is if `c_ast_unpointer_qual` returns `NULL`; and:
2. The code for `c_ast_is_tid_any_qual_impl` in listing 18.8 does nothing if `ast` is `NULL` — specifically, it does *not* use (the uninitialized) `qual_stids`.

```
static c_ast_t const*
c_ast_is_tid_any_qual_impl( c_ast_t const *ast,
                            c_tid_t tids,
                            c_tid_t qual_stids ) {
  if ( ast != NULL ) {
    c_tid_t ast_tids = c_type_get_tid( &ast->type, tids );
    ast_tids = c_tid_normalize( ast_tids );
    if ( c_tid_tpid( tids ) == C_TPID_STORE )
      ast_tids |= qual_stids;
    if ( c_tid_is_any( ast_tids, tids ) )
      return ast;
  }
  return NULL;
}
```

Listing 18.8: `c_ast_is_tid_any_qual_impl`

So what harm can there possibly be that `qual_stids` is uninitialized? In fact, since it's not used in the `NULL` case, how is that even undefined behavior? The problem is merely passing `qual_stids` to a function means it has to be read and, according to the C11 standard §6.3.2.1¶2, is undefined behavior:

> *If the ... object [has] automatic storage duration ... and ... is uninitialized (not declared with an initializer and no assignment to it has been performed prior to use), the behavior is undefined.*

And with undefined behavior, anything is possible. But does it matter in this case?

The Fix

Assuming the undefined behavior is responsible for the `if` disappearing, the fix is trivial: initialize `qual_stids` as shown in listing 18.9 on line 3. Compiling with `clang` 14.0.0 and running resulted in `cdecl` *not* crashing and the test passing!

```
c_ast_t const* c_ast_is_ptr_to_tid_any( c_ast_t const *ast,
                                        c_tid_t tids ) {
  c_tid_t qual_stids = TS_NONE;
  ast = c_ast_unpointer_qual( ast, &qual_stids );
  return c_ast_is_tid_any_qual_impl( ast, tids,
                                     qual_stids );
}
```

Listing 18.9: `c_ast_is_ptr_to_tid_any`, fixed

18.9 Profiling

If your program works correctly, but slowly, you can *profile* it to see where the CPU is spending the most time. Just as there are many choices of build tools (§13.9), there are many choices for profilers. Typically, a profiler on a Unix system requires one or more of giving special command-line options to the compiler, linking with special libraries, setting environment variables (§12.4.4), and perhaps running your program via a profiling program, to produce profiled output that you can then analyze.

Profilers include `callgrind` (part of `valgrind`), DTrace, `gperftools`, `gprof`, `perf` (Linux only), Tracy, VTune, and others. Some IDEs, such as CLion, Microsoft Visual Studio C, and Xcode, have integrated profilers. The details of any of the profilers are beyond the scope of this book — entire other books and web sites have been written about them.

18.10 Epilogue

Here's some advice for debugging:

- Enable more warnings.
- Enable debug information and disable optimization.
- Try every debugging technique at your disposal:
  - Print values.
  - Use a debugger.
  - Use `valgrind` (with the caveat that it works only on generated machine code, not optimized-out code).
  - Use address and undefined behavior sanitizers.
  - Use a rubber duck.[†]
- Bugs as a result of undefined behavior can be bizarre and make seemingly impossible things happen. If that seems to be the case, look at the generated assem-

---

[†]"Re: Not an awk question," Andrew Errington, `linux-users` mailing list, Nov. 7, 2002, `http://lists.ethernal.org/oldarchives/cantlug-0211/msg00174.html`

bly code. For example, when single-stepping in a debugger, if the next line of code you step to isn't where you think it should be, it's a hint that the compiler did something unexpected and the assembly code isn't what you think it is.

Exercises

1. Write a correct version of `slist_free` shown in listing 18.2 (p.270).
2. In addition to printing values (§18.1), it can sometimes be useful to trace your program's execution as it calls functions. For example, if `load_config` calls `read_file`, your program could print:

   ```
   entering load_config()
   entering read_file()
   ```

   Write a macro:

   ```
   #define TRACE_FUNC   /* ... */
   ```

   that should be inserted as the first line of every function you want to trace, for example:

   ```
   void load_config() {
       TRACE_FUNC;
       // ...
   ```

   that prints the function's name to `stderr`. Hint: use `__func__` (§9.9.1).
3. Modify your solution to the previous exercise to print anything only if the `ENABLE_TRACE` macro is defined to non-zero; if either undefined or zero, nothing should be printed. Your solution must not incur any run-time overhead.

Chapter 19
`_Generic`

C has the `_Generic` keyword that enables compile-time selection of an expression based on the type of its argument. The motivation is the ability for library authors to provide a veneer of C++ function overloading in C.

■ Personally, I think `_Generic` is too, well, generic of a name. It *should* have been called something like `_Typeswitch`. □

19.1 Motivating Example

The motivating example is the ability of the standard C library, e.g., `math.h`, to provide specialized functions for different floating point types (§2.5.6) yet only a single function in the API. For example, `math.h` provides these three functions:

```
double      sqrt ( double );           // square root of double
float       sqrtf( float );            // ... of float
long double sqrtl( long double );      // ... of long double
```

While you certainly can use those functions as they are, it would be nice if you could always use simply `sqrt` and have the compiler select the right function automatically based on the type of its argument:

```
double d;
float f;
long double l;

double      rv_d = sqrt( d );          // calls sqrt()
float       rv_f = sqrt( f );          // calls sqrtf()
long double rv_l = sqrt( l );          // calls sqrtl()
```

To make this work in C++, you'd simply overload the functions; to make this work in C, the math library defines a macro using `_Generic` as shown in listing 19.1.

```
#define sqrt(N)              \
  _Generic( (N),              \
    float        : sqrtf,     \
    long double: sqrtl,       \
    default      : sqrt       \
  )( (N) )
```

Listing 19.1: sqrt function using _Generic

The _Generic keyword is part of the C language proper, not part of the preprocessor (§8). However, the only way you can practically use _Generic is via a function-like macro (§8.7). For the above example, the ((N)) at the end is calling whichever function _Generic selected and passing N as its argument.

_Generic works as follows:

- It takes a single *controlling expression* followed by an *association list* of one or more type/expression pairs.
- If the type (not the value) of the controlling expression matches a particular type (before the :) in the association list, then the result of the _Generic expression is the expression for that type (after the :).
- There can be at most one occurrence of any particular type. (Remember that a typedef type (§2.6) is an alias, not a distinct type.)
- Optionally, one "type" may instead be default that will match only if no other type does.
- Expressions are *not* evaluated; only their type is considered. Hence, _Generic is strictly compile-time and has zero run-time overhead.

Additionally, when comparing types:

- Top-level _Atomic (§17), const (§4.5), restrict (§21), and volatile (§22) qualifiers are discarded. For example, an expression of type int const will match int.
- Array-to-pointer (§6.7) and function-to-pointer conversions happen as usual. For example, an array char s[8] decays to char* and a function's name like free becomes void (*)(void*) (pointer to function taking void*).
- However, no other conversions occur, including the usual arithmetic conversions. For example, short is *not* promoted to int.

_Generic solves its motivating example (though in a clunky manner), but it turns out that it's quite powerful and is capable of solving many other problems.

19.2 A printf Example

When using printf, it's sometimes difficult to remember the correct format specifier for particular types. Using _Generic, we can write helper macros as shown in listing 19.2. With those, we can now write this:

19.2 A printf Example

```
#define PRINTF_FORMAT(T)                                        \
  _Generic( (T),                                                \
    bool        : "%d",   char                   : "%c",        \
    signed char : "%hhd", unsigned char          : "%hhu",      \
    short       : "%hd",  unsigned short         : "%hu",       \
    int         : "%d",   unsigned int           : "%u",        \
    long        : "%ld",  unsigned long          : "%lu",       \
    long long   : "%lld", unsigned long long:      "%llu",      \
    float       : "%f",                                         \
    double      : "%f",   long double            : "%Lf",       \
    char*       : "%s",   char const*            : "%s",        \
    wchar_t*    : "%ls",  wchar_t const*         : "%ls",       \
    void*       : "%p",   void const*            : "%p"         \
  )

#define PRINTF(X)    printf( PRINTF_FORMAT( (X) ), (X) )
```

Listing 19.2: Helper macros for `printf`

```
PRINTF( 42 );          // printf( "%d", 42 )
PRINTF( -273.15 );     // printf( "%f", -273.15 )
PRINTF( "hello" );     // printf( "%s", "hello" )
```

One problem with this macro is that it won't work for any other kind of pointer. A way to fix this is shown in listing 19.3.

```
#define PRINTF_FORMAT(T)                          \
  _Generic( (T),                                  \
    /* ... */                                     \
    wchar_t*           : "%ls",                   \
    wchar_t const*     : "%ls",                   \
    default            : PTR_FORMAT(T),           \
  )

#define PTR_FORMAT(P)                             \
  _Generic( TO_VOID_PTR_EXPR( (P) ),              \
    void const*: "%p",                            \
    void*      : "%p"                             \
  )

#define TO_VOID_PTR_EXPR(P)   (true ? (P) : (void*)(P))
```

Listing 19.3: Helper macros for `printf`, version 2

That is, in PRINT_FORMAT, change the `void*` and `void const*` cases to a `default` case that calls PTR_FORMAT(T) to handle the pointer cases.

The macro TO_VOID_PTR_EXPR seems odd since `true` is always, well, true, so the result is always (P). That may seem pointless, but we want the side-effect of the `?:` operator (§3.7) which is:

- If either of *true-expr* or *false-expr* of `?:` is `void*`, then the type of the result shall also be `void*` (plus `const` if either is `const`).

Since we've explicitly cast P to void* for *false-expr*, that forces the type of the result also to be void* (or void const*) regardless of the pointer type.

■ A simple (void*)(P) (cast to void*) won't work because that would cast *any* type to void*. We want the type of the result to be void* only if P is a pointer. □

19.3 const Overloading

Recall the singly linked list structure from listing 6.2 (p.86):

```
struct slist {
  struct slist *next;
  void         *data;
};
```

and the slist_find function from listing 10.5 (p.161):

```
struct slist* slist_find( struct slist *list,
                          slist_pred_fn pred_fn,
                          void const *pred_data );
```

A problem you can encounter is if you try to pass a pointer to a const slist:

```
void f( struct slist const *list ) {
  // ...
  struct slist const *found =
    slist_find( list, &my_pred, nullptr );
```

That will generate a "discards const" warning because you're passing a pointer to a const slist to a function that takes a pointer to a non-const slist.

While you could ignore the warning, it's always best to write warning-free code. But how can it be fixed? You could cast away the const (§3.14.2), but that's ugly. In C++, you could overload slist_find that takes slist const*; in C, you'd have to write a distinctly named function as shown in listing 19.4 and call that instead for a const slist.

```
inline struct slist const*
const_slist_find( struct slist const *list,
                  slist_pred_fn pred_fn,
                  void const *pred_data ) {
  return slist_find( (struct slist*)list, pred_fn,
                     pred_data );
}
```

Listing 19.4: const_slist_find "overload" of slist_find

While it works, it's also ugly. _Generic can be used to hide the ugliness as shown in listing 19.5 (assuming you rename the original function to nonconst_slist_find).

```
#define slist_find(LIST,PRED_FN,PRED_DATA)        \
  _Generic( (LIST),                               \
    struct slist*      : nonconst_slist_find,     \
    struct slist const*: const_slist_find         \
  )( (LIST), (PRED_FN), (PRED_DATA) )
```

Listing 19.5: _Generic via macro for slist_find

Now, you can always call slist_find and it will "just work" for either a pointer to const or non-const slist.

19.4 Static if

_Generic can also be used to implement a "static if," that is an if that's evaluated at compile-time (similar to C++'s if constexpr) as shown in listing 19.6.

```
#define STATIC_IF(EXPR,THEN,ELSE)         \
  _Generic( &(char[1 + !!(EXPR)]){ },     \
    char (*)[2]: (THEN),                  \
    char (*)[1]: (ELSE)                   \
  )
```

Listing 19.6: Static if

This works by:

1. Converting EXPR to either 0 or 1 via !! (§3.6).
2. Creating a compound literal array (§6.11) having one element plus a second element only if EXPR is true.
3. Taking the compound array's address via & (§3.12), at which point its type is either "pointer to array 2 of char" (i.e., char(*)[2] if true) or "pointer to array 1 of char" (i.e., char(*)[1] if false).
4. If the type is char(*)[2], the result is THEN; else:
5. If the type is char(*)[1], the result is ELSE.

■ As first mentioned in §9.4.4, a "pointer to array N of T" (for some size N of some type T) is *not* the same as the "pointer to T" that results from the name of an array regardless of its size "decaying" into a pointer to its first element (e.g., array A being a shorthand for &A[0]). Pointers to arrays of different sizes are distinct types. □

Unlike #if (§8.5), STATIC_IF can use *any* constant expression and may reference C types, constants, variables, and functions.

We can build on `TO_VOID_PTR_EXPR` to make `IS_PTR_TO_CONST_EXPR` as shown in listing 19.7.

```
#define IS_PTR_TO_CONST_EXPR(P)            \
  _Generic( TO_VOID_PTR_EXPR( (P) ),       \
    void const* : true,                    \
    default     : false                    \
  )
```

Listing 19.7: Is an expression a pointer to `const`?

Given those macros, we can write a generalized macro that can `const` overload any function as shown in listing 19.8:

```
#define CONST_OVERLOAD(FN, PTR, ...)           \
  STATIC_IF( IS_PTR_TO_CONST_EXPR(PTR),        \
    nonconst_ ## FN,                           \
    const_ ## FN                               \
  )( (PTR) __VA_OPT__(,) __VA_ARGS__ )
```

Listing 19.8: `const` overload any function

19.5 No SFINAE (Substitution Failure is not an Error)

Recall the `string` structure from listing 1.9 (p.23):

```
struct string {
  char   *contents;  // pointer to actual contents
  size_t len;        // length (not including null at end)
};
```

Suppose you want to write a macro `STRLEN` that gets the length of either an ordinary C string or a `string`. You might write something like what's shown in listing 19.9.

```
#define STRLEN(S)                          \
  _Generic( (S),                           \
    char const*   : strlen((S))            \
    struct string*: (S)->len               \
  )
```

Listing 19.9: `STRLEN`, version 1

That is, if the type of s is:

- `char const*`, call `strlen(S)`; or:
- `string*`, return `(S)->len`.

That seems fairly straightforward. There's just one problem: it won't compile. Instead, you'll get:

1. `strlen(S)`: "**warning**: incompatible pointer types passing `string*` to a parameter of type `const char*`."
2. `(S)->len`: "**error**: type `const char` is not a structure or union."

The problem with `_Generic` is that *all* expressions *must* be valid — even expressions that are not selected. Specifically for this example:

1. You can't call `strlen` on a `string*`; and:
2. You can't refer to `->len` on a `char const*`.

In C++ with *SFINAE*, something that isn't valid when substituted is not an error: it's simply ignored; unfortunately, not so in C.

> ■ SFINAE is an (unpronounceable) acronym for "substitution failure is not an error." It's a principle in C++ where a substitution of a template parameter resulting in an invalid expression is not an error; it's simply ignored. □

The way to fix this is to make every `_Generic` expression similar. In this case, we can add a function:

```
inline size_t string_len( struct string const *str ) {
  return str->len;
}
```

Then rewrite STRLEN as shown in listing 19.10.

```
#define STRLEN(S)                    \
  _Generic( (S),                     \
    char const*   : strlen,          \
    struct string*: string_len       \
  )( (S) )
```

Listing 19.10: STRLEN, version 2

This works because each expression is the name of a function to call and each is passed a single pointer of the type it expects. Note that it's necessary to put the argument s outside the `_Generic`: if it were inside, then one function call would always be passing the wrong type.

19.6 Type Traits

Using `_Generic`, you can define macros similar to C++'s type traits functions. Note that some macros take expressions and others take types. Having one or the other (or sometimes both) is useful.

IS_ARRAY_EXPR

Gets whether A is an expression of an array (as opposed to a pointer) type:

```
#define IS_ARRAY_EXPR(A)            \
  _Generic( &(A),                   \
    typeof(*(A)) (*)[]: true,       \
    default           : false       \
  )
```

This works because if A is actually an array:

1. The &(A) yields "pointer to array of type T."
2. The A (inside typeof) "decays" into a pointer to its first element yielding "pointer to T," i.e., T*.
3. The *A dereferences T* yielding the element type T.
4. Finally, T (*)[] yields "pointer to array of type T" that matches #1 above and _Generic returns true.

If A isn't an array, e.g., a pointer, then none of the above works and _Generic matches the default case and returns false.

As written (p. 128), ARRAY_SIZE can be wrongly used on an "array" parameter (§9.4). For example, in the following code, ARRAY_SIZE returns the size of the pointer, not the actual array:

```
void print_csi( size_t n, int const vals[] ) {
  for ( size_t i = 0; i < ARRAY_SIZE(vals); ++i ) // WRONG
    // ...
```

To improve ARRAY_SIZE such that it will generate a compile-time error if used on anything but an array, we can use IS_ARRAY_EXPR with STATIC_ASSERT_EXPR (p.245):

```
#define ARRAY_SIZE(A) (                           \
  STATIC_ASSERT_EXPR( IS_ARRAY_EXPR(A),           \
                      #A " must be an array" )   \
  * sizeof(A) / sizeof(A[0]) )
```

(The compiler will optimize away the multiplication.)

19.6 Type Traits

IS_POINTER_EXPR

Gets whether P is an expression of a pointer (as opposed to an array) type:

```
#define IS_POINTER_EXPR(P)         \
  _Generic( &(typeof((P))){ },     \
    typeof(*(P)) **  : true,       \
    default          : false       \
  )
```

This works like STATIC_IF and IS_ARRAY_EXPR. The reason the &(typeof((P))){ } is necessary, instead of simply &(P), is for the case where you take the address of an object via & to yield a pointer rather than pass a pointer directly as shown in listing 19.11.

```
#define MEM_ZERO(P) do {                         \
  static_assert( IS_POINTER_EXPR(P),             \
                 #P " must be a pointer" );     \
  memset( (P), 0, sizeof( *(P) ) );              \
} while (0)

struct S { /* ... */ };
struct S s;
MEM_ZERO( &s );
```

Listing 19.11: Example use of IS_POINTER_EXPR

If &(P) were used, passing &s (an *rvalue*) would result in &(&s) which is illegal. However, when using &(typeof((P))){ }, the typeof((P)){ } results in a compound literal of type pointer to S and compound literals are *lvalues* that you can take the address of.

■ The terms *lvalue* and *rvalue* are used to describe values of expressions:

- An *lvalue* is a value, has a name, can appear on the left-hand-side of = (hence the "l" in lvalue), and can have its address taken via & (the address-of operator, §3.12).
- An *rvalue* is a *temporary* value, has no name, can appear *only* on the right-hand-side of = (hence the "r" in rvalue), and can *not* have its address taken via &.

The key thing that distinguishes an lvalue from an rvalue is: if something has a name, it's *not* an rvalue. Some examples are shown in listing 19.12. Both lvalues and rvalues have more significance in C++ with references. □

```
int a, b, *p;

a = b;              // "a" and "b" are both lvalues
a = a + b;          // "a" = lvalue; "a + b" = rvalue
a + b = 42;         // error: rvalue on left-hand-side of =

p = &a;             // address of lvalue
p = &(a + b);       // error: address of rvalue
```

Listing 19.12: Examples of lvalues and rvalues

IS_C_STR_EXPR

Gets whether E is an expression of a C string type:

```
#define IS_C_STR_EXPR(E)       \
  _Generic( (E),               \
    char*         : true,      \
    char const*   : true,      \
    default       : false      \
  )
```

This definition doesn't include the Unicode character types (§2.8) but you can make it include them if you want to.

As written (p. 131), STRLITLEN can be wrongly used on any char*, not only string literals. To improve STRLITLEN such that it will generate a compile-time error if used on anything but a string literal, we can use the improved ARRAY_SIZE (p. 290), STATIC_ASSERT_EXPR (p. 245), and IS_C_STR_EXPR:

```
#define STRLITLEN(S) (ARRAY_SIZE( (S) ) -         \
  STATIC_ASSERT_EXPR( IS_C_STR_EXPR( (S) ),       \
                    #S " must be a string literal" ) )
```

IS_SIGNED_TYPE and IS_UNSIGNED_TYPE

Gets whether T is a signed or unsigned integer type:

```
#define IS_SIGNED_TYPE(T)     !IS_UNSIGNED_TYPE(T)
#define IS_UNSIGNED_TYPE(T)   ((T)-1 > 0)
```

Note that IS_SIGNED_TYPE should not be ((T)-1 < 0) because some compilers will give an "expression is always false" warning for unsigned types.

19.6 Type Traits

IS_SIGNED_EXPR and IS_UNSIGNED_EXPR

Gets whether E is an expression of a signed integer type:

```
#define IS_SIGNED_EXPR(E)                      \
  _Generic( (E),                               \
    bool         : false,                      \
    char         : IS_SIGNED_TYPE(char),       \
    signed char: true,                         \
    short        : true,                       \
    int          : true,                       \
    long         : true,                       \
    long long    : true,                       \
    default      : false                       \
  )
```

Gets whether E is an expression of an unsigned integer type:

```
#define IS_UNSIGNED_EXPR(E)                         \
  _Generic( (E),                                    \
    bool                  : true,                   \
    char                  : IS_UNSIGNED_TYPE(char), \
    unsigned char         : true,                   \
    unsigned short        : true,                   \
    unsigned int          : true,                   \
    unsigned long         : true,                   \
    unsigned long long: true,                       \
    default               : false                   \
  )
```

As a reminder, it's implementation defined whether char is signed or unsigned (§2.5.3).

IS_INTEGRAL_EXPR

Gets whether E is an expression of an integer type:

```
#define IS_INTEGRAL_EXPR(E) \
  (IS_SIGNED_EXPR(E) || IS_UNSIGNED_EXPR(E))
```

For example uses, see TO_SIGNED_EXPR (p.296) and TO_UNSIGNED_EXPR (p.296).

IS_FLOATING_POINT_EXPR

Gets whether E is an expression of a floating-point type:

```
#define IS_FLOATING_POINT_EXPR(E) \
  _Generic( (E),                  \
    float          : true,        \
    double         : true,        \
    long double    : true,        \
    default        : false        \
  )
```

This definition doesn't include decimal-floating (§2.5.7), _Complex (§2.5.8), or _Imaginary (§2.5.9) types; but you can make it include them if you want to.

IS_ARITHMETIC_EXPR

Gets whether E is an expression of an arithmetic type:

```
#define IS_ARITHMETIC_EXPR(E) \
   (IS_INTEGRAL_EXPR(E) || IS_FLOATING_POINT_EXPR(E))
```

IS_TYPE_EXPR

Gets whether E is an expression of a specific type T:

```
#define IS_TYPE_EXPR(T,E) \
  _Generic( (E),          \
    T        : true,      \
    default  : false      \
  )
```

19.6 Type Traits

INT_MAX_EXPR and INT_MIN_EXPR

For an integer expression N, gets the maximum value for its type (§2.10):

```
#define INT_MAX_EXPR(N)                       \
    _Generic( (N),                            \
        bool                : 1,              \
        signed char         : SCHAR_MAX,      \
        char                : CHAR_MAX,       \
        short               : SHRT_MAX,       \
        int                 : INT_MAX,        \
        long                : LONG_MAX,       \
        long long           : LLONG_MAX,      \
        unsigned char       : UCHAR_MAX,      \
        unsigned short      : USHRT_MAX,      \
        unsigned int        : UINT_MAX,       \
        unsigned long       : ULONG_MAX,      \
        unsigned long long  : ULLONG_MAX      \
    )
```

For an integer expression N, gets the minimum value for its type (§2.10):

```
#define INT_MIN_EXPR(N)                       \
    _Generic( (N),                            \
        bool                : 0,              \
        signed char         : SCHAR_MIN,      \
        char                : CHAR_MIN,       \
        short               : SHRT_MIN,       \
        int                 : INT_MIN,        \
        long                : LONG_MIN,       \
        long long           : LLONG_MIN,      \
        unsigned char       : 0,              \
        unsigned short      : 0,              \
        unsigned int        : 0,              \
        unsigned long       : 0,              \
        unsigned long long  : 0               \
    )
```

Note that neither of these macros needs to use IS_INTEGRAL_EXPR(N) since the compiler will generate an error if the type of N doesn't match one of the types in the association list.

IS_SAME_TYPE

Gets whether T and U are the same type similar to C++'s std::is_same:

```
#define IS_SAME_TYPE(T,U)           \
  _Generic( *(T*)nullptr,           \
    typeof_unqual(U): true,  \
    default          : false \
  )
```

The *(T*)nullptr is needed to convert T (a type) into an expression required by _Generic. (Reminder: the expression isn't evaluated, so it doesn't matter that it's dereferencing a null pointer.)

The typeof_unqual(U) (§4.7) is necessary to remove qualifiers, otherwise it would never match if U had qualifiers. (Reminder: _Generic discards qualifiers from the type of the controlling expression.)

An example use for IS_SAME_TYPE is to write a generic SWAP macro as shown in listing 19.13.

```
#define SWAP(A,B) do {                                          \
    static_assert( IS_SAME_TYPE( typeof(A), typeof(B) ),        \
      "SWAP() arguments must have same type" );                 \
    auto const UNIQUE_NAME(tmp) = (A);                          \
    (A) = (B);                                                  \
    (B) = UNIQUE_NAME(tmp);                                     \
  } while (0)
```

Listing 19.13: Generic swap macro

TO_SIGNED_EXPR and TO_UNSIGNED_EXPR

Casts an integer expression N to a signed type of the same size:

```
#define TO_SIGNED_EXPR(N) (                       \
  STATIC_ASSERT_EXPR( IS_INTEGRAL_EXPR( (N) ),    \
    #N " must be integral" ) *                    \
  STATIC_IF( sizeof(N) == sizeof(char ),          \
    (signed char)(N),                             \
  STATIC_IF( sizeof(N) == sizeof(short),          \
    (short     )(N),                              \
  STATIC_IF( sizeof(N) == sizeof(int  ),          \
    (int       )(N),                              \
  STATIC_IF( sizeof(N) == sizeof(long ),          \
    (long      )(N),                              \
    (long long )(N) ) ) ) )
```

Casts an integer expression N to an unsigned type of the same size:

```
#define TO_UNSIGNED_EXPR(N) (                        \
    STATIC_ASSERT_EXPR( IS_INTEGRAL_EXPR( (N) ),     \
        #N " must be integral" ) *                   \
    STATIC_IF( sizeof(N) == sizeof(char ),           \
        (unsigned char     )(N),                     \
    STATIC_IF( sizeof(N) == sizeof(short),           \
        (unsigned short    )(N),                     \
    STATIC_IF( sizeof(N) == sizeof(int  ),           \
        (unsigned int      )(N),                     \
    STATIC_IF( sizeof(N) == sizeof(long ),           \
        (unsigned long     )(N),                     \
        (unsigned long long)(N) ) ) ) )
```

UNDERLYING_TYPE

Gets the underlying type of an enumeration (§7.3) similar to `std::underlying_type` in C++:

```
#define UNDERLYING_TYPE(ENUM_TYPE)                       \
    typeof( STATIC_IF( IS_SIGNED_TYPE(ENUM_TYPE),        \
                       TO_SIGNED_EXPR( (ENUM_TYPE)0 ),   \
                       TO_UNSIGNED_EXPR( (ENUM_TYPE)0 ) ) )
```

19.7 Epilogue

Here are some key points about _Generic:

- _Generic allows C library authors to provide a veneer of C++ function overloading in C by selecting among several expressions based on the type of a controlling expression.
- However, _Generic is capable of more including const overloading and C++-style type traits that allow more type-safe macros to be written.
- Even though _Generic is part of the C language proper, the only way you can practically use it is via a function-like macro.

Exercises

1. Modify your solution of ARRAY_END for exercise 8.2 (p.133) to check that ARRAY really is an array as opposed to a pointer. Hint: use IS_ARRAY_EXPR (p.290) and STATIC_ASSERT_EXPR (p.245).

Chapter 20
`setjmp` and `longjmp`

Unlike C++, C#, Java, or Python, C doesn't have exceptions. However, C does have two functions, `setjmp` and `longjmp`, that can be used together to return through more than one level of the call stack, typically as an error-handling mechanism when there's no other way for a deeply nested function to stop and return an error.

20.1 Basics

Let's jump (no pun intended) right in with an example given in listing 20.1.

- Line 1 includes the `setjmp.h` standard header needed to use `setjmp` and `longjmp`.
- Line 5 declares a global instance of `jmp_buf` that will be shared between the functions that call `setjmp` and `longjmp`.
- In `main`, line 21 calls `setjmp` that saves a copy of the current "execution context" into `env` and returns 0 that means "proceed normally."
- Line 22 calls `load_config` that in turn calls `read_file`.
- Now in `read_file` on line 9, we were unable to open the file so we call `longjmp` on line 10 passing `env` as the first argument. The second argument can be any `int` value. It's used to communicate a code of some kind, typically an error code.
- The program execution "jumps" back to the exact point where the `setjmp` was called on line 21 "returning" a *second* time with the value passed to `longjmp`, in this case 1. Note that control has returned from `read_file` directly to `main` bypassing `load_config`.
- Since 1 is not 0, execution transfers to the `else` on line 23.

That's it. While that doesn't seem complicated, the devil, as ever, is in the details.

```
1   #include <setjmp.h>
2   #include <stdio.h>
3   #include <stdlib.h>              // for exit()
4
5   static jmp_buf env;
6
7   void read_file( char const *path ) {
8     FILE *f = fopen( path, "r" );
9     if ( f == nullptr )
10      longjmp( env, 1 );           // "throw"
11    // ...
12  }
13
14  void load_config() {
15    // ...
16    read_file( ".config" );
17    // ...
18  }
19
20  int main() {
21    if ( setjmp( env ) == 0 ) {    // "try"
22      load_config();
23    } else {                       // "catch"
24      fprintf( stderr, "error loading configuration\n" );
25      exit( EXIT_FAILURE );
26    }
27  }
```

Listing 20.1: setjmp and longjmp example

20.2 setjmp Restrictions

Calls to setjmp *must* be done *only* in one of the following ways:

> (**void**)$_{opt}$ setjmp(*env*)
> *control-flow-keyword* (!$_{opt}$ setjmp(*env*) *relop-expr*$_{opt}$)

1. A plain call to setjmp (optionally cast to void); or:
2. For *control-flow-keyword*, one of for, if, switch, or while followed by:
   a. An optional !; followed by:
   b. The call to setjmp; followed by:
   c. An optional relational operator and an integer constant expression.

Additionally, the call to setjmp *must* constitute the entire controlling expression of the for, if, switch, or while which means you can't use && or ||.

Additionally, you may *not* save the return value from setjmp:

> **int** sj = setjmp(env); // not allowed

Calling setjmp in any other way results in undefined behavior (§15).

20.3 `volatile` Variables

Any variables local to the function in which `setjmp` is called that are modified between the calls to `setjmp` and `longjmp` *must* be declared `volatile` (§22). For example:

```
int volatile count = 0;
if ( setjmp( env ) == 0 ) {
  ++count;
}
```

Why? One of the things `setjmp` does is to save the values of all the CPU registers. If a local variable is put into a register by the compiler, then if `longjmp` is called and `setjmp` returns for the second time, it restores the values of the registers. For the above example, if count were not declared `volatile`, then:

1. The initial value of count (in a register) is 0.
2. `setjmp` saves this value.
3. The code then does ++count setting its value to 1.
4. If `longjmp` is called, `setjmp` returns for the second time restoring the values of all registers — including the register used by count whose value is 0.

The use of `volatile` prevents the compiler from storing the value of a variable in a register (among other things), hence it's stored in the local stack frame instead and so is unaffected by register value restoration.

20.4 `longjmp` Details

Calling `longjmp` returns to the function that called `setjmp`. That function *must* still be on the call stack. For example, you can't "wrap" calls to `setjmp` as shown in listing 20.2.

```
int wrap_setjmp( jmp_buf env ) {   // don't wrap setjmp
  if ( setjmp( env ) == 0 )
    return 0;
  return 1;
}

void read_file( char const *path ) {
  if ( wrap_setjmp( env ) == 0 ) {
    // ...
```

Listing 20.2: Don't wrap `setjmp`

The reason you can't is because `longjmp` jumps back to the `setjmp` — but in this case, that was inside `wrap_setjmp` that has already returned. This results in undefined behavior (§15).

The second argument to `longjmp` can be any non-zero value you want. It becomes the second return value of `setjmp`. For example, you can use it for error codes like in listing 20.3.

```
constexpr unsigned EX_FILE_IO_ERROR  = 0x0101;
constexpr unsigned EX_FILE_NOT_FOUND = 0x0102;

void read_file( char const *path ) {
  switch ( setjmp( env ) ) {
    case 0:
      read_file( path );
      break;
    case EX_FILE_IO_ERROR:
      // ...
      break;
    case EX_FILE_NOT_FOUND:
      // ...
      break;
  }
}
```

Listing 20.3: Using error codes with `setjmp`

Incidentally, you can't meaningfully pass 0 as the second argument to `longjmp`: if you do, it will silently be changed to 1.

Lastly, variable length arrays (§6.14) must *not* be used at all when using `longjmp`. If there are VLAs anywhere in the call stack between the `longjmp` and the `setjmp`, those likely will cause a memory leak (§18.6.7).

20.5 Exceptions in C?

Now that you know how `setjmp` and `longjmp` work, you might be wondering whether they can be used to implement exceptions in C. The answer can be best summed up as:

"Ooh ... Short answer: yes, with an if; long answer: no, with a but."
— Rev. Timothy Lovejoy, Jr.[†]

For a more detailed answer, see §27.

20.6 Epilogue

Here are some key points about and some advice for `setjmp` and `longjmp`:

[†]Harry Shearer (*Rev. Timothy Lovejoy, Jr.*), "Hurricane Neddy," *The Simpsons*, 8(8), Matt Groening (creator), Gracie Films, Dec. 29, 1996.

20.6 Epilogue

- Together, `setjmp` and `longjmp` can be used to "jump" back through multiple function calls, effectively a non-local `goto`, as an error-handing mechanism.
- Use `setjmp` to mark the point to jump back to and `longjmp` to perform the jump.
- Both `setjmp` and `longjmp` have many restrictions that you *must* adhere to.
- You may need to use `volatile` variables (§22).

Chapter 21
`restrict`

Among other things, C99 added the `restrict` keyword as a way for a programmer to specify that a pointer is the only pointer to a given object in a scope and, consequently, give the compiler a "hint" that it may perform additional optimizations when accessing the object via that pointer.

21.1 The Problem

To illustrate the problem that `restrict` solves, consider the function in listing 21.1.

```
void update_ptrs( int *p, int *q, int const *v ) {
  *p += *v;
  *q += *v;
}
```

Listing 21.1: Function to update pointers, version 1

The compiler will generate x86–64 assembly for it like:

```
1  mov eax, [rdx]    ; tmp = *v
2  add [rdi], eax    ; *p += tmp
3  mov eax, [rdx]    ; tmp = *v
4  add [rsi], eax    ; *q += tmp
```

You might wonder why it generates line 3 since it seems redundant with line 1. The problem is the compiler can't know you didn't do something like this:

```
int x = 1, v = 2;
update_ptrs( &v, &x, &v );   // x = 5, v = 4
```

In `update_ptrs`, p and v would alias the same `int`, so the compiler has to play it safe and assume that the value of `*v` can change between reads, hence the additional `mov` instruction.

In general, pointers in C confound optimization since the compiler can't know whether two pointers alias each other. In performance critical code, eliding memory reads could be a huge win if the compiler could do it safely.

21.2 The Solution

To solve the aforementioned problem, restrict was added to C to allow you to specify that a given pointer is the only pointer to an object in the pointer's scope, i.e., no other pointer in the same scope aliases it.

To use restrict, insert it *between* the * and the pointer's name in a declaration (like a const pointer, §1.7). An update_ptrs rewritten to use restrict is shown in listing 21.2.

```
void update_ptrs_v2( int *p, int *q,
                     int const *restrict v ) {
  *p += *v;
  *q += *v;
}
```

Listing 21.2: Function to update pointers, version 2, with restrict

(Read from right-to-left, e.g., v is a restricted pointer to a constant int.) By adding restrict, the compiler can now generate assembly like:

```
1  mov eax, [rdx]    ; tmp = *v
2  add [rdi], eax    ; *p += tmp
3  add [rsi], eax    ; *q += tmp
```

The compiler was able to elide the previous line 3 of the additional mov instruction.

Perhaps the best-known example where restrict is used is the standard function memcpy (§B.2):

```
void* memcpy( void *restrict dst,
              void const *restrict src, size_t n );
```

It's the fastest way to copy memory *if* the src and dst addresses do *not* overlap. The slightly slower memmove (§B.2) exists for use when the addresses do overlap.

21.3 Pitfalls

Misuse of restrict results in undefined behavior (§15), for example, by passing pointers that alias each other to update_ptrs_v2 or memcpy. In some cases, the compiler can warn you, but not in all cases, so don't rely on the compiler to catch misuses.

21.4 When (and When Not) to Use `restrict`

Note that `restrict` is for a given scope. Assigning one restricted pointer to another in the same scope results in undefined behavior:

```
void f( int *restrict d, int *restrict s ) {
    int *restrict p = s;     // undefined behavior
```

However, you can assign a restricted pointer to an unrestricted pointer just fine:

```
void f( int *restrict d, int *restrict s ) {
    int *p = s;              // OK
```

Even though p is unrestricted, the compiler can still perform the same optimizations.

It's also OK to assign a restricted pointer in an inner scope to another in an outer scope (but not the other way around):

```
void f( int *restrict d, int *restrict s ) {
    {                                   // inner scope
        int *restrict p = s;     // OK
        // ...
        s = p;                   // undefined behavior
    }
}
```

21.4 When (and When Not) to Use `restrict`

First, you should definitely profile your code (§18.9) and perhaps even look at the generated assembly code to see if using `restrict` actually makes a significant performance gain to justify risking the potential pitfalls. Diagnosing bugs caused by misuse of `restrict` is very hard to do.

Second, if use of `restrict` is confined to a function where the memory accessed via restricted pointers was allocated by you, then it's safer. For example, given:

```
void safer( unsigned n ) {
    n += n % 2 != 0;                 // make even by rounding up
    unsigned *const array = malloc( n * sizeof(unsigned) );
    unsigned *restrict half_1st = array;
    unsigned *restrict half_2nd = array + n/2;
    // ...
    free( array );
}
```

the code could operate on the first and second halves of array safely because they don't overlap (assuming you never access `half_1st[n/2]` or beyond).

Third, if `restrict` is used in a function's parameters, then it's potentially less safe. For example, contrast `safer` with `update_ptrs_v2` where the caller controls the pointers. For all you know, the caller got it wrong and passed pointers that alias.

21.5 Miscellaneous

Only pointers to objects (or `void`) can be qualified with `restrict`:

```
restrict int x;         // can't restrict non-pointer
int restrict *pi;       // can't restrict non-pointer
int (*restrict pf)();   // can't restrict pointer to function
```

You can use `restrict` for structure members as shown in listing 21.3.

```
struct node {
  void *restrict data;
  struct node *restrict left, *restrict right;
};
```

Listing 21.3: `restrict` with structure members

That says `data` will be the only pointer to that data and `left` and `right` will never point to the same node. Using `restrict` for structure members is very uncommon.

■ C++ never adopted `restrict` from C. Why not? The answer is fairly long and complicated, but the short version is that:

- `restrict` can be a source of hard-to-find bugs that the C++ committee didn't want to adopt from C.
- C++'s increased use of pointers, e.g., `this`, make using `restrict` safely even harder.

However, many C++ compilers offer `__restrict__` as an extension.[†] □

21.6 Epilogue

Here are some key points about and some advice for `restrict`:

- `restrict` exists to tell the compiler that a pointer is the *only* pointer to a given object in a scope so it can generate more efficient code.
- `restrict` is syntactically a qualifier like `_Atomic`, `const`, and `volatile`.
- Unlike the other qualifiers, `restrict` can be used only for pointers.
- In limited cases, using `restrict` can lead to performance gains.
- Diagnosing bugs caused by misuse of `restrict` is very hard to do.
- Before even considering using `restrict`, profile your code first (§18.9).

Use wisely.

[†]*Restricting Pointer Aliasing*, Free Software Foundation, *Using the GNU Compiler Collection*, §7.2, 1988–2025, https://gcc.gnu.org/onlinedocs/gcc/Restricted-Pointers.html

Chapter 22
`volatile`

C has the `volatile` keyword that's a qualifier (§4.5) just like `_Atomic` (§17), `const` (§4.5), and `restrict` (§21). As with `const`, `volatile` can be written to the right or "east" of the base type (§1.7):

```
volatile int x;    // "west" volatile
int volatile y;    // "east" volatile
```

In some code, there are uses of the `volatile` keyword that are simply *wrong*. This unfortunate situation is perpetuated by many articles on the Internet whose explanations of `volatile` are also simply *wrong*. So here, hopefully once and for all, is what `volatile` in C actually (and only) does.

■ Everything described in this chapter applies equally to C++ that also has the `volatile` keyword. □

There are *only* three legitimate uses of `volatile` in C:

1. To tell the compiler that objects qualified with it may either be modified or cause side effects in ways unknown to the compiler; therefore, not to optimize away accesses to such objects nor reorder their accesses with respect to other operations that have visible side effects.
2. For use in a signal handler.
3. For use with `setjmp` (§20).

That's it. Any other use of `volatile` is innocuous, inefficient, or simply *wrong*.

22.1 Optimization Suppression

The C23 standard §6.7.3¶8 says the following about the first use of `volatile`:

> An object that has a `volatile`-qualified type may be modified in ways unknown to the implementation or have other unknown side effects.

This typically means memory-mapped I/O, that is particular memory addresses are mapped either to specialized hardware or functions, so that reading from such an address actually reads a current value from such hardware (say, some kind of sensor) or writing to such an address actually causes a change in such hardware (say, sends a value over an old-fashioned modem).

For example, consider the code in listing 22.1 that sends all the characters of a C string over a modem that is mapped to the address 0x1000:

```
char *const MODEM = (char*)0x1000;   // memory-mapped

void modem_send_s( char const *s ) {
  while ( *s )
    *MODEM = *s++;
}
```

Listing 22.1: modem_send

Writing a character to *MODEM sends that character. The problem is that a compiler might be clever and optimize that code to be:

```
while ( *s++ )          // compiler-optimized version
  ;
*MODEM = s[-1];
```

Under ordinary circumstances, it would be within its rights to do so (because if MODEM were a pointer to ordinary memory, only the last write matters). But in the memory-mapped I/O case, it would be wrong (because the compiler doesn't know that address 0x1000 is special).

The C23 standard continues:

> Therefore any expression referring to such an object shall be evaluated strictly according to the rules of the abstract machine ...

That means *no* reads from *nor* writes to such an object will be optimized away nor instructions reordered by the compiler even if it normally would do so.

The way to tell the compiler not to optimize accesses to an object is by qualifying it with volatile:

```
char volatile *const MODEM = (char*)0x1000;
```

(Read from right-to-left: MODEM is a constant pointer to a volatile character.)

22.2 Signal Handling

The C23 standard §7.14.1.1¶5 says the following about the second use of volatile:

22.4 volatile in Other Languages

If the signal occurs ..., the behavior is undefined if the signal handler refers to any object with static or thread storage duration that is not a lock-free atomic object other than by assigning a value to an object declared as `volatile sig_atomic_t ...`

That means if you want to refer to any object outside of a signal handler function, the type of that object, *must* be `volatile sig_atomic_t` as shown in listing 22.2.

```
sig_atomic_t volatile last_sig_val;

void signal_handler( int sig_val ) {
  // ...
  last_sig_val = sig_val;
}
```

Listing 22.2: Use of `volatile` with signal handlers

22.3 setjmp

The C23 standard §7.13.2.1¶3 says the following about the third use of `volatile`:

... the representation of objects of automatic storage duration that are local to the function containing the invocation of ... `setjmp` *... that do not have* `volatile`*-qualified type and have been changed between the* `setjmp` *invocation and* `longjmp` *call is indeterminate.*

That means if you modify a local variable between the time `setjmp` is called and `longjmp` returns (§20), that variable *must* be declared `volatile` as shown in listing 22.3.

```
void f() {
  int volatile count = 0;
  if ( setjmp( jmp_buf ) != 0 )
    g( ++count );
  // ...
}
```

Listing 22.3: Use of `volatile` with `setjmp`

22.4 volatile in Other Languages

The explanation of `volatile` here pertains *only* to C (and C++). The `volatile` keyword also appears in other languages, for example C# and Java.

In those languages, `volatile` provides stronger guarantees regarding operations and therefore can be used for limited forms of thread-safety (§14). And this can sometimes cause confusion as to what `volatile` means in C (and C++).

22.5 Wrong Uses

In C, `volatile`:

- Is *not* a synonym for `_Atomic` (§17).
- Does *not* use memory barriers (§17.3).
- Therefore, does *not* guarantee thread-safety.
- Limits *only* what optimizations the compiler may do (§14).
- Does *not* limit what the CPU can do (§14).

In particular, the hardware is still free to do things like memory caching, instruction parallelization, and speculative execution.

22.6 Epilogue

Here are some key points about and some advice for `volatile`:

- `volatile` is used *only* for memory-mapped I/O, signal handlers, or with `setjmp`.
- Unless you're doing one of those things, do *not* use `volatile`.
- `volatile` is syntactically a qualifier like `_Atomic`, `const`, and `restrict`.
- For pointers, the pointer, the object pointed to, or both, can be `volatile`.

Part III
Extended Examples

Part III gives detailed examples with full source code of how features in other languages might be implemented including discussion of the trade-offs involved so you can understand what's really going on behind the curtain in whatever language you program in:

23. **Strings**: Illustrates proper string and string buffer types.
24. **Lists**: Illustrates initialization, clean-up, pushing, popping, removing elements, utility functions, and iterating for linked lists.
25. **Maps**: Illustrates initialization, clean-up, insertion, growing, finding, deleting, and iterating for hash tables that implement maps in languages like C++, Go, Java, Python, and Rust.
26. **Dynamic Dispatch**: Illustrates how pointers to function, function tables, and fat pointers are used to implement dynamic dispatch in languages like C++, C#, Go, Java, Python, Smalltalk, Rust, and Swift.
27. **Exceptions in C**: Illustrates how to use `setjmp` and `longjmp` to implement exception handling in C.

Chapter 23
Strings

Recall the proper string type that can grow automatically from §1.9:

```
struct string {
  char   *contents; // pointer to actual contents
  size_t len;       // length (not including null at end)
};
```

plus the functions:

```
void string_puts( struct string *str, char const *s );
void string_cleanup( struct string *str );
```

To make the string type more production-quality, it could use a few more functions. Additionally, a string buffer type is also quite useful.

23.1 `string` 2.0

Specifically, the string type could use few more "`put`" variants, formatted printing, and string ownership management.

23.1.1 More `put` Variants

The first new function is `string_putsn` that puts no more than n characters shown in listing 23.1. (It's an optimized version of the answer to exercise 1.4, p.26.)

- Line 3 sets n to the smaller of `strlen(s)` and n using `strnlen` (the answer to exercise 1.3, p.26).
- Line 6 calls `memcpy` (§B.2) to copy *exactly* n characters rather than however many characters are in s (that might be > n).

```
1  void string_putsn( struct string *str, char const *s,
2                     size_t n ) {
3    n = strnlen( s, n );
4    auto const new_len = str->len + n;
5    str->contents = realloc( str->contents, new_len + 1 );
6    memcpy( str->contents + str->len, s, n );
7    str->len = new_len;
8    str->contents[ str->len ] = '\0';
9  }
```

Listing 23.1: `string_putsn`

- Consequently on line 8, we must explicitly null-terminate the string.

Given that, `string_puts` can be rewritten as an `inline` function (§9.10) to call `string_putsn` and an additional `string_putc` can be written to append a single character as shown in listing 23.2.

```
inline void string_puts( struct string *str,
                         char const *s ) {
  string_putsn( str, s, strlen( s ) );
}

inline void string_putc( struct string *str, char c ) {
  string_putsn( str, &c, 1 );
}
```

Listing 23.2: `string_puts` and `string_putc`

Remember that inline functions need to be defined in a `.c` file (§9.10.4) like:

```
extern void string_puts( struct string*, char const* );
extern void string_putc( struct string*, char );
```

23.1.2 Formatted Printing

In addition to `printf`, the C standard library contains several variations, such as:

```
int snprintf( char *buf, size_t cap,
              char const *format, ... );
```

that "prints" the formatted string to the string buffer pointed to by `buf` having the capacity `cap`. The problem is the formatted string might not fit within `cap`. An implementation of `string_printf` that grows the string's size to accommodate the formatted string is shown in listing 23.3.

- Line 3 declares `args` and line 4 calls `va_start` per §9.11.

23.1 string 2.0

```
1   int string_printf( struct string *str,
2                      char const *format, ... ) {
3     va_list args;
4     va_start( args );
5     auto raw_len = vsnprintf( nullptr, 0, format, args );
6     va_end( args );
7     if ( raw_len <= 0 )
8       return raw_len;
9
10    auto const args_len = (size_t)raw_len;
11    auto const new_len = str->len + args_len;
12    str->contents = realloc( str->contents, new_len + 1 );
13    auto const buf = str->contents + str->len;
14
15    va_start( args );
16    raw_len = vsnprintf( buf, args_len + 1, format, args );
17    va_end( args );
18    str->len = new_len;
19    return raw_len;
20  }
```

Listing 23.3: string_printf

- Line 5 calls vsnprintf (variadic string of length n printf) that, fortunately, returns the number of characters that *would* have been printed if buffer were infinite.

  Normally, you pass the char array and its length you want the characters "printed" into, but here we pass nullptr and 0 since we don't yet have anywhere to print the characters, but we still want the number of characters that would have been printed.

- Alternatively, vsnprintf can return a negative value to indicate an error, so we check for this and return if necessary.
- Now that we know raw_len > 0, line 10 casts it to size_t.
- Now that the string is big enough to accommodate the formatted string, we call vsnprintf again on line 16 to print the arguments for real this time.

23.1.3 Taking Ownership

Another function that might be good to have is a way for the user to "take" a string's contents away from it in order to do something else with it, e.g., give it to some other function that will subsequently own it. Such a function is shown in listing 23.4 and is straightforward.

```
[[nodiscard]] char* string_take( struct string *str ) {
    auto const contents = str->contents;
    *str = (struct string){ };
    return contents;
}
```

Listing 23.4: `string_take`

23.2 `strbuf`: A String Buffer Type

The `string` structure and associated functions as presented in §23.1 are reasonable for production-quality use when managing the storage for and occasionally appending strings.

Another common use of strings is to append repeatedly while reading either from a file or socket. For such a use, calling `realloc` for every append is inefficient. It's better to give such strings additional capacity to grow into — a "buffer." Many languages provide such functionality. For example, C++ has `std::ostringstream`, Go has `strings.Builder`, Java has `StringBuilder`, and Python has `io.StringIO`.

To implement a string buffer in C, a *capacity* needs to be stored in addition to a length as shown in listing 23.5.

```
struct strbuf {
    char    *contents;  // pointer to actual contents
    size_t  len;        // length (not including null at end)
    size_t  cap;        // capacity
};
```

Listing 23.5: `strbuf`, version 1

While it's easy to add `cap`, it's not the most efficient in terms of storage. Assuming 8-byte pointers and `size_t`, `sizeof(strbuf)` would likely be 32 bytes, not 24, due to padding (§10.5).

One possible fix for that would be to use `uint32_t` rather than `size_t` so both `len` and `cap` would fit into 8 bytes making `sizeof(strbuf)` be 16 bytes. It's very unlikely that you'll be dealing with strings in excess of 4,294,967,294 ($2^{32} - 1$) characters. The updated `strbuf` declaration is shown in figure 23.6.

```
1  struct strbuf {
2      char      *contents;  // pointer to actual contents
3      uint32_t  len;        // length (not including null at end)
4      uint32_t  cap;        // capacity
5  };
```

Listing 23.6: `strbuf`, version 2, using `uint32_t`

23.2 strbuf: A String Buffer Type

23.2.1 Reserving Space

In cases where the user knows the length of a string (or sequence of strings) to append, it would be efficient to do *one* realloc in advance to reserve capacity. Such a function is shown in listing 23.7.

```
1   bool strbuf_reserve( struct strbuf *sbuf,
2                        size_t res_len ) {
3     if ( res_len < sbuf->cap - sbuf->len )
4       return false;
5     if ( sbuf->cap == 0 )
6       sbuf->cap = 2;
7     auto const new_len = sbuf->len + res_len;
8     while ( sbuf->cap <= new_len )
9       sbuf->cap <<= 1;
10    sbuf->contents = realloc( sbuf->contents, sbuf->cap );
11    return true;
12  }
```

Listing 23.7: strbuf_reserve

- Lines 3–4 check whether there is already capacity for res_len additional characters: if so, it returns false indicating that no reallocation was necessary, i.e., there is already sufficient capacity.
- Lines 5–6 check for the initial case of cap being 0: if so, sets it to 2.
- Line 7 calculates the new length.
- Lines 8–9 double the capacity while it's still $\leq$ new_len. The idea is to double the capacity every time you need to increase it so each subsequent doublings will be necessary half as often.
- Line 11 returns true indicating that a reallocation was necessary. (We'll see why this is useful shortly.)

23.2.2 Putting

Given strbuf_reserve, listing 23.8 shows strbuf_putsn, strbuf_puts, and strbuf_putc.

- Line 4 calls strbuf_reserve to ensure cap has room for n more characters.
- Line 5 now simply copies s into place using memcpy since we null-terminate the string ourselves on line 7.

```
void strbuf_putsn( struct strbuf *sbuf, char const *s,
                   size_t n ) {
  n = strnlen( s, n );
  strbuf_reserve( sbuf, n );
  memcpy( sbuf->contents + sbuf->len, s, n );
  sbuf->len += n;
  sbuf->contents[ sbuf->len ] = '\0';
}

inline void strbuf_puts( struct strbuf *sbuf,
                         char const *s ) {
  strbuf_putsn( sbuf, s, strlen( s ) );
}

inline void strbuf_putc( struct strbuf *sbuf, char c ) {
  strbuf_putsn( sbuf, &c, 1 );
}
```

Listing 23.8: `strbuf_putsn`, `strbuf_puts`, and `strbuf_putc`

23.2.3 Formatted Printing

The `strbuf_printf` function can be more efficient than `string_printf` from listing 23.3 (p.317) by using `strbuf_reserve` as shown in listing 23.9.

```
int strbuf_printf( struct strbuf *sbuf,
                   char const *format, ... ) {
  char *buf = sbuf->contents == nullptr ?
    nullptr : sbuf->contents + sbuf->len;

  va_list args;
  va_start( args );
  auto raw_len =
    vsnprintf( buf, sbuf->cap - sbuf->len, format, args );
  va_end( args );
  if ( raw_len <= 0 )
    return raw_len;

  auto const args_len = (size_t)raw_len;
  if ( strbuf_reserve( sbuf, args_len ) ) {
    buf = sbuf->contents + sbuf->len;
    va_start( args );
    raw_len = vsnprintf( buf, args_len + 1, format, args );
    va_end( args );
    assert( raw_len > 0 );
  }

  sbuf->len += args_len;
  return raw_len;
}
```

Listing 23.9: `strbuf_printf`

23.2 strbuf: A String Buffer Type

- Since strbuf might already have sufficient capacity, the first call to vsnprintf on line 9 might be able to "print" the entire formatted string into sbuf->contents.

  But first, lines 3–4 check for the special case of sbuf->contents being nullptr: if it is, then simply set buf to nullptr the same as in string_printf (listing 23.3, line 5, p.317).

- Line 15 calls strbuf_reserve. Reminder: if it returns false, there was already sufficient capacity, so we don't have to call vsnprintf again, which means we're done; if it returned true, simply call vsnprintf again on line 18 now that there's sufficient capacity.

23.2.4 Taking Ownership

Similarly to string_take from listing 23.4 (p.318), strbuf should have strbuf_take as shown in listing 23.10.

```
[[nodiscard]] char* strbuf_take( struct strbuf *sbuf ) {
  auto const contents = sbuf->contents;
  *sbuf = (struct strbuf){ };
  return contents;
}
```

Listing 23.10: strbuf_take

23.2.5 Resetting

If the same strbuf is being used repeatedly, it's more efficient simply to "reset" len to 0, but leave cap alone, i.e., don't discard the buffer we've already allocated. We can add a strbuf_reset function to do this by assigning a null character to contents[0] as shown in listing 23.11.

```
void strbuf_reset( struct strbuf *sbuf ) {
  if ( sbuf->contents != nullptr )
    sbuf->contents[0] = '\0';
  sbuf->len = 0;
}
```

Listing 23.11: strbuf_reset

One way to use strbuf_reset is in a function that keeps a strbuf between calls by making it static (§9.9). Consider a function that takes a nullptr-terminated array of strings and makes a single string out of them in "English list" form such that if the number of elements of this list is:

0. E.g., [nullptr] → "".
1. E.g., ["a", nullptr] → "a".
2. E.g., ["a", "b", nullptr] → "a or b".
3. E.g., ["a", "b", "c", nullptr] → "a, b, or c".

Such a function is shown in listing 23.12.

```
1  [[nodiscard]]
2  char const* str_list( char const *list[static 1] ) {
3    if ( list[0] == nullptr )
4      return "";
5
6    static struct strbuf sbuf;
7    strbuf_reset( &sbuf );
8    strbuf_puts( &sbuf, list[0] );
9
10   for ( unsigned i = 1; list[i] != nullptr; ++i ) {
11     auto const sep = list[i+1] != nullptr ?
12       ", " : i > 1 ? ", or " : " or ";
13     strbuf_printf( &sbuf, "%s%s", sep, list[i] );
14   }
15
16   return sbuf.contents;
17 }
```

Listing 23.12: str_list

- Line 2 declares list to be an "array" parameter (§9.4) using the non-null array syntax (§9.4.1) requiring at least 1 element.
- Lines 3–4 check for the trivial case of there being zero elements in list.
- Line 6 declares a static (§9.9) strbuf that will exist for as long as the program does. To make it thread-safe, add thread_local (§14.7).
- Instead of doing:

    sbuf = (struct strbuf){ };

  line 7 calls strbuf_reset simply to reset its length to zero, but leave cap alone.
- Line 8 puts the zeroth string in sbuf.
- Lines 10–14 put the remainder of the strings, if any. (The zeroth string is done outside the loop because if it were done inside, it would need an if (i > 0) for sep.)
- Line 11 peeks ahead at list[i+1] to know whether to put one of ", ", ", ", or ", or ".
- Line 16 returns the string's contents. Because sbuf is static, this won't result in a dangling pointer.

Subsequent times str_list is called can re-use the previously allocated buffer inside strbuf.

23.3 Epilogue

Strictly speaking, the memory used by `sbuf` is a memory-leak (§18.6.7) since it's never freed, but it doesn't grow indefinitely and, as mentioned in §1.8, its memory will be reclaimed by the operating system when the program terminates.

23.3 Epilogue

With only a few more core functions added, especially `string_printf`, `string` is now production-quality. Based on `string`, `strbuf` with the addition of a capacity, is efficient for building strings, hence is suitable for production-quality. Additional functions that could be implemented are left as exercises.

Exercises

1. Write a function:

   ```
   int string_cmp( struct string const *str1,
                   struct string const *str2 );
   ```

   that works like `strcmp` except that it takes advantage of the `len` member. For example, two strings can't be equal unless their lengths are equal.

2. Write a function:

   ```
   void string_etrim( struct string *str );
   ```

   that trims whitespace characters from the end of a string. Hint: no characters need to be moved.

3. Write a function:

   ```
   void string_strim( struct string *str );
   ```

   that trims whitespace characters from the start of a string. Hint: use `memmove` (§B.2).

4. Modify your solution of `string_paths` for exercise 8.1 (p.133) to work with `strbuf` shown in listing 23.6 (p.318):

   ```
   void strbuf_paths( struct strbuf *sbuf,
                      char const *comp );
   ```

Chapter 24
Lists

Recall the intrusive singly linked list structure from listing 10.9 (p.163):

```
struct islist {
  struct islist *next;
  alignas(max_align_t) char data[];
};
```

To make it more production-quality, it could use a couple of changes:

1. The first is to realize that the flexible array member (§10.6) for data can also be used to store data non-intrusively by simply making it store a void* to the actual data.
2. The second is to have separate list and link structures. The new link structure would be the same as the old list structure; the new list structure would have separate head and tail pointers. Having a tail pointer makes certain operations easier as we'll see.

The new structures are shown in listing 24.1. (Since the new list can be used either intrusively or not, the "i" prefix has been dropped.)

```
struct slink {
  struct slink *next;
  alignas(max_align_t) char data[];
};

struct slist {
  struct slink *head, *tail;
};
```

Listing 24.1: Singly linked list structures, version 2

24.1 Initialization and Clean-Up

The first functions to write are initialization and cleanup as shown in listing 24.2.

```
typedef void (*slist_free_fn)( void *data );

inline void slist_init( struct slist *list ) {
  *list = (struct slist){ };
}

void slist_cleanup( struct slist *list,
                    slist_free_fn free_fn ) {
  if ( list == nullptr )
    return;
  struct slink *curr = list->head, *next;
  if ( free_fn == nullptr ) {
    for ( ; curr != nullptr; curr = next ) {
      next = curr->next;
      free( curr );
    }
  } else {
    for ( ; curr != nullptr; curr = next ) {
      (*free_fn)( curr->data );
      next = curr->next;
      free( curr );
    }
  }
  slist_init( list );
}
```

Listing 24.2: Singly linked list initialization and cleanup functions

- The `slist_init` function isn't strictly necessary since the user could do what it does just as easily. But it's a good practice always to provide an "init" function. If initialization ever requires more, it can easily be added to the function.
- The `slist_cleanup` function takes a pointer to a function (§6.10) to free data for each link if necessary or `nullptr` if not. The cleanup function hoists the check for `nullptr` out of the loop and has two loops, one for each case since it's faster at the slight expense of double the code. As a nicety, if `list` is `nullptr`, the function does nothing.

24.2 Pushing

The next functions to write are "push-front" and, by virtue of having the `tail` pointer, "push-back" as shown in listing 24.3. The mechanics of manipulating the pointers should be straightforward to anyone who's had a data-structures course.

The curious part is that the functions take only a `size` of the data to push, not the data itself. Instead, both functions return a pointer to the newly pushed `slink`: it's

24.2 Pushing

```
[[nodiscard]]
struct slink* slist_push_back( struct slist *list,
                               size_t size ) {
  struct slink *const link =
    malloc( sizeof(struct slink) + size );
  if ( list->head == nullptr )
    list->head = link;
  else
    list->tail->next = link;
  list->tail = link;
  return link;
}

[[nodiscard]]
struct slink* slist_push_front( struct slist *list,
                                size_t size ) {
  struct slink *const link =
    malloc( sizeof(struct slink) + size );
  link->next = list->head;
  list->head = link;
  if ( list->tail == nullptr )
    list->tail = link;
  return link;
}
```

Listing 24.3: Singly linked list push functions

then up to the user either to copy the data into the node (if intrusive) or merely copy a pointer to it (if not). To facilitate accessing the data, we can define two macros:

```
#define SLIST_DINT(DATA)   ( (void*)(DATA) )
#define SLIST_DPTR(DATA)   ( *(void**)SLIST_DINT( (DATA) ) )
```

- **SLIST_DINT**: Gets a pointer to the data when stored intrusively. The cast to void* is to silence a warning about converting a char* to a pointer to a type having stricter alignment.

- **SLIST_DPTR**: Gets a pointer to the data when stored via pointer. Assuming 64-bit pointers, the pointer value is stored as char data[8]. As a reminder, when an array is used in an expression, it "decays" into a pointer to its first element (§6.7), in this case, the first byte of the pointer to the actual data. The cast to void** simply casts it to the pointer to the void* it really is. The left-most * then dereferences *that* pointer to read those 8 bytes comprising the pointer to the actual data.

Given those macros, we can either store, say, an int intrusively:

```
auto data = slist_push_front( list, sizeof(int) )->data;
*(int*)SLIST_DINT( data ) = 1942;
```

or store a pointer to data elsewhere:

```
auto data = slist_push_front( list, sizeof(void*) )->data;
SLIST_DPTR( data ) = p;
```

If you think those are verbose, you can enlist the help of a function-like macro (§8.7):

```
#define SLIST_PUSH_FRONT(LIST,T,V)                     \
  *((T)*)SLIST_DINT( slist_push_front( (LIST),        \
                       sizeof(T) )->data ) = (V)
```

24.3 Front, Back, and Empty

The next functions to write are "front," "back," and "empty" as shown in listing 24.4.

```
[[nodiscard]] inline
struct slink* slist_front( struct slist *list ) {
  return list->head != nullptr ? list->head : nullptr;
}

[[nodiscard]] inline
struct slink* slist_back( struct slist *list ) {
  return list->tail != nullptr ? list->tail : nullptr;
}

[[nodiscard]] inline
bool slist_empty( struct slist *list ) {
  return list->head == nullptr;
}
```

Listing 24.4: Singly linked list front, back, and empty functions

All are straightforward. For example, to use `slist_front` with intrusive data:

```
int i = *(int*)SLIST_DINT( slist_front( list )->data );
```

or with a pointer to data:

```
char *s = SLIST_DPTR( slist_front( list )->data );
```

24.4 Popping

The next functions to write are "pop-front" and "pop-back" as shown in listing 24.5. As with the push functions, the mechanics of manipulating the pointers should be straightforward to anyone who's had a data-structures course.

Unlike `slist_pop_front` that runs in $O(1)$ time, `slist_pop_back` runs in $O(n)$ time because it has to find the element *before* `tail`. The only way to do that in $O(1)$

24.5 Removing from the Middle

```
void slist_pop_front( struct slist *list ) {
  if ( list->head == nullptr )
    return;
  auto const new_head = list->head->next;
  free( list->head );
  list->head = new_head;
  if ( list->head == nullptr )
    list->tail = nullptr;
}

void slist_pop_back( struct slist *list ) {
  if ( list->head == nullptr )
    return;
  auto new_tail = list->head;
  while ( new_tail->next != list->tail )
    new_tail = new_tail->next;
  free( list->tail );
  new_tail->next = nullptr;
  list->tail = new_tail;
}
```

Listing 24.5: Singly linked list pop functions

---

time would be to implement a *doubly linked list*, i.e., `dlist` with a corresponding `dlink` that also had a `prev` pointer in addition to `next`. But it's a big price to pay due to `dlink` being twice the size of `slink`. Given that, `slist_pop_back` should be implemented and documented that it runs in $O(n)$ time.

Of course you can implement both `slist` and `dlist` where you use `slist` most of the time, perhaps with an occasional `slist_pop_back`. Use `dlist` only if you really need to use `slist_pop_back` frequently.

24.5 Removing from the Middle

Occasionally, you might need to remove a link from the middle of a list. It might seem that you can't do this with a singly linked list because, given a pointer to a link to remove, you can't get to `next` of the previous `slink` to update it to be the current link's `next`. What you can do instead is to write a function like what's shown in listing 24.6.

The function `slist_free_if` performs the mechanics of iterating over the list, keeping track of the pointers, and updating them, but delegates the decision of whether to remove a link to a predicate function that, given a pointer to a link, returns `true` only if it should be removed.

- For convenience, lines 1–2 declare a type for a predicate function. In addition to `link`, it also takes `pred_data` (so named so it's not confused with a link's `data`) that's passed along from `slist_free_if` possibly to be used to determine whether a link should be removed.

```
 1  typedef bool (*slist_pred_fn)( struct slink *link,
 2                                 void const *pred_data );
 3
 4  size_t slist_free_if( struct slist *list,
 5                        slist_pred_fn pred_fn,
 6                        void const *pred_data ) {
 7    size_t free_count = 0;
 8    struct slink **pcurr = &list->head, *prev = nullptr;
 9
10    for (;;) {
11      auto const curr = *pcurr;
12      if ( curr == nullptr )
13        break;
14      if ( !(*pred_fn)( curr, pred_data ) ) {
15        prev = curr;
16        pcurr = &curr->next;
17        continue;
18      }
19      if ( curr == list->tail )
20        list->tail = prev;
21      *pcurr = curr->next;
22      free( curr );
23      ++free_count;
24    }
25
26    return free_count;
27  }
```

Listing 24.6: Singly linked list remove-from-the-middle function

- Ordinarily, if the link to be removed is `head`, it requires a special case; this function uses "good taste" by using a pointer to the pointer (§6.6) pointing to the current link `pcurr` declared on line 8 that eliminates the special case.[†] The `prev` pointer is needed only because `slist` has a `tail` pointer and if the tail is the link to be removed.
- Line 14 calls the predicate function: if it returns `false` (don't remove), the pointers are updated and iteration continues (lines 15–17); if it returns `true`, the current link is to be removed.
- Lines 19–20 handle the special case of updating `tail`.
- Line 21 updates `*pcurr` (which is either the previous link's `next`, or `head`) to be the current link's `next` pointer effectively excising the current link.
- To be informative, line 26 returns the number of links removed.

An example predicate function that can be used with `slist_free_if` on a list of strings that removes links whose data (a string) does not contain the string given by `pred_data` is shown in listing 24.7.

[†] *The Mind Behind Linux*, Linus Torvalds, TED Talk, Vancouver, BC, Feb. 2016, 21:20, https://www.ted.com/talks/linus_torvalds_the_mind_behind_linux

```
bool slist_free_if_not_contains_str( struct slink *link,
        void const *pred_data ) {
  return strstr( SLIST_DINT( link->data ),
                 pred_data ) == nullptr;
}
```

Listing 24.7: Singly linked list not-contains-string predicate function

The `strstr` standard function (§B.2) searches a string for the occurrence of another string. An example of using the predicate function to remove links whose strings do not contain "`error:`" (effectively *grep*(1)) is:

```
slist_free_if( list, &slist_free_if_not_contains_str,
               "error:" );
```

You might be wondering why the predicate function takes an `slink*` rather than a pointer to the link's data directly. The answer is because it's slightly more flexible. An example predicate function that removes links whose data (a string) is a duplicate of its next link's string assuming the list of strings is sorted (effectively *uniq*(1)) is shown in listing 24.8.

```
bool slist_free_if_dup_str( struct slink *link,
                             void const* ) {
  return link->next != nullptr &&
         strcmp( SLIST_DINT( link->data ),
                 SLIST_DINT( link->next->data ) ) == 0;
}
```

Listing 24.8: Singly linked list is-duplicate-string predicate function

The function can not only look at the current link's data, but the next link's data also.

24.6 Iterating

As a convenience, we can write a macro to iterate over a list to reduce boilerplate:

```
#define FOREACH_SLINK(LINK,LIST)                     \
  for ( auto LINK = (LIST)->head; LINK != nullptr;   \
        LINK = LINK->next )
```

Using `auto` here is particularly good because, as mentioned in §4.2, for pointers, `auto` will preserve the "const-ness" of the pointed-to `slink`. That is, if `LIST` is `slist*`, `LINK` will be `slink*`; if `LIST` is `slist const*`, `LINK` will be `slink const*`.

24.7 Epilogue

With the addition of a separate `slink` structure and a `tail` member, `slist` is now production-quality. Additional functions that could be implemented are left as exercises.

Exercises

1. Add a `len` member to `slist` to keep track of a list's length. It's sometimes useful to have. Updating it simply requires either incrementing or decrementing it in push, pop, and free-if operations.
2. Change the `slist_pred_fn` signature to return an enumeration value:

    ```
    enum slist_pred_rv {
       SLIST_FALSE, SLIST_TRUE, SLIST_BREAK
    };
    ```

    where `SLIST_BREAK` causes `slist_free_if` to break out of its loop rather than always iterate to the end of the list.
3. Modify your solution of `slist_cmp` for exercise 6.1 (p. 98) to work with the version of `slist` presented in this chapter.
4. Modify your solution of `slist_dup` for exercise 6.2 (p. 98) to work with the version of `slist` presented in this chapter.
5. Write a function:

    ```
    void slist_push_list_back( struct slist *dst,
                               struct slist *src );
    ```

    to push the links of `src` onto the back of `dst`. After, `src` would be empty.
6. Write a function:

    ```
    void slist_push_list_front( struct slist *dst,
                                struct slist *src );
    ```

    to push the links of `src` onto the front of `dst`. After, `src` would be empty.
7. As mentioned in §24.4, implement `dlist`, a doubly linked list, also. Other than the addition of a `prev` pointer in `dlink` and some additional pointer manipulation for it, there's not much else that would be different from `slist`. There would be no need for a `dlink_free_if` function.

Chapter 25
Maps

A *map* is a data structure that "maps" *keys* to *values*, that is, given a key, you can find its associated value, if one exists. A map has two primary operations: *insert* and *find*; it also may have a third operation of *delete*. Operations in general have both average and worst-case running times as a function of the number of elements in a map, n, given in "big O" notation.

While there are both many uses of and choices for implementation, one way to decide on an implementation is whether iterating over the keys is:

- **Ordered**: Keys are iterated over in sorted order. Items must be at least less-than-comparable. This kind of map is typically implemented using a *balanced binary tree* that ensures the path from the root to every leaf is approximately the same length. The operations *insert*, *find*, and *delete* all run in $O(\lg n)$ time in the average and worst cases. C++ has map; Java has TreeMap; Rust has BTreeMap.
- **Unordered**: Keys are iterated over in an arbitrary order. Items must be both *hashable* and at least equality-comparable. This kind of map is typically implemented using a *hash table*, aka, *hash map*, for which the average *insert*, *find*, and *delete* all run in $O(1)$ time in the average case and $O(n)$ time in the worst case. C++ has unordered_map; Go has map; Java and Rust have HashMap; Python has dict.

Hence, if you don't need to iterate over keys at all or if you don't care about the iteration order, an unordered map is the better choice — provided you can both hash and equality-compare keys, and choose a good hash function (§25.1).

Unlike most modern languages, C has no standard map, so if you want one, you have to implement it yourself. In this chapter, we'll use a hash table to implement a map.

25.1 Hash Tables

A hash table uses a *hash function*, $h(k)$, that, given some data for a key k, returns a *hash* of k, that is an unsigned integer of a fixed size, say 64-bits. The trick is to derive a "good" hash function that:

- Is fast.
- Given either a wide range of data or nearly identical data, returns integers that are uniformly distributed over the entire integer range.
- Has a low occurrence of *collisions*, that is the number of different values of k that return the same hash.

If you know your data set, you can take advantage of that knowledge and write a specific hash function for it. A data set that contains unique things like IDs, e-mail addresses, or time-stamps are easier to create a good hash function for. But if you don't know the data set, then you need to write a good general hash function that meets those criteria anyway.

One hash function that satisfies those criteria and is therefore commonly used is "FNV–1a" hash function[†] shown in listing 25.1. The value of hash should be initialized to `FNV1A64_INIT`.

```
constexpr uint64_t FNV1A64_INIT  = 14695981039346656037UL;
constexpr uint64_t FNV1A64_PRIME = 1099511628211UL;

uint64_t fnv1a64_mem( uint64_t hash, void const *data,
                     size_t n ) {
  for ( size_t i = 0; i < n; ++i )
    hash = FNV1A64_PRIME *
            (hash ^ ((uint8_t const*)data)[i]);
  return hash;
}
```

Listing 25.1: FNV-1a hash function in C

■ Explaining the function and why it's good is beyond the scope of this book since it has nothing to do with C. There are many detailed explanations online.[‡] □

Once you have $h(k)$, you then use it as an index into an array of "buckets" B where k and its associated value v is stored. Of course you can't use a 64-bit integer as an index directly since it would require an array with over nine quintillion (9×10^{18}) entries; instead you have to *mod* it via the modulus operator (§3.2) by m, the size of the array, to get the actual index i into B to get (k, v), hence the steps are:

[†]*The FNV Non-Cryptographic Hash Algorithm*, Glenn Fowler, Landon Noll, and Kiem-Phong Vo, Comments to IEEE POSIX P1003.2 Committee, Sep. 1991.

[‡]*The FNV Non-Cryptographic Hash Algorithm*, Glenn Fowler, Landon Noll, Kiem-Phong Vo, and Donald Eastlake, *Internet Engineering Task Force*, Oct. 10, 2024,
https://datatracker.ietf.org/doc/html/draft-eastlake-fnv-29

25.1 Hash Tables

$$k \to h(k) \to \% \, m \to i \to B[i] \to (k, v)$$

Of course any value for m increases collisions. When a collision occurs, you have to compare k against every other key that also hashed to $B[i]$. Hence, it's a trade-off between using a larger m (more memory, but fewer collisions) vs. a smaller m (less memory, but more collisions). If you know n, the expected number of entries, say 2000, and you can live with, say, at most 3 comparisons per key due to collisions, then $m = \lceil 2000/3 \rceil = 667$. However, it's better for m to be both a prime number and as far away from a power of 2 as possible; hence a better m for 2000 entries would be 769.

■ Similarly, explaining why this is the case is also beyond the scope of this book. But, briefly, if m is not prime and the set of keys are *not* uniformly distributed, $h(k) \% m$ produces more collisions at i where it's a factor of m. If $m \approx 2^b$, then all but the lower b bits of $h(k)$ are discarded. □

When inserting a key and value and a collision occurs ($B[i]$ is not empty), what do you do? There are generally two approaches:

1. **Open addressing**: There are a few kinds including *linear probing* where you scan forward looking at $B[i+1]$, $B[i+2]$, ..., in general, $B[j]$ for j in $[i + 1 \ldots m-1] \% m$ looking for an empty $B[j]$. When you find one, put the key and value there. The advantages of linear probing include:

    + Good cache performance since the entries are directly in the array and therefore in the same cache line (§10.6).

    The disadvantages of linear probing include:

    - The hash table can become full by filling every element of B.
    - Deleting entries involves either marking them with a special "deleted" value (but this decreases performance as more entries are deleted) or moving existing entries to replace deleted ones.

2. **Chaining**: Every $B[i]$ is a linked list of all the keys that collided and their values. The advantages of chaining include:

    + The hash table can never become full since new entries can always be inserted into the linked lists (but see the first disadvantage).
    + Deleting entries involves only updating a few pointers.

    The disadvantages of chaining include:

    - Even though the hash table can never become full (in the sense that it's impossible to add more entries), its performance degrades from $O(1)$ to $O(n)$ as the length of the linked lists increases. However, you can "grow" the hash table.
    - Growing a hash table is time-consuming. In time-sensitive applications, you may not be able to afford it. (OK for compilers; bad for user interfaces.)

- Worse cache performance since the entries are scattered in memory.
- Wasted space due to the unused elements in B and extra space for the pointers in the linked lists.

For hash tables, there's a value known as its *load factor*, α, that's defined as:

$$\alpha = \frac{n}{m}$$

that is the percentage of B that's full. As the load factor increases due to increasing n, the performance of the hash table decreases because it takes longer to either insert or find entries. When α exceeds some threshold α_{max}, you can increase m, but that requires recalculating $h(k) \; \% \; m \to i$ for all entries. Nevertheless, that's what's typically done. For open addressing, α_{max} can never exceed 1; for chaining, α_{max} represents the maximum number of comparisons that need to be done per operation.

Whether you choose open addressing or chaining depends on your circumstances. In this chapter, we'll implement a hash table that uses chaining.

25.2 Hash Table Types

Types for our hash table implementation are shown in listing 25.2.

```
1   typedef int         (*ht_cmp_fn)(void const*, void const*);
2   typedef void        (*ht_free_fn)(void*);
3   typedef uint64_t    ht_hash_val;
4   typedef ht_hash_val (*ht_hash_fn)(void const*);
5
6   struct ht_entry {
7     struct ht_entry    *next;
8     union {
9       ht_hash_val       hash;      // for fake head entries
10      struct ht_entry   *prev;     // for real entries
11    };
12    alignas(max_align_t) char data[];
13  };
14
15  struct hash_table {
16    struct ht_entry    *buckets;
17    ht_cmp_fn           cmp_fn;
18    ht_hash_fn          hash_fn;
19    double              max_lf;    // maximum load factor
20    unsigned            size;      // number of entries
21    unsigned            prime_idx; // index into HT_PRIME
22  };
```

Listing 25.2: Hash table types

- Line 1 declares the signature for a conventional comparison function returning an integer < 0, 0, or > 0 for comparing `data`.

25.2 Hash Table Types

- Line 2 declares the signature for a function to free an entry's `data`.
- Line 3 declares a simple alias for a hash table value.
- Line 4 declares the signature for a function to calculate $h(k)$. It takes only a pointer to `ht_entry`'s `data`. To use it with `fnv1a64_mem` on a user-defined structure that has a `key` member such as:

  ```
  struct key_val {
    char const *key, *val;
  };
  ```

  we'll need an adapter function like:

  ```
  ht_hash_val hash_key_val( void const *data ) {
    struct key_val const *const kv = data;
    return fnv1a64_mem( FNV1A64_INIT, kv->key,
                        strlen( kv->key ) );
  }
  ```

- Lines 6–13 declare a structure for a hash table entry. Since this implementation uses chaining, each entry has a `next` and `prev` pointer to point to the next and previous entries, respectively, in a doubly linked list.

  Why a doubly linked list? As we'll see, having `prev` makes deletion (§25.7) trivial: you simply need to update a few pointers. For a singly linked list, deletion would always require recalculating $h(k)$ to get to the bucket, then iterating over the list until you find the entry. It's a trade-off between more memory and fast deletion vs. less memory but slower deletion. If your circumstance has either infrequent or no deletions, the singly linked list would be the obvious better choice.

  Why is `prev` in a union with `hash`? Since the head entry doesn't need `prev`, we might as well make use of the otherwise wasted space by storing $h(k)$ there since all keys in the same bucket have the same value. As we'll see, this eliminates recalculating $h(k)$ when growing (§25.5) the hash table.

- Line 12 declares `data` the same as for `slist` in listing 24.1 (p. 325) to allow entries to store data intrusively or not. Unlike a traditional hash table implementation where an entry's key and value are separate, here they're combined into `data`. The advantages are that either the key, value, or both, can either be intrusive or not; and that a value is optional, i.e., the hash table can implement a *set* rather than a map.

  A hash table needs to compare keys only for equality. Hence, the function could have returned `bool` instead where `true` means equal. However, that would rule out using conventional comparison functions like `strcmp` that return `int` where 0 means equal.

- Lines 15–22 declare a structure for a hash table itself. We'll allow the user to specify α_{max}, hence the `max_lf` member. The `prime_idx` member is an index into `HT_PRIME`, a table of prime numbers not near powers of two as shown in listing 25.3 to be used for the size of `buckets`.

```
static constexpr unsigned HT_PRIME[] = {
           53,       97,      193,      389,      769,
         1543,     3079,     6151,    12289,    24593,
        49157,    98317,   196613,   393241,   786433,
      1572869,  3145739,  6291469, 12582917, 25165843
};
```

Listing 25.3: Prime numbers not near powers of 2 for the number of buckets

25.3 Initialization and Clean-Up

The first function to write is initialization as shown in listing 25.4.

```
 1  void ht_init( struct hash_table *ht, double max_lf,
 2                unsigned est_size, ht_cmp_fn cmp_fn,
 3                ht_hash_fn hash_fn ) {
 4      unsigned prime_idx = 0;
 5      for ( ; prime_idx < ARRAY_SIZE(HT_PRIME); ++prime_idx ) {
 6          if ( HT_PRIME[ prime_idx ] * max_lf >= est_size )
 7              break;
 8      }
 9      *ht = (struct hash_table){
10          .buckets = calloc( HT_PRIME[ prime_idx ],
11                             sizeof(struct ht_entry) ),
12          .cmp_fn = cmp_fn,
13          .hash_fn = hash_fn,
14          .max_lf = max_lf,
15          .prime_idx = prime_idx
16      };
17  }
```

Listing 25.4: Hash table initialization function

- Lines 1–3 declare the function's signature where we allow the user to specify α_{max} and an estimated number of elements that will be used to determine the initial number of buckets.
- Lines 5–8 iterate through HT_PRIME looking for the first prime number times $\alpha_{max} \geq$ est_size to use *that* for the initial number of buckets.
- Line 10 uses the standard function calloc that's like malloc except that you specify the number of objects to allocate and the size of an object; calloc also initializes the memory to zero or equivalent that we need here so that all the pointers are nullptr.

The next function to write is cleanup as shown in listing 25.5 and is straightforward.

25.4 Insert

```
void ht_cleanup( struct hash_table *ht,
                 ht_free_fn free_fn ) {
  if ( ht == nullptr )
    return;
  for ( unsigned b = 0; b < HT_PRIME[ ht->prime_idx ];
        ++b ) {
    for ( struct ht_entry *entry = ht->buckets[b].next,
          *next;
          entry != nullptr; entry = next ) {
      if ( free_fn != nullptr )
        (*free_fn)( entry->data );
      next = entry->next;
      free( entry );
    }
  }
  free( ht->buckets );
  *ht = (struct hash_table){ };
}
```

Listing 25.5: Hash table cleanup function

25.4 Insert

When inserting a key into a hash table, you may find that an entry having the same key already exists. In that case, you should return a pointer to *that* entry rather than create a new one. But now you need to distinguish between returning a new entry and an existing one, hence a need for an "insert return value" structure ht_insert_rv as shown in listing 25.6. The ht_insert function itself is shown in listing 25.7.

```
struct ht_insert_rv {
  struct ht_entry *entry;   // entry found or inserted
  bool            inserted;
};
```

Listing 25.6: Hash table insert function return value structure

- Lines 4–7 calculate hash, n_buckets (the number of buckets, m), b (the index of the bucket), and sets head to point to the fake first entry of the linked list of the bucket.
- Lines 9–14 look through the linked list looking for an existing key that matches key: if found, returns an ht_insert_rv with that entry.
- Otherwise, line 16 allocates memory for a new entry including data_size.
- Lines 17–21 initialize the entry and update the bucket to point to it.
- Lines 23–25 calculate the load factor α: if it's $\geq$ max_lf, calls ht_grow to "grow" the hash table by increasing m and rehashing all entries as shown in listing 25.8.
- Line 27 returns an ht_insert_rv pointing to the new entry.

Note that ht_insert inserts only an ht_entry, not the data itself. To access the data, we need macros similar to those used for slist (p.327):

```
 1  struct ht_insert_rv ht_insert( struct hash_table *ht,
 2                                 void const *key,
 3                                 size_t data_size ) {
 4    auto const hash = (*ht->hash_fn)( key );
 5    auto const n_buckets = HT_PRIME[ ht->prime_idx ];
 6    auto const b = hash % n_buckets;
 7    struct ht_entry *const head = &ht->buckets[b], *entry;
 8
 9    for ( entry = head->next; entry != nullptr;
10          entry = entry->next ) {
11      if ( (*ht->cmp_fn)( key, entry->data ) == 0 )
12        return (struct ht_insert_rv)
13                 { entry, .inserted = false };
14    }
15
16    entry = malloc( sizeof(struct ht_entry) + data_size );
17    *entry =
18      (struct ht_entry){ .next = head->next, .prev = head };
19    if ( head->next != nullptr )
20      head->next->prev = entry;
21    *head = (struct ht_entry){ .next = entry, .hash = hash };
22
23    auto const lf = ++ht->size / (double)n_buckets;
24    if ( lf >= ht->max_lf )
25      ht_grow( ht );
26
27    return (struct ht_insert_rv){ entry, .inserted = true };
28  }
```

Listing 25.7: Hash table insert function

```
#define HT_DINT(ENTRY)   ( (void*)(ENTRY)->data )
#define HT_DPTR(ENTRY)   ( *(void**)HT_DINT( (ENTRY) ) )
```

Given those, you can do something like:

```
struct key_val kv = { "hello", "world" };
auto rv = ht_insert( ht, &kv, sizeof kv );
if ( rv.inserted )
  *(struct key_val*)HT_DINT( rv.entry ) = kv;
```

25.5 Growing

As mentioned, the `ht_grow` function "grows" the hash table by increasing m and rehashing all entries as shown in listing 25.8.

- Line 2 increments `prime_idx` to get the next larger prime number of buckets. Note that each prime number is roughly double the previous number. The doubling is done for the same reason as was done by `strbuf_reserve` in listing

25.6 Finding

```
static void ht_grow( struct hash_table *ht ) {
  auto const new_n_buckets = HT_PRIME[ ++ht->prime_idx ];
  struct ht_entry *const new_buckets =
    calloc( new_n_buckets, sizeof(struct ht_entry) );

  for ( unsigned b = 0; b < new_n_buckets; ++b ) {
    auto const hash = ht->buckets[b].hash;
    for ( struct ht_entry *entry = ht->buckets[b].next,
          *next;
          entry != nullptr; entry = next ) {
      auto const new_head =
        &new_buckets[ hash % new_n_buckets ];

      next = entry->next;
      entry->next = new_head->next;
      entry->prev = new_head;

      if ( new_head->next != nullptr )
        new_head->next->prev = entry;
      new_head->next = entry;
      new_head->hash = hash;
    }
  }

  free( ht->buckets );
  ht->buckets = new_buckets;
}
```

Listing 25.8: Hash table grow function

23.7 (p. 319), i.e., so each subsequent doubling will be necessary half as often especially since growing is an expensive operation.
- Lines 3–4 allocate a larger new_buckets array that entries will be moved into.
- Lines 6–23 iterate over all the buckets: for each bucket, iterates over each entry in the bucket's list to move it to a new linked list in new_bucket.
- Lines 11–12 set new_head to point to the fake first entry of the new linked list of the new bucket based on the bucket index using new_n_buckets.
- Lines 14–20 simply update all the pointers.
- Finally, lines 25–26 free the old buckets and set it to new_buckets.

A disadvantage of growing a hash table is that it invalidates all iterators (§25.8).

25.6 Finding

The next function to write is ht_find as shown in listing 25.9 and is straightforward.

```
struct ht_entry* ht_find( struct hash_table *ht,
                          void const *key ) {
  auto const b =
    (*ht->hash_fn)( key ) % HT_PRIME[ ht->prime_idx ];
  for ( auto entry = ht->buckets[b].next; entry != nullptr;
        entry = entry->next ) {
    if ( (*ht->cmp_fn)( key, entry->data ) == 0 )
      return entry;
  }
  return nullptr;
}
```

Listing 25.9: Hash table find function

25.7 Deleting

The next function to write is `ht_delete` as shown in listing 25.10.

```
void ht_delete( struct hash_table *ht,
                struct ht_entry *entry ) {
  entry->prev->next = entry->next;
  if ( entry->next != nullptr )
    entry->next->prev = entry->prev;
  free( entry );
  --ht->size;
}
```

Listing 25.10: Hash table delete function

As mentioned in §25.2, an advantage of using a doubly linked list is that it makes deletion trivial. Since every entry has a non-null `prev` pointer, deletion is simply a matter of updating a few pointers, freeing the entry, and decrementing `size`.

25.8 Iteration

It's sometimes useful to iterate over the entire hash table even if it's not in sorted order, say to print it for debugging. An iterator type and initialization function are shown in listing 25.11.

- Line 12 initializes `bucket_idx` (the index into `ht->buckets`) to `(unsigned)-1` so that the first time `ht_next` (listing 25.12) is called, it will be "incremented" to zero by "wrapping around."
- Rather than using `HT_PRIME[ht->prime_idx]` directly, line 13 copies its value to `n_buckets`. Why? See listing 25.12, line 3.

The `ht_next` function is shown in listing 25.12. Line 3 uses `assert` (§16) to ensure that `n_buckets` is still equal to the current number of buckets the hash table has. If it isn't, it means the hash table has since grown (§25.5) and any existing iterators

25.9 Epilogue

```
struct ht_iter {
  struct hash_table  *ht;
  struct ht_entry    *next;
  unsigned           bucket_idx;
  unsigned           n_buckets;
};

void ht_iter_init( struct ht_iter *it,
                   struct hash_table *ht ) {
  *it = (struct ht_iter){
    .ht = ht,
    .bucket_idx = (unsigned)-1,
    .n_buckets = HT_PRIME[ ht->prime_idx ]
  };
}
```

Listing 25.11: Hash table iterator type and initialization function

```
struct ht_entry* ht_next( struct ht_iter *it ) {
  for (;;) {
    assert( it->n_buckets == HT_PRIME[it->ht->prime_idx] );
    if ( it->next != nullptr ) {
      auto const entry = it->next;
      it->next = it->next->next;
      return entry;
    }
    if ( ++it->bucket_idx == it->n_buckets )
      return nullptr;
    it->next = it->ht->buckets[ it->bucket_idx ].next;
  }
}
```

Listing 25.12: Hash table iterator next function

are invalid. Not checking this would lead to undefined behavior (§15) on line 11 by attempting to access it->ht->buckets that would be a dangling pointer.

For the remainder of the code, there are three cases:

1. Lines 4–8 handle the case when there is a next entry in the linked list for the current bucket.
2. Lines 9–10 handle the case when there are no more entries in the linked list for the current bucket and there are also no more buckets.
3. Line 11 handles the case when there are no more entries in the linked list for the current bucket, but there is at least one more bucket.

25.9 Epilogue

As hinted at the outset of this chapter, there are many choices for implementing maps:

- Binary tree or hash table?
- For a binary tree, which type? AA, AVL, B, red-black, splay, or another? Each has its own trade-offs.
- For a hash table, which hash function? Open addressing or chaining? For chaining, single or doubly linked lists?

Some choices are influenced by your circumstances:

- Are your keys comparable, i.e., can you write a function $c(k_i, k_j)$ that returns an integer < 0, 0, or > 0 if key k_i is $<$, $=$, or $> k_j$, respectively? And is it fast? Or can your keys be checked only for equality?
- Do you *find* most of the time, but *insert* only occasionally?
- Does key iteration order matter?
- Can you afford to pause everything while growing a hash table?
- Do you need to delete keys?

Covering all these choices in detail could fill a semester-long computer science course. This chapter only scratched the surface, but hopefully gave you a peek behind the curtain for one implementation.

Exercises

1. Write a variation of `fnv1a64_mem` from listing 25.1 (p.334) that hashes the characters of a string (except the terminating null character) having a signature:

    ```
    uint64_t fnv1a64_str( uint64_t hash, char const *s );
    ```

2. Currently, doubly linked lists are used for the reasons mentioned in §25.2. Change the implementation to use a singly linked list. This requires:

    a. Deletion of `ht_entry`'s `prev` and `ht_bucket`'s `hash_val`.
    b. Recalculating `hash_val` in `ht_grow` (listing 25.8, p.341), line 8.
    c. Recalculating `hash_val` in `ht_delete` (listing 25.10, p.342) and iterating through the linked list of a bucket until you find the entry whose pointer matches the one to be deleted.

Chapter 26
Dynamic Dispatch

Dynamic dispatch means to select which function is called at run-time based on the type of some object (aka, *polymorphism*). It's one of the defining traits of object-oriented programming. Different languages that support dynamic dispatch, such as C++, C#, Go, Java, Python, Smalltalk, Rust, and Swift, implement it differently, each with its own trade-offs. C doesn't support dynamic dispatch directly, but you can implement it in the style of any programming language that does support it.

Recall the `token` structure from listing 11.1 (p.171). A simple example would be to have a function that prints a token's value no matter what type it is as shown in listing 26.1.

```
void token_print( struct token const *t ) {
  switch ( t->kind ) {
    case TOKEN_INT   : printf( "%ld", t->i ); break;
    case TOKEN_FLOAT : printf( "%lf", t->f ); break;
    case TOKEN_CHAR  : printf( "%c" , t->c ); break;
    case TOKEN_STR   : printf( "%s" , t->s ); break;
  }
}
```

Listing 26.1: Simple dynamic dispatch

While that *is* dynamic dispatch, it's fairly restrictive. Why? Suppose you want the option to print tokens in different ways, e.g., integers in hexadecimal or binary, or with separators; or floating-point numbers in exponent form. You could add members to `token` to store all those options and make `token_print` take them all into account when printing. The caveats are that all tokens would have that additional data when only some need it and that printing options are restricted to what you thought of in advance.

26.1 Pointers to Function

Rather than having additional `token` members storing printing options, you can instead store pointers to function (§6.10) and delegate printing to them as shown in listing 26.2.

```
struct token {
  // ...
  void (*print_int)( long );
  void (*print_float)( double );
  void (*print_char)( char );
  void (*print_str)( char const* );
};

void token_print( struct token const *t ) {
  switch ( t->kind ) {
    case TOKEN_INT   : t->print_int   ( t->i ); break;
    case TOKEN_FLOAT : t->print_float ( t->f ); break;
    case TOKEN_CHAR  : t->print_char  ( t->c ); break;
    case TOKEN_STR   : t->print_str   ( t->s ); break;
  }
}
```

Listing 26.2: Dynamic dispatch, version 2, using pointers to function

When a `token` is created, its pointers would be set to point to a default set of printing functions. To change the way tokens print, you simply change one or more of the pointers to point to different printing functions. To print using the pointers, we can rewrite `token_print` as also shown.

As a reminder from §6.10, if you know C++, then a statement like:

```
t->print_float( t->f );       // not C++; shorthand for ...
```

might look like a C++ member function call, but it's still really C and a shorthand for calling a pointer to function:

```
(*t->print_float)( t->f );    // ... this
```

■ Even though I commented in §6.10 that I personally prefer using the explicit (*...) form, when implementing dynamic dispatch like this, the shorthand form seems more natural. □

While having one pointer per function is very flexible, it takes 32 bytes for the pointers (assuming 64-bit pointers), and that triples the total size of `token`.

26.2 Function Tables

To reduce the size of a `token`, instead of having one pointer per function, you can have one pointer to a table of functions as shown in listing 26.3.

```
struct token_fn_tbl {
  void (*print_int)( long );
  void (*print_float)( double );
  void (*print_char)( char );
  void (*print_str)( char const* );
};

struct token {
  // ...
  struct token_fn_tbl const *fn_tbl;
};

static struct token_fn_tbl const TOKEN_FN_TABLE_DEFAULT = {
  &print_int, &print_float, &print_char, &print_str
};

void token_print( struct token const *t ) {
  switch ( t->kind ) {
    case TOKEN_INT:
      t->fn_tbl->print_int( t->i );
      break;
    case TOKEN_FLOAT:
      t->fn_tbl->print_float( t->f );
      break;
    case TOKEN_CHAR:
      t->fn_tbl->print_char( t->c );
      break;
    case TOKEN_STR:
      t->fn_tbl->print_str( t->s );
      break;
  }
}
```

Listing 26.3: Dynamic dispatch, version 3, using a function table

Notice that all tokens share a single default function table. To change the way tokens print, create a different `token_fn_table` instance with its pointers pointing to different functions and change `fn_tbl` to point to it only for those tokens to print differently. The caveat is that calling a function now requires an extra level of indirection through the `fn_tbl` pointer. Like many other things in computer science, it's a trade-off.

Function tables are the way C++, C#, Java, and Swift implement dynamic dispatch. In C++ specifically, a token class would have its `fn_tbl` named `vptr` ("vee pointer," short for "virtual function pointer") instead and point to an instance of a token `vtbl` ("vee table," short for "virtual function table") but otherwise would be the same. A C++ member function call like:

```
            t->print_int();          // C++ member function call ...
```

is simply syntactic sugar and rewritten by the compiler to be:

```
            t->vptr->print_int( t );  // ... is this behind the curtain
```

passing `token` to become the function's `this` pointer.

There would be one `vtbl` per class. A derived class that overrides a base class's function would have its `vtbl` pointer pointing to a different table. Non-overridden functions would have their pointers pointing to the base class's functions.

The "in-object" way of implementing `vptrs` has the following disadvantages:

- They increase the object's size by the size of a pointer (typically, 8 bytes). For small objects, that's significant since it means they'll will likely no longer fit in a register nor be efficient to pass by value. (For `token`, its size increased by 50%.)
- They're intrusive (§10.6). In order to perform dynamic dispatch, an object must have a `vptr`. That means objects *must* be derived from a base object, hence inheritance is required to get dynamic dispatch. For example, listing 26.4 shows this for C++.

```
            struct token {                      // C++ base class
              // ...
              struct token_vtbl const *vptr;
            };

            struct derived_token : token {     // derived inherits vptr
              // ...
            };
```

Listing 26.4: Intrusive `vptrs` need inheritance for dynamic dispatch in C++

26.3 Fat Pointers

As an alternative to intrusive `vptrs`, languages like Go and Rust use "fat pointers" as shown in listing 26.5 where `itoken` is a fat pointer.

■ In Go, fat pointers are used to implement "interfaces," hence the "i" in `itoken`. In Rust, fat pointers are used to implement "traits" that are essentially the same. In this section, the Go terminology is used. □

A fat pointer is simply a structure that contains two pointer members:

1. A pointer to the object's function table, i.e., a `vptr`, that's the same as it is was before except that it moved from the object to the fat pointer.
2. A pointer to the object.

26.3 Fat Pointers

```
struct itoken {              // fat pointer
  struct token_vtbl const *vptr;
  struct token *token;
};

void token_print( struct itoken const *it ) {
  auto const t = it->token;
  switch ( t->kind ) {
    case TOKEN_INT  : it->vptr->print_int  ( t->i ); break;
    case TOKEN_FLOAT: it->vptr->print_float( t->f ); break;
    case TOKEN_CHAR : it->vptr->print_char ( t->c ); break;
    case TOKEN_STR  : it->vptr->print_str  ( t->s ); break;
  }
}
```

Listing 26.5: Dynamic dispatch, version 4, using a fat pointer

Because only fat pointers have vptrs now, only fat pointers and not ordinary pointers can be used to do dynamic dispatch. Hence, the corresponding token_print takes a fat pointer as a parameter. Using fat pointers to implement dynamic dispatch has the following advantages:

+ They don't increase the object's size.
+ They're not intrusive. This means dynamic dispatch can be performed for an object without requiring that it be derived from a base object, hence, inheritance is not required to get dynamic dispatch. For example, listing 26.6 shows this for Go. *Any* object type that implements those four functions would be able to participate in dynamic dispatch without inheritance.

```
type IToken interface {
  PrintInt(int32)
  PrintFloat(float64)
  PrintChar(rune)
  PrintString(string)
}
```

Listing 26.6: Interfaces in Go don't use inheritance for dynamic dispatch

But fat pointers also have the following disadvantages:

- They're twice as big as ordinary pointers. If you have arrays of fat pointers, you can fit only half as many in a cache line (§10.6).
- Because they're not intrusive, once an interface "decays" into a pointer for a function's *receiver* (the object to which the function applies) there's no way to do dynamic dispatch *again* using the pointer in that function.

For example, given the following in Go:

```
func (t *Token) PrintFloat(n float64) {
  // ...
  t.PrintInt(int64(n))   // not fat: no dynamic dispatch :(
}
```

Even though this function may have been called via an interface, it received a *pointer* (not interface) into t. If the function calls PrintInt via t to print the integer portion of the floating-point number, it would call Token's version of PrintInt, not the dynamic dispatch version, since only interfaces can do dynamic dispatch. Hence, polymorphism in Go is "shallow" in that it "decays" from an interface one call level down to a pointer and no further.

In C++, t would point to the token that contains a vptr from which dynamic dispatch can be done again. Hence, polymorphism in C++ is "deep" in that it can go any number of call levels down from a pointer.

26.4 Epilogue

As stated at the outset of this chapter, C doesn't support dynamic dispatch directly, but you can implement it in the style of any programming language that does support it — you just have to be explicit about it.

Here are some key points about dynamic dispatch as illustrated in this chapter:

- Regardless of technique, pointers to function are needed.
- Use of function tables (structures with pointers to function members) are used in many languages.
- Intrusive virtual function pointers increase an object's size, but allow deep polymorphism. They also often require inheritance.
- Fat pointers don't require inheritance, but only allow shallow polymorphism.

Like many other things in computer science, there are always trade-offs.

Chapter 27
Exceptions in C

Continuing from §20.5, this chapter provides a more detailed answer to whether `setjmp` and `longjmp` can be used to implement exceptions (or at least something exception-like) in C. While it's somewhat possible, the restrictions of `setjmp` and `longjmp` unfortunately bleed into using them for exception-like handling in C. Despite this, we'll derive and implement such a mechanism noting the "ifs" and "buts." Not surprisingly, this implementation will be modeled after exceptions in C++.

27.1 Requirements

A self-imposed requirement is that a proper exception-like mechanism in C should look as similar as possible to C++ exceptions. Many exception-like implementations for C out there require using ugly macros in stilted ways. What we want is to be able to write "natural looking" code like what's shown in listing 27.1.

```c
void read_file( char const *path ) {
  auto f = fopen( path, "r" );
  if ( f == nullptr )
    throw ( EX_FILE_NOT_FOUND );
  // ...
}

int main() {
  try {
    read_file( ".config" );
  }
  catch ( EX_FILE_NOT_FOUND ) {
    // ...
  }
}
```

Listing 27.1: Natural looking exception-like code in C

We also want to be able to nest `try` blocks, either directly in the same function, or indirectly in called functions. This means we'll need multiple `jmp_buf` variables and a list linking a `try` block to its parent, if any. We can declare a structure to hold this information and a pointer to the head of the linked list as shown in listing 27.2.

```
struct cx_impl_try_block {
  jmp_buf                       env;
  struct cx_impl_try_block *parent; // parent, if any
};

static thread_local
struct cx_impl_try_block *cx_impl_try_block_head;
```

Listing 27.2: `cx_impl_try_block`, version 1

The use of `thread_local` (§14.7) for `cx_impl_try_block_head` means that each thread can be in the process of throwing or catching an exception independently of any other.

27.2 try

To implement `try`, it will clearly have to be a macro (§8.3); but that expands into what? What's needed is something that allows:

1. Storage of a `cx_impl_try_block` local to the scope of the `try`.
2. Code to be specified between `{ }` for the `try` block.

The only thing in C that gives us both is a combination of `for` and `if` as shown in listing 27.3.

```
#define try                                                        \
  for ( struct cx_impl_try_block cx_tb = { }; ???; ??? )           \
    if ( setjmp( cx_tb.env ) == 0 )
```

Listing 27.3: `try`, version 0

But what do we put for the `for` loop condition and next expressions? The loop needs to execute only once, so the condition has to return `true` the first time and `false` the second. We can add a "state" to `cx_impl_try_block` as shown in listing 27.4.

We can then write a function `cx_impl_try_cond` for the `for` loop condition expression as shown in listing 27.5.

- On line 2, we `switch` on the current state. Initially, it will be `CX_IMPL_INIT`.
- Lines 4–5 push `tb` onto the head of the `try` block list.
- Line 6 sets the state to `CX_IMPL_TRY`.
- Line 7 returns `true` for the `for` loop condition in the `try` macro.

```
enum cx_impl_state {
  CX_IMPL_INIT,                         // initial state
  CX_IMPL_TRY,                          // no exception thrown
};

struct cx_impl_try_block {
  jmp_buf                     env;
  struct cx_impl_try_block    *parent;
  enum cx_impl_state          state;    // new exception state
};
```

Listing 27.4: cx_impl_try_block, version 2, with state

```
 1  bool cx_impl_try_cond( struct cx_impl_try_block *tb ) {
 2    switch ( tb->state ) {
 3      case CX_IMPL_INIT:
 4        tb->parent = cx_impl_try_block_head;
 5        cx_impl_try_block_head = tb;
 6        tb->state = CX_IMPL_TRY;
 7        return true;
 8      case CX_IMPL_TRY:
 9        cx_impl_try_block_head = tb->parent;
10        return false;
11    }
12  }
```

Listing 27.5: cx_impl_try_cond, version 1

- The second time cx_impl_try_cond is called, it'll be in the CS_IMPL_TRY state. Line 9 will pop tb from the head of the try block list.
- Line 10 returns false so the for loop will exit.

With this, we can augment the definition of try to be as shown in listing 27.6. Given that, we don't need anything for the for loop next expression.

```
#define try                                              \
  for ( struct cx_impl_try_block cx_tb = { };            \
        cx_impl_try_cond( &cx_tb ); )                    \
    if ( setjmp( cx_tb.env ) == 0 )
```

Listing 27.6: try, version 1, with cx_impl_try_cond

27.3 throw

When implementing throw, it will be extremely helpful if the "exception" thrown contains the file and line whence it was thrown. We therefore can define throw as a macro to pass said information:

```
#define throw(XID) \
  cx_impl_throw( __FILE__, __LINE__, (XID) )
```

where XID is an integer "exception ID." But that means we need another data structure to hold the exception information and a global exception object as shown in listing 27.7.

```
struct cx_exception {
  char const *thrown_file;  // thrown from this file
  int         thrown_line;  // thrown from this line
  int         thrown_xid;   // thrown exception ID
};

static thread_local struct cx_exception cx_impl_exception;
```

Listing 27.7: cx_exception

Similarly to the declaration of cx_impl_try_block_head in listing 27.2, the use of thread_local (§14.7) for cx_impl_exception means that each thread will have its own exception object.

We also need to add more to cx_impl_try_block as shown in listing 27.8.

```
struct cx_impl_try_block {
  jmp_buf                   env;
  struct cx_impl_try_block *parent;
  enum cx_impl_state        state;
  int                       thrown_xid;
  int                       caught_xid;
};
```

Listing 27.8: cx_impl_try_block, version 3, with thrown_xid and caught_xid

Given that, we can write cx_impl_throw as shown in listing 27.9.

```
 1  [[noreturn]] void cx_impl_throw( char const *file,
 2                                   int line, int xid ) {
 3    cx_impl_exception =
 4      (struct cx_exception){ file, line, xid };
 5    if ( cx_impl_try_block_head == nullptr )
 6      cx_terminate();
 7    cx_impl_try_block_head->state = CX_IMPL_THROWN;
 8    cx_impl_try_block_head->thrown_xid = xid;
 9    longjmp( cx_impl_try_block_head->env, 1 );
10  }
```

Listing 27.9: cx_impl_throw, version 1

- Lines 3–4 store the file, line, and exception ID into cx_impl_exception.
- Line 5: if cx_impl_try_block_head is null, it means throw was called, but there's no active try block, which means the exception can't be caught. In this

27.3 throw

case, there's no choice but to terminate the program by calling `cx_terminate` shown in listing 27.10. (This is similar to what C++ does when it calls its standard `std::terminate` function.)

```
[[noreturn]] static void cx_terminate() {
  fprintf( stderr,
    "%s:%d: unhandled exception %d (0x%X)\n",
    cx_impl_exception.thrown_file,
    cx_impl_exception.thrown_line,
    cx_impl_exception.thrown_xid,
    (unsigned)cx_impl_exception.thrown_xid
  );
  abort();
}
```

Listing 27.10: Function to terminate program when no `try` in effect

It prints a message to standard error including the file and line of the `try` and the exception ID in both decimal and hexadecimal; then calls `abort`.

- Otherwise, lines 7–9 set `state` to `CX_IMPL_THROWN`, `thrown_xid` to the thrown exception ID, and call `longjmp` to "throw" the exception using the current `try` block's `env`.

`CX_IMPL_THROWN` and `CX_IMPL_CAUGHT` are two new states needed to distinguish the cases. The updated `cx_impl_state` is shown in listing 27.11.

```
enum cx_impl_state {
  CX_IMPL_INIT,           // initial state
  CX_IMPL_TRY,            // no exception thrown
  CX_IMPL_THROWN,         // exception thrown, but uncaught
  CX_IMPL_CAUGHT,         // exception caught
};
```

Listing 27.11: `cx_impl_state`, version 2

To handle the new states, the updated `cx_impl_try_cond` is shown in listing 27.12.

- Lines 1–7 are the same as in listing 27.5 (p.353).
- Lines 9–10 add cases for `CX_IMPL_THROWN` and `CX_IMPL_CAUGHT`.
- Line 12 checks if `state` is `CX_IMPL_THROWN` which means it wasn't caught by the current `try/catch` block so line 13 rethrows the exception by calling `cx_impl_do_throw` split off from `cx_impl_throw` so it can be called directly as shown in listing 27.13.

```
 1  bool cx_impl_try_cond( struct cx_impl_try_block *tb ) {
 2    switch ( tb->state ) {
 3      case CX_IMPL_INIT:
 4        tb->parent = cx_impl_try_block_head;
 5        cx_impl_try_block_head = tb;
 6        tb->state = CX_IMPL_TRY;
 7        return true;
 8      case CX_IMPL_TRY:
 9      case CX_IMPL_THROWN:
10      case CX_IMPL_CAUGHT:
11        cx_impl_try_block_head = tb->parent;
12        if ( tb->state == CX_IMPL_THROWN )
13          cx_impl_do_throw();    // rethrow uncaught exception
14        return false;
15    }
16  }
```

Listing 27.12: `cx_impl_try_cond`, version 2

```
[[noreturn]] void cx_impl_do_throw() {
  if ( cx_impl_try_block_head == nullptr )
    cx_terminate();
  cx_impl_try_block_head->state = CX_IMPL_THROWN;
  cx_impl_try_block_head->thrown_xid =
    cx_impl_exception.thrown_xid;
  longjmp( cx_impl_try_block_head->env, 1 );
}

[[noreturn]] void cx_impl_throw( char const *file,
                                 int line, int xid ) {
  cx_impl_exception =
    (struct cx_exception){ file, line, xid };
  cx_impl_do_throw();
}
```

Listing 27.13: `cx_impl_throw`, version 2, split into `cx_impl_do_throw`

27.4 catch

We can #define catch as:

```
#define catch(XID) \
  else if ( cx_impl_catch( (XID), &cx_tb ) )
```

and write `cx_impl_catch` as shown in listing 27.14.

- The `if` on line 3 checks for the case when the same exception is thrown from a catch block. Once an exception is caught at the current try/catch level, it can never be re-caught at the same level. By returning `false` on line 4 for all catches at the current level, the code in `cx_impl_try_cond` will pop us up to the parent level, if any, where this check will fail (because the parent's `caught_xid` will be 0) and we can possibly re-catch the exception at the parent level.

27.5 finally

```
bool cx_impl_catch( int catch_xid,
                    struct cx_impl_try_block *tb ) {
  if ( tb->caught_xid == tb->thrown_xid )
    return false;
  if ( tb->thrown_xid != catch_xid )
    return false;
  tb->state = CX_IMPL_CAUGHT;
  tb->caught_xid = tb->thrown_xid;
  return true;
}
```

Listing 27.14: `cx_impl_catch`

- Lines 5–6 check if `catch_xid` matches the `thrown_xid`: if not, return `false`.
- Otherwise, we're catching `thrown_xid`: mark `state` as `CX_IMPL_CAUGHT`, set `caught_xid`, and return `true`.

27.5 finally

Even though C++ doesn't have `finally` like Java does, C doesn't have destructors to implement *RAII*, so having `finally` would be useful to clean up resources (free memory, close files, etc.).

■ RAII is an (unpronounceable) acronym for "resource acquisition is initialization." It's a foundational technique in C++ for managing resources (memory, files, etc.). The basic idea is that a resource is acquired by a local (stack-based) object via its *constructor* ("init" function) and is held only as long as the object exists. When the object gets destroyed, the resource is released via the object's destructor ("cleanup" function). □

It turns out that adding `finally` isn't difficult. The big difference is that the `for` loop has to execute *twice*: once to run the original `try`/`catch` code and a second time to run `finally` code. The second time, `setjmp` must *not* be called again. This can be achieved by adding another state of `CX_IMPL_FINALLY` and an `if` in the definition of `try` as shown in listing 27.15.

```
#define try                                       \
  for ( struct cx_impl_try_block cx_tb = { }; \
        cx_impl_try_cond( &cx_tb ); )             \
    if ( cx_tb.state != CX_IMPL_FINALLY )         \
      if ( setjmp( cx_tb.env ) == 0 )
```

Listing 27.15: `try`, version 2, for `finally`

The implementation of `finally` therefore trivially becomes:

```
#define finally    else /* setjmp() != 0 */; \
                   else /* cx_tb.state == CX_IMPL_FINALLY */
```

where the first else is for the second if (listing 27.15, line 5) and the second else is for the first if (line 4). The implementation of cx_impl_try_cond also needs to account for the new CX_IMPL_FINALLY state as shown in listing 27.16.

```
1   bool cx_impl_try_cond( struct cx_impl_try_block *tb ) {
2     switch ( tb->state ) {
3       case CX_IMPL_INIT:
4         tb->parent = cx_impl_try_block_head;
5         cx_impl_try_block_head = tb;
6         tb->state = CX_IMPL_TRY;
7         return true;
8       case CX_IMPL_CAUGHT:
9         tb->thrown_xid = 0;       // reset for finally case
10        [[fallthrough]];
11      case CX_IMPL_TRY:
12      case CX_IMPL_THROWN:
13        tb->state = CX_IMPL_FINALLY;
14        return true;
15      case CX_IMPL_FINALLY:
16        cx_impl_try_block_head = tb->parent;
17        if ( tb->thrown_xid != 0 )
18          cx_impl_do_throw();     // rethrow exception
19        cx_impl_exception = (struct cx_exception){ };
20        return false;
21    }
22  }
```

Listing 27.16: cx_impl_try_cond, version 3, for finally

- The CX_IMPL_TRY, CX_IMPL_THROWN, and CX_IMPL_CAUGHT states now return true on lines 7 and 14 to execute the for loop once more for the finally block.
- We need to remember if the exception was caught or not. We could have added a separate flag for this, but we can alternatively simply reset tb->thrown_xid to 0 on line 9 and check for non-0 later to know whether to re-throw the exception.
- Lines 15–19 add a case for the CX_IMPL_FINALLY state. Line 17 checks whether to re-throw an uncaught exception.

With the addition of finally, we can now write "natural looking" code as shown in listing 27.17.

27.6 Restrictions

Even though this implementation meets all of our requirements (§27.1), there are still a number of restrictions:

- The requirement of volatile variables (§20.3) and prohibition of VLAs (§20.4) still apply. There's simply no way around these.
- Within a try, catch, or finally block, you must *never* break unless it's within your own loop or switch due to the use of the for loop for the try.

```
void read_file( char const *path ) {
  auto const f = fopen( path, "r" );
  if ( f == nullptr )
    throw ( EX_FILE_NOT_FOUND );
  try {
    // ... do something with f ...
  }
  finally {
    fclose( f );
  }
}
```

Listing 27.17: Example C code using exception-handling

- Similarly, within a `try`, `catch`, or `finally` block, you must *never* either `goto` outside the blocks nor `return` from the function. In addition to the `finally` block, if any, not being executed, `cx_impl_try_block_head` will become a dangling pointer to the defunct `cx_tb` variable. (Fortunately, this situation can be detected.)
- Within a `try` or `catch` block, `continue` will jump to the `finally` block, if any. (Perhaps this is a good thing?)
- If you were to use this implementation with your own code, you'd have to use the compiler options `-Wno-dangling-else` and `-Wno-shadow` (or equivalent for your compiler) to suppress warnings (§18.7). There's simply no way to use `{}` to suppress "dangling else" warnings nor use unique names for `cx_tb` to avoid the "shadows" warnings and keep the natural looking code.

Without direct language support, it's impossible to implement exceptions in C such that they behave exactly like exceptions in C++ (or any other language).

27.7 Epilogue

What sort of C programs might benefit from using an exception implementation such as this? Obviously, smaller, simpler programs can continue to use more traditional error-handling mechanisms (§9.6). Classes of C programs that might benefit from exception handling are those that either employ long function call chains or callbacks where it's either too difficult or impossible to check for and handle errors all the way back through the call stack.

Actual projects written in C that use similar macros (or simply `setjmp` and `longjmp` directly) include the Lua and R programming languages, the PostgreSQL relational database, and the Wireshark network protocol analyzer.

While this particular C exception implementation works, the aforementioned restrictions are easily forgotten because wrong code doesn't look wrong. It's unclear whether the utility of being able to throw and catch exceptions with it outweighs the restrictions. Only actual users of this implementation will be able to answer. Hopefully, this implementation has at least been illuminating as to what's similarly going on behind the curtain in languages that do support exceptions.

Exercises

Currently, `cx_impl_catch` (listing 27.14, p. 357) catches only exception IDs that are equal via the lines:

```
5      if ( tb->thrown_xid != catch_xid )
6          return false;
```

It would be nice if the user could install a custom "exception ID matcher" function that could, for example, catch exceptions in a range of IDs.

1. Given:

   ```
   typedef bool (*cx_xid_matcher)( int thrown_xid,
                                   int catch_xid );
   ```

   write a function:

   ```
   cx_xid_matcher cx_set_xid_matcher( cx_xid_matcher fn );
   ```

   that sets a global "exception ID matcher" pointer-to-function (§6.10) to `fn` and returns the previous such function that was set or `nullptr` if none.

2. Using your solution to the previous exercise, change `cx_impl_catch` lines 5–6 to call the global exception ID matcher function, if any. Consider the exception caught only if the function returns `true`.

Appendix A
Standard Headers

Table A.1 shows summaries of the standard library headers that either have been mentioned in this book or that you are most likely to use in your programs.

Table A.1: Standard Headers

Header	Description
`assert.h`	Assertions (§16).
`complex.h`	Complex numbers and functions (§2.5.8).
`ctype.h`	Character functions, e.g., `isprint` (§B.1).
`dirent.h`	Directory types, e.g., `dirent` and functions (§12.3).
`errno.h`	Global `errno` variable and constants.
`fcntl.h`	Low-level file I/O (§12.2.5).
`limits.h`	Numeric limits (§2.10).
`locale.h`	Locale related (§B).
`math.h`	Math functions, e.g. `fmod`.
`pthreads.h`	POSIX threads, aka, pthreads (§14).
`setjmp.h`	`setjmp` and `longjmp` (§20).
`stdarg.h`	Variadic argument types and functions (§9.11).
`stdatomic.h`	`_Atomic` functions (§17).
`stdbit.h`	Bit-level functions, e.g., `stdc_leading_zeros`.
`stddef.h`	Various types, e.g., `max_align_t` (§2.9).
`stdint.h`	Fixed-width integer types, e.g., `uint64_t`, and limits (§2.7).
`stdio.h`	Input and output types and functions (§12).
`stdlib.h`	Miscellaneous types and functions, e.g., `malloc`.
`string.h`	String functions, e.g., `strlen` (§B.2).
`sys/stat.h`	File information types and functions, e.g., `stat` (§12.2.2).
`threads.h`	Standard threads (§14).
`time.h`	Time types, e.g., `time_t`, and functions (§B.3).
`unistd.h`	Unix types and functions.
`wctype.h`	Wide character types and functions (§2.9).

Appendix B
Standard Functions

This appendix lists various standard functions, their signatures, and brief descriptions, by header that you are most likely to use in your programs. For full descriptions, see their respective manual pages either on your system or online.

The standard C library has the concept of a *locale*, that is a set of cultural conventions used either to classify or format data like numbers, dates, times, and currency. The default locale is the "C" (aka, "POSIX") locale. Many functions in the standard library are locale-sensitive.

B.1 `ctype.h`

These functions take `int` rather than `char` to allow the value of `EOF` as an argument (§1.2). They return `int` rather than `bool` since they pre-date the addition of a Boolean type to C (§C.6). As always, zero means `false` and non-zero means `true`.

`int isalnum(int c)`
: Returns non-zero only if c is either an alphabetic or numeric character in the current locale. (See also `isalpha`, `isdigit`, `isxdigit`.)

`int isalpha(int c)`
: Returns non-zero only if c is an alphabetic character in the current locale. (See also `isalnum`.)

`int isblank(int c)`
: Returns non-zero only if c is a blank character in the current locale. In the default locale, only space and tab are considered blank characters. (See also `isspace`.)

`int iscntrl(int c)`
: Returns non-zero only if c is a control character, that is either in the range `'\x00'`–`'\x1F'` or `'\x7F'`.

int isdigit(int c)
Returns non-zero only if c is a decimal digit, that is one of 0123456789. (See also isxdigit.)

int isgraph(int c)
Returns non-zero only if c is one of a decimal digit, alphabetic, punctuation, or any graphical character in the current locale. (See also isprint.)

int islower(int c)
Returns non-zero only if c is a lower-case alphabetic character in the current locale. (See also isupper.)

int isprint(int c)
Returns non-zero only if c is one of a decimal digit, alphabetic, punctuation, or blank character in the current locale. (See also isgraph.)

int ispunct(int c)
Returns non-zero only if c is a punctuation character in the current locale. In the default locale, !"#$%&'()*+,-./:;<=>?@[\]^_'{|}~ are punctuation.

int isspace(int c)
Returns non-zero only if c is one of a space (' '), carriage return ('\r'), form feed ('\f'), horizontal tab ('\t'), line feed ('\n'), or vertical tab ('\v'). (See also isblank.)

int isupper(int c)
Returns non-zero only if c is an upper-case alphabetic character in the current locale. (See also islower.)

int isxdigit(int c)
Returns non-zero only if c is a hexadecimal digit, that is one of 0123456789, abcdef, or ABCDEF. (See also isdigit.)

int tolower(int c)
Returns c converted to lower-case according to the current locale. (See also toupper.)

int toupper(int c)
Returns c converted to upper-case according to the current locale. (See also tolower.)

B.2 string.h

Some of these functions use the types *QChar* or *QVoid*. (The "Q" means cv-qualified, §4.5.) These are generic functions (§19) that preserve the "const-ness" of the argument. For example, the strchr function is documented as:

QChar* strchr(QChar *s, int c)

That means the const-ness of s and the return type match, i.e., if the type of s is:

B.2 string.h

- `char*`, then the return type is `char*`; or:
- `char const*`, then the return type is `char const*`.

The same is true for *QVoid**, i.e., the return type is either `void*` or `void const*` depending on the const-ness of the argument.

The difference between the `mem` and `str` versions of similar functions is that the latter require their arguments to be null-terminated strings whereas the former don't.

QVoid* memchr(QVoid *p, int c, size_t n)
Returns a pointer to the first occurrence of `(char)c` in p of length n, or `nullptr` if not found. (See also `strchr`, `strrchr`.)

int memcmp(void const *p1, void const *p2, size_t n)
Compares at most the first n bytes pointed to by p1 and p2. Returns an integer $< 0, 0,$ or > 0 if `p1[`i`]` is $<, =,$ or $>$ `p2[`i`]`, respectively. (See also `strcmp`, `strncmp`.)

void* memcpy(void *restrict dst, void const *restrict src, size_t n)
Copies the first n bytes from `src` to `dst`. The memory ranges *must not* overlap. Returns `dst`. (See also `memmove`, `strcpy`, `strncpy`.)

void* memmove(void *dst, void const *src, size_t n)
Copies the first n bytes from `src` to `dst`. The memory ranges may overlap. Returns `dst`. (See also `memcpy`, `strcpy`, `strncpy`.)

void* memset(void *dst, int c, size_t n)
Sets n bytes starting at `dst` to `(unsigned char)c`. Returns `dst`.

char* strcat(char *restrict dst, char const *restrict src)
Appends a copy of the null-terminated string `src` onto the end of the null-terminated string `dst`. Returns `dst`.

QChar* strchr(QChar *s, int c)
Returns a pointer to the first occurrence in the null-terminated string s of `(char)c`, or `nullptr` if not found. (See also `memchr`, `strrchr`.)

size_t strcmp(char const *s1, char const *s2)
Compares the null-terminated strings s1 and s2. Returns an integer $< 0, 0,$ or > 0 if s1 is $<, =,$ or $>$ s2, respectively. (See also `memcmp`, `strncmp`.)

char* strcpy(char *restrict dst, char const *restrict src)
Copies from the null-terminated string `src` to `dst`. Returns `dst`. (See also `memcpy`, `strncpy`.)

size_t strcspn(char const *s, char const *set)
Returns the length of the maximum initial span of the null-terminated string s that consists only of characters *not* comprising (**c**omplement of) `set`. (See also `strspn`.)

char* strdup(char const *s)
Returns a duplicate of the null-terminated string s. (See also `strndup`.)

char const* strerror(int err_num)
Returns the error message corresponding to the error number err_num.

size_t strlen(char const *s)
Returns the length of the null-terminated string s.

char* strncat(char *restrict dst, char const *restrict src, size_t n)
Appends at most n characters of a copy of the null-terminated string src onto the end of the null-terminated string dst. Returns dst. (See also strcat.)

size_t strncmp(char const *s1, char const *s2, size_t n)
Compares at most n characters of the null-terminated strings s1 and s2. Returns an integer $< 0, 0,$ or > 0 if s1 is $<, =,$ or $>$ s2, respectively. (See also memcmp, strcmp.)

char* strncpy(char *restrict dst, char const *restrict src, size_t n)
Copies at most n characters from the null-terminated string src to the null-terminated string dst stopping before n if the null character is encountered. Returns dst. (See also memcpy, strcpy.)

char* strndup(char const *src, size_t n)
Returns a duplicate of at most n characters of the null-terminated string s. (See also strdup.)

QChar* strpbrk(QChar *s, char const *set)
Returns a pointer to the first occurrence in the null-terminated string s of any character comprising set, or nullptr if none are found. (See also strspn.)

QChar* strrchr(QChar *s, int c)
Returns a pointer to the last occurrence in the null-terminated string s of (char)c, or nullptr if not found. (See also strchr.)

size_t strspn(char const *s, char const *set)
Returns the length of the maximum initial span of the null-terminated string s that consists only of characters comprising set. (See also strbbrk, strcspn.)

QChar* strstr(QChar *s, char const *sub)
Returns a pointer to the first occurrence in the null-terminated string s of sub, or nullptr if not found.

B.3 time.h

Many of the functions described in this section take a pointer to a tm structure that stores a date and time. Its members are shown in listing B.1. (There may be other esoteric members as well.)

Several functions in the standard library take a pointer to a timespec structure that stores a number of seconds and nanoseconds. Its members are shown in listing

B.3 time.h

```
struct tm {
  int    tm_sec;      // seconds (0-60)
  int    tm_min;      // minutes (0-59)
  int    tm_hour;     // hours (0-23)
  int    tm_mday;     // day of month (1-31)
  int    tm_mon;      // month of year (0-11)
  int    tm_year;     // year - 1900
  int    tm_wday;     // day of week (0-6, 0 = Sunday)
  int    tm_yday;     // day of year (0-365)
  int    tm_isdst;    // is daylight saving time in effect?
  char   *tm_zone;    // timezone name abbreviation
  long   tm_gmtoff;   // offset from UTC (in seconds)
};
```

Listing B.1: Members of `tm` structure

B.2. The type *T* is implementation defined. (There may be other esoteric members as well.)

```
struct timespec {
  time_t tv_sec;      // whole seconds ≥ 0
  T      tv_nsec;     // nanoseconds [0, 999999999]
};
```

Listing B.2: Members of `timespec` structure

Note that the order of the members shown here (and in the C standard) is merely illustrative; the actual order is implementation defined.

■ To define a type equivalent to an implementation defined type such as `timespec`'s `tv_nsec`, you can do:

```
typedef typeof((struct timespec){}.tv_nsec) nsec_t;
```

making use of `typeof` (§4.6) and a structure compound literal (§10.4). □

`double difftime(time_t end, time_t start)`
Returns the difference between `start` and `end` times in seconds.

`struct tm* gmtime(time_t const *t)`
Converts `*t` to a `tm` structure representing its Greenwich Mean Time (UTC). Returns a pointer to an internal, `static` `tm` and is therefore not thread-safe. (See also `gmtime_r`, `localtime`, `localtime_r`.)

`struct tm* gmtime_r(time_t const *t, struct tm *tm)`
Converts `*t` to a `tm` structure representing its Greenwich Mean Time (UTC). Returns `tm`. (See also `gmtime`, `localtime`, `localtime_r`.)

`struct tm* localtime(time_t const *t)`
Converts `*t` to a `tm` structure representing its local time. Returns a pointer to an internal, `static` `tm` and is therefore not thread-safe. (See also `gmtime`, `gmtime_r`, `localtime_r`.)

struct tm* localtime_r(time_t const *t, struct tm *tm)
   Converts *t to a tm structure representing its local time. Returns tm. (See also gmtime, gmtime_r, localtime.)

time_t mktime(struct tm *tm)
   Returns the time since epoch (§2.9) of *tm representing local time on success or −1 on failure.

**size_t strftime(char *restrict buf, size_t buf_size,
              char const *restrict format,
              struct tm const *restrict tm)**
   Similar to printf (§12.1.1), uses a *format* string that is composed of zero or more *directives* where a directive is either:

   - A sequence of ordinary characters (not containing %) that are copied verbatim to the output.
   - A sequence of characters containing one or more *conversion specifications* starting with % of the form %*specifier* where the specifiers are shown in table B.1.

   Returns the number of characters written to buf (not including the terminating null character) or zero if buf_size is too small to accommodate the string.

time_t time(time_t *t)
   Returns the current time since epoch (§2.9). If t is not nullptr, then also stores the time in *t.

int timespec_get(struct timespec *ts, int base)
   Puts the current time relative to base into *ts. Returns base on success or zero on failure. The members of the timespec structure are shown in listing B.2. The only value for base that's defined is TIME_UTC.

B.3 `time.h`

Table B.1: `strftime` conversion specifiers

Year
- `C` First two digits of year (00–99).
- `g` Last two digits of ISO 8601 week-based year.
- `G` ISO 8601 week-based year.
- `y` Last two digits of year (00–99).
- `Y` Year.

Month
- `b` Localized, abbreviated month name, e.g., `Nov`.
- `B` Localized, full month name, e.g., `November`.
- `h` Same as `b`.
- `m` Decimal month (01–12).

Week
- `U` Week of the year (00–53) where Sunday is the first day of the week.
- `W` Week of the year (00–53) where Monday is the first day of the week.
- `V` ISO 8601 week of the year (01–53).

Day of the Year or Month
- `d` Decimal day of the month (01–31).
- `e` Decimal day of the month (1–31).
- `j` Day of the year (000–366).

Day of the Week
- `a` Localized, abbreviated weekday name, e.g. `Fri`.
- `A` Localized, full weekday name, e.g., `Friday`.
- `u` Decimal weekday (1–7, 1 = Monday).
- `w` Decimal weekday (0–6, 0 = Sunday).

Hour, Minute, Second
- `H` Decimal hour (00–23).
- `I` Decimal hour (01-12).
- `M` Decimal minute (00–59).
- `p` Localized `a.m.` or `p.m.`.
- `r` Localized 12-hour clock time.
- `R` Same as `%H:%M`.
- `S` Decimal second (00–60).
- `T` Same as `%H:%M:%S`, the ISO 8601 time format.

Other
- `c` Localized standard date and time, e.g. `Tue Sep 09 01:23:45 1941`.
- `D` Same as `%m/%d/%y`.
- `F` Same as `%Y-%m-%d`, the ISO 8601 date format.
- `n` Newline.
- `t` Horizontal tab.
- `x` Localized date.
- `X` Localized time.
- `z` Offset from UTC in the ISO 8601 format, e.g., `-0800`.
- `Z` Localized time zone name or abbreviation, e.g., `PST`.
- `%` Literal `%`.

Appendix C
C23 Differences

As of this writing, C23 is the latest version of C. This appendix lists its differences from C17, the previous version of C. Because of C23's newness, many existing C programs are written in older versions of C. If you need to maintain such programs and can't switch to compiling with a C23 compiler, alternatives for C23 features are given when possible.

C.1 Aggregate Initialization

Prior to C23, array (§6.2) structure (§10.3), and union (§11.2), collectively *aggregates*, that were initialized via the = { } syntax could not have the {} empty. At a minimum, you had to do {0}, i.e., include a zero, that you can still do.

C.2 alignas and alignof

Prior to C23, alignas was named _Alignas (§2.2 #7, p.29) and alignof (§3.17) was named _Alignof. There was also the stdalign.h standard header that did:

```
#define alignas _Alignas
#define alignof _Alignof
```

so you could use the lower-case names if you wanted to. Both _Alignas and _Alignof are still supported and likely will continue to be for many years.

C.3 Attributes

Prior to C23, attribute syntax (§4.9) was either implementation defined or had specific keywords:

    `__attribute__((`*attribute-list*`))`   `clang` and `gcc`
    `__declspec(`*attribute-list*`)`   Microsoft C

The implementation defined syntax for their respective compilers will likely be supported indefinitely.

C.4 `auto`

Prior to C23, `auto` could be used only as a storage class (§4.3.1). Objects had to be declared to be of a specific type. Use of `auto` to deduce the type automatically is not supported. However, both `clang` and `gcc` offer `__auto_type` as an extension.[†]

C.5 Binary Literals

C23 adopted binary literals from C++. Previously, only decimal, octal, and hexadecimal integer literals (§2.5.4) were supported. This includes the standard library functions `strtol`, `strtoll`, `strtoul`, and `strtoull` (§12.4.2) not supporting either the `0b` or `0B` prefix. As an alternative, you can write a wrapper around those functions to accept either prefix. Such a wrapper for `strtol` is shown in listing C.1.

C.6 `bool`

Originally, C didn't have any Boolean type; `int` was used instead. C99 added one, but it was called `_Bool` (§2.2 #7, p.29), so you may see that in older code. However, the `false` and `true` keywords were *not* added: you still had to use zero or non-zero, respectively. Alternatively, C99 also added the `stdbool.h` standard header that did:

```
#define bool   _Bool
#define false  0
#define true   1
```

[†] *Referring to a Type with* `__auto_type`, Free Software Foundation, *GNU C Language Manual*, §20.4, 1988–2025,
https://www.gnu.org/software/c-intro-and-ref/manual/html_node/Auto-Type.html

```
long c23_strtol( char const *s, char **pend, int base ) {
    s += strspn( s, " \n\t\r\f\v" );    // skip whitespace
    int const sign = 1 - 2 * (s[0] == '-');
    if ( sign == -1 )
        ++s;
    if ( (base == 0 || base == 2) &&
         s[0] == '0' && (s[1] == 'b' || s[1] == 'B') ) {
        s += 2;                          // skip binary prefix
        base = 2;
    }
    return strtol( s, pend, base ) * sign;
}
```

Listing C.1: Wrapper for `strtol` to support binary prefix for integer literals

so you could use the more natural-looking `bool`, `false`, and `true`.

After 24 years, C23 finally renamed `_Bool` to `bool` (though `_Bool` is still supported and likely will continue to be for many years) and added `false` and `true` as keywords.

C.7 constexpr

Prior to C23, `constexpr` is not supported. As an alternative, you can simply use `const` in most cases with two exceptions. Integer literals declared `const`:

1. Can not be used to specify array sizes (§6.1). If you do, you'll get a VLA (§6.14), not a fixed-sized array:

    ```
    int const MAX = 10;
    int a[MAX];              // VLA
    ```

2. Can not be `case` values within a `switch` statement (§5.8).

C.8 Declarations After Labels

Prior to C23, declarations after either `goto` labels (§5.10) or `case` values (§5.8) are not supported:

```
error: int status;          // error prior to C23
// ...
case 'x': int n;            // same
```

As an alternative, you can include the empty statement (§5.11) after the label:

```
error:; int status;        // OK prior to C23
// ...
case 'x':; int n;          // same
```

C.9 Digit Separators

Prior to C23, digit separators (′) for numeric literals (§2.5.4, §2.5.6, §2.5.7) are not supported. Unfortunately, there is no pre-C23 alternative.

C.10 #embed

The #embed preprocessor directive (§8.15) that reads the raw bytes from a file and converts them into a comma-separated list of integer literals corresponding to the binary values effectively "embedding" the binary data into a program. Unfortunately, there is no pre-C23 alternative.

C.11 Fixed-Type Enumerations

Prior to C23, fixed-type enumerations (§7.3) are not supported. Unfortunately, there is no pre-C23 alternative.

C.12 Function Definition Unnamed Parameters

Prior to C23, function definitions (§9.1) required that unused parameters (§9.2) still be named and cast to void to suppress a warning (§3.14.1 #2, p.55), for example:

```
bool visit( void *node_data, void *user_data ) {
    (void)user_data;       // suppress "not used" warning
    // ...
```

C.13 K&R-Style Function Declarations and Definitions

In K&R (first edition) C, function declarations didn't have prototypes, hence:

```
char* strncpy();           // K&R function declaration
```

C.13 K&R-Style Function Declarations and Definitions

declared `strncpy` (§B.2) as a function returning `char*` without saying *anything* about what parameters, if any, it required. You simply had to *know* by reading the documentation or source code and get it right. If you didn't, the compiler wouldn't even warn you and your program would likely crash.

■ Originally, in addition to `cc`, there was also `lint`, a program that did static analysis of C program source code.[†] Among other things, `lint` did much better type-checking than `cc` including function arguments matching types used in definitions and would warn you if anything was amiss. But using `lint` was optional, so you could forget to use it to check your programs. Most modern C compilers subsumed `lint`, but there are also modern static analysis tools that are still known as *linters*.

The name "lint" itself comes from catching dubious constructs in your programs is similar to how a lint trap in a clothes dryer catches the short fibers that shed from clothing. □

Function definitions weren't much better:

```
char* strncpy( dst, src, n )   // K&R function definition
  char *dst, *src;
{
  // ...
}
```

Only parameter *names* were listed between `( )`; their declarations were given separately between the `)` and `{`. Additionally, if a parameter was of type `int`, its declaration was optional since `int` was the default type.

Function prototypes were adopted from C++ into C89 with one addition:

```
void f();              // K&R: no parameter information
void g( void );        // C89: zero parameters
```

That is, a function with only `( )` was still a K&R-style declaration in that no parameter information is given; but a function declaration (or definition) with `(void)` explicitly means the function takes zero parameters. If you want to write code that means the same thing in versions of C prior to C23, use `(void)` for function declarations and definitions that have zero parameters.

■ For inter-language compatibility, C++ also adopted `(void)` to mean zero parameters even though `( )` has always meant that in C++. □

Prior to C23, K&R-style function declarations and definitions were *still* legal to remain backwards compatible. Finally, 34 years after function prototypes were adopted into C, the C committee removed the ability to declare and define functions in K&R style.

[†]*Lint, a C Program Checker*, Stephen C. Johnson, *Computer Science Technical Report*, 78, Bell Laboratories, Murray Hill, New Jersey, July 6, 1978.

C.14 `noreturn`

Prior to C23, the `noreturn` attribute (§4.9.5) was `_Noreturn` (§2.2 #7, p. 29), and didn't use the `[[]]` syntax. Instead, `_Noreturn` was used by itself:

```
_Noreturn void fatal_error( int status,
                            char const *format, ... );
```

`_Noreturn` is still supported and likely will continue to be for many years.

C.15 `nullptr`

Prior to C23, `nullptr` was `NULL`. While `NULL` is still supported and likely will continue to be indefinitely, if you want to use `nullptr`, but be able to compile with a C17 or earlier compiler, you could do the following:

```
#if __STDC_VERSION__ < 202311L && !defined nullptr
# include <stddef.h>          // for definition of NULL
# define nullptr NULL
#endif
```

■ `NULL` itself is just a macro, typically:

```
#define NULL  ((void*)0)   // one possible definition
```

However, some platforms define it differently:

```
#define NULL  0            // alternative definition
#define NULL  0L           // ... or this
```

In C, the integer literal `0` is special in that it can implicitly convert to a pointer — that happens to be the value used to represent the null pointer. (No other integer literal implicitly converts to a pointer.) At the time of C's creation, using `0` and `NULL` seemed simple and convenient.

However, both `0` and `NULL` (regardless of how it's defined) cause problems in certain cases. For example, if `NULL` is defined as only `0`, then passing `NULL` as an argument to a variadic function such as `vstr_is_any` from listing 9.9 (p. 150) that expects a pointer will result in undefined behavior (§15) if `sizeof(int)` is not the same as `sizeof(void*)` on the platform. It's for this and other cases why `nullptr` was (finally) added to C.[†] □

[†]*Introduce the nullptr constant*, Jens Gustedt and JeanHeyd Meneide, *ISO/IEC JTC1/SC22/WG14: Programming Language — C*, N3042, July 22, 2022, https://www.open-std.org/jtc1/sc22/wg14/www/docs/n3042.htm

C.16 `static_assert`

Originally, C didn't have `static_assert` (§16.5). C11 added it, but it was called `_Static_assert` (§2.2 #7, p.29), so you may see that in older code. Alternatively, C11 also added the following to the `assert.h` standard header:

```
#define static_assert(EXPR,MSG) \
    _Static_assert( (EXPR), MSG )
```

Prior to C11, you could do something like:

```
#define static_assert(EXPR, MSG) \
    typedef int static_assert[(EXPR) ? 1 : ((void)(MSG), -1)]
```

If EXPR evaluated to false, then it would attempt to declare an array type with a negative size that's illegal and you'd get an error message like:

```
error: 'static_assert' declared as an array with a
    negative size
```

that might also include MSG. While the error message is a nonsequitur, at least the macro would fulfill its purpose of not compiling your program.

C.17 Storage Classes for Compound Literals

Prior to C23, storage classes (§4.3) for compound literals (§6.11, §10.4) are not supported. Unfortunately, there is no pre-C23 alternative.

C.18 `thread_local`

Originally, C didn't have `thread_local` (§14.7). C11 added it, but it was called `_Thread_local` (§2.2 #7, p.29), so you may see that in older code. Alternatively, C11 also added the following to the `threads.h` standard header:

```
#define thread_local    _Thread_local
```

C.19 `typeof` and `typeof_unqual`

Prior to C23, `typeof` and `typeof_unqual` are not supported. However, `clang`, `gcc`, and Microsoft C, offer `typeof` (or `__typeof__`) as an extension.[†] Unfortunately, they do not offer an extension for `typeof_unqual`.

C.20 `__VA_OPT__`

Prior to C23, the `__VA_OPT__` preprocessor macro (§8.7.3) was not supported, but some compilers supported it as an extension. As an alternative, `clang`, `gcc`, and Microsoft C, support a non-standard extension[‡] to the preprocessor's `##` concatenation operator (§8.7.5), for example:

```
#define INTERNAL_ERROR(FORMAT, ...)                     \
    fatal_error( EXIT_INTERNAL,                         \
                 "%s:%d: internal error: " FORMAT,      \
                 __FILE__, __LINE__, ##__VA_ARGS__ )
```

When `##` is placed between a comma and `__VA_ARGS__`, the comma is deleted if `__VA_ARGS__` expands into nothing, hence this equivalence:

Extension	Standard C23
`, ##__VA_ARGS__` ≡	`__VA_OPT__(,) __VA_ARGS__`

Note that `##__VA_ARGS__` works *only* in the specific case of the token before the `##` being a comma, hence `__VA_OPT__` is more general.

C.21 Variadic Functions

Prior to C23, variadic functions (§9.11) required at least one non-variadic parameter, for example:

```
int printf( char const *format, ... );
```

and you had to supply that parameter as a second argument to `va_start`:

```
va_start( args, format );
```

[†] *Referring to a Type with* `typeof`, Free Software Foundation, *Using the GNU Compiler Collection*, §6.7, 1988–2025, https://gcc.gnu.org/onlinedocs/gcc/Typeof.html

[‡] *Variadic Macros*, Free Software Foundation, *The C Preprocessor*, §3.6, 1987–2025, https://gcc.gnu.org/onlinedocs/cpp/Variadic-Macros.html

Neither is required in C23, though you can still have non-variadic parameters, of course, and even still supply the last one as an argument to va_start (but it's ignored).

C.22 #warning

The #warning preprocessor directive (§8.11) prints a message and continues. Unfortunately, there is no pre-C23 alternative.

Index

A bold number (like **42**) means the page contains a primary reference for a term; a plain number means the page contains only a mention of a term.

Symbols

! (logical-not operator) — 48
!= (not-equal-to operator) — 6, **48**
== precedence — 6
\" (double quote character literal) — 33
\' (single quote character literal) — 33
( ) (function-call operator) — 52
* (dereference operator) — 16, **53**
* (multiplication operator) — 16, **46–47**
/ (end comment of /) — 5, **27**
*= (multiply-assign operator) — 52
+ (addition operator) — 46–47
+ (unary-plus operator) — **47**, 124
++ (increment operator) — 11, 20, **47–48**
+= (increment-assign operator) — 52
, (comma operator) — **56–57**
  misuse warning — 272
  single statement — 242
- (subtraction operator) — 46–47
- (unary-minus operator) — 47
-- (decrement operator) — 11, **47–48**
-= (decrement-assign operator) — 52

-> (pointer-member-access operator) — 23, **53**
. (designated initializer) — 23, **159**, 170
. (member-access operator) — 23, **53**
... (ellipsis)
  variadic function — 149
  variadic macro — 118
/ (division operator) — 46–47
/* (comment to */) — 5, **27**
// (comment to end-of-line) — 5, **27**
/= (divide-assign operator) — 52
< (less-than operator) — 48
<< (left-shift operator) — 49–51
  bit flag creation — 108
<<= (left-shift-assign operator) — **52**, 319
<= (less-than-or-equal-to operator) — 48
= (assignment operator) — 16, **52**
== (equal-to operator) — **48**
  != precedence — 6
> (greater-than operator) — 12, 14, **48**
>= (greater-than-or-equal-to operator) — 48

`>>` (right-shift operator) — 12, 13, **49–51**
`>>=` (right-shift-assign operator) — 12, 14, **52**
`?:` (conditional operator) — 48–49
  `void*` side-effect — 285
`[]` (array index operator) — **52–53**, 84
`[]` (designated initializer) — 84
`#` (preprocessor stringification operator) — *see* stringification
`%` (modulus operator) — 33, **46–47**, 77, 334, 339–341
`%=` (modulus-assign operator) — 52
`&` (address-of operator) — 16, **53**
`&` (bitwise-and operator) — 16, **49–51**
`&=` (bitwise-and-assign operator) — 52
`&&` (logical-and operator) — 48
  `&` confusion, origin — 50
  `assert` — 245
  `assert` message — 244
  warning — 274
`\\` (backslash character literal) — 33
`\0` (null character literal) — 9
`^` (bitwise-exclusive-or operator) — 49–51
  hash function — 334
`^=` (bitwise-exclusive-or-assign operator) — 52
`~` (bitwise-not operator) — 12, 13, **49–51**
`|` (bitwise-or operator) — **49–51**, 108
  bit flags — 108
  `mtx_init` — 226
`||` (logical-or operator) — 12, 14, **48**, 274
  `|` confusion, origin — 50
2D array — *see* multidimensional array

A

`\a` (alert, aka, bell, character literal) — 33

`a.out` — **4**, 208
`a2d_ij` — 95
ABA Problem — 257, 258, **259–261**
`abort` — **142**, 267, 276, 355
  `assert` — 241–242
`abs` — 41
abstract syntax tree — 172
actual parameter — *see* function, argument
`ad` — **203**, 212, 213
Ada — 240
Alexandrescu, Andrei — 261
ALGOL — xviii
`alignas` — **69**, 130, 163, 336
  C23, prior to — 371
  false sharing — 263
alignment (data) — **58**, 130
  `_Atomic` — 247
  cast — 272
  `max_align_t` — **39**, 163
  padding (2D array, allocating) — 94
  padding (structure) — 162
  `SIGBUS` — 267
  warning — 327
  `-Wcast-align` — 272
alignment (printing) — 182
`alignof` — **58**, 69, 95
  C23, prior to — 371
`alloc2d` — 94–95
anonymous union — **171**, 175
`ansi_color` — 104
Apache — xvii
APFS — 184
`__APPLE__` — 114
`argc` — **143**, 184
`argv` — **143**, 185
ARMv8 — 220
array — 83–99
  `[]` syntactic sugar — 88
  bounds checking — 84, 238, **268**
  declaration — 8, **83**
  designated initializer — 84
  indexing — 52–53, **84**
  initialization — 9, **83–84**
    C23, prior to — 371

INDEX 383

multidimensional — *see* multidimensional array
non-null parameter syntax — 138, 322
of pointers — 89–90
parameter — *see* parameter, array
pointer difference — 89
pointer equivalence — **88**, 94
pointer, and — 88
pointer, decay to — **88**, 139, 151, 290
qualified parameter syntax — 138
variable length — *see* variable length array
`ARRAY_SIZE` — 117, **128**, 131, **290**, 292, 338
ASCII — 9, 14, 33, 39, 50
assembler — 4
assembly language — 235, 279
   ARMv8 pre-decrement — 220
   bit-field — 165–166
   C compiler output — 4
   C statements, mapping/translation — 266
   call function — 146
   compare-exchange — 256
   `return true` — 237, 238
`assert` — **241–246**, 267, 277, 278, 342
   disabling — 243–244
   implementation, possible — 119
   implementation, sample — 241–242
   message, custom — 244
`assert.h` — **241**, 377
associativity — 45, 48
   `else` with `if` — 74
   evaluation order difference — 45–46
`at_quick_exit` — 211
`atexit` — 210–211
`_Atomic` — 67, 113, 138, **247–264**, 284, 312
   mutex alternative — 248
atomic (meaning) — **219**, 248
`atomic_exchange`, etc. — 249
`atomic_fetch_add`, etc. — 249

`atomic_fetch_and`, etc. — 249
`atomic_init` — 252
`atomic_load`, etc. — **249**, 251
`atomic_store`, etc. — **249**, 251
attribute — 70–72
   C23, prior to — 372
   namespace — 30
   placement in declaration — 70
   `__attribute__` — 372
`AUTHORS` — 212
auto
   C23, prior to — 372
   deduced type — **62–63**, 331
   history — 64–65
   storage class — 64–65
   `typeof` difference — 67–68
`__auto_type` — 372
autoconf — 213
automake — 213
Autotools — **213**, 214

B

`\b` (backspace character literal) — 33
B (programming language) — 3, 50, 64, 65
big endian — *see* endianness
big O notation — **xix**, 328–329, 333, 335
binary compatibility — 205
binary literal — 34
   C23, prior to — 372
binary tree — 333
bit-field — 165–166
   `int` signedness — 166
`_BitInt` — 32, **34–35**
`BLOCK` — 129
block — 73
block scope — **30**, 31, 63
   `_Atomic` initialization — 252
   `thread_local` — 230
BNF — 185
`bool` — 12, 14, **32**
   atomic read — 222
   atomic write — 222
   atomic, not — 219

C23, prior to — 372–373
function return type — 142
`bootstrap` — 213
bottleneck
  `memory_order_seq_cst` — **250**, 251
  mutex — 223
Bourne, Steve — 278
`break` — 75, **76**, 78
breakpoint — 278
BSD — 207
buffer overflow — 21, **268**
bug — 268–271
  array bounds — 84, 238, **268**
  buffer overflow — 21, **268**
  double free — 269
  memory leak — 22, 71, **270–271**
  null pointer dereference — 269
  off-by-one — 269
  thread leak — 218
  uninitialized variable — **271**, 280
  use after free — 269–270
build tools — 213–214
  warning specification — 272
built-in types — 31–37
bus error — 267
Butenhof, David R. — 217, 223, 226

C

C Programming Language, The — **xviii**, xxi, 3, 29, 235, 374
C# — 347
  dynamic dispatch — 345
  exception — 299
  `volatile` — 311
C++ — xviii–xix
  abstract class — 90
  `_Atomic()` — 247
  `auto` — 65
  binary literal — 372
  C code, using — 208
  `const` — 17
  `constexpr` — 17
  `decltype` — 68
  destructor — 24

  dynamic dispatch — 345
  embedded system — xviii
  exception — 242, 299, 351, 359
  `extern "C"` — *see* `extern "C"`
  `final` — 172
  flexible array member — 165
  function overloading — 136, 283, 286
    linker — 208
  function prototype adoption — 375
  identifier compatibility — 29
  `if constexpr` — 287
  language linkage — 208–209
  member function call — 348
  name mangling — 208
  name origin — 11
  namespace — 30
  non-null array parameter syntax — 138
  paste avoidance — 126
  polymorphism — 350
  qualified array parameter syntax — 138
  RAII — 357
  reference — 68
  `register` — 66
  `__restrict__` — 308
  `restrict` — 308
  scoped enumeration — 103
  SFINAE — 289
  `std::exchange` — 256
  `std::is_same` — 296
  `std::map` — 333
  `std::swap` — 256
  `std::unordered_map` — 333
  structure nesting — 158
  type punning — 171
  type trait — 289
  variable length array — 97
  version — 113
  `(void)` — 375
C++ Programmer's Handbook, The — xxiii
`c_ast_is_ptr_to_tid_any` — 278–280

INDEX 385

c_ast_is_tid_any_qual_impl — 278, **280**
c_ast_unpointer_qual — **277**, 278, 280
c_int_fmt (enumeration) — 108
c_int_fmt (structure) — 165
c23_strtol — 372
cache coherent — 220
cache line — 163
    false sharing, and — 262–263
    fat pointer, and — 349
    hash table, open addressing — 335
    size — 263
call stack — 242
call_once — 229–230
callgrind — 281
calloc — **338**, 340
case — **77–78**, 373
cast — 11, **54–56**
    away const — 55
    implicit conversion warning — 273
    pointer — 56
    return type, to — 79
    unsigned, to — 41
    void, to — **55**
    void*, from — 86
catch — **356–357**, 357, 358
cc — **3**, 112, 143, 213, 375
cdecl
    maintainer — xxiii
cdecl — **91**, 280
    argv[0] — 143
    debugging — 276–280
    macros, expanding — 133
    restricted class hierarchy — 172–176
cexp — 37
cfront — xxiii
chaining (hash table) — 335–336
ChangeLog — 212
char — 32–33
    implementation defined signedness — **33**, 293
    literal — 33
    signed — 33
    unsigned — 33
CHAR_BIT — 33
char16_t — 39
char32_t — 39
char8_t — 38
character
    alert, aka, bell — 33
    backslash — 33
    backspace — 33
    carriage return — 33
    char — 33
    char16_t — 39
    char32_t — 39
    char8_t — 38
    double quote — 33
    form feed — 33
    hexadecimal literal — 33
    literal — 33
    newline — 5, **33**
    null — *see* null character
    octal literal — 33
    signed — 33
    single quote — 33
    string — *see* string
    tab — 33
    Unicode — 38–39
    unsigned — 33
    vertical tab — 33
    wchar_t — 39
check_open — 184
clang — 4, 71, 72, 78, 111–113, 266, 276, 277, 279, 280, 372
clearerr — 187
CLion — 214, 281
close — 189
closedir — **192**, 193
CMake — 213
cnd_destroy — 228
cnd_init — 228
cnd_signal — 228
cnd_timedwait — 229
cnd_wait — **228–229**, 256
COBOL — 209
code bloat — 148, 149
Cohen, Danny — 56

collision (hash table) — 334
`color_string` — 123
comment — 5, **27–28**
`comp.lang.c` — 240
   Frequently Asked Questions — 235
`comp.programming.threads` — 223, 226
compare-and-swap — 255–258
compilation phases — 111
compiler optimization — 266
   disable — **266**, 278
   Heisenbug — 278
   observable behavior — 216
   order — 238–239
   pointer, and — 306
   `register`, and — 66
   `restrict`, and — 305
   return value — 142
   undefined behavior — 238–239
   `volatile` — 309–310
`_Complex` — 32, **36–37**
`complex.h` — **36–37**, 113
compound literal
   array — **92–93**, 226
   lifetime — 93
   scope — 93
   storage class — 93
      C23, prior to — 377
   structure — 24, 141, 142, **160–162**, 270, 317, 321, 338, 339, 342, 354, 355
      `typeof`, with — 367
   union — 170
compound statement — 73
concatenation (string) — 20, **21**
   `mstrcat` — *see* `mstrcat`
   `strcat` — *see* `strcat`
concatenation (token) — **120**, 129
   pitfalls — 120–121
condition variable — 226–229
   timed — 229
conditional compilation — **113–116**, 263
`configure.ac` — 213
`const` — 17–20, 62, **67**, 284

   casting away — 55
   `constexpr` difference — 18, **67**
   east — 19
   overloading — 286–287
const-ness — 364–365
   `auto` — **63**
   `auto`, and — 331
   casting away — 55
`CONST_OVERLOAD` — 288
`constexpr` — 7, 17, 33, 39, **67**, 77
   C23, prior to — 373
   compound literal — 93
   `const` difference — 18, **67**
`continue` — 9, 11, 13, 33, **76**, 77, 78
conversion specification
   `printf` — 181
   `scanf` — 195
   `strftime` — 368
`coord` — 158–159
`COPYING` — 212
copying (file) — 184–186
copying (input to output) — 5–8
core dump — xxi, 21, 142, 241, 242, **266–267**, 268, 276
   origin — 267
   signal, triggered by — 267
`__cplusplus` — **113**, 209, 247
CPU
   alignment — *see* alignment (data)
   architecture, predefined macro — 114
   atomic value operation — 219
   cache coherent — 220
   cache line — *see* cache line
   compare-and-swap — 261
   dependent — 172
   endianness — *see* endianness
   illegal instruction — 267
   integer size — 41
   opcode — 267
   performance — 216
   process — 215
   register — *see* register (CPU)
   right shift of signed type — 51
      warning — 275

INDEX 387

spike — 227
strongly-ordered — **254**, 257
`thrd_yield`, and — 225
value visibility — 219
`volatile` — 312
weakly-ordered — **254**, 257
`ctype.h` — 10, **363–364**
Curious Case of the Disappearing `if`, The — 276–280
cURL — xvii
cv-qualified — **67**, 364
cvr-qualified — 67
`cx_exception` — **354**, 358
`cx_impl_catch` — 356
`cx_impl_do_throw` — 355
`cx_impl_exception` — **354**, 355
`cx_impl_state` — **352**, 354, **355**
`cx_impl_throw` — 354, 355
`cx_impl_try_block` — 230, **352**, 353, **354**, 355–358
`cx_impl_try_block_head` — 230, **352**, 354, 355, 358
`cx_impl_try_cond` — **352**, 353, **355**, 357, **358**
`cx_set_xid_matcher` — 360
`cx_terminate` — 355
`cx_xid_matcher` — 360

D

`-D` (Unix compiler option) — 42, **112**, 114
`/D` (Microsoft compiler option) — **112**, 114
`d_name` — 193
dangling pointer — **93**, 261, 343
data race — 216
  bit-field — 166
  `__DATE__` — 113
`df`, `DD` (`_Decimal64` literal suffix) — 36
deadlock — 224–226
`/DEBUG` (Microsoft compiler option) — 266
debugger — 278
debugging — 265–282

information — 266
printing values — 266
rubber duck — 281
decimal floating-point — 36
decimal literal — 34
`_Decimal32`, etc. — 32, **36**
`DECL_UNUSED` — 69, **130**, 173
declaration — 61–72
  empty statement, after, prior to C23 — 374
  label, after, prior to C23 — 373–374
  multiple — 62
  syntax rationale — 61–62
`__declspec` — 372
`decltype` — 68
default
  `_Generic` — **284**, 285
  `switch` — **77–78**, 274
  enumeration values — 107
deprecated — 70
dereference — **16**, 53, 56, 87, 88, 91, 92, 255, 290, 327
  null pointer — 269
  pointer to array — 139
  use after free — 269
  `void*` — 86
Descent to C, The — 25
designated initializer
  array — 84
  structure — 23, **159**
  union — 170
Development of the C Language, The — 25, 50, 137
`df`, `DF` (`_Decimal32` literal suffix) — 36
`difftime` — 367
digit separators — 34, 36
  C23, prior to — 374
Dijkstra, Edsger W. — 223
`DIR` — 192, 193
directory — 192–193
  deletion — 191–192
`dirent` — 192–193
`dirent.h` — 193
disk — 183–184

dl, DL (`_Decimal128` literal suffix) — 36
do-while — 8, **75**, 150, 184
 multiple statements in macro — 122
double — 32, **35–36**
double free — 269
double precision — 32, **35**
Doxyfile — 212
Doxygen — **28**, 212
DTrace — 281
dynamic dispatch — 345–350
dynamic memory — 20–22

E

-E (Unix compiler option) — 111
/E (Microsoft compiler option) — 111
east `const` — 19
`EINVAL` — 197, 198
`else` — 12, **74**
 dangling — 359
#embed — 126–127
 C23, prior to — 374
embedded system — xviii
empty statement — 80
 declaration after, prior to C23 — 374
end of file — *see* `EOF`
endianness — 56
 bit-field — 166
 origin — 56
 `__STDC_ENDIAN_BIG__`, etc. — 113
enum — 102
enumeration — 30, 38, **101–110**, 203
 constant — 102–103
  collision — 102–103
 declaration — 102
 fixed type — 103
  C23, prior to — 374
 function return value — 141
 implicit conversion — 103
 scoped — 103
 tag — 102
 underlying type — 103
 values — 104–109
  bit-flag — 108–109

 checking — 106–107
 counting — 107
 duplicate — 105–106
 externally imposed — 104
 none, not set, unspecified — 106
 serializing — 105
environment variable — 192, **200–201**
EOF — 5, **6–7**, 11, 77, 179, 186–188, 194, 196, 198, 200, 363
 distinguish from error — **194**, 199
 type — 6
epoch — **39**, 368
`EPRINTF` — 180
`EPUTC` — 180
`EPUTS` — 180
`ERANGE` — **198**, 199
Errintgon, Andrew — 281
errno — **142**, 180, 184–186, 188–194, 197–199, 201, 230, 361
errno.h — 142
#error — 124–125
error handling — 142
euler — 37
evaluation order
 associativity difference — 45–46
 `case` — 77
 left-to-right
  , — 57
  ?: — 49
  && and || — 48
 short-circuit of && and || — **48**, 50
 unspecified behavior — 45
exception — 142, **351–360**
 `assert` and errors, vs. — 242–243
 C# — 299
 C++ — 299, 351
 `catch` — *see* `catch`
 `finally` — *see* `finally`
 Java — 299
 Python — 299
 requirements — 351–352
 restrictions in C — 358–359
 `try` — *see* `try`
Exim — xvii
`_Exit` — 210

exit — 72, 122, 142, 185, **210**
exit status — 144
EXIT_FAILURE — 8, **144**
EXIT_SUCCESS — 8, **144**
exponent — 36
expression statement — 73
Ext4 — 184
extern — 65
  inline — 148–149
  thread_local — 230
extern "C" — **208–209**, 211
external linkage — 64–65
  leading underscore — 29

F

\f (form feed character literal) — 33
f, F (float literal suffix) — 36
fallthrough — 70, **78**, 106, 274, 358
false sharing — 262–263
fat pointer — 348–350
fatal_error — 118, **276**, 378
  C23, prior to — 376
fclose — 184, **185**, 358
fdopen — 190
feof — 187
ferror — 7, 184, **188**
fflush — 188
fgetc — 194
fgets — 115, **198–200**
__FILE__ — **113**, 118, 119, 122, 124, 153, 354
file — 183–192
  as memory — 191
  deletion — 191–192
  descriptor — 189
  inclusion — *see* #include
  information — 186–187
  low-level — 189–190
  memory as — 190
  open mode — 186
  position — 188–189
  source organization — 212–213
  state — 187–188
  temporary — 192

file scope — **30**, 65–67, 106, 145, 158, 159, 230
  _Atomic initialization — 252
  const initializer — 67
FILE_OFFSET_BITS — 42
fileno — 190
filesystem — **183–184**, 191
finally — 357–358
Fishburne, Laurence — 25
fl_print_error — 152
flexible array member — **162–165**, 251, 325
  sizeof — 165
float — 32, **35–36**
float.h — 40
floating-point — 35–36
  cast to — 54
  decimal — 36
  equality — 273
  modulus — 47
  rounding or truncation — 54
  type conversion — 43
FLPRINTF — 129
flush (buffer) — 185–186
fmemopen — 190
fmod — 47
FNV–1a hash function — 334
fnv1a64_mem — 334
fopen — **185**, 299, 358
for — 12, 13, **76**
  while equivalence — 13, **76**
FOR_ALL_COLORS — 122–123
FOREACH_SLINK — 331
formal parameter — *see* function, parameter
Fortran — 209
fprintf — 122, 152, **179**, 184, 276
fputc — 179
fputs — 9, 12, 107, **179**, 217
fread — 7, 8, 184, 189, **194**, 236
free — 21, **22**, 24, 95, 97, 164, 231, 270, 326, 328, 329, 338, 340, 342
  double — 269
  nullptr — 269
  use after — 269–270

`fscanf` — 194
`fseek` — 188
`fstat` — 186
`ftell` — **188**, 236
fully buffered — 185
`__func__` — 145
function — 12–14, 52, **135–155**
  argument — 5, **135–136**
  body — 4, **135**
  call — 52
    mechanism — 146
    pointer — 91
  declaration — 4
  declaration vs. definition — 135
  error handling — 142
  inline — *see* `inline`
  K&R style — 374–375
  `main` — *see* `main`
  overloading — 209
    linker — 208
  parameter — 4, **135–136**
    array — 136–141
    `register` — 66
    unnamed — 135
  pointer — 52, **90–92**, 147, 151, 210, 231, 284, 326, 346, 360
    call — 91
  prototype — 62, **135**
  return value — 4, **141–142**
  scope — 30
  signature — 135
  `static` — 144–145
    local variable — 145–146
  variadic — *see* variadic function
`fwrite` — 7, 8, **180**, 184, 189

G

`-g` (Unix compiler option) — 266
garbage collection — 22
`gcc` — 4, 71, 72, 78, 111–113, 266, 276, 372
`gdb` — 108, **265**
`_Generic` — 283–297
  `const` overloading — 286–287
  motivation — 283

  `printf` example — 284–286
  SFINAE — 288–289
  type traits — 289–297
`geo_loc` — 158–159
`getc` — 194
`getchar` — 5–7, 33, 77, 189, **194**
`getdelim` — 199
`getenv` — 200
`getline` — 115, 189, **199**
Git — xvii
`gmtime` — 367
`gmtime_r` — 367
GN — 213
Go
  dynamic dispatch — 345
  interface — 90, **348–350**
    decay to pointer — 349
`goto` — 7, 8, 75, 78, **79–80**, 109, 373
  label — *see* label
`gperftools` — 281
`gprof` — 281
`grep` — 152, 158, 331
  exit status — 144
Groening, Matt — 302

H

`__has_c_attribute` — 116
`__has_include` — 116
hash function — 334
  FNV-1a — 334
hash table — 333–344
  chaining — 335–336
  clean-up — 338
  collision — 334
  deletion — 342
  finding — 341
  growing — 340
  initialization — 338
  insertion — 339
  iteration — 342
  load factor — 336
  open addressing — 335–336
`hash_table` — 336–338
hazard pointer — 261

INDEX 391

header file — 5, **116**
  example — 211
  include everything necessary — 207
  including header file — 206
  including in .c file — 209–210
  `inline` function — 148
  interdependency — 207–208
  self-sufficient — 206–208
heap memory — **21**, 97, 165
heisenbug — 278
hello, world — 3
hexadecimal literal
  character — 33
  floating-point — 36
  integer — 34
higher-order macro — *see* X macro
hint
  `inline` — 147
  `register` — 66
  `restrict` — 305
`ht_cleanup` — 338
`ht_cmp_fn` — **336–338**, 341
`ht_delete` — 342
`HT_DINT` — 340
`HT_DPTR` — 340
`ht_entry` — 336–338
`ht_find` — 341
`ht_free_fn` — 336–338
`ht_grow` — 340
`ht_hash_fn` — 336–338
`ht_init` — 338
`ht_insert_rv` — 339
`ht_iter` — 342
`ht_next` — 342
`HT_PRIME` — 338–342

I

`-I` (Unix compiler option) — 116
I (imaginary number i constant) — 37
`/I` (Microsoft compiler option) — 116
IDE — 6, **214**
identifier — 29
IEEE Std 1003.1-2024 — *see* POSIX
`if` — 12, **74–75**

`if_empty` (#embed parameter) — 127
`#ifndef` — 112
illegal instruction — 267
`_Imaginary` — 32, **37**
implementation defined — 235–236
  `argc, argv` — 143
  `atexit`, number of calls — 210
  attributes, prior to C23 — 372
  bit-field endianness — 166
  bit-field word boundary — 166
  C++ name mangling — 208
  `char` signedness — **33**, 293
  `d_name` array size — 193
  directory entry iteration order — 193
  enumeration default underlying type — 103
  `EXIT_FAILURE` — 144
  I/O buffer capacity — 185
  `if-else`, number of chained — 75
  `int` bit-field signedness — 166
  language linkage — 209
  local variable memory order — 268
  rationale — xxi
  right shift of signed type — 51
  `tv_nsec` type — 367
`#include` — 5, **116**, 203, 213
include guard — 115, 127, 128, **203–205**, 207, 211
include path — 116
incomplete type — 205
infinite loop — 75, 76
  recursion — *see* recursion
`inline` — 146–149
  code bloat — 148, 149
  definition — 148–149
  hint — 147
  macro, difference from — 146–147
  `static` — 148
  when to — 147–148
Inline Disease, The — 148
`INSTALL` — 212
`int` — 32, **34**, 42
  bit-field signedness — 166
  omission — 13, 32
`INT_MAX` — 40, 237

INT_MAX_EXPR — 295
INT_MIN_EXPR — 295
int32_t — 56
int8_t, etc. — **38**, 41
   choosing appropriate — 42
integer
   choosing appropriate — 41–42
   fixed-width — 38
   int — see int
   natural size — 41
   numeric limits — 39
   overflow — 40–41
   promotion — 43
     _BitInt — 35
   rank — 43
   underflow — 40–41
interface — 90, **348–350**
internal linkage — 64–66
   function — 144–145
INTERNAL_ERROR — 118, 122
intrusive — 163–164
IS_ARITHMETIC_EXPR — 294
IS_ARRAY_EXPR — 290
IS_C_STR_EXPR — 276, **292**
IS_FLOATING_POINT_EXPR — 294
IS_INTEGRAL_EXPR — **293**, 295
IS_POINTER_EXPR — 291
IS_PTR_TO_CONST_EXPR — 288
IS_SAME_TYPE — 296
IS_SIGNED_EXPR — 293
IS_UNSIGNED_TYPE — 292
IS_TYPE_EXPR — 294
IS_UNSIGNED_EXPR — 293
isalnum — 81, **363**
isalpha — 363
isblank — 363
iscntrl — 363
isdigit — 363
isgraph — 364
islist_lfpush — 258
islower — 364
ISO — xx
isprint — 9, 10, **364**
ispunct — 364
isspace — 364

isupper — 364
isxdigit — 364

J

Java — 25, 347, 357
   dynamic dispatch — 345
   exception — 299
   interface — 90
   Map — 333
   sealed — 172
   virtual machine — 25
   volatile — 311
jmp_buf — **299**, 311, 352, 354
Johnson, Stephen C. — 124, 375

K

K&R (book) — xviii, xxi, 3, 235, 374
K&R (style) — 29, **374–375**
Kernighan, Brian W. — **xviii**, 3
Kotlin — 172

L

l, L (long double literal suffix) — 36
l, L (long literal suffix) — 34
label — 8, **79–80**
   declaration after, prior to C23 — 373–374
   namespace — **30**, 80
LANG_IS — 121
language linkage — **208**, 211
Lesk, Michael E. — 124
lex — 124
lib (subdirectory) — 213
life, the universe, and everything — 42
limit (#embed parameter) — 127
limits.h — 40
__LINE__ — **113**, 118–122, 124, 153, 354
#line — 124
linkage — 64
   external — see external linkage
   internal — see internal linkage
   language — see language linkage

none — *see* no linkage
linked list — 163–165, 325–332
   iteration — 331
linker — 208
`lint` — 375
Linux — xvii, 184
   kernel coding style — 148
   `__linux__` — 114
literal
   binary — 34
   `_BitInt` — 35
   `bool` — 32
   `char` — 33
   compound — *see* compound literal
   decimal — 34
   `_Decimal32`, etc. — 36
   digit separators — 34, 36
   `double` — 36
   `float` — 36
   hexadecimal
     floating-point — 36
     integer — 34
   `int` — 34
   `long` — 34
     `double` — 36
     `long` — 34
   octal — 34
   string — 5, **33**
   `unsigned` — 34
little endian — *see* endianness
`ll`, `LL` (`long long` literal suffix) — 34
`lldb` — 265
load factor (hash table) — 336
`load_bool_mtx` — 221
local variable
   declaration — 5
   initialization — 9–10
   no linkage — 64
   `register` — 66
   register (CPU), `longjmp` — 301
   stack frame — 21
   `static` — 145–146
     inline function — 149
   `volatile` — 311
locale — 363

`localtime` — 367
`localtime_r` — 368
lock-free — 258
`long` — **32**, 41, 42
   `double` — 35–36
   `long` — 41, 42
`long long` — 32
`longjmp` — 75, 78, 299, **301–302**, 311, 351, 354, 355, 359
   variable length array, and — **302**, 358
Lovejoy, Rev. Timothy — 302
`lstat` — 186–187
Lua — 359
lvalue — 291

M

`m4` (macro processor) — 111
`m4` (subdirectory) — 213
macOS — 184
macro
   argument — 117–118
   function-like — 117–121
   higher-order — *see* X macro
   `inline`, difference from — 146–147
   multiple statements — 122
   not expanding — 125
   object-like — 112
   parameter — 117
   paste avoidance — 125–126
   predefined — 113
   variadic — *see* variadic macro
   X — *see* X macro
magic values — 7
`main` — 3, 4, **143–144**, 266
   parameters — 143
   return type — 144
   return value — 144
     omission — 5, **144**
main thread — 215
Make — 213
Makefile — 213
`Makefile.am` — 212
`malloc` — **21–22**, 94, 95, 97, 164, 199, 269

`calloc`, difference — 338
    failure return value — 96
    `realloc`, difference — 23
    `sizeof`, use with — **57**, 88, 252, 258, 326, 339
man (subdirectory) — 213
manual pages — 213, 363
map — 333
`math.h` — 47, 283
Matrix, The — 25
`MAX` — **117**, 271
`max_align_t` — **39**, 163, 336
`maybe_unused` — 70, **71**, 245, 275
`MEM_ZERO` — 291
member
    structure — 157
    union — 170
member namespace — 30
    structure — 157
    union — 170
`memchr` — 365
`memcmp` — 255, **365**
`memcpy` — 255, 268, 270, 271, 306, 315, 319, **365**
`memmove` — 86, 306, 323, **365**
memory — 14–15
    array vs. pointer — 89
    dynamic — 21
    global — 21
    heap — **21**, 97, 165
    leak — 22, 71, **270–271**
        VLA — 302
    multidimensional array layout — 85
    page size — 8
    post office box analogy — **14**, 15
    stack — **21**, 97
    static — 21
memory barrier — **250–255**, 312
memory-mapped I/O — 310
`memory_order_acq_rel` — 255
`memory_order_acquire` — 253–255
`memory_order_consume` — 254–255
`memory_order_relaxed` — 251–252
`memory_order_release` — 253
`memory_order_seq_cst` — 250

`memset` — 291, **365**
Meson — 213
Michael, Maged — 261
Microsoft C — 111, 112, 116, 213, 214, 281
    warnings — 272
Microsoft Windows
    b (file mode) — 186
    epoch — 39
    file deletion — 192
    NTFS — 184
    pthreads — 216
    `wchar_t` — 39
    `_WIN32` — 114
Mind Behind Linux, The — 330
minidump — 267
`mktime` — 368
`mmap` — 191
modifier — 12, **31–32**
module — 203
Morpheus — 25
`mstrcat` — **21**, 55, 65, 71
    documentation — 28
`mtx_destroy` — 221–222
`mtx_init` — **221–222**, 224, 226
`mtx_lock` — **221**, 225, 227
`mtx_lockall` — 225–226
`mtx_plain` — **221–222**, 226
`mtx_recursive` — 226
`mtx_t` — 221
`mtx_timed` — 226
`mtx_timedlock` — 224
`mtx_trylock` — 225
`mtx_unlock` — **221**, 225, 227
multidimensional array — 84–86
    dynamically allocating — 94–95
    indexing — 85
    initialization — 85, 86
    memory layout — 85
    parameter — 139–140
        VLA — 140
    pointer, vs. — 93–94
    row-major order — 85
multithreading — 215–232
    bad example — 219–220

condition variable — *see* condition variable
mutex — *see* mutex
`munmap` — 191
mutex — 221–226
  bottleneck — 223
  lock — 221
  recursive — 226
  timed — 224
  unlock — 221

N

\n (newline character literal) — 5, 9, **33**
`NAME2` — 129
namespace — 30
nasal demons — 240
`NDEBUG` — 112, 241, 242, **243–244**
New B (programming language) — 137
newline character — 5
`NEWS` — 213
NFS — 184
Ninja — 213
no linkage — 64
  local variable — 64
  `register` — 66
`nodiscard` — **71**, 131, 164, 321, 322, 326, 328
non-null array parameter syntax — **138**, 322
`_Noreturn` — 376
`noreturn` — **72**, 184, 185, 211, 354, 355
  C23, prior to — 376
NTFS — 184
`NULL` — 277, **376**
null character — **9**, 10, 20, 90, 131, 190, 200
  append to string — **9**, 84
  literal — 9
  string, last character — **9**, 53, 196, 344
null pointer dereference — 269

`nullptr` — **15**, 28, 92, 93, 119, 125, 150, 151, 160, 164, 190, 193, 198, 199, 218, 219, 221, 231, 238, 245, 246, 248, 260, 266, 277, 317, 321, 326, 338
  array parameter — 137
  C23, prior to — 376
  error indication — 96, **142**, 185, 190, 191, 200
  `free` — 269
`nullptr_t` — 39
numeric limits — 39

O

`-o` (Unix compiler option) — **266**, 278
`/o` (Microsoft compiler option) — 266
`objdump` — 279
observable behavior — **216**, 250
observer effect — 278
octal literal — 34
off-by-one — 269
`off_t` — 41
`offsetof` — 176
`OK_DISCARD` — 131
`once_flag` — 230
`ONCE_FLAG_INIT` — 230
one definition rule — 148
opaque type — 205
`open` — 189
open addressing (hash table) — 335–336
open source — xvii
`open_memstream` — 190
`opendir` — **192**, 193
OpenSSL — xvii
operating system
  `main` as interface — 143
  memory reclamation — **22**, 323
  predefined macro — 114
  semi-portable C — 235
  signal — 267
  system call — 189
operator — 45–59
  associativity — **45**, 48, 49
  precedence — 6, 23, **45**, 48, 49

& and | — 50
  macro substitution — 117
optimization
  compiler — *see* compiler
    optimization
  return value — 142
  small size — 96
ordinary namespace — 30
owning pointer — **269**, 270

P

padding
  2D array allocation — 94–95
  bit-field — 166
  flexible array member — 165
  structure — 162
parameter
  function — *see* function, parameter
  macro — *see* macro, parameter
Pascal — 61
PASTE — 120, **121**
paste avoidance — 125–126
perf — 281
perror — 7, **8**, 185, 199
PL/I — 209
PLUS_ONE — 124
pointer — 15–17
  alias — 306
  arithmetic — 88
  array difference — 89
  array equivalence — **88**, 94
  array, decay from — **88**, 139, 151, 290
  array, to — 139
  cast — 56
  dangling — **93**, 261, 343
  declaration — 15
  fat — 348–350
  function — 52, **90–92**, 147, 151, 210, 231, 284, 326, 346, 360
    call — 91
    dynamic dispatch — 346
  hazard — 261
  one past last array element, to — 88
  owning — **269**, 270
  pointer, to — 87
  self — 24
  this — 24
  versioned — 261–262
  virtual function — 347
  void — 86
POSIX — xx
  locale — 363
  threads — *see* pthreads
Postfix — xvii
PostgreSQL — xvii
  exceptions — 359
#pragma — 127–128
  disable warning — 276
prefix (#embed parameter) — 127
preprocessor — 111–134
  concatenation — *see* concatenation (token)
  directive — 112
  macro — *see* macro
  rationale — 111
  stringification — *see* stringification
Princess Bride, The — 242
print_color — 105, 107
printf — 5, 17, 180, **181**, 284
  consecutive spaces — **33**, **77**, 198
  variadic arguments — 151–152
PRINTF_FORMAT — 284
process — 215
profile — 281
  assertions — 243
  inline — 148
  restrict — 307
program organization — 203–214
Programming with POSIX Threads — 217
pthreads — 216–217
PTR_FORMAT — 285
ptrdiff_t — 39
putc — 179
putchar — 5–7, 33, 77, **179**, 189
puts — 21, 22, **179**
putubin — **12**, 31, 63, 64, 66, 131
pwd.h — 207
Python — xvii

INDEX

dict — 333
dynamic dispatch — 345
exception — 299
interpreter — 25

Q

qsort — 90–91
qualified array parameter syntax — 138
qualifier — 67
quick_exit — 211

R

\r (carriage return character literal) — 33
R (programming language) — 359
race condition — 216
RAII — 357
rank (integer) — 43
read — 189
readdir — **192**, 193
README.md — 213
realloc — 315, 316, 318–320
   getdelim — 199
   malloc, difference — 23
recursion — *see* infinite loop
recursive mutex — 226
register — **66**, 147
   compiler optimization — 66
   compound literal — 93
register (CPU) — 14, 66, 220, 348
   function call — 146
   longjmp — 301
   setjmp — 301
   volatile — 301
Reiner, Rob — 242
remove — 191
resource acquisition is initialization — 357
restrict — 67, 138, 284, **305–308**
   C++ — 308
   pitfalls — 306–307
   this, and — 308
restricted class hierarchy — 172–176

return — 7, 75, 78, **79**
return value optimization — 142
rewind — 189
Ritchie, Dennis M. — **xviii**, xxi, 25, 41, 50, 61, 64, 137, 138
round_half_up — 54
row-major order — 85
rubber duck debugging — 281
rup — 51
rup2 — **51**, 94
Rust
   BTreeMap — 333
   dynamic dispatch — 345
   traits — 348
rvalue — 291

S

S_IFREG, etc. — 186
S_ISREG, etc. — 187
scan-build — 279
scanf — 194, **194**
   buffer overflow — 268
Schmidt, Eric — 124
scope — **30–31**, 64, 130
   array declaration — 88
   enumeration constants — 102
   extern — 65
   for variable declaration — 13, **76**
   pointer aliasing — 306
   preprocessor — 112
   restrict — 305, 307
   try — 352
   typedef tag injection — 102, 158, 170
scoped enumeration — 103
segmentation fault — **267**, 268
self — 24
self-sufficient header — 206–208
semi-portable C — 114, **235**
Sendmail — xvii
setjmp — 299, **300**, 351–353, 357, 359
   restrictions — 300
   volatile, and — **301**, 311
setvbuf — 266

SFINAE — 288–289
Shawn, Wallace — 242
Shearer, Harry — 302
`short` — **32**, 41, 42
`sig_atomic_t` — 311
signal — 267
  handler — 310–311
`signed` — 32
  `char` — 33
  `int` in bit-field — 166
significand — 36
Simpsons, The — 302
single precision — 32, **35**
single-threaded — **215**, 229
`size_t` — 18, 26, **39**, 51, 62, 86, 90, 95, 141, 142, 158, 190, 211, 289, 306, 317
  `alignof` return type — 58
  conversion specification — 182
  number of bytes — 41
  number of objects — 42
  sentinel value — 54
  `sizeof` — 318
  `sizeof` return type — 57
  `strlen` return type — 62, 64
  VLA — 140
`sizeof` — **57**, 69, 91, 95, 141
  flexible array member — 165
  `malloc`, use with — **57**, 88, 252, 258, 326, 339
`slist_back` — 328
`slist_cleanup` — 326
`SLIST_DINT` — **327–328**, 330, 331
`SLIST_DPTR` — 327–328
`slist_empty` — 328
`slist_find` — 286
`slist_free` — 270
`slist_free_if` — 329
`slist_front` — 328
`slist_init` — 326
`slist_pop_back` — 328
`slist_pop_front` — 328
`slist_push_back` — 326
`slist_push_front` — 326
small size optimization — 96

Smalltalk — 345
`snprintf` — 316
Solaris — 157
spaghetti code — 8
spawn (thread) — 215
spin lock — **227**, 253
spurious failure — 256–258
spurious signal — 229
`sqrt` — 85, 159, 283
`src` (subdirectory) — 213
`ssize_t` — 39
`st_mode` — 186–187
stack frame — **21**, 64, 142, 266, 268, 301
stack memory — **21**, 97
standard floating-point — *see* floating-point
standard input — 6, 8, 183, **194**
standard output — 6, 8, **179**, 183, 265–266
`stat` (function) — 186
`stat` (structure) — 186
`static`
  compound literal — 93
  function — 144–145
    `inline` — 148
  local variable — 145–146
    `inline` function — 149
  non-null array parameter syntax — **138**, 322
  storage class — 65–66
  `thread_local` — 230
`static_assert` — 176, **244–245**, 291, 296
  C11, prior to — 377
  C23, prior to — 377
`STATIC_ASSERT_EXPR` — **245**, 290
`STATIC_IF` — 287–288
`-std` (Unix compiler option) — 4, 113
`/std` (Microsoft compiler option) — 113
`std::terminate` — 355
`std::underlying_type` — 297
`stdalign.h` — 371
`stdarg.h` — **149**, 152

INDEX 399

stdatomic.h — 247, 248
stdbool.h — 372
stdbuf — 266
__STDC__ — 113
__STDC_ENDIAN_BIG__, etc. — 113
__STDC_IEC_60559_DFP__ — 36, **113**
__STDC_NO_ATOMICS__ — **113**, 248
__STDC_NO_COMPLEX__ — 36, 37, **113**
__STDC_NO_THREADS__ — **113**, 217
__STDC_NO_VLA__ — 113
__STDC_VERSION__ — **113**, 376
stddef.h — **39**, 176, 211, 376
stderr — 184, **189**, 276
STDERR_FILENO — 189
stdin — 8, 185, 189, **194**
STDIN_FILENO — 189
stdint.h — **38**, 40
stdio.h — 3, **5**, 179, 194
stdlib.h — 7, 8, 210
stdout — 8, **179**, 185, 189
   unbuffered — 266
STDOUT_FILENO — 189
storage class — 63–66
   automatic — 63
   compound literal — 93
      C23, prior to — 377
   static — 63
   thread — **63**, 230
store_bool_mtx — 221
str_is_any — **92**, 125, 150
strbuf — 318–323
strbuf_printf — **320**, 322
strcat — 20, **365**
   buffer overflow — 268
strchr — 44, 199, 200, **365**
strcmp — 92, 150, 160, 193, **365**
strcpy — 22, 24, 71, 169, **365**
   buffer overflow — 268
   implementation — 19
strcspn — 365
strdup — 270, 271, **365**
strerror — 201, **365**
string — 9–12, **315–317**
   literal — 5, **33**
string_printf — 316

string_putc — 316
string_puts — 316
string_putsn — 315
string_take — 317
string.h — 20, **364–366**
stringification — **119**, 242
   pitfalls — 120–121
STRINGIFY — 119, 120, **121**
strlcat — 268
strlcpy — 268
strlen — 21, 53, 62, 64, 131, 269,
   288, 289, 337, **366**
STRLITLEN — **131**, 292
strncat — 366
strncmp — 366
strncpy — 366
strndup — 366
strnlen — 315
strongly-ordered — *see* CPU,
   strongly-ordered
Stroustrup, Bjarne — 62
strpbrk — 366
strrchr — 366
strspn — 366
strstr — 330, 331, **366**
strtod — 199
strtol, etc. — **197–198**, 372
struct — 23, **157**
structure — 23–24, 30, 38, 52,
   157–166, 203
   bit-field — *see* bit-field
   compound literal — 24, 141, 142,
      160–162, 270, 317, 321, 338,
      339, 342, 354, 355
      typeof, with — 367
   definition — 157–158
   designated initializer — 23, **159**
   function return value — 141
   initialization — 23, **159–160**
      C23, prior to — 371
   member — 157
      access — **23**, 53
      flexible — *see* flexible array
         member
      namespace — 30

nesting — 158–159
opaque type — 205
padding — 162
tag — 157
substitution failure is not an error — 288–289
subsystem — 213
`suffix` (#embed parameter) — 127
`sum_to_zero` — 273
Summit, Steve — 235
`SWAP` — 296
Swift (programming language) — 347
    dynamic dispatch — 345
Swift, Jonathan — 56
`switch` — **77–78**, 373
    enumeration values — **106–107**, 109
syntactic sugar — 9
    -> — 53
    [ ] — 88
    array function parameter — 137
    C++ member function call — 348
    multidimensional array — 85
`sys/mman.h` — 191
`sys/stat.h` — 186
`sys/types.h` — 207
`sysexits.h` — 144
system bus — 267
system call — 189

T

\t (tab character literal) — 33
tag
    enumeration — 102
    `typedef`, and — 38
    namespace — **30**, 102, 158, 170
    structure — 157
    union — 170
Tatham, Simon — 25
temporary file — 192
`test` (subdirectory) — 213
`this` — **24**, 348
    `restrict`, and — 308
`thrd_busy` — 225
`thrd_create` — **217**, 219, 221, 248

`thrd_current` — 218
`thrd_detach` — 218
`thrd_exit` — 218
`thrd_join` — **218**, 219, 221, 248
`thrd_t` — **217**, 221, 248
`thrd_timeout` — **224**, 229
`thrd_yield` — 225
thread — 215–232
    create — 217–218
    detach — 218–219
    join — 217–218
    leak — 218
    producer and consumer — 226
`thread_local` — **230**, 352, 354
    C23, prior to — 377
    compound literal — 93
    thread-specific storage — 231
thread-safe — **216**, 219, 220
    `gmtime` — 367
    `localtime` — 367, 368
    `volatile`, other languages — 311
thread-specific storage — 231
`threads.h` — 217
throw — **353–355**, 358
__TIME__ — 113
time — 368
`time_t` — 39
`time.h` — 39, **366–368**
`timespec` — 366–367
    `cnd_timedwait` — 229
    `mtx_timedlock` — 224
`timespec_get` — 224, 229, **368**
`tm` — 366
`TMPDIR` — 192
`tmpfile` — 192
`TO_SIGNED_EXPR` — 296
`TO_UNSIGNED_EXPR` — 296
`TO_VOID_PTR_EXPR` — **285**, 288
token — 111
`token_print` — 345
    fat pointer — 348
    function table — 347
`tolower` — 364
toolchain — xviii, **208**
Torvalds, Linus — 148, 330

toupper — 44, **364**
Tracy — 281
transaction — 219
triangular matrix — 95
troff — 111
try — 352, **352–353**, 358
tss_create — 231
tss_delete — 231
tss_get — 231
tss_set — 231
tss_t — 231
Tutorial Introduction to the Language B, A — 3
two's complement — **40**, 47, 54
two-dimensional array — *see* multidimensional array
type cast — *see* cast
type conversion — 42–43
    variadic function argument — 151
type punning — 171–172
typedef — **37–38**, 103, 261, 284
    tag name injection — 102, 158, 170
typeof — **67–68**, 290, 291, 296, 378
    C23, prior to — 378
typeof_unqual — **69**, 296
    C23, prior to — 378

U

u, U (unsigned literal suffix) — 13, **34**
uchar.h — 39
uint8_t, etc. — **38**, 41
    choosing appropriate — 42
uintptr_t — 261
uncertainty principle — 278
#undef — 126
undefined behavior — 235–240
    ++, -- — 47
    array indexing — 88
    _Atomic structure member — 248
    compiler optimization — 238–239
    different inline function definitions — 148
    flexible array member — 165
    implications — 236–237
    main thread termination — 219
    modifying constant — 55
    nasal demons — 240
    other languages — 239–240
    pointer dereferencing — 88, 93
    race condition — 216
    reading uninitialized variable — 9, 271, **280**
    sanitizer — 279
    setjmp — 300, 301
    signed integer overflow — 40–42
    signed integer underflow — 40–41
    specifier mismatch — 152
    variadic argument
        accessing — 151
        type mismatch — 151
UNDERLYING_TYPE — 297
Unicode — 33, 292
    character types — 38–39
    in identifier — 29
uninitialized variable — **271**, 280
union — 30, 38, 52, **169–177**, 203, 337
    anonymous — **171**, 175
    compound literal — 170
    definition — 169–170
    designated initializer — 170
    function return value — 141
    initialization — 170
        C23, prior to — 371
    member — 170
        access — 53
        namespace — 30
    restricted class hierarchy — 172–176
    safeguard — 175–176
    tag — 170
    type punning — 171–172
    which member — 171
union — **170**, 336
uniq — 331
UNIQUE_NAME — **130**, 296
unistd.h — 189, 207
unportable C — 235
unsigned — 12, **32**, 33, 77
    char — 33
unspecified behavior — 235–236

case evaluation order — 77
evaluation order — 45
use after free — 269–270
uwb, UWB (unsigned _BitInt literal
    suffix) — 35

V

\v (vertical tab character literal) — 33
va_arg — 149–152
__VA_ARGS__ — **118**, 122, 125, 132,
    150, 180, 226, 288
    ## extension — 378
VA_ARGS_COUNT — **131**, 150, 151, 226
va_end — **149–150**, 152, 276, 316,
    320
va_list — **149–150**, 152, 153, 276,
    316, 320
__VA_OPT__ — **118**, 122, 132, 288
    C23, prior to — 378
va_start — **149–150**, 152, 276, 316,
    320
    C23, prior to — 378
valgrind — 281
VALUE_COMMA — 123
variable — 5
variable length array — 96–97
    C++ — 97
    longjmp, and — **302**, 358
variadic function — 138, **149–153**,
    286, 296
    C23, prior to — 378–379
    calling variadic function — 152–153
    pitfalls — 150–152
variadic macro — 118
VERS_PTR — 261
versioned pointer — 261–262
vfprintf — 152, **180**, 276
vfscanf — 194
vim — 214
virtual function pointer — 347
virtual function table — 347–348
Vizzini — 242
VLA — *see* variable length array
vnsum — 149–150
void

casting to — 55
pointer — 86
return type, instead of — 16, **135**
zero parameters — **136**, 375
volatile — 67, 138, 249, 284,
    309–312, 358
    compiler optimization
        suppression — 309–310
    east — 309
    other languages — 311
    setjmp, and — **301**, 311
    signal handler, and — 310–311
    wrong use — 220, **312**
Voyage to Lilliput, A — 56
vprintf — 152, **180**
vscanf — 194
vsnprintf — **180**, 316–317, 320
vsscanf — 194
vstr_is_any — 150–151
VTune — 281

W

Wachowski, Lana and Lilly — 25
wait-free — 258
-Wall (compiler option) — 272
warning — 272–276
    0 as nullptr — 276
    cast alignment — 272
    comma operator misuse — 272
    comparison is always true or
        false — 275
    const, discard — 286
    const, modify — 18
    deprecated — 70
    disable — 276
    else, dangling — 359
    enumeration constant case — 107
    enumeration value, duplicate
        assigned — 273
    enumeration, different — 273
    expression is always false — 292
    fallthrough — **78**, 274
    floating-point equal — 273
    format string nonliteral — 274
    format string sign mismatch — 274

format string type mismatch — 274
implicit conversion — 272
implicit fallthrough — **78**, 274
incompatible pointer — 289
`inline` — 147
`maybe_unused` — 71
`nodiscard` — 71
non-null array parameter syntax — 138
`noreturn` — 72
`#pragma` — 127
`printf` specification — 181
recommended — 272–276
`restrict` — 306
`scanf` specification — 195
shadow — 130, **274**, 359
shifting sign overflow — 275
`sizeof` — 141
string literal to `char*` — 275
`struct`, nested — 158
suppress via cast — 54–56
uninitialized variable — 10, 127, 271, **275**
 conditionally — 272
 sometimes — 275
unreachable code — 275
unused variable, function, or label — 55, 245, **275**
`#warning` — 124–125
 C23, prior to — 379
wb, WB (signed `_BitInt` literal suffix) — 35
`-Wcast-align` (compiler option) — 272
`wchar_t` — 39
`wchar.h` — 39
`-Wcomma` (compiler option) — 272
`-Wconditional-uninitialized` (compiler option) — 272
`-Wconversion` (compiler option) — 272
`wctype.h` — 39
`-Wduplicate-enum` (compiler option) — 273

weakly-ordered — *see* CPU, weakly-ordered
`-Wenum-enum-conversion` (compiler option) — 273
`-Wextra` (compiler option) — 273
`-Wfloat-equal` (compiler option) — 273
`-Wfor-loop-analysis` (compiler option) — 273
`-Wformat-nonliteral` (compiler option) — 127, 274
`-Wformat-signedness` (compiler option) — 274
`-Wformat-type-confusion` (compiler option) — 274
`while` — 6, **75**
whitespace — 4
 in declaration — 62
 in function-like macro — 117
`-Wimplicit-fallthrough` (compiler option) — 78, 274
`_WIN32` — 114
Windows — *see* Microsoft Windows
`-Winline` (compiler option) — 147
`wint_t` — 39
Wireshark — xvii
 exceptions — 359
`-Wlogical-op-parentheses` (compiler option) — 274
`-Wno-dangling-else` (compiler option) — 359
`-Wno-shadow` (compiler option) — 359
Woods, John F. — 240
`write` — 189
`-Wshadow` (compiler option) — 274
`-Wshift-sign-overflow` (compiler option) — 275
`-Wsometimes-uninitialized` (compiler option) — 275
`-Wuninitialized` (compiler option) — 127, 271, 275
`-Wunreachable-code` (compiler option) — 72, 275
`-Wunused` (compiler option) — 71, 275

-Wutological-type-limit-compare (compiler option) — 275
-Wwrite-strings (compiler option) — 275
-Wzero-as-null-pointer-constant (compiler option) — 276

X

\x*hh* (hexadecimal character literal) — 33
X macro — 122–124
   enumeration values
      counting — 124
      serializing — 123–124
x86–64 — 58, 114, 237, 238, 267, 279, 305, 306
Xcode — 213, 214, 281
XL C/C++ — 209

Y

yacc — 124

Z

ZFS — 184
Zlib — xvii

GPSR Compliance
The European Union's (EU) General Product Safety Regulation (GPSR) is a set of rules that requires consumer products to be safe and our obligations to ensure this.

If you have any concerns about our products, you can contact us on

ProductSafety@springernature.com

In case Publisher is established outside the EU, the EU authorized representative is:

Springer Nature Customer Service Center GmbH
Europaplatz 3
69115 Heidelberg, Germany

www.ingramcontent.com/pod-product-compliance
Lightning Source LLC
LaVergne TN
LVHW010333260326
834688LV00036B/695